Sicilian Queenship

Also by Jacqueline Alio

Queens of Sicily 1061-1266
(Sicilian Medieval Studies)

The Ferraris Chronicle
(Sicilian Medieval Studies)

Margaret, Queen of Sicily
(Sicilian Medieval Studies)

Sicilian Studies
A Guide and Syllabus for Educators

Women of Sicily
Saints, Queens and Rebels

The Peoples of Sicily
A Multicultural Legacy

Norman-Arab-Byzantine
Palermo, Monreale and Cefalù
(Time Traveler's Guides)

Sicilian Food and Wine
The Cognoscente's Guide

SICILIAN MEDIEVAL STUDIES

Sicilian Queenship

Power and Identity
in the
Kingdom of Sicily
1061-1266

Jacqueline Alio

Copyright © 2019 Calogera Jacqueline Alio. All rights reserved.

Published by Trinacria Editions, New York.

This book may not be reproduced by any means whatsoever, in whole or in part, including illustrations, photographs and maps, in any form beyond the fair-use copying permitted by the United States Copyright Law and the Berne Convention, except by reviewers for the public press (magazines, newspapers and their websites), without written permission from the copyright holder.

The right of Calogera Jacqueline Alio to be identified as the author of this work has been asserted by her in accordance with the Copyright, Design and Patents Act, 1988 (UK).

Legal Deposit: Library of Congress, British Library (and Bodleian Libraries, Cambridge University Library, Trinity College Library, National Libraries of Scotland and Wales), Italian National Libraries (Rome, Florence).

The title of this book was assigned a Library of Congress Control Number on 26 June 2019. On 1 July 2019, copyright of this work was pre-registered with the United States Copyright Office under number PRE000010903 (case number 1-7841068801) in the class "Literary Work in Book Form" with the title *Sicilian Queenship: Power and Identity in the Kingdom of Sicily 1061-1266*. Identifying information was registered by the British Library through Bibliographic Data Services on 24 June 2019. Some material contained herein previously appeared in *Queens of Sicily* © 2019 Calogera Jacqueline Alio, and is used by permission.

Except where otherwise indicated, all translations contained herein are by Calogera Jacqueline Alio. Illustrations, photographs, maps, image editing and cover design by Louis Mendola with a copyright license to the author. Additional credits in acknowledgments. The text of this monograph was peer-reviewed.

ORCID identifier, Calogera Jacqueline Alio: 0000-0003-1134-1217

Printed in the United States of America on acid-free paper.

ISBN 9781943639212 (softcover)
ISBN 9781943639229 (ebook)

Library of Congress Control Number 2019944485

A CIP catalogue record for this book is available from the British Library.

PREFACE

Historians are intellectual voyeurs, retrospective observers, travelers through time, commentators about a past that is generally forgotten. Each historian is unique, at least slightly different from every other. Our commonality is our quest for information about our subjects in an attempt to turn raw facts into eternal truths. Only through its dissemination can information become knowledge. Known facts are more useful than those that are not known. This book is part of an effort to bring heretofore little-known information to a curious readership.

If, until recently, the history of medieval women has received less attention than it should, that sad predicament was particularly evident here in Italy, where social, political and academic realities marginalized the study of women, and restricted the rights of women themselves, into the middle years of the twentieth century. Long before researching this history formally, in libraries and archives, the author, as a teenager, had heard stories about the "old" Italy from her mother, grandmother, aunts and other Sicilian women of generations past.

Some of what is presented in the following pages is the result of rather recent revelations brought to us through the efforts of diligent researchers. Although the thesis had been advanced earlier, it was only in the nineteenth century that scholars began to seriously contemplate the possibility of the presence of a woman amongst the poets of the Sicilian School that flourished under the patronage of Frederick II, and two poems attributed to Nina of Messina appear in translation in this volume. It was during the same century that both known codices of the Assizes of Ariano were found. The rediscovery of sources such as Sicily's rite of reginal coronation and the long-lost Ferraris Chronicle, both translated into English by the author for other books, is also quite recent.

The objective of this concise thematic collection, a supplement to *Queens of Sicily 1061-1266,* is to expound upon a few topics which, though relevant, are not necessarily integral to "conventional" biographies of those eighteen countesses and queens as they were presented in that long-overdue compendium. *Queens of Sicily* is essentially a traditional reference work intended to fill a void in the field, not a forum for detailed examinations of queenship, which may be defined as the study of the power, agency and identity of queens, including such topics as diplomacy, patronage and culture.

That was stated in its introduction: "This work is not a general disquisition on queenship or the role of women in medieval society, important as both topics are, although it provides source material for scholars writing about these subjects."

It went on to explain: "While the nature of queenship, with special reference to the queens of Sicily in the context of Norman and Swabian tradition, is considered from time to time, this volume is essentially a biographical reference work. Though queenship, feminism and gender identity are certainly, immediately pertinent to our study, and must not be overlooked, they are not, as an object of exhaustive analysis, the central focus of this work."

In other words, that book is an essential foundation in the tradition of published biographies.

This book, conversely, presents a few details gleaned from sundry sources during the research for *Queens of Sicily*. Some of these topics were contemplated by the author for a decade or more and occasionally discussed with colleagues and friends. A few found their way into books, articles or lectures.

Before embarking upon specialized studies in queenship, particularly if a study embraces the life of more than one woman — let's say it considers the relationship between Beatrice of Rethel and Margaret of Navarre — it is useful to have at hand a grounding in the essential biography of each one, or at least something to which the reader may refer for basic biographical information. Until recently, a reference of that kind did not exist for Sicily's first eighteen countesses and queens, and no single volume included biographical information on all of them. That made research for biographical facts cumbersome.

Until now, most of the few biographies of these women have been written by Italians and published here in Italy. That makes sense. Exceptionally, *Margaret, Queen of Sicily* was written in English in the original, though there are plans afoot to translate it into Italian. This is not quite so unusual as it may seem, since the major biographies of Frederick II published during the twentieth century (by Kantorowicz, Van Cleve and Abulafia) first appeared in other languages before making their way into Italian; that was largely because he was claimed by peoples and nations beyond southern Italy. Those biographies, though quite different from each other, were models for *Margaret*.

In the middle of the nineteenth century, Mary Anne Everett Green wrote about two Plantagenet princesses, Joanna and Isabella, who were crowned as Sicilian queens, in greater detail than what was theretofore published about either woman in Italy, where biographies of medieval women were as rare as the saola. In the south, an exception was Joanna of Anjou, a Queen of Naples born around 1326, about whom much was written in Italian.

Some of the subjects addressed in the following pages were considered in *Queens of Sicily* but not at great length. Usually, they were presented as little more than endnotes, appendices or even photo captions. As we have seen, that book's focus was conventional biography rather than the study of queenship as a phenomenon. Yet colleagues, students and Siculophiles clamored for more information, and so did readers curious about such things as the food served at court or the poems read there. This book is a response to that need to bring the queens of Sicily, and prominent women such as Matilda Hauteville, daughter of Roger I, into the wider conversation about the prominent women of the *Regnum Siciliae* during its Norman-Swabian era.

Most of what is included in this monograph is broadly social, considering those contextual details that don't always make their way into a conventional biography as much more than footnotes: What did our queens say? What did they read? What did they write? What did they eat? What did they hear? What did they build? Whom did they destroy?

We'll seek the elusive answers to a few slightly more recondite questions: What kind of challenges did these women and their contemporaries face in marriage and motherhood? What was their rapport with their children? How did their status as part of a social elite affect their lives? How did they help to forge the identity of the place they ruled?

Because it was written by a Sicilian woman in Sicily, this book reveals the legacy of our queens as part of Sicilian society, not only in such pursuits as their patronage of churches but in things that can be seen, heard and tasted today — things more likely to be known to, and perhaps appreciated by, those of us who live here in southern Italy, the former *Regnum Siciliae,* than those curious Siculophiles who live elsewhere. These pages reflect an effort to bring these sociocultural aspects of medieval queenhood to life as something more than shadows.

The author invites you, the reader, on this journey to discover Sicilian queenship and to explore the place our queens knew, experiencing something of what they have bequeathed us that survived the Middle Ages, making these women and their society more than a memory.

The queens' experiences may be viewed as an international metaphor because what we shall find says something about the roles of queens in medieval society beyond southern Italy.

This book is only a beginning, offering a few succinct ideas based on primary sources. It is a framework for what is to come, and an invitation to other scholars to engage in the field. A few already have, and some of their work is listed in a special chapter.

While many scholars consider Sicily's Norman age distinct from our Swabian era, your author is inclined to regard the second epoch as a continuation of the first.

Another difference involves the scope and implications of *Sicilian* queenship specifically; unlike books and papers written by historians less familiar with Sicily and Sicilians (and such topics as our language, literature and cuisine), this one examines the more general influence of our queens and their era on the social culture of southern Italy, which had its own kingdom until 1860. Not every medieval queen had a great personal impact on the events of subsequent centuries. Collectively, however, the queens, and the civilization they cultivated, had a lasting effect in shaping what was to come.

Our first queens were not merely consorts or regents but, with the kings, threads running through the social fabric of a nation that flourished as a monarchy for seven centuries.

A biography, and certainly a compendium of biographies, should include information about the place a queen was crowned and perhaps passed most of her life. For us, this country is the erstwhile Kingdom of Sicily. In *Queens of Sicily,* the necessity of a detailed background chapter on the kingdom and its multicultural society was largely obviated by the existence of another book, *The Peoples of Sicily,* which introduces the place and its people to those who may not be very conversant with that history. In the study of the biography of an important historical figure, what comes before and after her life facilitates useful insights into context; the book *Sicilian Studies* includes a capsule history of Sicily.

Such work may be viewed as part of a resurgence of interest in Norman Sicily amongst scholars writing in English over the last two decades. Antedating that trend, however, your author's interest in the Normans and Swabians who ruled the land of her ancestors places her slightly "ahead of the curve" in this field, as she first attended an international academic conference on this subject in Italy in 1994. Some of the work included in this book was conceived years ago but left unpublished until now; two of the poems were translated by the author from the Sicilian around 1998 (this book's poetry chapter comprises the entire "Frederican Canon" of poems attributed to the emperor), and the chapter on the queens as "she-wolves" is based on a lecture given in Palermo to a group of American women in 2011.

Curiosity is intrinsically personal. It may be that every scholar arrives at her field of study by following a path different from that of each of her peers. Writing in 1913, Evelyn Jamison, whose contribution to these studies was truly remarkable, expressed herself with her characteristic eloquence when she wrote that, "Some fifteen years ago, when this wave of interest was as yet hardly suspected, I was attracted, as all students of the Middle Ages must be, not only by the dramatic story of the Norman adventure in the South, but by the extreme importance of the constitutional and administrative system which grew up in the conquered regions."

Here Professor Jamison's language is slightly reductive, for those "conquered regions" became the Kingdom of Sicily, which was founded a few years before the Kingdom of Portugal and lasted nearly as long, spawning a distinctive culture in the southern half of what is now Italy. Like the first King of Sicily, the first King of Portugal wed a lady of northern Spain's powerful Jiménez dynasty.

Belatedly addressing a need in the field, *Queens of Sicily* should have been written at least seventy years ago, around 1950, when freedom of expression had already been instituted in Italy following the defeat of Fascism, and *this* book should have been written a generation ago. The penultimate chapter addresses such questions. While these books on the queens of Sicily may interest a few medievalist and gender scholars working outside southern Italy, their chief purpose transcends this in making available to the reader beyond academia information that was not previously accessible in many publications, and far less so in English than in Italian. The story of our first queens is not merely an object of study but a precious part of Sicilian, Italian, European and Mediterranean heritage, and the history of women generally.

As this book was going to press, there was a fine exhibit about Norman Sicily at Palermo's royal palace, an imposing edifice erected in the eleventh century on high ground where Phoenician and Arab citadels once stood. The exhibit, *Castrum Superius,* brought together a large number of objects and manuscripts (such as the charter in figure I in the chapter on seals) contemporary to the Hautevilles' reigns. Drawn from various collections, these items are rarely displayed together. The setting was significant. One of the things that made the exhibit truly special was its physical and social (perhaps even spiritual) place in the home of the Norman monarchs, a few steps away from the sights they knew, near the Arab souk, the charming churches, the Palermitans speaking a language rooted in the Norman era, and foreign visitors enjoying local food based on medieval recipes familiar to our queens.

This is *living* history, connecting the past to the present. Another word for it is *Sicilianità,* a concept of historical and cultural identity to which an entire chapter is dedicated.

Queenship transcends a dry history consisting of facts, words and images. It's about important women as real people. It should be viewed as something more than a museum or a lecture. As the keepers of this legacy, Sicily and Sicilians, and southern Italians generally, are an important part of this story of medieval women. The queens' story is our story, and it has much to teach us.

Books such as this one are a necessary prelude to placing our medieval Sicilian queens into the wider European and global narrative about the role of these elite women in society.

While there are various approaches and paradigms of historiography, feminist theory and even research methodology, the present work is the result of a pragmatic examination of the existing corpus of sources rather than theses to which the evidence was adapted selectively, as one sometimes finds in papers and monographs. The author has sought to avoid the pedantic and the semantic so as to bring you a work of value that may serve as a springboard for further efforts. Unlike much of the work that is published relating to the study of queenship, this book is intended to be useful to casual readers as well as specialist scholars.

In the continuum of the study of medieval queenly biography, this volume is not a destination but a starting point. It is not the last word but the beginning of a new conversation which, one hopes, can be advanced further in the years to come.

If we are to find the answers, we must first formulate the questions.

Avvertenza

As this book is intended to be read in conjunction with *Queens of Sicily,* only a few essential maps and figures from that volume are (redundantly) included in these pages for the benefit of readers who may not have that book, which contains numerous genealogical tables and other material. Most of what is presented in the following chapters presupposes consultation of *Queens of Sicily.*

It is not the purpose of this work to rebut or critique the efforts of colleagues currently working in this field, where new theses are frequently being advanced, but to focus instead on topics that may be of genuine interest to readers.

It is not the author's intent to engage in lengthy, contentious debates over historiography, feminism or anthropology, nor endless polemics about what the study of Sicilian queenship should (or should not) be, as if, by way of analogy, Camille Paglia and Gloria Steinem were debating the scope and purpose of the newest wave of feminism in America. Interesting though it would be, an exhaustive examination of feminism (or its absence) in the field of medieval studies in the Italian academy, or feminism in Italian society more generally, is fodder for works yet to be contemplated.

In academia one encounters eclectic ideas about even the simplest subjects. Nevertheless, a biographer's authorial point of view must strive for neutrality. The author resides in Sicily, where she attended high school and university. Like the queens of Sicily, she is Roman Catholic. However, she is not affiliated with any political party or movement, nor has she received any form of funding to write this book beyond a modest advance from its publisher.

Acknowledgments

Contrary to what seems to be a widespread belief, not all medieval charters are available online. For the consultation and photography of these manuscripts, I would like to express my thanks to the staffs of the Palermo Archive of State, the Vatican Apostolic Library, the Palermo Diocesan Archive, the Fundación Casa Ducal de Medinaceli in Toledo, and the Burgerbibliothek in Berne, among others. For the photograph of the gold reliquary pendant of Queen Margaret, thanks to the Cloisters of the Metropolitan Museum of Art in New York. Thanks also to the Regional Art Gallery in Palermo, the Cathedral Tesoro Gallery of the Palermo Archdiocesan Museum and others. My thanks to Salvatore Insenga, the president of Trinacria Editions, for publishing this book, and to Gabriella Carcagnolo, his associate editor. Special thanks to Karen La Rosa, John Keahey, Francesca Lombardo, Mary Ann Kuchera, Professor Virginia Agostinelli, Archbishop Lorenzo Casati, Baron Robert La Rocca and Commendatore Louis Mendola for their suggestions and encouragement. Except where it is stated otherwise, any positions or opinions expressed in this book are those of the author alone.

— C. Jacqueline Alio

Pietratagliata, Palermo, October 2019

CONTENTS

Preface v
Introduction 1
Maps 31
1. She-Wolves 37
2. Queenly Words 55
3. Seals and Appellations 69
4. Reginal Heraldry 103
5. Sexuality and Marriage 113
6. Queenly Cuisine 151
7. Poetry for Queens 191
8. Margaret's Matronage 217
9. Queens Dubbing Knights 267
10. Queens and Sicilianità 289
11. A Sicilian Biographer's Notes 321
12. Queenship Studies 365
Appendix 1: Places 371
Appendix 2: Nina of Messina 381
Sources and Bibliography 391
Index 413

Courtesy Metropolitan Museum of Art

Given to Queen Margaret in 1177, this pendant depicting her is the only object of its kind to survive from the Kingdom of Sicily. See pages 70 and 100.

INTRODUCTION

This book is the beginning of a journey. It is not the destination. Our first stop is Sicily, but it will not be our only stop.

The study of medieval queenship has been defined by a number of historians.[1] Until now, most papers and monographs about the queens of the Norman-Swabian era have tended to focus on Adelaide del Vasto and Constance Hauteville, at least partly because these women were the mothers of our greatest medieval kings, Roger II and his grandson, Frederick II.

Some of those papers were published in thematic edited collections with an emphasis on medieval queenship generally rather than one kingdom specifically, or in journals that focus on medieval studies. In the present volume, this author has sought to avoid duplicating those efforts, listed in a special chapter dedicated to the work of fellow scholars.

Most of the following chapters concentrate on history over historiography, but a few remarks about the latter are appropriate in considering the way we study the lives of the medieval queens of a specific kingdom. Some of these topics are disparate, unified only through our examination of queenhood in medieval Sicily.

Meeting the Queens of Sicily

The queens of Sicily, like medieval women generally, have often been relegated to the margins of published history. Here in Italy, simple sexism accounts for much of this. Into the middle decades of the twentieth century, books about the history of medieval Italian women were almost as rare as female historians. The most obvious exceptions were biographies about saints and martyrs. An aristocratic lady like Caterina Sforza might be mentioned in a general history if she played a major role in important events; apart from the obscene gesture at a siege for which she is remembered in the popular mind, Caterina wrote a book of medicinal recipes.

As stated in the preface, most of what is included in this book constituted part of the preliminary research for *Queens of Sicily* and is obviously complementary to it. The queens' charters, seals and heraldry were part of that research, but so were certain social and cultural topics. Each biography reflects the uniqueness of its subject, and the peculiarities of one kingdom may make it quite different from another.

Several significant affirmations resulted from that research undertaken over the course of a number of years in several countries. Perhaps the most salient of these is the determination that Margaret be considered the Sicilian queen who stands out from the others based on the complexity of her regency and what we know about it compared to the equally arduous regencies of Adelaide del Vasto and Constance Hauteville.

The coronation of Elvira of Castile as queen consort in 1130 was not just a union between the Hauteville family, rulers of a third of Italy, and the Jiménez dynasty, masters of a third of Spain, important as such a union was. It was the beginning of Sicilian queenhood, which ended only with the death of Maria Sophia, the last Queen of Sicily, eight centuries later.

Sicilians' rediscovery of our first queens is a belated

epiphany. Though a curious foreign scholar might well pursue successful research in this area, the Sicilians among us have a scholarly responsibility and social obligation to make this history known beyond Sicilian shores, and the on-site resources to make that a reality. Here a simple analogy is that although we may occasionally meet a foreign woman, one lacking a Sicilian grandmother or two, who, through her own diligent efforts, has mastered the preparation of caponata, espresso and cannoli, in Palermo or Catania one is far more likely to encounter a woman who knows how to make these things and others because here in Sicily there are *many* grandmothers and chefs available to assist her in the nuances of the art of Sicilian cookery, and plenty of arcane "secret" ingredients or methods to make the result a success.

Another reason for the Italians among us to lead the field is that the study of historical Italian women, our foremothers, is an important point of reference for a wider Italian feminism, and it is up to today's Italians, especially those of us living in Italy, to actively marshal this effort (or movement) from within Italian society. While a woman in Wales or Wisconsin might well sympathize with the objectives of this initiative, it is the women of Italy ourselves who must steer it if it is to be anything more than an exercise in theory. Here in Italy, the field of women's studies, as an academic discipline, is not criticized so much as ignored. It is unrealistic to expect a foreigner, an outsider, to take up the cause of women's studies and women's rights in the Italian academy, with its peculiar social practices (considered under "Feminism" in Chapter 11), which your author has witnessed firsthand. Moreover, a foreign Italianist *professoressa* who publicly draws attention to this entrenched misogyny is likely to find herself the target of reprisals, henceforth being excluded from academic conferences here in Italy.

This book is part of an effort to bring some heretofore unpublished information to the public, not only to others having ancestral roots in the Kingdom of Sicily but to readers everywhere. Authorial motivations of that kind are explained in Chapter 11. Here we may suffice it to note that this author contemplated a biography of Queen Margaret for over two decades, during which it was hoped that somebody would write it.

That experience is typical in Italy, where the exceptions were the hagiographic biographies of the women of the ruling House of Savoy published after 1860 to bolster the prestige of the reigning dynasty.

This book is not about "Italian" medieval studies *per se*. Here the Kingdom of Sicily is treated as an important part of Europe and the Mediterranean, not simply a constituent element of what, in the nineteenth century, became the ill-fated Kingdom of Italy.

A few of these topics may prove controversial. In truth, it is the very polemics of certain subjects that make them worth studying at all; it is sometimes difficult to add much of value to a historiographical conversation when controversy is deliberately avoided.

Queenship

In common parlance, the essential difference (though not the only one) between the definitions of queenship and queenly biography is that the former explores the status and condition of being a queen, often with an emphasis on arcane or previously-unexplored details. It is the study of female agency and the use of power based largely on various analytical considerations, some reflecting a modern point of view shaped by feminist theory. "Traditional" biography, the chronological story of one's life and experiences, concentrates on factual events, but usually with less sociological analysis.

To some degree, the difference between the two reflects the

editorial distinction between "political" and "social" history mentioned in Chapter 11. These are not perfect definitions.

Both forms of scholarship are nourished by facts, and they obviously overlap because no thesis involving queenship can be advanced without a knowledge of biography. That is to say, whilst a reginal biography can exist without the modern study of queenship, no examination of any aspect of queenship is complete where a solid grounding in essential biography is lacking.

This usage of the word *queenship*, though popularized during the last few decades, is not entirely novel. In the Catholic Church the twenty-second day of August is the feast of the "Queenship of Mary," known here in Italy as *la festa della Regalità di Maria*. This transcends the status of queenhood of the Mother of God, or *Theotokos*, as Queen of Heaven or *Regina Coeli*, considering the unique power of Mary, in her spiritual realm, to oversee and perhaps even intervene. Not coincidentally, this was what earthly medieval queens like Margaret of Sicily often did. It was the exercise of queenly power.

Keys to the Kingdom

Our journey shall focus on the nature of being a queen of *Sicily*, or, more precisely (considering the extent of the kingdom), Sicily, Campania, Apulia, Calabria, Basilicata, Abruzzi and Molise. This necessarily brings us to the topic of the "ethnic" culture(s) of the place and its people(s). The kingdom's polycultural, multiconfessional nature makes the study of Sicilian queenship somewhat intricate. Not many studies of queenship consider such topics as poetry, language and cuisine, but ours does, *per forza*, because we are seeking, to the extent it is possible, to discover something of the "whole" woman, not just a facet or two.

How "different" was the Kingdom of Sicily? Despite important Norman and Swabian influences, it was much more similar to multicultural Spain, Jerusalem and the Byzantine lands than it was to northern and central Europe. Significantly, the Kingdom of Sicily had queens from all of these regions.

Can we touch the polyglot, cosmopolitan spirit of the place most of our queens knew? Obvious examples are places like Monreale's cathedral, but there is much more.

Though it isn't possible to return to the Sicily of eight centuries ago, a shadow of it can be seen in a few corners of the larger cities. The influx of new immigrants has brought back to Palermo's Ballarò street market, once a souk, something of the vibrant multicultural flavor it enjoyed during Norman times. Nearby, beneath a Jesuit cloister, is Europe's oldest mikveh, still fed by the Kemonia springs, and a synagogue re-established by a resurgent Jewish community.

The focus of Ian Mortimer's book, *The Time Traveller's Guide to Medieval England,* is a specific region during the fourteenth century, and Sicily is mentioned only in connection with pasta being present in Italy but absent in England. Yet anybody reading that book who is familiar with the social aspects of medieval Sicily will discern numerous differences, from the landscape to the law to the food. Only at their own peril do historians ignore the social and cultural side of the place about which they are writing.

We cannot study the Sicilian monarchy in the absence of the Sicilians any more than we could study Japan's eternal monarchy in the absence of the people of Japan.

A chapter speaks to the *Sicilianità* intrinsic to the study of Sicilian queens collectively and the importance of these women to the formation and evolution of Sicilian social culture and identity over time. Until very recently, however, precious little of value was written about our earliest queens by Sicilian women, or indeed by anybody, and virtually none of it was published in English.

INTRODUCTION

An entrenched sexism was not the only reason for this. Among the factors complicating the modern historiography was the Italians' generally negative perception of royalty and the nobility. Lacking a Queen Victoria, Italy never experienced the same trend toward philanthropy and *noblesse oblige* that England saw during the nineteenth century. The absence of a true industrial revolution left the country with a dearth of new plutocrats and a surfeit of reactionary landholders. In southern Italy, the modern image of the baron and his wife was far removed from that of the lord and lady of the manor in rural England. At the dawn of the twentieth century, Palermo boasted two grandiose opera houses to entertain the rich but no public hospital to cure the poor. As recently as 1949, when the Italian government undertook to break up Sicily's vast rural estates, the *latifondi,* that still covered much of the island, aristocrats were despised by most people. The lack of prosperity and opportunity prompted a new wave of emigration, not only from Sicily and Calabria but from northern regions like Tuscany and Piedmont, following the Second World War.

Into the middle of the thirteenth century, when a pope tried to place an English prince, Edmund "Crouchback," on the Sicilian throne, the Kingdom of Sicily could still be compared to the Kingdom of England in some ways since both had been ruled by Norman dynasties and there was much contact between the two realms. Yet, as has been stated, government and law in the two kingdoms differed notably, and the differences became ever more pronounced in successive centuries when Sicily was ruled, for the most part, from Spain. What existed in the Kingdom of the Two Sicilies, a tenuously constitutional state, at its demise in 1860 bore little resemblance to Britain's monarchy, or even to the monarchy founded by Roger II. It was, if anything, rather similar to Spain's Catholic monarchy, which was ruled by the same Bourbon dynasty.

It may be observed, though it is rarely discussed very openly, that many medieval studies undertaken by Italians here in southern Italy differ somewhat in their approach, emphasis and tone from those pursued by foreign historians visiting our country.[2] In practice, most of the native medievalists in southern Italy generally take little account of the historiographical views of their foreign colleagues who publish abroad about the Norman and Swabian dynasties, just as a Briton might ignore an Italian author's perspective expressed in a biography of Henry II of England. The study of the Norman-Swabian Kingdom of Sicily is, in fact, highly eclectic; certain views that prevail in England are not widely accepted in Italy. This leaves us with several schools of thought on certain historical topics: Italian, German, Anglophone, Francophone, and so forth.

Some of these differences are reflected in the insightful analyses presented by the historian Santi Correnti (see Chapter 10), whose views of Sicily and Sicilians were rather different from those embraced by outsiders like his contemporary, the late Denis Mack Smith, whose Italian mentor was the onetime Fascist Benedetto Croce. An obvious explanation for this phenomenon, which likewise occurs amongst populations in other countries, is Sicilians' everyday contact with the history and culture of Sicily, something that permits closer scrutiny and evaluation of many details. Here what is needed is the eye of an astute Luigi Barzini or, in medieval studies, the late Salvatore Tramontana.

Significantly, Santi Correnti wrote not only about the place but about its people. Unless you were educated in southern Italy, it is quite likely that he is the greatest historian you've never heard of. Yet for decades Correnti's history of Sicily, a book virtually unknown outside Italy (though its author, a professor at the University of Catania, was fluent in English and taught in the United States), was what most Sicilians read when seeking a greater knowledge about our island's complex past.

That made sense, just as it is reasonable for a Chinese to read a native historian's book about China rather than something written by a visitor who can barely speak that nation's language. Applying the same principle, the point of view expressed in a biography of Eleanor of Aquitaine written by an Italian in Italy might well differ from that of a woman raised and educated in England or France, not because the English version is necessarily Anglocentric or parochial but because it is more likely to be better-informed, with fewer misperceptions.

A result of this phenomenon is that what is published about, for example, the history of the United States by a publisher in Moscow or Beijing may differ in emphasis and tone from what is published about the same subject in New York or Chicago. The American perspective of the Russian Revolution may not be the most accepted Russian view, and the typical British view of George Washington is not always as flattering as the American view of him. If siblings can have contrasting memories about the mother they share, it should not surprise us that historians having different backgrounds might entertain opposing perspectives. Historiography brings us a world of complexities (see note 11).

This is not to discourage passionate scholars from writing medieval histories or biographies involving countries other than their own; Evelyn Jamison and Lynn Townsend White were noteworthy contributors to our knowledge of Italy's medieval Normans, and Charles Haskins also left his mark in the field.

Until the fall of the dystopic Italian monarchy, and indeed for a decade or two thereafter, access to original records was somewhat restricted, with most of Italy's public libraries and archives controlled by uncooperative bureaucrats. Researching in southern Italy before archival material was available to the general public, Jamison and White faced obstacles to access that were eliminated only through the kind auspices of sympathetic Italians like Carlo Alberto Garufi.

In reality, not every historian born in England, Tuscany or Texas has the opportunity to spend many years in Sicily learning the Sicilian language and every detail of the art, culture and cuisine we have inherited from the Middle Ages (and those raised in Italy should work harder to master English in order to communicate with their foreign colleagues). However, the importance of understanding Sicily and its people has generally been overlooked, leading to a few bizarre misperceptions in certain material published outside Italy since Professor Jamison's death in 1972.

Context is important to avoid errors about geography, topography and, more importantly, society. In some cases these are mere details, like not knowing the precise location of a certain church mentioned in a chronicle.

In other instances the errors are somewhat more egregious, such as attributing the origin of the Mafia to Arabs living in Palermo during the twelfth century or, conversely, claiming that the Mafia is an idea but not an organization (both are examples of bizarre ideas about Sicilian society entertained by foreign historians holding tenured professorships outside Italy).

It is also important to know what came before and after the period one is studying in order to consider causes and effects. For our purposes, this concerns more than the Roman Empire that preceded the Middle Ages, and the patchwork of states that succeeded Italy's medieval era to survive into the nineteenth century. Everything about the multiethnic, polycultural, multiconfessional Kingdom of Sicily known to our queens was rooted in the civilizations that flourished here into the Norman era, and a few social influences of the Hauteville-Hohenstaufen golden age were still evident in modern times. Even the fact that Italy and Germany were not formed into unitary nation states until 1860 and 1870, and the fact that these two unifications were achieved so differently, owes something to the complex medieval past. It is indeed difficult to adequately assess the impact of our kings and queens without scrutinizing the more general history of southern Italy.

Were we to subtract any significant element from the mix, the history of southern Italy, and our collective memory of it, would be different than what it is. This includes its queens, not that the stories of their lives were always expressed in very clear or flattering terms. In the first published history of Sicily, written by Thomas Fazello in the sixteenth century, the regency of Margaret for her young son, William II, is summarized in a single line of text: *Margaritam Reginam eius uxorem voluit totius regni administratricem.* This Fazello drew from the chronicle of Hugh Falcandus, who, however, describes Margaret and her regency at far greater length than what she is accorded by a friar born in 1498. Successive general histories by Francesco Maurolico, Francesco Ferrara and Giovanni Di Blasi, amongst others, were not much more generous.

In no small measure was the popular perception of the role of women, even most queens, dictated by the fact of their stories being written, for the most part, by men. This has constrained us to "read between the lines" when examining the lives, the true experiences, of medieval women.

In our haste to write history based on the written record, which of course must be our primary source of information, we sometimes overlook the unwritten evidence staring us in the face. Chapter 8 includes a fair number of photographs because it is important to *see* the evidence of Queen Margaret's influence at Monreale. Nevertheless, a cynical devil's advocate (the papal *advocatus diaboli* is a man) might try to attenuate this by stating that the queen's likeness does not appear to be depicted in the monastic complex. Therefore, your author, like Sicilian historians before her, looks to a larger body of evidence for convincing signs of the queen's patronage.

Sometimes the evidence speaks to us, as it does through

the poetry of the Sicilian School considered in Chapter 7, and over the years a knowledge of the Sicilian language spoken in the author's family has proven invaluable in translating and appreciating this tongue. Chapter 6, which deals with cuisine, was the beneficiary of the author's personal knowledge of recipes known in her family for generations, perhaps since the Middle Ages.[3] Here she rebuts the ahistorical claim (made by foreign historians) that the medieval Sicilians imported rice but did not cultivate it.

La Fimmina Siciliana

Through all of this, the accomplishments of medieval women are not easily discerned. A good example is the physician Trota of Salerno, mentioned in Chapter 5, about whom precious little is known, but there are others.

As a widow, Lucy of Cammarata, a kinswoman of Roger II, administered vast lands in Sicily's Sicanian Mountains during the middle of the twelfth century on behalf of her young son. She is just one of many aristocratic women of southern Italy who oversaw feudal tasks in the absence of their husbands during the Norman period. Most of these heroines are unsung in the annals of history because their husbands, being minor vassals, held smaller estates and left only tenuous paper trails. There were also a number of such women in the Swabian era.

Exceptionally for a woman of the thirteenth century, Macalda of Scaletta was afforded a military education, as if destined to be a knight, and could wield a sword. The War of the Vespers of 1282 found her governing Catania while her husband, Alaimo of Lentini, was away in Messina doing battle against the Angevins. She then became a lady-in-waiting to Constance, the daughter of King Manfred of Sicily, and she knew John of Procida, who had been a counsellor of Frederick II. Macalda is known to posterity for her court intrigues; she infamously, if unsuccessfully, seduced Constance's husband, Peter III of Aragon. In 1285, she was placed under arrest and imprisoned in Mategriffon, the castle erected by Richard Lionheart at Messina. The chronicler Bartholomew of Nicastro tells us that Macalda was a chess master, and played against the emir Margam bin Sebir, who was held captive at Mategriffon following an Aragonese raid on his Tunisian dominions (Arabs playing chess are depicted in the painted Fatimid ceiling of Palermo's royal chapel). Macalda's eventful life bears the marks of what today would be called *feminism*.

Queenhood is part of womanhood. The extent to which feminism, as an ideology, is part of our study of queenship depends in some measure on how we define feminism. The field of women's studies is not monolithic, and there are various currents within academic feminism.

For the purpose of the most essential historiography, the author is inclined to accept the simplest paradigm. This means that women and their history should be given the same attention as that of men, and ascribed the same importance. It recognizes that we cannot always apply certain modern ideas, or ideals, to medieval circumstances; serfdom, for example, was an entrenched part of life during the twelfth century, and so was the role of religion, particularly Catholicism. This approach is broadly "historicist" in that it views each queen in the context of her time.

While it has important societal implications, this view of queenship is more historical than political. Often, the feminist conclusions are best left to the reader.

Looking beyond rudimentary feminist theory, one scholar of medieval women's studies draws clear, if nuanced, distinctions between women's history, feminist history and gender history.[4] Valuable as they are, such definitions (and others) are somewhat more subtle than what is required for our immediate purposes, which necessitate only the most essential sense of scholarly feminism.

The nature of what is usually called *patriarchy* was well-established as an integral part of medieval society that was generally accepted because most women knew no other way of life, and were virtually powerless to effect change even if they posited another social order.

In this social milieu, queens, and particularly queens regent, were exceptional because they wielded more power than other women, and more than most men.

The reason there is a need for specific, empirical studies of queenship (as a topic) rather than kingship is because, until recently, nearly *all* studies involving medieval monarchies were, in effect, studies of kingship. Here one is reminded of a response by the American writer and activist Tim Wise to a man who complained about Black History Month by saying there is no White History Month. Wise patiently explained that none was needed because *every* other month is "White History Month."

Queenhood was an international affair, the Kingdom of Sicily was initially a multicultural realm, and most of our first queens hailed from regions beyond what is now Italy (a map in *Queens of Sicily* indicates their birthplaces). Nevertheless, the kingdom itself was in southern Italy, which was sovereign into the nineteenth century, and it is here that one would expect to find a focus of scholarship on these women, hopefully with the participation of a few of us Italian women who actually live here. It is important to publish such work in English if it is to find an international readership.

This book is part of a multidisciplinary effort to bring attention to the stories of these women but also the place and its people. The early queens of Sicily are just as important to southern Italians as the first queens of England are to the English. They are equally relevant to the history of Europe. It should be remembered that four of our queens were also crowned Holy Roman Empress. An English chronicler reported that many viewed the marriage of Isabella, the daughter of King John, to Frederick II, an emperor, as a sign of prestige for the Kingdom of England.

E Dio Creò la Regina

The Italian *regalità* seems an antiquated word for queenship or queenhood, which in Italy might be better expressed in the neologisms *reginalità* or perhaps even *reginezza*. In English, we might pedantically distinguish between *queenhood* and *queenship,* with the former as a more general term for the state of being a queen (though it is not used exclusively in that sense in this book).

Terminology aside, universities here in Italy seldom offer undergraduate courses on the study of women as a specific historical subject, much less the study of *Italian* women. This is a reflection of the general social status of women in this country. True, a fair (though by no means overwhelming) number of women will be found in parliament and in the professions, where Maria Montessori and Rita Levi-Montalcini were trailblazers, but most Italian women joined the workforce late in the last century out of raw necessity rather than the noble aspirations expressed in the seminal work of Betty Friedan, Gerda Lerner, Germaine Greer and Gloria Steinem.

Granted, it could be argued that the motivation is irrelevant so long as the result achieved is the same. But is it? Recent social movements (such as #MeToo) have had very little effect on Italy's surreal social landscape, where sexual harassment is still fairly commonplace and rape cases are only rarely prosecuted.[5] Where these matters are concerned, Italian women, not normally a stoic lot, are largely silent, and those who speak out are rabidly divided politically. If we add to this mix the rivalries and jealousies among academics and within other segments of the female population, such as lawyers and politicians, the current Italian environment sometimes looks less like a sisterhood and more like a catfight.

Some of the social issues affecting women were mentioned, though not thoroughly examined, in my *Women of Sicily,* a slender volume intended as a very simple introduction rather than an academic study. Yet, being the only book of its kind published in English about the historical women of Sicily, it has been received quite well. It was the first book propounding Sicilian feminism to be written in English by a woman in Sicily. A foreign Siculophile author might well support this effort, but it is Sicilian women, first and foremost, who must bring the stories of our queens, as part of our island's history, to the attention of the wider world. These historical women are an important part of Sicilian feminism, just as England's queens are integral to British feminism.

The first modern Italian feminist of note was Laura Cereta, a writer who died in 1499 aged just thirty. Much of Italy's feminist ideology, as we know it, was forged by pioneers such as Anna Maria Mozzoni. Mozzoni, who died in 1920, famously questioned the value of the exclusively patriarchal mentality that dominated Italian families and law. She worked tirelessly to achieve women's suffrage but did not live long enough to see her efforts bear fruit.

Owing, perhaps, to the comparatively embryonic state of the Italian women's movement into the last decades of the last millennium, outspoken proponents such as Carla Lonzi, Carla Accardi and Oriana Fallaci tended to emphasize fundamental rights over sophisticated feminist theory. Perhaps it has something to do with Italian social culture. The candid, pragmatic, feminist commentary of Italian descendants like Camille Paglia, Nancy Pelosi and Alyssa Milano (Americans and respectively an atheist, a Catholic and a deist) might lead one to believe that this emphasis on activism and practice over theory is an Italian thing, perhaps rooted in the role of strong mothers in Italian families.

There are several schools of feminist thought, even where historiography is concerned, and in these pages it is not the author's intent to explicate or advocate one or the other.[6] She shall leave it to others to develop those concepts regarding medieval European and Mediterranean women.

In this complex milieu, your author is only a messenger, here to tell you that an elite cadre of eighteen countesses and queens of Sicily, and a few kindred women like Sichelgaita of Salerno and Matilda Hauteville, left a mark on the history and culture of southern Italy. That millions of other women likewise influenced this society is beyond cavil, but it is only the notable ones about whom much was written during the Middle Ages, and even in some of those cases it is very little indeed.

In this volume space is made for a few women of Norman-Swabian Italy other than our queens, such as the aforementioned Sichelgaita and Matilda, and the ever-elusive Trota of Salerno and Nina of Messina.

Because human nature has changed little over time, we find that certain situations or challenges present in Italy's Norman-Swabian era were not too different from those facing women in modern centuries, and that our Sicilian queens have left us a greater legacy than has generally been recognized.

Naturally, such a legacy is based on what we know, and certain details will never be known to us. Beatrice of Rethel, the widow of Roger II, was sometimes present at court when Margaret was regent for William II, who was about the same age as Beatrice's daughter, Constance. Beatrice and her daughter spent much of their time at the Hauteville castle at San Marco d'Alunzio up the coast, probably to avoid the incessant court intrigues of Palermo but perhaps as Margaret's eyes and ears along the gateway leading to Messina and Calabria. The court was full of men, including two of Margaret's troublesome kinsmen, namely her half-brother Rodrigo (Henry) and her cousin Gilbert, but as queen regent, and the most powerful woman in Europe, the rose from Pamplona was the kingdom's ultimate voice of authority. Beatrice, who was raised in the Ardennes just south of what is now Belgium, was likewise a "foreigner." Did the two queens, both in their mid-thirties, commiserate with each other, perhaps cultivating a sisterly friendship? Interesting as that information would be, it is lost to time. Not that the Sicilian monarchy was ever a matriarchy, but for these few years, from 1166 to 1171, it likely boasted a subtle female influence under these two women, neither of whom remarried, or departed the kingdom, in widowhood.

For Queen and Country

With the prominent exception of Constance of Sicily, whom the Guelphs of Tuscany infamously despised for giving birth to their nemesis Frederick II, these women were generally overlooked by historians until the last few decades except in connection with their weddings or their regencies.

Not surprisingly, therefore, most of the topics considered in the following pages were ignored for centuries. Specific aspects of a few have been examined only in papers published in journals that are not present in many libraries or are not available online except beyond a pay wall. Several have been addressed exclusively in articles published in Italian. This does not apply only to reginal biography itself; it is astounding that most of the medieval recipes included in Chapter 6 were never translated into English until now.

The research methods leading to publication of this material are similar to those employed by diligent investigative journalists when unearthing facts that always existed in abstract form but were never previously made public. They reveal an evolution from the arrival of the Hautevilles early in the eleventh century, when the region was truly multicultural, to the fall of the Hohenstaufens in 1266 that left southern Italy with its own, very distinct culture, laws and languages. Frederick II probably recognized this when he composed poetry in Sicilian and promulgated his legal code, the Constitutions of Melfi. Whether this cultural symbiosis was a positive development is a debate that lies beyond this discussion, but it is a reality that explains why a Latin monoculture dominated southern Italy by 1300, when the transmogrification was essentially complete, Sicilian society having abandoned cosmopolitanism for ethnocentrism.

That is not, however, the only reality that we shall explore in these pages. Power and identity, though distinct concepts, are often linked. One can support the other, and both change over time.

As mentioned above, an important, even personal, aspect of the study of queenhood is its sociocultural legacy, particularly, but not exclusively, in the place where the queens ruled. For us this country is now the southern part of the Italian Republic, and it makes sense that a reginal biographer whose focus is the countesses and queens of Sicily should be intimately familiar with this region, its people, language and culture. As we shall see, the Sicilian language known to Dante has survived, along with some Sicilian medieval traditions and even a few vestiges of the cuisine of the Middle Ages.

The Kingdom of Sicily left us some interesting hallmarks of the Norman-Swabian era, colored by Lombard, Byzantine Greek and Muslim Arab ideas. Not all of these survived into modern times. Nevertheless, the Normans and Lombards permitted women to inherit patrimonial property, while the Byzantines and Arabs fostered a high rate of literacy among girls.

Italianists, or "Tuscanists," and especially foreign Italophiles, often fail to grasp the implications of the historical differences between Italy's north and south. Rooted in antiquity, when the culture of the Greeks of *Magna Graecia* overshadowed that of the Etruscans and inspired the aspirations of Rome, this divergence survived into the Renaissance era and through the *Risorgimento*. In some ways it is still with us. An analogy of sorts may be drawn with the regions of Spain, but for all their individuality Navarre, Andalusia and Catalonia have been part of a united nation since the end of the fifteenth century, whereas "Italy," as a modern unitary state, has existed only since the reign of Queen Victoria and the presidency of Abraham Lincoln.

Right up until that time, Italy's greatest, most prosperous realm was not in its northern or central regions but here in the south. This was the tangible legacy of the first kings and their intrepid wives.

Sicily's medieval queens were not the only ones to be at least partially obscured by modern Italian historiography, sometimes for political reasons. Maria Sophia of Bavaria, the widowed consort of King Francesco II of the Two Sicilies, whose kingdom was lost to Piedmontese forces in 1861, lived until 1925, yet very little was written about her in a biographical vein before 1961, when Harold Acton's history, *The Last Bourbons of Naples,* was published.

The idea — and misperception — that medieval queens who held actual power were extremely anomalous for their times finds less acceptance today than it did just a few decades ago. Hopefully, the author's examination of the lives of the queens of Sicily will contribute something to this reassessment by helping to dispel that antiquated notion as it pertains to this part of Europe, just as others are writing about the medieval queens of other regions.[7]

Significantly, what is presented in this volume, as well as in

INTRODUCTION

Queens of Sicily and the works listed in Chapter 12, serves to complement and bolster what has been reported elsewhere based on recent research about the medieval queens of other parts of Europe, specifically that their participation in monarchical society as wives and mothers, but also regents, governors, judges, benefactresses and (when necessary) warriors was extremely important, generally considered normal, and usually accepted. Women like Adelaide, Margaret and the two Constances certainly had their male detractors (typically in the *Regnum Siciliae* these were disgruntled barons), but one is struck by how rarely they were subjected to overt misogyny even by these troublesome men. As regents, Adelaide and Margaret found themselves ruling a large population of Muslims, yet the men who occasionally challenged their authority were not Muslims, Jews or Greek Orthodox but Roman Catholic. King Tancred may have resented Constance Hauteville, the kinswoman whose birthright he usurped, but there is no evidence to suggest that he openly disparaged her simply because she was a woman, and he refused to kill her when he could. Like Empress Maude, Constance was a Norman heiress, a king's daughter, ever steadfast in her will to stand her ground against adversaries. Like Maude, she was successful in getting her son crowned king despite occasional opposition.

Viewing the question of female power in a wider temporal context, the social rise of Italian women has been laggard, and this goes far to explain the delay in the publication of our queens' biographies.[8] As this is written, the most powerful Italian woman in the world is not a native of Italy but a descendant, the Honorable Nancy Pelosi, née D'Alesandro, Speaker of the United States House of Representatives, whose ancestral roots are in Abruzzi and Molise.[9]

Among feminists having Italian roots, the contrarian voice of Professor Camille Paglia is the most resonant, though, like Nancy Pelosi, she was born and educated not in Italy but in the United States. With the possible exception of the audacious Oriana Fallaci, no Italian-born feminist has seen her views become so influential outside Italy; Italian journalists such as Lilli Gruber are virtually unknown beyond Italy's shores. An exploration of Paglia's positions, expressed in such books as her *Free Women, Free Men: Sex, Gender, Feminism* (2017), will be left to the reader.

While the feminism in these pages is not explicitly *Italian* feminism, it is impossible to overlook our queens in the context of the history of what is now Italy. Gender biases are still with us. As an everyday example, the preference for daughters over sons didn't end with the Middle Ages or even the last century. It still exists in some countries, including Italy. Here one observes that amongst most of the middle-class couples having two children the elder is a girl because the wife/mother was convinced to try having a son on a second attempt that might not have been encouraged were the first child a boy; it is an obvious but unspoken verity that in a disproportionate number of Italy's one-child families the only child is a boy.[10] There is even a traditional expression addressed to pregnant wives: *Speriamo che sia maschio.*

Those outside humanistic fields may well deride a modern study of historical women or a specific region (or ethnicity) as a subtle manifestation of "identity politics" or even self-interest (a woman writing about women) as if an emphasis on them consisted of unjustified platitudes. In actuality, such studies usually reflect nothing more than a balanced attempt to cast an eye upon people given less attention by historians in times past. There is certainly a localized aspect to this. Whereas a British girl studying her country's history in Britain might learn something of Eleanor of Aquitaine, a young *studentessa* here in Sicily would, one hopes, learn about Eleanor's contemporary and *consuocera*, Margaret of Navarre. Sadly, that has not always been the case.

Here in Italy, it is facile to point to Fascism's repression as an obstacle to the modern study of women by women until after the Second World War, but even before the advent of that regime, which was no less sexist than any other, there were extremely few Italian women in academia. In the first decade of the twentieth century, Evelyn Jamison, as an outsider, was granted greater opportunities to peruse Italian archives and libraries to study Italy's Norman history than any Italian woman of that era was afforded. Even at Professor Jamison's death at ninety-five in 1972 there were very few Italian women in the field, where Professor Marina Scarlata stood out. By then, Marjorie Chibnall, once a student of Jamison, was publishing studies of the Normans, and she eventually wrote a notable biography of Empress Maude, the mother of Henry II of England. Jamison's work, though it does not focus on a queen, at least takes account of Margaret's regency for William II.

In our times, the critical study of history, of which biography is an important part, is usually taken for granted. Leaving aside the conditions that existed in Italy (which led to a *de facto* censorship), notable thinkers have struggled with the question of writing about a certain people, place or gender, engaging in the inexorable debate over the purpose of history and the best approaches to historiography and the historical method.[11]

Were it not for the defeat of the Hohenstaufens at Benevento and Tagliacozzo and their subsequent disparagement by the victorious Guelphs, followed by a series of developments into the twentieth century, the queens of Sicily and the culture they represent would have received more attention than they have thus far.

This volume is meant to be an impetus to encourage a belated movement to give them the recognition they deserve. Your author apologizes for not bringing this book to you twenty years ago.

As stated earlier, this volume is merely a starting point, reflecting an effort to focus study of medieval queenship on the monarchy of southern Italy, of which the Hauteville and Hohenstaufen reigns are the cornerstones. It is part of a trend in the study of the aristocratic women of the Middle Ages somewhat more profound than what was usually undertaken before the last decades of the twentieth century.[12]

Sicilian Studies

We see that, among the many topics and disciplines with which a study of Sicilian queenship before 1300 is concerned to one degree or another, those that stand out focus on several pivotal areas, most notably female agency, medieval multiculturalism, and the sociohistorical fabric of southern Italy. Naturally, these elements must be viewed in the context of the flow of history and not as isolated developments.

In Sicily's high schools and universities, certain humanistic and social studies are emphasized more than others. As stated above, women's studies are not usually taught as a specific subject; however, the general history of Sicily is covered quite well, indeed far better than it has ever been. As part of this, students might read a book like *The Leopard,* by Giuseppe Tomasi di Lampedusa, a work of literature that has been compared to Margaret Mitchell's *Gone with the Wind.*

The Leopard, or *Il Gattopardo,* is set in 1860, but that era was preceded by some thirty centuries of rather complex history on the world's most conquered island.

Students in Britain, the United States or elsewhere may well study something about the history, philosophy and culture of the ancient Greeks as a fundament of western civilization. In Sicily, however, this legacy is ubiquitous, not only in museums but at the archeological sites that dot the island.

Outside Italy, studies of Sicilian (or southern Italian) history and culture are usually integrated into programs or courses on Italian studies. That is not inappropriate. However, the author commends professors' efforts to teach about Sicily in specific courses. *The Peoples of Sicily* has been used as a text for introductory undergraduate courses of this kind, some using medieval Sicily as a metaphor for a wider multiculturalism. *Sicilian Studies: A Guide and Syllabus for Educators* was a response to the specific requests of academicians seeking a framework for such courses.

Sicily's lengthy, detailed history leaves little time in a survey course for the intense study of a specialized topic. Yet it is the author's contention that an examination of the lives of our first queens must be included even in an introductory course because it tells us so much about the importance of these women in medieval society.

We should never tolerate a telling of history that virtually ignores the female half of the population. To that end, the study of the history of women must be encouraged.

If democracy cannot survive without diligent journalists, it cannot thrive without thorough historians.

Summary

In view of the foregoing comments, the objectives of the following chapters may be summarized in fairly succinct terms.

• Unlike some monographs and edited collections relating to European and Mediterranean queenship, this one is written not only for scholars but for readers beyond academia; it is intended for anybody interested in the lives and social culture of the countesses and queens of Sicily until 1266.

• Several topics are considered that transcend in scope what is typically included in studies of queenship, with an emphasis on the cultural and social significance of these women to southern Italy and for the people of the former Kingdom of Sicily, latterly the Kingdom of the Two Sicilies, and their many descendants around the world as a significant part of our heritage and culture, just as the historical queens of other kingdoms (e.g. England, France) are part of the social culture of those countries.

• To the extent that every biographical study reflects an inherent (if sometimes unintended) authorial view, the historiographical emphasis is international rather than Italocentric or Siculocentric since most of our countesses and queens, via exogenous marriages, were from European regions such as Normandy, Spain and England beyond what is now Italy, yet it ascribes importance to these women as an integral element in the modern culture of southern Italy as this began to develop during the Norman-Swabian era.

• Unlike most books about the reigns of the Hauteville and Hohenstaufen dynasties, this one considers these eras together even while recognizing the unique distinctions between the Norman and Swabian cultures and their impacts on southern Italy; the Norman-Swabian period is thus viewed against subsequent Angevin and Aragonese rule in southern Italy.

• In the interest of discerning historical context, this work examines, or at least considers, what occurred in southern Italy before and after our Norman-Swabian era, along with certain parallel developments regarding such phenomena as queenly patronage elsewhere by our queens or others.

• The perspective of this work is intrinsically feminist without identifying with a specific school of feminist theory or historiography.

INTRODUCTION

• This book fills a void by presenting much information that, for the most part, has not been published very extensively elsewhere, nor in a single volume; it does not include critiques of the work of fellow scholars currently working in this field.

• This work presents accurate information without its tone infringing upon the dignity of the historical women described here, viewed as real people and not simply objects of study.

• There is no political motive or "agenda" in this work and it does not reflect the views of any government, movement, organization or other institution.

• In our times, historical studies are collegial and international in nature (which often necessitates publication in English), yet it is appropriate that research on Sicily's medieval queens and queenship be encouraged via means emanating from Sicily, ideally from Palermo as the medieval royal capital; an organized initiative of that kind does not presently exist but should be established, with foreign scholars invited to participate, and this book is an early phase of that effort. Although it is the first book on Sicilian queenship, one hopes that it will not be the last.

NOTES

1. See Chapter 12 and the notes in Chapter 11.

2. For diplomatic comments on this by British scholars, see Abulafia, David, *Frederick II: A Medieval Emperor* (second edition, 2002), page 457; Matthew, Donald, "Modern Study of the Norman Kingdom of Sicily," *Reading Medieval Studies,* volume 18 (1992), pages 34-56. Correnti's remarks about the biases of Denis Mack Smith are candid enough; see his *Storia di Sicilia come Storia del Popolo Siciliano.* For an important example of Sicilian historiographical views generally (before unificationist ideas affected the field), see Gregorio, Rosario, *Considerazioni sopra la Storia di Sicilia dai Tempi Normanni sino ai Presenti* (1816).

3. Culinary research referring to familial knowledge is not extremely unusual (or at least should not be) because many Sicilian recipes can be traced to medieval times, if not the Norman era specifically. A leading scholar of this subject recounts how, whilst delivering a paper to the Culinary Historians of New York in 1995, she was informed by an attendee of Sicilian ancestry that there is a Sicilian recipe called "Turk's Head," and subsequent correspondence from other Sicilian readers yielded several recipes having the same name. See Hieatt, Constance, "How Arabic Traditions Travelled to England," *Food on the Move: Proceedings of the Oxford Symposium on Food and Cookery 1996* (1997), page 123.

4. Skinner, Patricia, *Studying Gender in Medieval Europe: Historical Approaches* (2018), pages 14-15.

5. See Van Cleave, Rachel, "Rape and Querela Law in Italy: False Protection of Victim Agency," *Michigan Journal of Gender and Law,* volume 13, January 2007 (Ann Arbor 2007), pages 273-310; Galli, Natalie, *The Girl Who Said No: A Search in Sicily* (2019); Bubola, Emma, "Locker-room talks: Italian politics and normalized sexism," *Al Jazeera* (11 March 2018); Donadio, Rachel, "The Missing Piece in Italian Politics: Women," *The Atlantic* (10 March 2018); Pianigiani, Gaia, "Women Could Decide Italy's Election, but They Feel Invisible," *The New York Times* (3 March 2018); Siri, Simona, "Having a misogynist leader has consequences. And no, I don't mean Trump." *The Washington Post* (14 December 2017); Soncini, Guia, "The Failure of Italian Feminism," *The New York Times* (26 October 2017); Giuffrida, Angela, "Italy's highest court accused of victim blaming over rape case," *The Guardian* (17 July 2018); Horowitz, Jason, "In Italy, #MeToo is More Like 'Meh'" in *The New York Times* (16 December 2017); Vigo, Julian, "Tight Jeans, Rape and Technology," *Forbes* (22 July 2018); Winfield, Nicole, "Italian Court Ruling That a Woman Was Too Ugly to Be Raped Sparks Outrage," *Time* (14 March 2019). In 2018, the *Global Gender Gap Report* published by the World Economic Forum found Italy in 70th place compared to France in 12th, Britain in 15th and Spain in 29th. During the same year, Italy (with a population of some 55 million), had 142 femicides. ISTAT, the Italian national statistics agency, reports that 43.6 percent of Italian women (nearly 9 million) between the ages of 15 and 65 have been sexually harassed in the workplace, 15.4 percent in the three years immediately prior to the report; see *Statistiche Report: Le molestie e i ricatti sessuali sul lavoro 2015-2016* (13 February 2018), published

INTRODUCTION

in English in condensed form under the same date as *Sexual Harassment and Sexual Blackmail at Work*. The Italian version of #MeToo is #QuellaVoltaChe.

6. See, for example, Mairey, Aude, "Gender and Written Culture in England in the Late Middle Ages," *Clio: Women, Gender, History* ("Working Women, Working Men"), volume 38 (2013), pages 264-288.

7. Amongst other recent works along these lines is *Medieval Elite Women and the Exercise of Power 1100-1400: Moving Beyond the Exceptionalist Debate,* edited by Heather Tanner and published in 2019.

8. See the works by Bianca Beccalli, Liviana Gazzeta, Fiamma Lussana and Eleonora Missana in the bibliography, and also note 5 above.

9. Nancy Patricia Pelosi first served as Speaker from 2007 to 2011. See Stolberg, Sheryl Gay, "Nancy Pelosi, Icon of Female Power, Will Reclaim Role as Speaker and Seal a Place in History," *The New York Times* (2 January 2019); Clinton, Hillary Rodham, "Nancy Pelosi," *Time Magazine: The 100 Most Influential People* (29 April 2019); Allen, Nick, "Nancy Pelosi: Donald Trump's Steely Nemesis Shattered Glass Ceilings Along the Way," *The Telegraph* (25 September 2019); Rogers, Katie, "Inside the Derailed White House Meeting," *The New York Times* (16 October 2019).

10. Ascertaining a precise national statistic is difficult because, among other factors, 31 percent of Italian children are born outside marriage (ISTAT 2017).

11. In Chapter 11 the author cites Barbara Tuchman. For the views of others whose stances have influenced the discipline, see Carr, Edward, *What is History* (1961); Elton, Geoffrey, *The Practice of History* (1967); Marwick, Arthur, *The Nature of History* (1970); Tosh, John, *The Pursuit of History* (1984); Jenkins, Keith, *Rethinking History* (1991); Munslow, Alun, *Deconstructing History* (1997); McCullagh, C. Behan, *The Truth of History* (1997); Evans, Richard, *In Defence of History* (1997); Cannadine, David, *What is History Now?* (2002); Mortimer, Ian, *What Isn't History?* (2017).

12. A fine example is Johns, Susan, *Noblewomen, Aristocracy and Power in the Twelfth-Century Anglo-Norman Realm* (2003). For many others see chapters 11 and 12.

F. THOMÆ FAZELLI
SICVLI OR PRÆDICA/
TORVM

DE REBVS SICVLIS DECADES DVAE, NVNC
PRIMVM IN LVCEM EDITAE.

HIS ACCESSIT TOTIVS OPERIS IN-
DEX LOCVPLETISSIMVS.

CAVTVM EST PHILIPPI ANGLIAE, HISPANIAE,
Siciliæq; Regis, Pauli. IIII. Pont. Max. ac Veneta Reip. priuilegio, ne
cui has Decades de Siculis rebus ad decennium in eorum di-
tione vel imprimere, vel alibi impressas venales
habere, neue in sermone Italico iniuſ-
sii authoris vertere sub mul
cta liceat.

First published history of Sicily, by Thomas Fazello, in 1558

MAPS

Regnum Siciliae: The Norman-Swabian Kingdom of Sicily

MAPS

SICILIAN QUEENSHIP

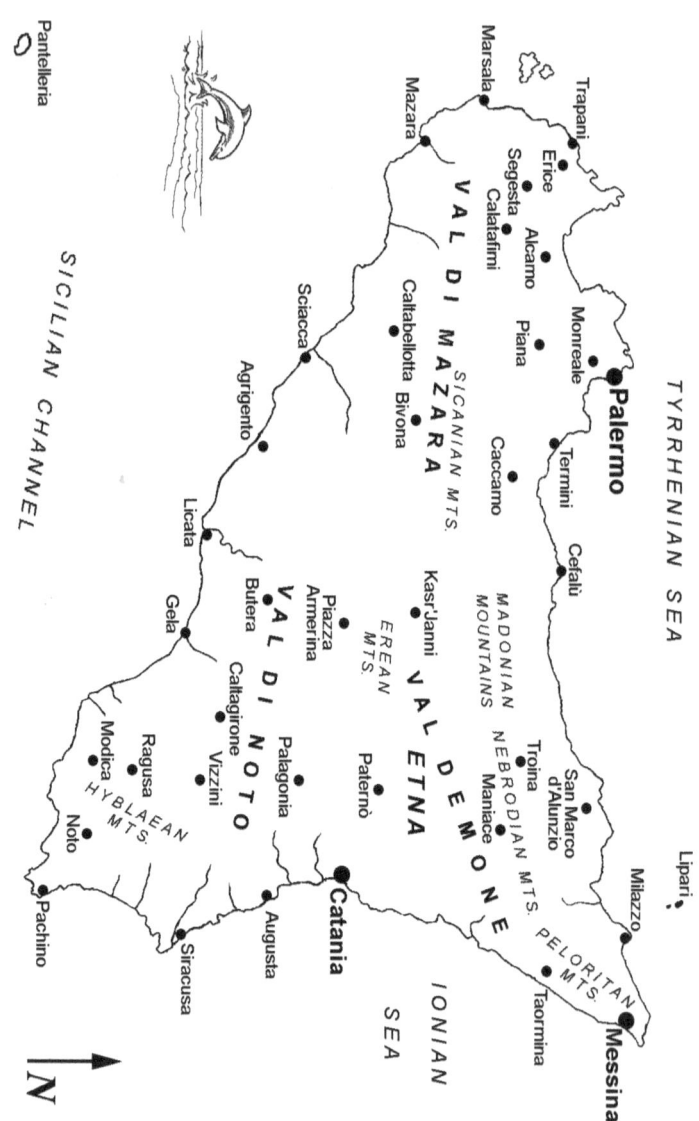

MAPS

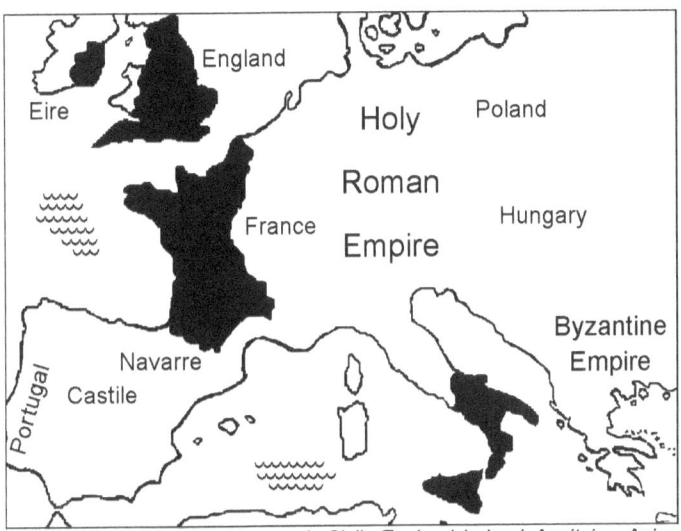

Norman control in 1171: Normandy, Sicily, England, Ireland, Aquitaine, Anjou

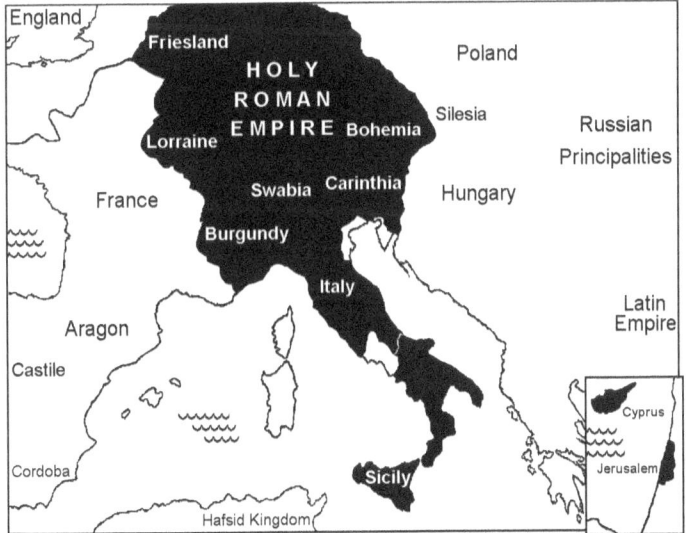

Greatest extent of Hohenstaufen dominion under Frederick II - 1229

SICILIAN QUEENSHIP

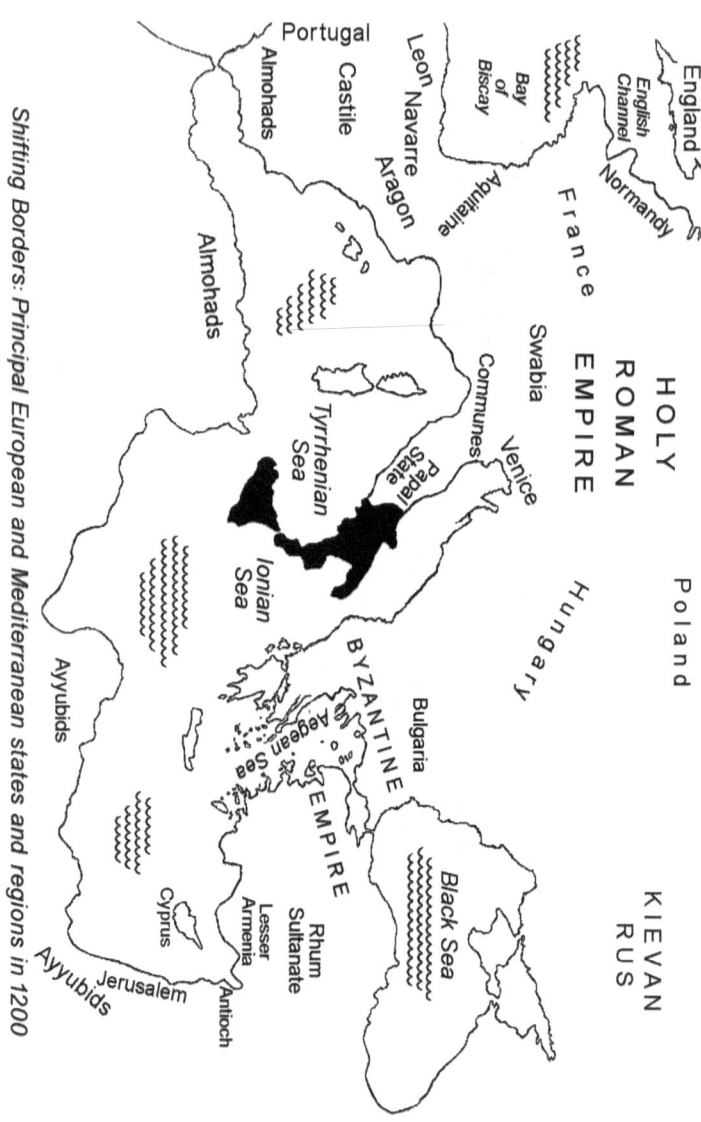

Shifting Borders: Principal European and Mediterranean states and regions in 1200

Chapter 1
SHE-WOLVES

What makes a woman a she-wolf? In simplest terms, it is her willingness to act, or react, expediently, even violently, against adversaries. Several English authors have posited that there was a touch of the she-wolf's fierce survival instinct in most of England's early queens, and two of these biographers have given their books the very title "She-Wolves."[1] Here in Italy the term *lupa* is an old one.[2]

That a woman might be a mother does not seem to detract from her behaving as if she were an aggressive canine. Her defense of her children may encourage such behavior. (For our purposes, the term "she-wolf" has no sexual connotations.)

Much is written nowadays about queenly power. Arguably, the ultimate form of authority is the power over life and death.

In seeking our own she-wolves, three queens exemplify this character trait more obviously than others based on precise information drawn from specific sources. Margaret was regent for young William II and Joanna was his consort. Constance, the closest thing to a Sicilian queen regnant, was regent for her young son, Frederick II.

This is not to suggest that Adelaide and the others were not equally courageous or even aggressive; as regent, Adelaide had to suppress a baronial revolt that potentially threatened the succession of her son, the future Roger II. However, there are fewer explicit records of the actions of these other women against named adversaries. Ladies worthy of mention are intrepid Sichelgaita of Salerno, consort of Robert Guiscard, and Matilda, sister of Roger II.

In each of these cases (Margaret, Joanna, Constance), there is at least some basis for believing that the woman was capable of violence, even homicide, if needs be. The actual deeds, of course, were handled by proxy. We have no evidence of any of our queens ever assaulting or killing anybody herself. What little we know of the queens' words and behavior (see Chapter 2) alludes to nothing like a violent outburst. On the contrary, it seems that all three women were generally adept in the use of power.

Absence of evidence is not evidence of absence, and it is quite possible that our intrepid queens involved themselves in acts and intrigues unknown to us.

Nevertheless, there is sufficient evidence, either explicit or implicit, that our three queens were directly involved in the cases described here. Other cases, for which there is insufficient proof of direct involvement through a reginal command or evident complicity, are not included.

This is not the appropriate forum for rationalizing; it is clear enough that, in most instances, these women were motivated, in one way or another, by the instinct for survival and justice more than raw vendetta or caprice. Nevertheless, there seem to have been situations when indignation clouded wisdom.

As we shall see, some of our conclusions are colored by conjecture because extant accounts do not always attribute specific actions to the initiative of the queens themselves. It should be noted that none of these three women is usually depicted by historians as a "victim." Indeed, a case could be made that no contemporary chronicler, however sympathetic, ever portrayed these queens in such a light.

Even so, they had to endure trials and challenges. Margaret's power was curtailed somewhat following the expulsion of her cousin, Stephen of Perche. Joanna's brother considered betrothing her to a Muslim leader in Palestine, and her second marriage, to the Count of Toulouse, seems to have been a sour one. Constance had to contend with much adversity, from her cousin usurping her Sicilian throne to German barons in the Kingdom of Sicily challenging her authority following her husband's death.

Through all of this, it sometimes took the courage and audacity of a she-wolf just to survive.

Were these women "alpha" females? If they did not begin life that way, they certainly became able leaders and, to their enemies, formidable adversaries. Most of the queens' targets were men. Given the paucity of surviving information, it is rather difficult to extrapolate much from what chroniclers tell us about these queens' actions. Although it may have been considered pragmatic, at a certain moment, to bolster a regent's prestige, the chroniclers themselves were invariably men, typically monks, and probably not inclined to overstate a woman's power, intellect or charisma. Here Peter of Eboli seems exceptional, for his chronicle was written at the command of Henry VI and Constance, the quintessential medieval "power couple," at least partly to justify their rule of the Kingdom of Sicily and the punishment of those who had opposed them.

Conversely, even Hugh Falcandus, one of the more caustic commentators, may have been reluctant to denigrate his queen directly for fear of reprisal. Instead, he reserved his most vehement vitriol for those, like Stephen of Perche, who were Margaret's allies.

Significantly, the actions noted were reactions to threats, or perceived threats, to royal authority. It was logical that such matters would be addressed in some way if the existing social order were to be preserved. Draconian though some of these strategies and tactics may have been, they were effective.

Moreover, as the actions of queens, they were beyond contestation, as if they were tantamount to natural (even divine) justice. As the ultimate authority, the monarch was the law. Commentary in our times often overlooks the blunt social realities of medieval life. A detractor or traitor could not be "rehabilitated" or controlled through psychotherapy or other means.

Our sources are chronicles; a decree (charter) is unlikely to offer much more than the scarcest detail about events such as these.

Interestingly enough, the specific circumstances of the incidents resulting in each queen's actions differ notably from those of the other two. The women of our trio never lacked for individuality, if not originality. There's more than one way to skin a cat, and these ladies were more than ready to rise to the occasion. Indeed, they may even have relished the experience of defeating their nasty adversaries.

It is difficult to speculate about a medieval woman's personality or state of mind. What can be said is that these incidents occurred after each of our queens had gained a few years of experience in dealing with the political realities entailed in their status. They were not newly-crowned women who had lived sheltered lives. If they were in any way cynical or embittered, it was with good reason.

Margaret

Margaret's aggressiveness as a she-wolf takes two essential forms, namely homicide in targeted killings and, as regent, the harsh sentencing of opponents or those perceived as rivals.

These accounts come to us from the chronicle of Hugh Falcandus, whose precise identity is disputed. Whoever he was, Falcandus was present at court. Though he is generally viewed as a disagreeable person, cynical and perhaps pernicious, he is reasonably accurate despite sometimes repeating court gossip. Except for a few cases of questionable chronology, occasionally making the reader wonder which event came first, Hugh's worst flaw is an opinionated tone expressed through a poison pen. He is not a great apologist for Margaret, but neither is he her worst critic. Perhaps he was writing just critically enough to be able to defend himself against accusations of disloyalty, if it ever came to that. He does not seem to have liked William I very much.

We first learn of Margaret's sense of retribution, if not vengeance, in 1162 while her husband was away on the mainland asserting his authority over the restless baronage. The reprisals followed the recent revolt that had claimed the life of her eldest son.

Margaret was assisted by the courtier Caïd Martin, an Arab eunuch who had converted to Christianity but seemed to dislike Catholics (as opposed to Orthodox) because his brother had died at their hands during the revolt.

There were two named targets.

Henry Aristippo, the lecherous archdeacon of Catania, had abducted some concubines from the king's harem during the riots, setting up his own little harem in his home (yes, this was a Catholic cleric). He was apprehended and cast into a dark dungeon to die, probably in the royal palace or the seaside castle.

Sylvester of Marsico, one of the king's cousins, was also caught, and he met with the same fate.

According to Hugh Falcandus: *Henricus enim Aristippus, antequam in Apuliam pervenisset, iubente rege, captus fuerat et Panormum reductus, qui etiam in carcere, post non multum temporis, miserie simul et vivendi modum sortitus est electus ergo Siracusanus et Silvester comes diu multumque regi supplicantes, multis ei rationibus persuadere conabantur urbem opinatissimam totique regno non parum decoris afferentem, ob paucorum scelera non oportere destrui, cum omnes ex urbe proditores aufugerint, ac si forte quospiam illorum remansisse contigerit, eorum incumbendum suppliciis, neque populum immeritum ob aliena crimina puniendum.*

This is significant because both Henry and Sylvester formed, with Matthew of Aiello, the chancery council of three *familiares* appointed to replace the murdered Maio of Bari. Indeed, Sylvester may well have been a party to the plot of Matthew Bonello to depose William.

We do not know how the assassinations were planned. It seems that these men were lured to the royal palace and, once there, apprehended and imprisoned. This would be similar to the way Matthew Bonello was killed. It would not attract undue attention among the baronage or populace. The men would simply "disappear." The palace is located at the southern end of the old city, near its outer walls, overlooking the Genoard park (now Piazza Indipendenza and Corso Calatafimi). Henry and Sylvester probably lived in the Kasr district, not more than a ten-minute walk from the palace. One imagines them being accompanied inconspicuously by guards through the crowded streets to the palace. The other, unnamed, targets, being less important than these two, were likely arrested, taken from their homes and put to death immediately, perhaps at the seaside castle. We know of no public executions of these men.

The deaths of Henry and Sylvester left Matthew as a counsellor, joined by Richard Palmer and Caïd Peter. It would later develop that Margaret, as regent, was not enthralled by the personalities of Matthew and Richard, but for now she would tolerate them. She trusted Peter.

This reprisal incident has led some historians to suppose that Margaret was inclined to act when William, her husband, was not. We can never know if William himself, before his departure, ordered the capture of Henry and Sylvester, though it seems unlikely that he would ask his wife to oversee such an action.

There seem to have been other targets, but they were not important enough for Falcandus to mention their names. This was not a purge so much as a surgical strike.

The other incidents, which did not involve actual homicide, occurred during Margaret's time as regent. Most of her decisions to mete out justice were juridically sound, and she left these to her justiciars or to her chancellor, Stephen of Perche, rarely exercising her right of veto. At least one known case deviated from this norm. It involved Richard of Molise (Mandra) and it is rather disturbing, even at this distance of time.

Richard, who held estates in the Molise region, was invested with lands by Margaret early in her regency to counterbalance the power of other barons on the mainland. The record does not show any disloyalty on his part. Yet, in 1168 Margaret imprisoned him based largely on the testimony of Bohemond of Manopello, who accused him of supporting her half-brother, Henry (Rodrigo), in a conspiracy to unseat her.

Among the accusations was the claim that Richard held Mandra and some royal lands illegally. This was untrue, Richard explained, because Mandra itself was already his, and it had been confirmed to him by the chamberlain Caïd Peter. The other towns were granted him, temporarily, by Turgisio, Apulia's governor. By now, Peter, fearing for his life, had fled the kingdom. Turgisio, for his part, failed to vouch for Richard. Falcandus does not mention any charters being produced as evidence.

The trial was, to say the least, irregular. The overzealous justiciars ruled that Richard held Mandra and the Apulian towns lawfully so long as Caïd Peter guaranteed his rights, but lost his feudal tenure *ipso facto* when Peter left the kingdom.

Richard, a royal *familiare* (counsellor), vigorously denied these accusations, going so far as to challenge to trial by single combat anybody accusing him of treason. We have no record of this challenge being accepted.

Further allegations followed, apparently intended to erode Richard's credibility in Margaret's eyes. The substance of these charges involved illegal feudal tenure rather than any actual moves against the crown. Nobody seems to have accused Richard of plotting to kill anybody.

The accused, though a nobleman, was not permitted the right to exonerate himself. Instead of his accusers being required to prove his guilt, Richard was expected to prove his innocence. He was arrested without any venue of appeal, and then imprisoned in the castle on the rocky cliffs overlooking Taormina to the south of Messina.[3]

It is difficult to know what to make of this. Did Margaret truly believe in Richard's guilt? Were other machinations involved? Did Stephen, her chancellor, have a motive for convincing her of the man's complicity in a conspiracy? The trial, as it unfolded, bore every sign of a pretext based on imaginary crimes.

Yet Margaret was present at the trial, and she alone had the authority to sentence Richard of Molise or grant him clemency. Perhaps she knew not whom to trust.

In the event, Richard was eventually freed when Henry, Margaret's troublesome half-brother, escaped his own imprisonment across the strait in Calabria and released the erstwhile *familiare* at Taormina.

Henry's treason, on the other hand, seems to have been supported by the evidence and his pattern of behavior.

In both cases, Margaret, like many queens regent of her era, was steadfast in her determination to punish adversaries.

Joanna

We know virtually nothing of Joanna's life from the time of her marriage to William II in 1177 until his death in 1189.

For Joanna's she-wolf temperament, we look to her second marriage, following her widowhood. In 1196, she wed Raymond VI, Count of Toulouse, as his third wife, but the marriage does not seem to have been a happy one.

By this time, Joanna had been deprived of most of her Sicilian dower. For a few months following William's death, her movements were restricted by the newly-crowned Tancred, who knew of her loyalty to Constance Hauteville, the daughter of Roger II who contested Tancred's claim to the throne, and the widow was housed in Palermo's Zisa palace under guard. She was finally released to her brother, Richard, when he came through Messina *en route* to the Holy Land during the Third Crusade. Joanna had to be rescued at Cyprus after having been shipwrecked there; Richard imprisoned the island's ruler. Then she sailed to Palestine, where she was nearly betrothed by Richard to Al Adil (Saphadin), Saladin's brother, though historians debate whether this was a serious proposal. Later, whilst Richard was imprisoned by Constance's husband in the German lands, Joanna stayed with the pope until she could return along a safer route.

Philip II of France seems to have thought of marrying Joanna, but she ended up with Raymond.

As if she had not already proven her mettle, Joanna undertook to defend her husband's position by besieging a castle, Les Cassés, near Toulouse, in spring 1199. She was forced to lift the siege when some of her own people secretly armed the rebels and set fire to her camp.

She went northward to seek the aid of her brother, Richard, who was besieging Chalus, in Aquitaine. This was late in her pregnancy, and the spring rains were heavy. When she finally arrived at Chalus, or perhaps even before, she was apprised of Richard's death from a crossbow dart.

The arbalester, Bertram of Gurdun was brought before Joanna. Richard had forgiven the man but the besieger Marchadés, something of a freelance warrior, had imprisoned him anyway.

Joanna, the she-wolf, ordered the man tortured to death in what was tantamount to a summary execution. The crime was regicide. More precisely, the offense was killing Richard as Duke of Aquitaine.

According to the "Winchester Chronicle" (the Annals of Winchester), Joanna had Bertram's eyes torn out and he died following a bout of torture: *Sed Marchadeus misit eum clam rege ad Johannam comitissam Sancti Egidii sororem regis, qui fecit ei evelli ungues pedum et manuum et oculos, et postea excoriari et equis detrahi.*[4]

Roger of Howden recounts the episode slightly differently, though with the same fatal destiny for Bertram, and here is Henry Riley's eloquent translation of the relevant passage published in 1853:

The king then ordered Bertram de Gurdun, who had wounded him, to come into his presence, and said to him, "What harm have I done to you, that you have killed me?" On which he made answer, "You slew my father and my two brothers with your own hand, and you had intended now to kill me. Therefore, take any revenge on me that you may think fit, for I will readily endure the greatest torments you can devise, so long as you have met with your end, after having inflicted evils so many and so great upon the world." On this, the king ordered him to be released, and said, "I forgive you my death," but the youth stood before the feet of the king, and with scowling features, and undaunted neck, did his courage demand the sword. The king was aware that punishment was wished for, and that pardon was dreaded. "Live on," said he, "although thou art unwilling, and by my bounty behold the light of day. To the conquered faction now let there be bright hopes, and the example of myself." And then, after being released from his chains, he was allowed to depart, and the king ordered one hundred shillings of English money to be given him. Marchadés, however, the king not knowing of it, seized him, and after the king's death, first flaying him alive, had him hanged.[5]

Either way, Bertram, who seems to have been in his twenties when captured, never loosed another crossbow dart.

Clearly, Joanna had strong opinions about royal authority and justice, and she was unafraid to use her power to achieve them.

Joanna did not long outlive her brother or the man she ordered to be tortured to death. She died from complications of giving birth in September 1199.

Her legacy is a complicated one. Her son, Raymond VII, was often known not only as the son of a countess but as "the son of a queen."

Constance

Following Constance's birth in late 1154 as the posthumous daughter of Roger II, we hear virtually nothing about her until 1168 when Henry (Rodrigo), the half-brother of Queen Margaret, seized control of the city of Messina with a violent revolt. Falcandus tells us that there was a rumor that Geoffrey, the brother of the chancellor Stephen of Perche, was coming to Sicily to marry Constance and rule in her name, *sed Gaufridum quemdam eius fratrem regnaturum, et ob hoc Odonem Quarrellum cum ingenti pecunia transiturum in Gallias ut eius opera ductuque predictus Gaufridus in Siciliam transfretaret, et Constantiam, Rogerii regis filiam, uxorem duceret, inde sibi dandam occasionem existimans ut videretur regnum iustius occupare.* Such a rumor may well have existed, but it was based on nonsense.

Constance passed her childhood with her mother, Beatrice of Rethel, in Palermo and at the royal castle crowning a mountain at San Marco d'Alunzio. Upon reaching the age of majority, she did not immediately marry, and it is possible (though unproven) that she lived for a few years in one of the nunneries founded by Margaret in the Nebrodian Mountains.

In 1185, she wed the future Henry VI, destined to become the Holy Roman Emperor. Her childless nephew, William II, named Constance his universal heir, but following his death in 1189 Matthew of Aiello, Roger of Andria, Margaritus of Brindisi and other magnates of the kingdom elected Tancred of Lecce, Constance's bastard cousin, King of Sicily. Constance had her supporters, including, as we have seen, Joanna of England, William's widow, but they could not immediately help her cause.

Constance was hardly invisible during her years in Germany, when she sought to intervene with her husband to resolve a conflict involving one of her mother's kinsmen.[6] Later, one of the motives for Henry VI accepting Richard Lionheart as his prisoner was the English king's support of Tancred over Constance.

Otherwise, little that was known of Constance's strength of character is reported before this time. That was to change.

Several sources refer to Constance's attempts to take by force the kingdom that was hers by right of inheritance as the daughter of Sicily's first king, but the two chroniclers nearest the action in time and place were Richard of San Germano and Peter of Eboli, although the Cassino Chronicle and Cassino Annals also mention these events, while the Fossanova Chronicle is also informative.

Following a failed incursion, when she was taken prisoner but then released through papal intervention, Constance finally returned to the *Regnum* in 1194 during an invasion partly financed with funds from the ransom paid by England, in the person of Eleanor of Aquitaine, to liberate the Lionheart.[7]

The Sicilian she-wolf had not forgotten the people who had deprived her of her throne five years earlier.

In late 1194, while Constance was in Apulia, where she gave birth to a son, her husband was in Palermo, where he was crowned King of Sicily *jure uxoris*. Supposedly, he had agreed to permit Sibylla of Acerra, Tancred's widow, along with her young son, William III, safe conduct to a comfortable place of exile, perhaps Tancred's County of Lecce. Not long afterward, it was alleged, a plot was uncovered that was being planned by several courtiers, including the vice chancellor Matthew of Aiello and the general Margaritus of Brindisi. This led to their exile and imprisonment, although some less important persons were burned alive.[8]

Young William was blinded, castrated and eventually killed, while Sibylla and her daughters were sent to live in a convent north of the Alps.[9]

None of this was unusual for the times, and most of it was decided long before Constance finally arrived in Palermo in 1195. The only act she may have overseen was casting the remains of the late Tancred, and his son Roger III, out of the Magione church erected by Matthew of Aiello.[10]

Sibylla's brother, Richard of Acerra, was executed on Henry's orders late in 1196. Henry himself died at Messina in September of the following year.

How much did Constance know about the arrests and executions? Did she encourage her husband? The known records attribute the deeds not to Constance but to Henry.

Yet the preponderance of the evidence suggests that Constance knew of these acts and was in agreement with what her husband was doing. Certainly, as Queen of Sicily, she could have intervened if she thought his policy overzealous.

As she most likely saw it, the people being punished were traitors getting what they deserved.

Like Joanna, Constance died soon after the violent events. Her death from natural causes came in November 1198.

Conclusion

The behavior of our three she-wolves probably reflects the harsh realities of medieval life more than the women's personalities, about which we can know very little. Much like a soldier who would not deliberately kill in civilian life, these women were thrust into situations that they might not otherwise have had to confront. Other important women, such as abbesses, were not necessarily preoccupied with survival in the face of predatory adversaries.

There is not enough information to imply anything like a pattern of behavior for Margaret, Joanna or Constance. From what little we know, it seems that they usually operated behind the scenes. Therefore, there may well be other examples, now lost to the eyes of history, of their efforts, successful or not, to suppress opponents. It could be argued that unsuccessful attempts would not likely be mentioned by chroniclers, even those, like Hugh Falcandus, who were fixtures at court.

Margaret, Joanna and Constance were not alone. Queens elsewhere had to resort to the same tactics to survive. We could even posit that it was a normal part of a queen's life.

The twelfth century did not lack for strong queens willing to do whatever was necessary to defend their families. Some of these women were related to the three discussed here. We should note, in particular, Urraca "the Reckless" of Castile and León (1079-1126), like Margaret a Jiménez, Empress Maude (1102-1167), mother of Henry II of England, Melisende of Jerusalem (1105-1161), Constance of Antioch (1128-1163), a Hauteville as daughter of Bohemond II, and of course Eleanor of Aquitaine (1122-1204).

NOTES

1. Castor, Helen, *She-Wolves: The Women Who Ruled England before Elizabeth* (2012); Norton, Elizabeth, *She-Wolves: The Notorious Queens of Medieval England* (2008).

2. An obvious symbolic reference is Rome's famous bronze Capitoline She-Wolf, which scientific dating indicates is medieval, but the metaphor is not completely absent from Sicilian tradition. The she-wolf inspired the title of a story by Giovanni Verga, *La Lupa*, about a wealthy peasant woman of the nineteenth century. This was published in 1880, when actual wolves still roamed Sicily; today there are red and gray foxes (the author recently saw one of these in the Madonian Mountains) but no wolves. There are, however, wolves of the protected species *canis lupus italicus* in regions of the former *Regnum Siciliae* such as Calabria's Sila Mountains.

3. The account of Hugh Falcandus: *Dum hec adversus comitem agerentur, Robertus comes Casertinus adiecit eundem auctoritate sua dudum in Apulia Mandram et quedam oppida regis in Troianorum finibus invasisse furtimque adhuc, eadem ignorante curia, possidere. Ad hec ille respondit quod gaytus Petrus, qui tunc preerat curie, Mandram ei tenendam ad tempus eo tenore dederat, ut inde singulis annis curie certam redderet pecunie quantitatem; oppida vero que in partibus Troianorum invasisse dicebatur, itidem sibi a Turgisio terre illius camerario fuisse concessa. Interrogatus idem Turgisius, qui tunc forte presens aderat, negavit eum hec oppida sua licencia tenuisse. Iussi sunt itaque proceres omnes, preter curie familiares, in partem secedere, super hiis que adversus comitem dicta fuerant iudicialem sentenciam prolaturi. erant autem hii qui ad iudicium faciendum surrexerant: Boamundus Monopolis comes, Robertus de Lauro comes Casertinus, Rogerius eius filius Tricarici comes, Rogerius comes Avellini, Symon comes Sangrensis, Rogerius comes Giracii, Rogerius Tironensis magister comestabulus, Florius Camerotensis, iudex quoque Tarentinus et Abdenago Hannibalis filius, qui magistri erant iusticiarii. Quibus invicem super hiis disceptantibus, visum est Richardum Molisii comitem, antequam gaytus Petrus fugeret, Mandram quam ab eo acceperat licentia curie tenuisse. Post illius autem discessum, cum eam teneret occulte, neque rem, ut oportebat, ad regis notitiam referret, non iam precario possidentem, sed invasorem rectius estimandum, ut qui sua tantum auctoritate, non consentiente sed ignorante curia, possideret, eumque de tota terra quam tenuerat in misericordia regis esse tum propter id, tum propter dicta oppida que constabat eum sua itidem auctoritate contra fidem regi debitam occupasse. Hanc ergo sententiam, vice consensuque omnium, Boamundus comes, ut erat vir eloquens, in presentia regis exposuit. tunc Richardus comes exclamavit: iniuste se gravari; odium equitati manifeste preferri; paratum se probare quod iniquam falsamque protulisset sententiam. quibus verbis Boamundus comitem prohibuit curie respondere, dicens iniuriam hanc non in eos qui iudicaverant, sed in caput regium principaliter redundare. Dehinc iniunctum est archiepiscopis et episcopis qui ader[ant ut in aucto]rem tante contumelie quod equum esset de iuris severitate decernerent. At illi, iuxta constitutiones regum Sicilie, decreverunt Richardum comitem non solum de terra sua, verum etiam de membris et corpore regis misericordie subiacere, eo quod iudicium curie falsum dicere presumpsisset. Captus igitur et militum custodie deputatus, Tauromineum iussus est perduci et ibidem in castello quod in ardua rupe positum oppido supereminet summa diligentia custodiri.*

4. Reported in the *Winchester Chronicle*, page 71, where the editor, Henry Luard, refers in marginalia to the "frightful cruelty of the Princess Joanna." Howden claims that it was the warrior Marchadés who had the man killed, q.v. *The Annals of Roger de Hoveden*, volume 2, page 454.

5. Ibid, pages 454-455.

6. *Queens of Sicily,* pages 386-387.

7. Ibid, pages 388-393.

8. The events are recounted by Richard of San Germano for the year 1194. In the chronicle of Peter of Eboli, particula 42, verses 1329-1362, folio 136v in the manuscript: *Al Deus, inpaciens fraudis scelerisque nefandi, Puplicat in lucem quod tegit archa nephas; Nam nichil admittit felix fortuna sinistrum, Nec possunt quod obest prospera fata pati. Hec tria felices comitantia Cesaris actus Quam bene dispensant sors bona, fata, Deus! Conscius archani quidam secreta revelat Et docet insidias enumeratque viros; Detegit et scriptum nocturna lampade factum, Quod docet in Caypha presule posse capi. Ostupet armipotens famulos miratus iniquos, Ducit et in dubiam verba relata fidem. Postquam certa ftdes super hiis datur, indice scripto, Coniuratorum dissimulatur opus; Curia contrahitur, resident in iure vocati, Quisque sibi dubitans multa timenda timent. Iamque silere dato, solio redimitus ab alto, Exolvit querulo Cesar in ore moras: "Quis pro pace necem, vel quis pro munere dampnum, Aut quis pro donis dampna meretur?" ait. "Nec Christo Cayphas fedt, nec sevius Anna, Quam michi conscripte disposuere manus." Protinus armiferis pieno iubet ore ministris, Ut capiant quosquos littera lecta notat. Qui cito mandatis inplent pia iussa receptis, Infectos capiunt prodicione viros. Dampnalos ex lege viros clementia differt et suffert pietas inpietalis bonus; In condempnatos meritum sententia tardat, Quo datur ut vinctos Apula dampnet humus, Quam Cesar properans, ex parte licenciat agmen, Ne gravet urbanos maxima turba suos. Bavuarus et Scavus, Lonbardus, Marchio, Tuscus, In propriam redeunt Saxo, Boemus humum.* See also the *Cassino Chronicle,* page 476; *Annales Casinenses,* entries for 1194 and 1195.

9. *Queens of Sicily,* pages 364-365; *Ottonis de Sancto Blasio Chronica,* pages 65-66; *The Annals of Roger de Hoveden,* volume 2, page 341. See also *Patrologiae Cursus Completus,* book 214, sections 20-22: *Sed et Sibilia, relicta regis Tancredi, cum filiabus suis, ergastulum captivitatus evasit, et in regnum Francorum confugiens, porgenitam suam Gualtero, Brenensi comiti, tradidit in uxorem.* In English translation see *The Deeds of Pope Innocent III,* pages 20-21.

10. *The Annals of Roger de Hoveden,* volume 2, page 341.

Sibylla and her son (upper right) as prisoners of Henry (shown) and Constance in 1194 in the chronicle of Peter of Eboli. Constance was in Apulia with her infant son.

Chapter 2
QUEENLY WORDS

Apart from just a few records, we have virtually no evidence of what our countesses and queens ever actually said. Notably, Margaret is quoted by Hugh Falcandus and Constance by Peter of Eboli, and the lengthiest known passages of these words are published here.

Precious little evidence survives of letters between queens that would confirm an active "reginal sisterhood." For example, we know of no correspondence between Margaret and her *consuocera,* Eleanor of Aquitaine, though it is theoretically possible that they met in Palermo in 1149; it seems more likely that Sibylla of Burgundy met Eleanor on that occasion.[1] Although Thomas le Brun, Gervase of Tilbury, Peter of Blois and others once present at the Sicilian court ended up in the service of English monarchs, there is no known evidence of them transmitting actual letters between queens, interesting as it would be to discover such correspondence as a note from Eleanor to Margaret on the occasion of the marriage of young Joanna of England to William II.

Even if letters were never actually written, concise messages could well have been relayed by couriers who memorized a text to recite, perhaps to augment what was contained in a letter being delivered. An example of this, though the letter's bearer was no mere courier, is the verbal message borne by Thibald, Prior of Saint-Arnouldt de Crepy, to Margaret on behalf of Thomas Becket (see the text below).

A mounted courier could make it from Naples to Messina in two weeks. Couriers, or courier relays, could get a letter from Messina to Palermo in three days, although travel by sea was sometimes preferred for that route. This is how Margaret, as regent, stayed in touch with her treasury at Palermo whilst she and her court were at Messina.

Heralds, who sometimes carried messages between monarchs or princes, were not couriers but, in effect, diplomats in the service of kings; by the end of the twelfth century they also kept records of blazons, not only at battles but at tournaments, hence the term *heraldry,* described in another chapter. In the Kingdom of Sicily, actual heralds, as court officers, are not mentioned explicitly until the thirteenth century, and some were present at the Battle of Benevento in 1266.

Here, apart from words spoken in actual conversation, we are referring to correspondence of a personal nature, rather than charters or public letters (considered in another chapter) issued as part of the official duties of a regent. In stark contrast to the very few known words of Sicily's countesses and queens, those of certain contemporaries, such as Eleanor of Aquitaine, are legion.[2]

A diary would be enlightening, but during this period most such works were accounts of such experiences as journeys undertaken by pilgrims or crusaders. In the event, nothing like a journal survives for any of our ladies.

An additional problem in Sicily and parts of Spain was the use of paper, which was introduced by the Arabs. Eventually, the Constitutions of Melfi, promulgated by Frederick II in 1231, proscribed the use of paper for important charters, but what of less important documents? Clearly, a significant number of charters and letters written on fragile paper, particularly before 1231, have been lost, presumably destroyed by humidity, fire or other hazards. It is quite possible, therefore, that certain (hypothetical) letters written by our queens might have survived were these inscribed on parchment or vellum rather than paper, but this is conjecture.

Circumstantial evidence and situational context strongly suggest that there were conversations between certain queens living at the same court at the same time. Margaret must have spoken with Beatrice of Rethel. Sibylla of Acerra certainly conversed with Constance Hauteville, who slept in the same chamber as her while detained in Palermo. Unfortunately, we have few indications of what was said during these conversations, interesting as such dialogue would be, although we know that Sibylla wanted her husband, Tancred of Lecce, to kill Constance.

What language did our queens speak?

Until the end of the regency of Constance Hauteville at her death in 1198, the chief language spoken at court was Norman French. Even Sichelgaita of Salerno, despite her Lombard upbringing, was conversant in the language of her husband, Robert Guiscard; Norman French was probably the tongue she spoke when leading the knights she sometimes commanded. It is the language Adelaide del Vasto most often spoke to her sons and, as regent following her husband's death, to the oft-rebellious Norman barons. A form of French was what Adelaide spoke at court in Jerusalem, where she was briefly queen.

Hugh Falcandus explicitly mentions the fact that Margaret's wayward half-brother, Rodrigo (Henry), had difficulty communicating at the Sicilian court because his mastery of French was limited: *Quibus ille Francorum se linguam ignorare, que maxime necessaria esset in curia, nec eius esse, respondebat, industrie ut oneri tanto sufficeret.*[3]

However, there was a certain German influence during the last decade of the twelfth century and the minority of Frederick II, particularly following the death of Constance, because Henry VI had brought with him many speakers of that language. Constance, who spoke German as well as French, was not only a dynastic bridge but a linguistic one.

The earliest form of the Sicilian language (Middle Sicilian) came into common use during Frederick's reign, perhaps being widely spoken as early as his first marriage, to Constance of Aragon, in 1209. This was the language of the first native court poetry composed in Palermo. It was spoken in Sicily, much of Calabria, and the western parts of Apulia, such as Taranto. The inception of a new language is gradual, and Sicilian may have been evolving long before Constance's reign, but our most reliable record of its use dates only from the early years of the thirteenth century (an example follows in note 12). The modern Sicilian one occasionally hears spoken today bears the mark of Catalan and other languages.

Most of Sicily's earliest countesses and queens were, by necessity, at least bilingual; Adelaide may have learned some Greek and Margaret some Arabic, though we do not know to what extent this was the case.

We may speculate that an early form of Sicilian was already spoken around the time of Margaret's death in 1183. By then, the *Regnum Siciliae* was largely Latinized, with ever fewer speakers of Greek. Many, if not most, Muslims had converted to Catholicism, and though there were trilingual Latin-Greek-Arabic missals, such as the Harley Psalter, the liturgy was celebrated in Latin. Indeed, the Arabs may have been the first segment of the Sicilian population to embrace the new language.

Sicilian, though Latin-based, reflects various influences, from French and German to Arabic, Greek and Lombardic.[4]

Margaret of Navarre

We find Margaret addressing her court in Norman French upon the arrival of her cousin, Stephen of Perche:

"Here I see myself finally achieving what I have so ardently desired. To the sons of the Count of Perche I owe the same honor one accords a brother. The work of their father, in truth, gave my own father his kingdom. It was the Count of Perche who granted to my mother as his niece, and thereby to my father, a dowry of vast lands conquered in the face of great dangers and prolonged effort from the Muslims of Spain. You need not be surprised that I regard his son, Stephen, my mother's kinsman, as if he were my brother, welcoming him with joy the moment he arrives here from faraway lands. I desire and command that all who declare good wishes to me and my son will sincerely respect and honour Stephen. From your kind treatment of him, I will infer the depth of your fealty and affection toward us."[5]

On another occasion, Margaret is quoted responding to a request by the papal delegate that Richard Palmer be sent to Rome for archiepiscopal consecration:

"The presence of the archbishop-elect is needed at court, so for now he cannot leave. He can depart in another moment when circumstances permit."[6]

Only a few letters survive that were written to our queens directly, rather than to the young kings for whom they were regents. Here a notable exception is a letter sent to Margaret by Thomas Becket:

"To the most serene lady and dearest daughter in Christ, Margaret, the illustrious Queen of Sicily, Thomas, by divine appointment humble minister of the church of Canterbury, sends health, and thus to reign temporally in Sicily, that she may rejoice forever with the angels in glory! Although I have never seen your face, I am not ignorant of your renown, its fame supported by nobility of birth and by greatly numerous virtues. But amongst other perfections which we and others praise, we owe a debt of gratitude to your kindness, which we are now endeavouring to acknowledge, for the generosity with which you gave refuge to our fellow exiles, Christ's poor ones, our own kin who fled to your realm from him who persecutes them. You have consoled them in their distress, which is a great duty of religion. Your wealth has relieved their indigence, and the amplitude of your power protected them in their needs. By such sacrifices God is well pleased, your earthly reputation is enhanced and made known, and every blessing is poured upon you. By these means you have bound ourself also to you in gratitude, and we devote all that we possess and all we are to your service. As the first fruits of our devotion, we have used our good services to present your request to the most Christian king, as you may know by the requests which he had made to our dear friend, the King of Sicily, and by the words of the venerable prior of Crepy, whose literary attainments, single-mindedness and sense of justice make him dear to all good men. He is a man of correct life, sound doctrine, and perfect sanctity in human judgment. We beg of you to hear him with as much reverence as you would listen to the entire Western Church were it assembled at your feet. And I beseech you, not only out of respect for his person, but in high regard for the Church of Cluny, whose necessities he is charged with and which is reputed throughout all the Latin world to have possessed, within its walls, all the glory of virtue and perfection from the time of our first ancestors. In other respects also, I ask you, if it so please you, to place as much confidence in all that he shall tell you as coming from me, as if I myself had said it. Farewell."[7]

Unfortunately, there exists no known letter that Margaret wrote to Thomas Becket, although one may have been written and later lost or destroyed. Becket's nephews, to whom his letter refers, resided in Palermo, probably in the vicinity of Vicolo del Lombardo and Via del Protonotaro, where a church was erected to the archbishop's memory shortly after his death.[8]

Constance Hauteville of Sicily

Speaking to Tancred of Lecce upon meeting him as his prisoner, upon which he asked why his kinswoman, who was Holy Roman Empress, claimed what was allegedly his dominion, Constance's response was quite explicit:

"Do not forget what I am saying to you now, Tancred. Before long, your rising star shall turn against you, just as my star has fallen upon me. Destiny cannot be changed. I do not seek your kingdom but that of my father, which is mine by right. Are you Roger's son? Not by any means. I am the king's universal heiress because I am his legitimate child by my mother. The legal rights of both my parents bequeath me the realm you presently hold as a usurper. You have not yet confronted the man [Emperor Henry VI] who shall obtain these lands for me by the sword. What laws and oaths gave you the realm that appertains to me? It was only the benevolent grace of King William that permitted you to keep even Lecce."[9]

In which language did Constance speak to Tancred? It was most likely Norman French or perhaps even a very early form of Sicilian (see Chapter 7).

Peter of Eboli "quotes" Constance elsewhere, where her words may be rather more conjectural. For example, he quotes her prayer that God take vengeance upon Tancred. Although it seems doubtful that Constance actually said these words, she probably would have prayed in Latin:

"Alfa Deus, Deus O[mega], mundi moderator et auctor, Ex hiis vindictam, supplico, sume dolis; Alfa Deus, Deus O[mega], liquide scrutator abyssi, In me periuras contine, queso, manus; Alfa Deus, Deus O[mega], stellati rector Olimpi, Pena malignantes puniat alta viros; Alfa Deus, Deus O[mega], iuris servator et equi, Iam tua conflictus vindicet ira meos; Alfa Deus, Deus O[mega], terre fundator amicte, In me pugnantes ferrea fiamma voret; Alfa Deus, Deus O[mega], rerum Deus omnicreator, Supplicis anelile respice, queso, preces; Iram congemines, acuas penamque, furorem accendas, tumidos comprime, perde feros; Contine faustosos, instantes perde feros; Da pacem, gladios divide, scinde manus, arma cadant, arcusque teras, balista cremetur; Rumpe polum, specta, collige, scribe, nota; Hos notet exilium, scribat proscriptio, plures obprobrium signet. Rumpe polum, transmitte virum romphea gerentem; Eruat ancillam, dissipet ora canum. Alfa Deus, Deus O[mega], genitor, genitura creatrix, Quod precor acceptes, Alfa Deus, Deus O[mega]." [10]

We know that her prayers were answered with the demise of Tancred and imprisonment of his consort, Sibylla of Acerra.

Sibylla of Acerra

In a citation that is highly hypothetical, indeed apocryphal, Peter of Eboli quotes the deposed Sibylla, consort of the late Tancred. It is extremely unlikely that Sibylla herself ever pronounced these words of lament about her life as Queen of Sicily and consort of Tancred, as if she were a condemned criminal repenting of her misdeeds.[11]

Constance Hohenstaufen

Unlike the prose chronicle of Hugh Falcandus, Peter's chronicle quoting Constance Hauteville and (perhaps) Sibylla of Acerra is written in verse. Contemporary literary references of this kind refer to Sicilian women rather rarely unless they were queens regnant or regent.

An obvious exception was the *Rebellamentu di Sichilia contra Re Carlu,* probably the memoir of John of Procida, onetime counsellor of Frederick II. Composed in Middle Sicilian about a century after Peter of Eboli wrote his chronicle, this recounts the story of the War of the Vespers of 1282. It is one of the oldest surviving works of prose, rather than poetry, written in one of the Italian languages (Tuscan, Umbrian, Neapolitan, etc.) and the lengthiest narrative text composed in any of these vernaculars at such an early date.

Significantly, this work refers to Constance, the daughter of King Manfred of Sicily and wife of Peter III of Aragon:

"To the magnificent, great and powerful lord the King of Aragon, Count of Barcelona, in all your exalted power, to which we commend ourselves for your favor. First among us, Count Alaimo of Lentini, Lord Palmeri Abate and Lord Walter of Caltagirone, joined by all the brethren barons of the island of Sicily. We greet you with every reverence. Ruled by our present sovereign [Charles of Anjou], we have come to view ourselves as men who have been sold, subjugated as beasts. We wish to submit our fealty to your authority and that of *your consort, our Lady,* to whom we must convey our homage, praying that you may deign to free us of our enemies just as Moses freed his people from the hands of the Pharaoh, so that we may ensure our children's future, secure from the deceitful, devouring wolves. We shall write to you every day, or otherwise credit to you Lord John our secretary."[12]

Conclusions

Any record of the words actually spoken by our queens is a rare treasure. Unfortunately, the dominance of Latin for writing means that nothing in the original tongues (French, German, Sicilian) has been conserved. There is no conclusive evidence that a Sicilian queen composed poetry, though it is a possibility.

What little survives reflects actions that are steadfast and decisive, even in the face of adversity.

NOTES

1. *Queens of Sicily,* pages 149, 641n446.

2. For some examples, see Richardson, Henry, "The Letters and Charters of Eleanor of Aquitaine," *The English Historical Review,* volume 74, number 291 (April 1959), pages 193-213.

3. Chapter 50 in the chronicle; *Cronisti e Scrittori Sincroni Napoletani,* volume 1 ("Normanni"), edited by Del Re, Giuseppe (Naples 1845), page 366.

4. For a few examples, along with an introduction to the faiths and cultures, see *The Peoples of Sicily: A Multicultural Legacy* (2014), pages 288-289.

5. The text, recorded in Latin, comes to us from Hugh Falcandus, probably a witness, as: *"Ecce, completum video quod plenis semper votis expetii. Nec enim aliter quam fratres proprios diligere quidem et honorare debeo filios comitis Perticensis per quem, ut verum fatear, pater meus regnum obtinuit. Nam idem comes patri meo terram amplissimam cum nepte sua, matre mea, dotem dedit, quam in Hispania multis periculis ac diuturnis laboribus expugnatam, Sarracenis abstulerat. Nec ergo mirari debetis si filium eius, matris meae consobrinum, loco mihi fratris habendum censeam, et de remotissimis partibus ad me venientem gratanter excipiam, quem quidem volo jubeoque, ut qui me filiumque meum diligere se fatentur, propensius diligant et honorent, ut eorum gratia erga nos ex hoc ipso fidei dilectionisque quantitatem emetiar."* This is the lengthiest verbatim quotation of the words of a Sicilian queen of this era that is known to us.

6. This comes to us from Hugh Falcandus: *Regina mutato consilio respondit: "Electi praesentiam curie necessariam esse, nec eum ad praesens posse quopiam proficisci, alias iturum, cum temporis oportunitas pateretur."*

7. The English translation is from the book by John Allen Giles published in 1846. The original: *Serenissime domine, et in Christo carissimae Margarete, illustri reginae Siculorum, Thomas divina dispensatione Cantuariensis ecclesiae minister humilis, salutem, et sic temporaliter regnare in Sicilia, ut cum angelis aeternaliter exultet in gloria. Licet faciem vestram non noverimus, gloriam tamen non possumus ignorare, quam et generosi sanguinis illustrat claritas, et multarum magnarumque virtutum decorat titulus, et famae celebritas numerosis praeconiis reddit insignem. Sed inter caeteras virtutes, quas cum aliis auditoribus gratanter amplectimur, liberalitati vestrae debemus, et qua nunc possumus devotione, gratias referimus ampliores, quae coexules nostros, proscriptos Christi, et consanguineos nostras, fugientes ad partes vestras a facie persecutoris, consolata est in tribulatione sua, quae profecto magna pars verae et Deo gratissimae religionis est, si pro justicia patientibus clementia ferat solatium, si pauperibus opulentia suffragetur, si sanctorum necessitatibus absoluta potestatis communicet amplitudo. Talibus enim hostiis promeretur Deus, exhilarescit et dilatatur gloria temporalis, et omnium bonorum gratiosus conciliatur affectus. His meritis inter alios specialiter tamen promeruistis et nos, qui totum id quod sumus et possumus ad vestrum devovimus obsequium. Cujus devotionis primitias, quas pro tempore potuimus excellentiae vestrae nuper optulimus, preces vestras apud regem Christianissimum promoventes, sicut perpendere potestis ex precibus ejus dilecto nostra illustri regi Siciliae porrectis, et ex verbis venerabilis prioris*

Crispiniacensis, quem et eruditio litterarum, et vitae sinceritas et integritas famae bonis omnibus amabilem et commendabilem reddunt. Est enim vir probatissime conversationis sanae doctrinae, et quantum ad humanum spectat examen, perfectae pro tempore sanctitatis, quem tanta reverentia a sublimitate vestra desideramus et petimus exaudiri, quanta totam occidentalem ecclesiam, si vestris pedibus assisteret, audiretis. Et hoc quidem tum pro suae personae reverentia, tum pro merito et auctoritate Cluniacensis ecclesiae, cujus procurat necessitates, quae in orbe Latino dinoscitur, a diebus patrum nostrorum in monastica religione perfectionis gloriam quasi propriam possedisse. In caeteris, quae vobis ex parte nostra dixerit, ei, si placet, credatis ut nobis. Valete.

8. This church has escaped the notice of most historians because no foundation charter or other contemporaneous record seems to survive that mentions it explicitly, and the structure was later reconstructed as a Baroque chapel. It is mentioned in the so-called *Ruolo dè Tonni* compiled in 1439. See *Opere Storiche Inedite sulla Città di Palermo* (1873), volume 3, by Gioacchino Di Marzo, page 489, footnote 1.

9. From the chronicle of Peter of Eboli (rubrics in Giovanni Battista Siragusa's *Liber ad Honorem Augusti di Pietro da Eboli*, pages 56-57), particula 25, verses 729-741; folio 119v in the manuscript: *"Quod ais, Tancrede, recordor: Ut michi retrogradum, iam tibi sidus erit. Quidquid fata volunt, stat inevitabile semper, per varias vario curritur axe vices. Non tua regna peto, set patris iura requiro. An tu Rogerii filius? Absit. Ego. Heres regis, ego matris iustissima proles, lex patris et matris dat michi quicquid habes. Regna tenes tantum usurpata, set illa. Vivit inexperta qui petat ense suo. Que leges, que iura tibi mea regna dederunt? Nam Lichium vobis gratia sola dedit."*

10. Particula 22, verses 620-648, folio 116v in the manuscript; the prayer uses words from the Book of Revelation, for example 2:12 in the vulgate, *Haec dicit qui habet rompheam urraque parte acutam.*

11. Particula 40, verses 1269-1300, folio 134v in the manuscript: *"O utinam Lichio comitissa manerem! Terrerent animos prelia nulla meos, Vir michi forsan adhuc superesset et inclita proles. Nunc Lichium tristis orba duobus eo. Vidisset nunquam visus Trinacria nostros! Nunc michi deserte dos mea tuta foret. Quam cito falsus honor nos deserit et fugit omen! Ut nova furtivus bruma liquescit honor. Ardeat in medio vicecancellarius Orco, Qui fuit excicii sedula causa mei. Quantum nequicie, quantumve tirannidis ausus Vir meus, in penas hec tulit liora meas. Et michi, quid prodest quod rex tulit Anglicus aurum? Ei michi, quid prosunt que tibi, Roma, dedi? Thesauros exausta meos succurre relicte, Auxilium perhibe, si potes, ipsa michi. Cur tua carta virum tibi dantem dona fefellit? Hen tuus egrotus regnat et arma tenet. Mortuus hen vincit, tuus eger in urbe triumphat; Sic tua decepit littera falsa virum. Ei michi, nec tutum est Romane credere puppi, Que, quas insequitur, has imitatur aquas. Nec michi Greca norus prodest, dulcissime fili, Quam, nec adhuc visa fronte, Philippus amat. Ergo, quod est tutum, veniam summissa precabor, Effundens lacrimas Cesaris ante pedes. Singultus, lacrime, gemitus, suspiria, fletus. Hec vir et hec proles, hec mihi frater erunt; Pro me pugnabunt, pro me dominumque rogabunt; Plus facient lacrime quam mea tela michi; Plus poterit pietas quam milia mille Quintum; Plus prece quam telis Cesar habendus erit."*

12. The original Sicilian: *A lu magnificu et egregiu et putenti signurj Re di Aragona, et Conti di Barsilona, cum tuctu vostru putiri et signuria, di ki nui ni arricumandamu tucti a la gracia vostra. Imprimu lu Conti di Lintini, zo esti Misser Alaymu, et Misser Palmeri Abati, et Misser*

QUEENLY WORDS

Galteri di Calathagiruni, et tucti li altri baruni di la ysula di Sichilia, sì vi salutanu cum omni reverencia. Havendu sempri mercì di li nostri persuni, sì comu homini vinduti et subiugati comu bestii, ricomandamuni a la vostra Signuria et a la signura vostra mugleri, la quali è la nostra Donna a ccui nui divimu purtari liancza, mandamuvi prigandu chi vui ni digiati liberari et trayri et livari di li manu di nostri et di li vostri nimichi, sì comu liberau Moises lu populu di li mani di Faraguni, actali chi nui poczamu tiniri li vostri figloli per signurj et diviniari di li perfidi lupi malvasi devoraturi, di zò chi omni jornu vi scrivirimu, et quandu non potissimu per nostri lictri scriviri, criditi a Misser Iohannj lu quali esti nostru secretu.

Chapter 3
SEALS AND APPELLATIONS

The most evident aspect of a medieval woman's identity was what she was called and what she looked like; the most obvious vestiges of comital and reginal identity are the seals and titles by which these more famous women were known.

What tangible evidence is there of the status of Sicily's countesses and the kingdom's first queens? Only a few of their tombs survive. Except for chronicles and letters, very little contemporary literature refers to the women specifically. All but one crown, that of Constance of Aragon (shown on this book's front cover), are lost to time.

In the absence of portraiture beyond simple renderings in illuminated manuscripts such as that of Peter of Eboli (on this volume's back cover), it was a woman's seal, title and coat of arms that defined her social image in the eyes of kindred royalty, the nobility and the literate classes.

The mortal remains of our queens have not been well-preserved. Some have been lost, others conserved poorly; the two consorts of Frederick II interred in the cathedral of Andria, Yolanda of Jerusalem and Isabella of England, are in a collective tomb of notable personages in the crypt.

The only surviving effigy which may be true to life, that of Adelaide preserved at Patti near Messina, was sculpted centuries after her death, even though its inscription seems to reflect medieval usage and may have been adapted from what was inscribed on the original tomb (see *Queens of Sicily*, page 126). The image of Margaret on the pendant given to her at her son's wedding in 1177 may be reasonably accurate, but what was left of her body was largely destroyed by a fire at Monreale's cathedral two centuries ago. In their seals, Constance of Sicily and Joanna of England seem to be depicted rather generically, but one doubts that a designer would have rendered either queen as obese even were that the case. (See the photos at the end of this chapter.)

Though the study of reginal seals and appellations found on charters raises a few complexities in interpretation, for contemporaries it was generally a transparent, even banal, question of identity and communication taken for granted. It is thus unsurprising that we read very few accounts of a queen, or anybody else, fretting over how the lady should be styled in a charter or letter, or portrayed in a seal. Once established, these norms became consistent over time.

Contrary to popular belief, queens regent and regnant who sealed charters were not the only queens to use seals. A queen consort might well seal a letter. Even some abbesses had seals. However, despite "Sicilian Succession" (in Italy modern jurists used the term *Successione Siciliana* for the transmission of titles and baronies to women approved with the Constitutions of Melfi in 1231), it was rare for noblewomen to use seals in the Kingdom of Sicily before 1300.

In the case of Sicily's regents, some seals survive, and in most cases the seal displayed was that of the queen's husband or son.

While the appellations (titles and styles) of those who issued charters are known, these phrases also appeared in letters and epitaphs.

Although several later queens, such as Isabella of England, presumably inherited the right to use ancestral coats of arms, we find extremely few examples of the use of heraldry in royal and reginal seals in the Kingdom of Sicily before the Angevin period (beginning in 1266), and at all events the inception of heraldry, the arrangement of symbols on a shield in a prescribed form as hereditary insignia, can be traced with certainty only to the second half of the twelfth century (heraldry is considered in the next chapter).

Appellations, styles, seals, heraldry. These topics involving identity are connected to each other through what came to be accepted usage. A related area worthy of mention is the use of royal likenesses and heraldic symbols in coinage, though this is not directly relevant to the queens of Sicily before 1266; none of our queens appears on a coin.

Background

The earliest Hauteville rulers of southern Italy, whose Norman toponym (or surname) was not ordinarily used in charters and letters, were identified by their Italian dominions, thus *dux apuliae* for "Duke of Apulia." We find, for example, a charter issued by Roger I in 1092, two decades after the conquest of Palermo, bearing the appellation "Roger, Count of Calabria and Sicily."[1] There was no reason to identify these rulers by their hereditary surname, the French toponym *de Hauteville*. Likewise, their knights, once enfeoffed in Italy, usually abandoned any French toponyms or patronyms in favor of the names of their Italian counties, baronies or manors.

Into the thirteenth century, the seals used in southern Italy by royals, nobles and clerics took several forms. Gold seals attached to a document were rare; these were used by kings for extremely important charters, and the finest surviving exemplars in southern Italy are those of the Staufens. Wax seals were either attached by string or affixed directly upon the surface of the document onto which the wax was melted. Charters were written either on parchment or paper (more about this later). Leaden seals were usually attached by string or ribbon. As an alternative to this, and sometimes in addition to a wax seal suspended from a charter, seals were sometimes drawn in red ink; this method, somewhat more commonplace in Norman Italy than elsewhere in Italy, offered the obvious advantage of durability, as the drawn seal could not be broken or detached, though it could be forged more easily than an impression in gold, wax or lead.

The materials were consistent with general European use. For gold seals, which in Sicily were inspired by their use by the Holy Roman Emperors beginning with Henry VI, a very high level of metal purity was the norm. Wax seals were red, colored with such substances as vermilion and cinnabar, which contain mercury sulphide. They were formed from a mixture of beeswax and the resin of the Nebrodian fir of Sicily or other coniferous trees present in southern Italy. Elsewhere in Europe, the resin of such trees as the European larch was used. The English vogue for seals of green wax, a practice that seems to have been begun out of economy by Richard Lionheart, never became favored in the Kingdom of Sicily.

One may decry the lack of studies dedicated specifically to Sicilian reginal sigillography, but in fact there are very few exemplars to study.

Forgery was not unheard of, and several abbeys were known for it. Here in Sicily, Santa Maria della Scala, the fortified *Badiazza,* in Contrada Badiazza in the Peloritan Mountains northwest of Messina, was infamous for its forgeries. It should be mentioned that, more generally, some surviving exemplars may have been nothing more than the work of young scriveners using palimpsests to perfect their art, with no intention to deceive.

In this connection, it should be remembered that many unsealed charters are not "forgeries," as some modern scholars assert, but contemporary copies which may contain occasional, unintentional errors. Experts do not always agree on whether a particular document is, in fact, a forgery (see note 8).

Apart from paleography and the examination of the documents themselves (parchment, paper, ink), the study of identifying titles and insignia depends upon language (Latin, Greek, Arabic) and tradition.

This research is based on the consultation of published transcriptions as well as actual charters, and here a few observations are in order. It is the author's experience that most of the Latin and Greek charters published in Italy into the twentieth century are generally accurate and clear. The same can be said for most chronicles of the Norman-Swabian era, despite occasional criticisms by scholars. The Ferraris Chronicle, for example, existed only in its *editio princeps,* published in 1888, when my work was begun on the English translation (a new Latin edition was published in 2008). A comparison of the 1888 publication to the only manuscript, with its tiny writing, revealed very few actual errors so much as necessary interpretation where the script was not very legible. True, there may be minor errors in conjugation and declension in the original documents, and some editors may wish to correct these, but the published texts are usually faithful to the manuscripts. Potential pitfalls are more frequent where several contemporary medieval copies exist for the same material.

This chapter is an introduction rather than an exhaustive study.

Titulature and Usage

Apart from the usual nuances found in Latin records, titles written in Greek and Arabic vary somewhat depending on when a phrase was written and by whom. While phraseology may well reflect perceptions and is important in that respect, often it is simply the result of local usage.

By the time Robert Guiscard died in 1085 he was Duke of Apulia. Roger I, as we have seen, was Count of Sicily. The Latin titles, *dux* and *comes,* gave rise to their modern cognates in Italian and English. In Greek we find *doukas* and *komes.* The Greek for *countess* was *komessa.* The translations of *rex* and *regina* are equally clear.

The Arabic record should be considered in its medieval context. The words *malik* and *malikah* were connoted to mean "great leader" but also "king" and "queen." Nevertheless, the use of such terms in the Hauteville dominions before 1130 reflects the limitations of language rather than the premature elevation of our rulers to the status of royalty by their Muslim subjects. There was no universal Arabic word for *count,* as the medieval European ranks of nobility differed from those in the Arab world. The term *emir,* for a leader or commander, was sometimes used rather loosely.

In charters, there was rarely any distinction between such titles as "queen regnant" and "queen mother." We occasionally find a regent, such as Margaret, referred to as "the king's mother" or, in a rather modern interpretation of the Latin, "the queen-mother," but to most subjects *regina* was simply a queen, there being no need to explain her precise status in every charter that was written. Scribes can be forgiven for what a historian may view as "laxity."

Although nobiliary and knightly ranks and titles evolved during the two centuries of the Norman-Swabian era (see Chapter 9), that was less the case of reginal titles.

Precedent and law form the framework for usage. Historians' analyses of evidence such as the diplomatic record sometimes overlook the essential historiographical principle that, in the first instance, we are examining the *effects* of facts and events, not the phenomena themselves. Adelaide was not countess or malikah (and later Queen of Jerusalem) because an artefact indicates this but, rather, because the fact of her being such was a physical reality. Such artefacts as seals, coins, charters and letters, significant as they are, merely reflect the facts rather than establish them. Although they may indicate usage, their existence does not establish legal precedent or alter history. At best, the surviving records may tell us when a certain appellation or phrase was used in a particular time or place, or by a specific population.

Owing to these differences, as well as the individuality and idiosyncrasies of scribes and copyists, too much should not be made of inconsistencies, or *apparent* contradictions, between the prescriptions present in the historical record. That oversights, errors or sundry lacunae find their way into the historical record does not change fundamental facts. For a modern comparison, a driving license reporting the bearer's name in a certain form, such as *Karl* for *Carlo,* or even with an outright misspelling like *Carrl,* does not alter the person's name or identity in actuality.

Pedantry serves no purpose in aiding our understanding of the true relevance and intent of the object of our study.

Let us cast an eye over a few charters and seals with a view to considering general practice. (The letters identifying these documents correspond to those indicated in the key at the end of this chapter.)

Sichelgaita

Sichelgaita of Salerno, the wife of Robert "Guiscard" Hauteville, issued a number of charters in which she is styled "Duchess of Apulia and Princess of Capua" based on her husband's status. The exemplar shown here (figure A) is typical. This was issued after Robert's death.

Sichelgaita, a Salernitan lady of Lombard extraction, was a remarkable woman. She studied at her city's medical school and later led troops on her husband's behalf.

It is interesting that Robert and Sichelgaita, though based chiefly in Apulia (Puglia), continued to have occasional dealings in Sicily even after 1072 despite Roger I, Robert's younger brother, being the island's nominal and actual ruler. This charter of 1089 is typical. In it, Sichelgaita cedes to Alcherio, the (Latin) Archbishop of Palermo, the right to tax some local Jews. This differed from the authority of the city's former (Greek) bishop, Nicodemus, who enjoyed no such authority under the Kalbids. It reflects a process of endowing the archdiocese with land, serfs and various rights lacking during the Arab era.[2]

An inscription dedicating a Palermitan church in 1081 mentions Robert and Sichelgaita rather than Roger (see page 101). The church in question, Saint Peter's, seems to have begun its life as a Greek Orthodox chapel.

Adelaide

Adelaide del Vasto was Countess of Sicily and later Queen of Jerusalem. Following the death of her husband, Roger I, she became regent for her young sons, Simon and Roger, whose inheritance included the island of Sicily as well as the mainland region of Calabria. Several of Adelaide's charters survive.

Of particular interest is a letter of 1109 confirming the rights of a monastery under comital patronage to a salt mine near Kasr'Janni (Enna), where there was then an Ibadi community.[3] Written in Greek and Arabic, this is the oldest surviving paper document of local manufacture in Italy. The oft-repeated claim of it being the oldest such document extant in Europe is erroneous, as there are earlier exemplars in Spain.

The document (figure C) and its wax seal are severely damaged. Unfortunately, there are no other seals of this kind in legible condition in any of Adelaide's various charters, some of which survive only as copies.

Paper making was introduced in Sicily by the Arabs, who acquired the craft from China and India. The frequent use of fragile paper in comital and royal charters explains its later proscription for the recording of important documents. This was explicated in the Constitutions of Melfi of Frederick II in 1231, but even before then the most important royal charters were written on parchment or vellum.

The wax seal affixed to the document was most likely that of Adelaide's late husband rather than her own. It was not very large, less than three centimeters (slightly more than an inch) in diameter. In both languages the last line refers to the presence of the wax seal on the document. Inclusion of such phraseology was normal; it was intended, among other things, to discourage forgeries.

The appellation is interesting. In Greek Adelaide is simply "Countess of Calabria and Sicily." In Arabic she is "the great lady, ruler of Sicily and Calabria" but also "defender of the Christian faith." That one medieval language expressed a certain idea in more flowery or poetic terms than another comes as no great revelation.[4]

Bilingual documents provide us with a sense of how terms were translated in everyday parlance, but they were the exception.

Many of Adelaide's earliest charters were in Greek. Several of these survive (and at least three of Adelaide's unpublished charters are held in private collections).

A charter issued in Greek in 1101, shortly after her husband's death, cedes four serfs and their families to an Orthodox abbey in the Nebrodian Mountains near the familial castle of San Marco d'Alunzio to commemorate thanks to God for the recovery of young Roger from a severe ear infection (figure B). Interestingly, Adelaide commemorated this with a similar donation in 1112, probably to mark her son reaching the age of majority (see Chapter 9 on dubbing knights) or her own impending wedding to King Baldwin I of Jerusalem.

Some charters were copies of earlier ones or simple decrees reiterating the rights guaranteed by earlier charters that had been lost. This was the case of a charter issued by Adelaide in 1110 (figure D). Perhaps the earlier charter, issued by Roger I, was written on fragile paper.

Margaret

Margaret of Navarre, regent for William II and later a patron of abbeys and churches (see Chapter 8), features in a number of charters. None of her personal seals are known to survive.

Some charters refer to Margaret as "queen mother," others, especially after her son reached the age of majority, simply as *Regina Margarita*.

In a very distinct exemplar from 1168 we see William II described as "King of Sicily and Duke of Apulia," with Margaret as "glorious Queen Margaret his mother," *Margarita gloriosa Regina matre sua* (figure E). This wording was typical of charters issued during this period; another example from 1168 is preserved in Spain (figure F, bottom).

A charter of 1169 bears an ink seal drawn on the document (figure G). Contrary to what seems to be a popular belief, some of these charters also had wax or metal seals attached.

Charters issued by Margaret in her own name became the norm during William's majority; an interesting example was issued in 1176 (figure F, top). Here a particularly significant example is a charter of 1171 (figure H).

There are instances of bilingual charters, such as one issued during the regency in 1166, that indicate only Margaret's name in one language (in this case Greek) and only William's name in the other (Arabic).[5]

The inscription above her tomb (Chapter 8) states merely that Margaret was Queen of Sicily.

Joanna

There is a dearth of surviving letters written by Joanna as Queen of Sicily compared to the substantial epistolary record of her mother, Eleanor of Aquitaine. Joanna's known seals were designed later, when she was Countess of Toulouse.[6]

The legends in some of these referred to her as "Queen of Sicily." Over time, her son, Raymond VII, was occasionally described by historians as "the son of a queen" even though his father, Raymond VI, was not a king. Here we may draw an analogy of sorts to the situation of Roger II, sometimes described as "the son of a queen" even though his mother, Adelaide, was crowned Queen of Jerusalem long after Roger's birth.

Constance of Sicily

Constance Hauteville was the nearest thing in the Kingdom of Sicily to a queen regnant. However, the wax seal used by her appears chiefly, though not exclusively, in diplomas issued during the few years of her widowhood that she was regent for her young son. Before then, her husband, Henry VI, ruled as King of Sicily in her name, *jure uxoris*.

Pictorially, Constance's seal is not unlike those used by her father, husband and son, or by monarchs across Catholic Europe. She is depicted enthroned, holding, in her right hand a scepter crowned by a lily or fleur-de-lis as a sign of rule by divine right of the Holy Trinity. This is similar to the representation of her in the illuminated chronicle of Peter of Eboli, where a similar scepter or stem is shown. (The seal and manuscript are both shown on this book's back cover.) The use of the fleur-de-lis is considered in Chapter 4.

In the seal, Constance is referred to simply as "Roman Empress and Queen of Sicily," without further equivocation as "queen regnant" or "queen regent." The Latin reads *Constantia dei Gratia Romanorum Imperatrix Semper Augusta et Regina Sicilie.*

Accompanying the photograph of her seal at the end of this chapter is a drawing from a book published before the advent of photography.

A well-preserved charter issued in April 1196 cedes authority over some serfs (figure I). This is perhaps the best-known of Constance's charters, distinguished by its state of preservation and the fine condition of its seal, mentioned above.

Constance of Aragon

Constance of Aragon occasionally issued charters or letters on behalf of her husband, Frederick II, while she was overseeing his affairs in Sicily during his travels in his imperial dominions in Germany and peninsular Italy. Historians sometimes refer to her as Frederick's "regent" for Sicily, though "governor" might be a more appropriate term.

More precisely, Constance was regent for her young son, Henry, whom Frederick had crowned King of Sicily to appease papal concerns about Germany, the Holy Roman Empire, the Italian communes and the Kingdom of Sicily being ruled by the same monarch.

An interesting exemplar issued in Palermo in 1213 refers to "Constance, by the Grace of God Queen of Sicily, Duchess of Apulia and Princess of Capua with her son Henry King of Sicily" (figure J).

Whereas the widowed Joanna wed for a second time following her Sicilian queenhood, Constance was a widow when she married Frederick, and in Hungary she had issued charters for the son, Ladislas III, who died very young.[7]

Lucy

Little is known about Lucy of Cammarata. She held a castle in the Sicanian Mountains guarding a town overlooking the Platani Valley. The locality is identified by the royal geographer Idrisi. She seems to have been a niece of Roger I, perhaps the daughter of one of his many brothers. It is possible that she was a young cousin.

By 1141, when she issued the first of half a dozen known charters ceding property and Berber villages to the diocese of Cefalù, Lucy was a widow caring for Adam, her son. Adam, her only surviving child, is invariably identified as her heir.

Cefalù was erected into a diocese by the Byzantine Greeks in the seventh century but suppressed by the Aghlabids during the ninth. Bishop Jocelmo was installed in 1131 as part of the refoundation of the diocese when the Norman cathedral was being constructed, serving until 1150. Lucy's donations of churches and lands were part of the endowment of this Latin foundation even though Cammarata itself was some distance away, in the diocesan territory of Agrigento. Her patronage, which may be seen as part of the Norman effort to convert the local Muslims living in the villages under her manorial control, had King Roger's approval. Besides a mosque, there was a synagogue at Cammarata; it survived until 1493 but the precise date of its foundation is not known.

In most of the charters, Lucy is styled simply "Lady of the Castle of Cammarata" (figure K), as if she held the fortified town and the surrounding manors by her own feudal right rather than as "regent" for her son.[8] Indeed, the formula is rather similar to what we find in some of the charters issued by Margaret as regent for William II.

It seems that Roger II gave Cammarata to Lucy following her husband's death but this cannot be stated with certainty; she may simply have succeeded her late spouse, of whom virtually nothing is known, with the king confirming her tenure. Her estates were fairly extensive, including fertile lands in what are now the townships of Cammarata, Casteltermini and Mussomeli. After Adam died around 1154, the territory reverted to the crown during the reign of William I.

Adelisa of Adernò, et alia

Lucy was not unique. The names of several ladies having Hauteville bloodlines or other connections to the royal family occur in charters of the twelfth century. An interesting case is Adelisa of Adernò, named in her charter of 1134 as *Adelecia neptis domini regis Rogerii*. Indeed, she is invariably identified as the granddaughter of Roger I, even when her husband is mentioned.[9]

Specifically, Adelisa was the daughter of Emma Hauteville and Rudolf of Montescaglioso. Emma was a daughter of Roger I and his first wife, Judith of Evreux.

By 1134, Adelisa was the widow of Rainald of Avenella, a baron descended from the Drengot family; Matilda Hauteville, Adelisa's sister (or half-sister), whom we shall meet in Chapter 5, also wed into this family.

Over time, Adelisa donated some churches and estates in her dominions to the diocese of Catania and other episcopal jurisdictions in Sicily.[10]

By Rainald, she had at least two children, Adam and Matilda.

Our information about Adelisa may be considered typical of what we find regarding the noblewomen of this era, for whom a charter or two, or perhaps a fleeting reference in a chronicle, is the most we can expect.

Conclusions

This concise examination of a few charters is intended merely as an introduction to the subject to establish a few parameters.

The study of our queens' titles, charters and seals is not an isolated one if considered more generally in the context of the field, about which fine works have been published.[11]

There is little, if anything, to suggest that Sicilian usage was very different from what existed elsewhere, nor that it influenced other kingdoms very greatly. In 1283, Edward I of England, whose younger brother, Edmund, was once the papal choice for the Sicilian throne eventually ascended by Charles of Anjou, ordered that letters sent to the Kingdom of Sicily should be sealed in red wax (rather than the more economical green), presumably to conform to what was then the papal and Italian norm.[12]

The next chapter addresses the topic of heraldry, often related to sigillography and numismatics insofar as medieval seals and coins sometimes bore coats of arms. Yet the queens of our Norman-Swabian era do not seem to have used heraldic insignia for any purpose.

What should not be overlooked is the fact of queenly identity expressed through the use of certain titles and seals. The authority of these women was rarely in doubt. Like Empress Maude, Melisende of Jerusalem and others, they were part of an elite sisterhood adept in the use of power, and not timid about showing it or using it.

FIGURES

One of the reasons these charters were selected is their ready legibility and physical condition. However, most have been published. These may be consulted in Palermo and Toledo.

A. Archivio Storico Diocesano di Palermo, Tabulario della Cattedrale di Palermo: Manuscript number 3.

B. Archivio di Stato di Palermo, Tabulario dei Monasteri di San Filippo di Fragalà e di Santa Maria di Maniace: Manuscript 7 (charter written in Greek on goatskin vellum).

C. Archivio di Stato di Palermo, Tabulario dei Monasteri di San Filippo di Fragalà e di Santa Maria di Maniace: Manuscript 9 (paper letter of March 1109 in Greek on upper half and Arabic on lower half from Adelaide commanding jurats of Kasr' Janni, now Enna, to protect the monastery of Saint Philip of Demenna, in the San Marco Valley, under her personal patronage).

D. Archivio di Stato di Palermo, Tabulario dei Monasteri di San Filippo di Fragalà e di Santa Maria di Maniace: Manuscript 6 (charter of 1110 replacing an earlier one issued by Roger I).

E. Archivio di Stato di Palermo, Tabulario di Santa Maria Maddalena of Messina: Manuscript number 50 (Margaret and William order nobles to exempt a monastery from taxation based on established policy, in 1168).

F. Fundación Casa Ducal de Medinaceli (Toledo, Spain), Fondo Messina: Manuscripts number 528 (top) and number 109 (bottom).

G. Archivio Storico Diocesano di Palermo, Tabulario della Cattedrale di Palermo: Manuscript number 21 (royal concession of the feudal rights of the mills on the manor of Brucato, the Arabic *Bur-Ruqqad,* to Walter, the newly-consecrated Archbishop of Palermo, in September 1169).

H. Archivio di Stato di Palermo, Tabulario dei Monasteri di San Filippo di Fragalà e di Santa Maria di Maniace: Manuscript 17, 27 November 1171 (unsealed, probably a copy of an original, sealed charter; recorded in Greek and Latin, confirms privileges of Roger II protecting said monasteries, exempting them from the obligation to provide timber and livestock, lodge men-at-arms, and so forth, effectively exempting them from local civic authority).

I. Archivio Storico Diocesano di Palermo, Tabulario della Cattedrale di Palermo: Manuscript number 29.

J. Archivio Storico Diocesano di Palermo, Tabulario della Cattedrale di Palermo: Manuscript number 42.

K. Biblioteca Comunale di Casa Professa, Palermo: Manuscript QqD3, folio 76 recto (near-contemporary copy of charter issued by Lucy of Cammarata in August 1141).

NOTES

1. For two amongst many exemplars see Garufi, Carlo Alberto, *I Documenti Inediti dell'Epoca Normanna in Sicilia*, document 1, pages 3-6; document 2, pages 7-9. These charters were issued by Roger I at Messina in 1092.

2. See Archivio Storico Diocesano di Palermo, Tabulario della Cattedrale di Palermo, Manuscripts number 1, 2, 4, 5, 8.

3. For the Ibadi community of Kasr'Janni see Chiarelli, Leonard, "The Ibadi Communities in Muslim Sicily," *Ibadi Jurisprudence: Origins, Development and Cases*, in the series *Studies on Ibadism and Oman,* volume 6 (2015), pages 159-166.

4. For a good description and bibliography see Johns, Jeremy, "Paper versus Parchment: Countess Adelaide's Bilingual Mandate of 1109," *Documenting Multiculturalism* (November 2018).

5. For a recent study of such a charter see von Falkenhausen, Vera, and Johns, Jeremy, "An Arabic-Greek Charter for Archbishop Nicholas of Messina, November 1166," *Rivista di Ricerche Bizantinistiche,* number 8, for 2011 (2012), pages 153-170. The original manuscript is conserved in the Fondo Messina of the archive of the Fundación Casa Ducal de Medinaceli in Toledo as number 1118; this was issued by Caïd Martin in the name of the king and his mother.

6. See *Queens of Sicily,* page 355.

7. Ibid, pages 411-412.

8. For the texts of the Latin diplomas (two are in Greek) see Garufi, Carlo Alberto, *I Documenti Inediti dell'Epoca Normanna in Sicilia*, document 27, pages 64-65; Pasca, Cesare, "Cenno Storico e Statistico del Comune di San Giovanni e Camerata," *Giornale di Scienze Lettere e Arti per la Sicilia,* volume 60, number 178 (October 1837), pages 41-46. For an additional charter and commentary, see White, Lynn Townsend, *Latin Monasticism in Norman Sicily,* pages 192-193, 257-259. Having examined both charters of 1141 (QqD3, pages 66-68 and 76-79 at Palermo's Biblioteca Comunale di Casa Professa), one of which being thought by Professor White to be a near-contemporary forgery, the author believes the diploma in question more likely to be a slightly inaccurate transcription rather than a malicious deception; in either case, the reason for mentioning Lucy here is to recognize the title in her charters (see figure K) and her role as a benefactress, not to scrutinize every minute detail of one charter among several.

9. For these charters see Garufi, Carlo Alberto, "Per la Storia dei Secoli XI e XII," *Archivio Storico per la Sicilia Orientale,* volume 9 (1912), number 2, pages 342-343, 353-365.

10. Ibid. For a donation to the diocese of Cefalù see also Garufi, Carlo Alberto, *Documenti Inediti dell'Epoca Normanna in Sicilia,* document 15, pages 38-41 (the original

charter from June 1140 is in the Tabulario di Cefalù, number TVC008, formerly 8, at the Catena division of the Archive of State of Palermo); for another donation, document 31, pages 76-77 (number TVC011, formerly 11, in the Tabulario di Cefalù).

11. See Whatley, Laura (editor), *A Companion to Seals in the Middle Ages* (2019); Schofield, Phillipp (editor), *Seals and their Context in the Middle Ages* (2014); also Johns, Susan, *Noblewomen, Aristocracy and Power in the Twelfth-Century Anglo-Norman Realm* (2003).

12. See Maxwell-Lyte, Henry, *Historical Notes on the Use of the Great Seal of England* (1926), page 309.

Unsealed charter issued in 1089 by Sichelgaita, the widow of Robert Guiscard, granting to Alcherio, the Latin archbishop of Palermo, the right to taxation of some local Jews

SEALS AND APPELLATIONS

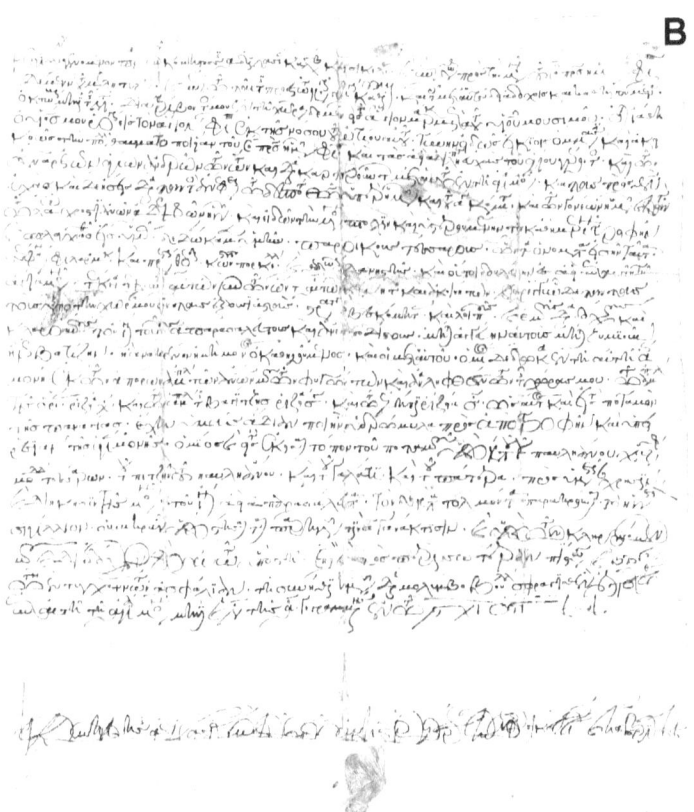

Courtesy Palermo Archive of State

This charter issued by Adelaide in Greek in 1101 cedes four serfs and their families to an Orthodox abbey in the Nebrodian Mountains as a donation in memory of the recovery of her son, Roger, from a severe ear infection. It is one of her first decrees, made just four months after the death of her husband. She made a similar donation for the same miracle in November 1112 around the time Roger II reached the age of majority.

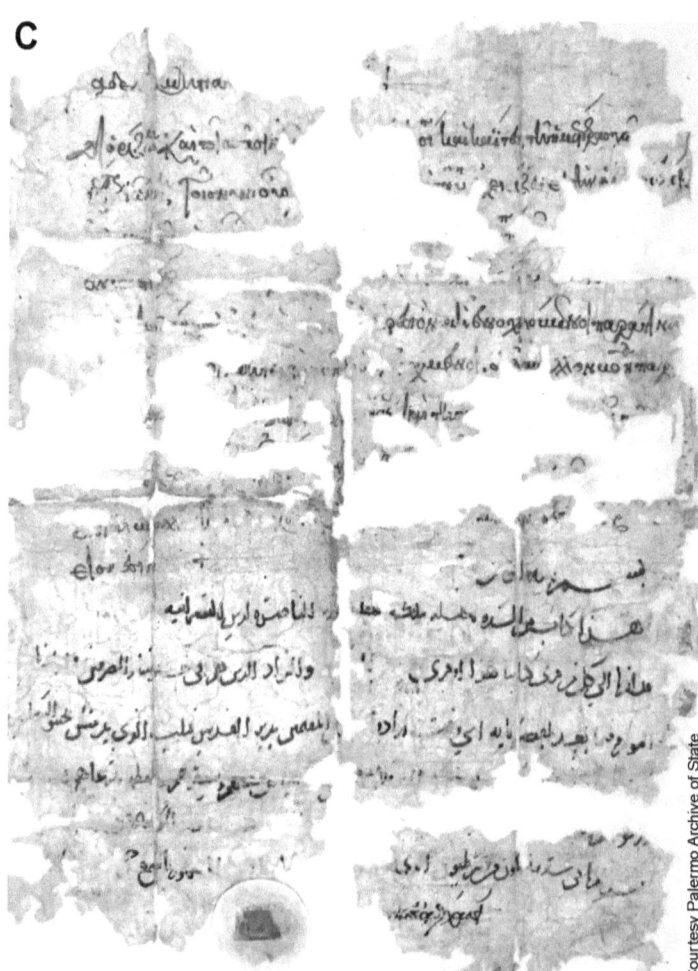

This charter issued by Adelaide in 1109 in Greek and Arabic is the oldest surviving paper document in Italy and one of the oldest in Europe (only Spain has earlier exemplars). The damaged seal may be Adelaide's.

SEALS AND APPELLATIONS

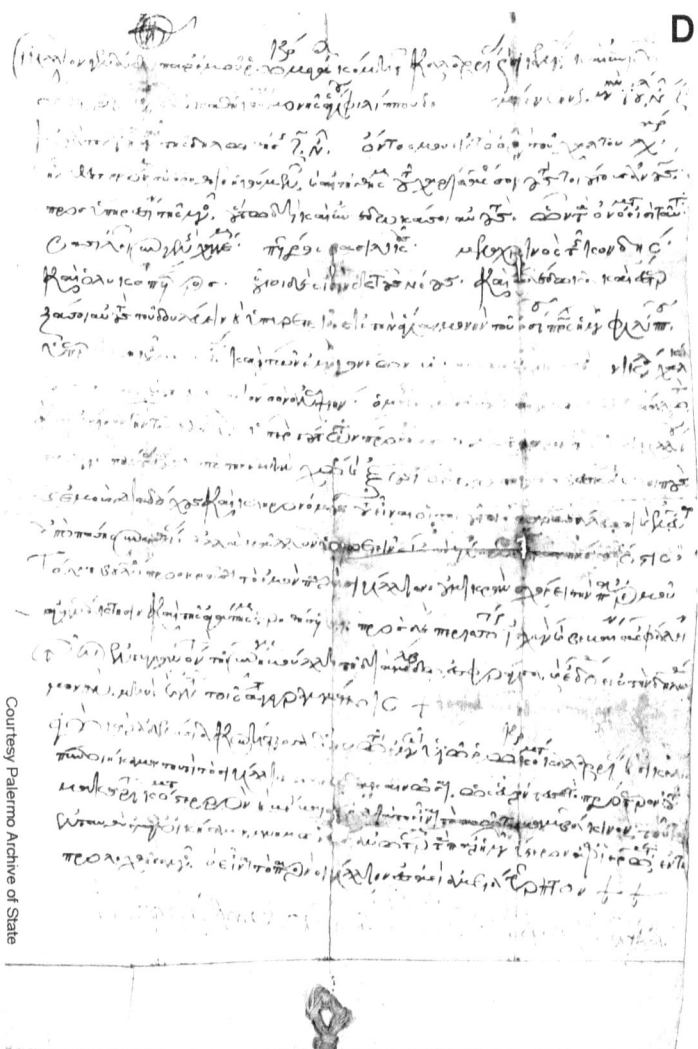

Adelaide issued this charter around 1110 to replace one that her husband had issued a decade earlier.

In this charter issued in March 1168 (the date was later altered) in William's name, Margaret's name is also indicated as she was regent.

Charter of Margaret in her own name in 1176 (top) and as regent with William II, her son, in 1168

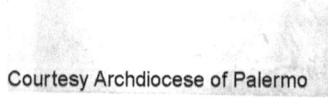

Feudal charter issued by Margaret to Walter, Archbishop of Palermo, in the name of her son, King William II, in 1169, a rarity as very few charters issued during her regency survive. The seal was designed in deep red ink, a common practice in Sicily during this period. The charter on the following page appears to be granted in the queen's name.

Margaret's charter of November 1171 in Latin and Greek confirming privileges granted by Roger II to abbeys in the Nebrodian Mountains

On 15 April 1196 Constance issued this charter under her own name and seal, ceding authority over some serfs (named in the decree) to a certain jurisdiction. Here she is referred to as Roman Empress and Queen of Sicily.

J

Courtesy Archdiocese of Palermo

Charter issued by Constance of Aragon at Palermo in January 1213 acting on behalf of her son, the young Henry, who her husband, Frederick II, had crowned King of Sicily. Frederick delegated regnal authority to his wife as his administrator (regent) in the Kingdom of Sicily while he was in his imperial realms to the north. The seal once attached to this document does not survive, but some crimson silk cord suggests that one existed, probably Henry's. This decree cedes a spring to Palermo's cathedral parish for an annual feudal rent of four gold tarì.

K

In nomine sce & individue trinitatis. Anno abincacione dni nri ihu x. o. c. L.iij. Regni aut felicissimi dni nri Rogerii invic tissimi regis sicilie & italie vicesimo & dni W. filii sui cu eode patre suo feliciter reg nantis tercio vicesimo pmo die madii in dictoe. Ego lucia una cu meo filio ada castelli camerate dnatx bona mea volun tate & puoluntate & consensu mei filii ada p di amore & aie mee parentuq; nror mer cede laboraui qnda ercti ext castello ca merato ad honore di & beate marie sep vir ginis qua inter & uineis. baccis ditam & totata eccla sci saluatoris de chephi mo bed entia obtuluit recipiente ea mee ipsi eccle rocelino coside eccle electo quatus ornib; binficiis pducte eccle & eor ppr participes fud Qua etia cu dns i.. barensis archieps puolun tate dni regis Rogerii inviris uenit partib; roga tu nro & dni barduim chigo electi & puoluntate & cosensu decani & canonicor agregentune mais eccle in cui tritorio e aba... dedicare seco & p amore di ecclieq; pficuo & p honore

Courtesy Biblioteca Comunale di Palermo

"I, Lucy, Lady of the Castle of Cammarata, with my son, Adam..." in a charter issued in Sicily in 1141

SEALS AND APPELLATIONS

Wax seal of Constance Hauteville and modern drawing

Margaret's pendant and Joanna's seal

SEALS AND APPELLATIONS

Courtesy Sicilian Regional Art Gallery, Palermo

Dedication of the church of Saint Peter la Bagnara near the Sea Castle of Palermo in 1081 mentioning Robert Guiscard and his consort, Sichelgaita. The first pastor and congregants were Orthodox, hence the inscription in Greek. Only after the death of Robert four years later did Roger I assume complete control of Sicily. This restored stone plaque is virtually all that remained of the church following the bombings of 1943.

101

SICILIAN QUEENSHIP

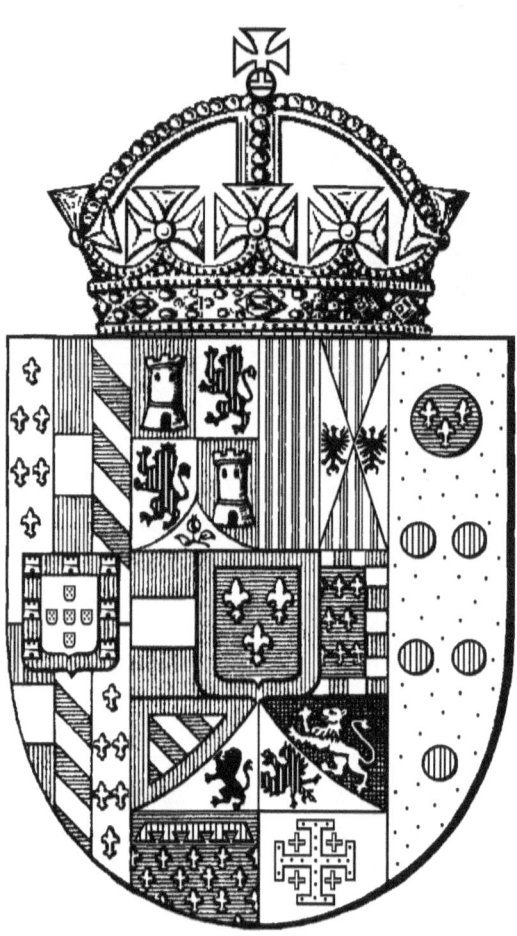

The coat of arms of Naples and Sicily beginning with the reign of Charles de Bourbon (later Charles III of Spain) in 1734. This was the coat of arms used in the Kingdom of the Two Sicilies until its demise in 1861.

Chapter 4
REGINAL HERALDRY

Apart from seals, appellations and the rare portrait or effigy, queens were represented by their coats of arms. It so happens that none of the queens of Sicily of the Hauteville or Hohenstaufen eras was known to make use of a coat of arms, although several could have, particularly during the thirteenth century.

Heraldry is defined as the arrangement of patterns or symbols on an escutcheon (shield) as a form of hereditary, identifying insignia. Coats of arms became popular during the second half of the twelfth century, especially after 1170, as knights in western Europe began to emblazon their shields and surcoats with these colorful designs for ready identification by heralds during battle and tournaments. Beyond its history, armorial heraldry is a methodical "science" with its own rules and conventions.[1] Yet it is widely misunderstood, partly because not every use of what became heraldic symbols (such as the eagle, lion, crosslet and fleur-de-lis) was, strictly speaking, heraldic.

In the period under discussion, heraldry was inseparably linked to the aristocracy. In those times, only monarchs, prelates, abbots, vassals and knights were entitled to the use of coats of arms. For a peasant to design and display one would be seen as usurping a prerogative of the upper classes and punished accordingly, as if the man were impersonating a knight; this was a grave offense. However, since peasants did not normally possess shields, war horses (vested with surcoats displaying heraldic designs) or seals, this kind of thing was unlikely to occur. Only later did guilds, which in southern Italy were known as *maestranze,* begin to use heraldic insignia.

One of the oldest coats of arms known to us is that of Geoffrey of Anjou, who died in 1151. This was the father of Henry II of England. The shield rendered in the effigy on Geoffrey's tomb (see the photo at the end of this chapter) depicts gold *lions rampant* on a blue background. An early example of an armigerous knight is William Marshal, who died in 1219, but we have no record of any tourneyer of his renown in Sicily.

Though it later came to be regulated by law, heraldry in Sicily was not legislated during the Norman-Swabian era. Indeed, it was not widely used in the *Regnum Siciliae* until the thirteenth century.[2]

Nevertheless, the bestowal of feudal knighthood (see Chapter 9) was closely regulated beginning around 1140 with the Assizes of Ariano, where we read that "no man shall be knighted who is not of a knightly family."[3]

Coats of arms came to be used on seals and coinage. Although certain heraldic symbols, such as the Staufens' imperial eagle, found their way onto coins struck during the thirteenth century, the formal use of royal heraldry (devices rendered on shields) in the Kingdom of Sicily flourished in earnest after 1266 at the Angevin and Aragonese courts.

This is significant because the use of a symbol other than its rendering on a shield is not, strictly speaking, armorial, although some symbols (charges) were used as crests (atop helmets) and are heraldic in that sense.

We find no evidence of any Queen of Sicily using a heraldic device before the fall of the Staufen dynasty in 1266, either on a seal or elsewhere (such as clothing). Although the chronicle of Peter of Eboli depicts a bird atop the crowns of Tancred and Sibylla, this probably was not intended as a heraldic crest.[4]

None the less, symbols were known that later found their way into coats of arms. Besides the imperial eagle, the most frequent royal symbols in use in the Kingdom of Sicily before 1266 were the lion and the fleur-de-lis.[5]

At first glance, some of these symbols may seem to have originated as royal insignia elsewhere. In fact, the use of the lion and the fleur-de-lis was rather general beyond the kingdoms, respectively England and France, where they became known as royal insignia.

The fleur-de-lis, or something very similar to it, appears at the end of the sceptre of Constance of Sicily shown in her seal and in contemporary illuminations (see this volume's back cover). A similar motif is shown in the crown of Constance of Aragon (on the front cover) and on the lower part of the walls in Monreale's cathedral. To Normans and Greeks it symbolized the triune God of Christianity; to Fatimids it was a geometric design consistent with the aesthetic precepts of Islam.

The fleur-de-lis — if we identify it as such — at the end of royal sceptres as these ceremonial staffs were sometimes depicted before the advent of heraldry was displayed in seals used by many European dynasties, particularly in the west. In earlier times, royal sceptres were occasionally depicted ending in crosses, spheres, eagles or other symbols.

Whether the golden objects on a blue field depicted in the rendering of the robe of Roger II in a mosaic in the Martorana church are fleurs-de-lis or crosses is a matter of debate.[6] (See the drawing at the end of this chapter.) In either case, the creation of the mosaic probably antedates the introduction of heraldry.

The lion *passant guardant* appears in the Palatine Chapel on the wall behind the throne dais and as a repeating motif on the external walls of the apses of Palermo Cathedral. Lions were also embroidered on the crimson coronation robe of Roger II. Later, they were produced in mosaic above the royal throne dais in Monreale's cathedral. However, we find no evidence of the lion as a reginal badge.

Remarkably, the seals used by the widowed Joanna as Countess of Toulouse in the years shortly before her death are not of heraldic design even though, by then, both her husband and her brother used coats of arms. An oft-cited letter that King Richard sent to the Archbishop of Canterbury in 1194 setting forth rules for tournaments did not address heraldry.[7]

The natal families of the first countesses and queens of Sicily were armigerous or eventually became so, and their coats of arms are shown at the end of this chapter. It should be borne in mind that some of these blazons were assumed by kinsmen *after* the deaths of these women, and that the Hautevilles did not make use of the coat of arms later attributed to them.

Yet we see the Hauteville arms, blazoned *azure a bend checky argent and gules,* rendered in mosaic above the royal throne dais in Monreale's cathedral (see the photograph in Chapter 8). The addition of this detail to the church's wall was probably part of a later movement to retroactively ascribe coats of arms to kings and even early saints.

NOTES

1. Information regarding the origins of heraldry will be found in Fox-Davies, Arthur, *A Complete Guide to Heraldry* (1909); Brooke-Little, John, *Boutell's Heraldry* (1978); Neubecker, Ottfried, *Heraldry: Sources, Symbols and Meaning* (1976). See also Mendola, Louis, *Sicilian Genealogy and Heraldry*, pages 137-158. To place medieval heraldry in the context of practical military use, see Funken, Liliane and Fred, *Arms and Uniforms: The Age of Chivalry*, part 1, (1977), pages 42-83.

2. Mendola, Louis, "English and Italian Legacy of the Norman Knight Figures of Monreale," *The Coat of Arms*, journal of The Heraldry Society, London, NS volume 10, number 166 (1994), pages 245-254.

3. Assizes of Ariano: *Codex Vaticanus 8782*, statute 19; *Codex Casinensis 468*, statute 31 (the author's numeration). See *Queens of Sicily*, pages 509-531.

4. Siragusa, Giovanni Battista, *Liber ad Honorem Augusti di Pietro da Eboli* (1906), page 139. For commentary on the bird, which may be a hoopoe, see Hood, Gwenyth, *Book in Honor of Augustus by Pietro da Eboli*, pages 111 (citing Theo Kölzer) and 375. Folio 18v (upper-right of the page) of the falconry treatise of Frederick II, *Codex Palatinus Latinus 1071*, shows a bird which appears to be a yellow-crested cockatoo (possibly cacatua galerita), perhaps a gift from Sultan al Kamil; see Dalton, Heather, "Frederick II of Hohenstaufen's Australasian Cockatoo: Symbol of Detente between East and West and Evidence of Ayyubids' Global Reach," *Parergon*, number 35, volume 1 (January 2018), pages 35-60. Various explanations have been advanced for the presence of this crested bird, whatever the species may be, in Peter's chronicle; it probably reflects the chronicler's attempt to ridicule Tancred's reign as illegitimate. It is sometimes seen atop Queen Sibylla's crown (folio 125r in the manuscript and Hood, page 232). As it does not always appear on her crown (folios 124r and 134r in the manuscript and Hood, pages 226 and 280), it seems to represent a live bird rather than a crest in the form of one; thus it presumably flew away when Sibylla was deposed following Tancred's death. The bird does not always appear atop Tancred's crown, either (folio 124r). A crest would normally be depicted on a helmet, where it was intended to deflect direct blows, but not atop a crown, where one might expect to see a cross.

5. Mendola, Louis, "Pre-Armorial Use of the Lion Passant Guardant and the Fleur-de-Lis as Heraldic Badges in Norman Sicily," *The Coat of Arms*, journal of The Heraldry Society, London, NS volume 10, number 165 (1994), pages 210-212. Mendola believed that the symbols may be fleurs-de-lis; contrarily, in his biography of Roger II published a few years later Hubert Houben identified these as crosses. A similar mosaic of William II (being crowned directly by Christ) appears in Monreale's cathedral, but in another mosaic (depicting him offering the church to the Virgin Mary) in the same church the symbols are very clearly stylized Greek crosses. See also the following note.

6. It is highly unlikely that the presence of the fleurs-de-lis on the robe is in some way connected to Roger's marriage to a Capetian princess, Sibylla of Burgundy. It

should be noted that the event depicted is Roger's coronation two decades earlier than that (in 1130), and that there is no reliable evidence that the Capetians were already using the blazon *azure semé-de-lis or* in 1150 as a coat of arms in this form (in this composition and with these tinctures); the earliest coat of arms of the dukes of Burgundy, shown at the end of this chapter, was blazoned *bendy or and azure a bordure gules,* with no fleurs-de-lis, and the first French king to use the blazon associated with his dynasty was probably Philip II after 1180. See note 5 above and also (for a contrasting view) Hayes, Dawn Marie, "Significance of the Fleurs-de-Lis in the Mosaic of King Roger II of Sicily in the Church of Santa Maria dell'Ammiraglio, Palermo," *Viator,* volume 44, number 1 (January 2013), pages 201-252. For more about the heraldry of the House of Burgundy as a cadet branch of the Capetian dynasty see Louda, Jiri, and Maclagan, Michael, *Heraldry of the Royal Families of Europe* (1988), pages 146-149. See also note 1 above.

7. *The Historical Works of Ralph de Diceto, Dean of London,* volume 2, pages lxxx and lxxxi; *The Annals of Roger de Hoveden,* volume 2, page 339; *Chronicles of the Reigns of Stephen, Henry II and Richard I,* volume 2, pages 422-423 (William of Newburgh).

This engraving reflects the prevailing notion that the repeating symbols on the king's robe are crosses

Roger II depicted as a Byzantine basileus crowned by Christ in engraving based on mosaic in Martorana church, Palermo

SICILIAN QUEENSHIP

Coats of Arms of the Natal Families of Sicilian Queens

 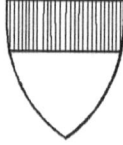  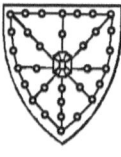 

Judith	Adelaide	Eremburga Joanna Isabella	Elvira Margaret	Sibylla of Burgundy

 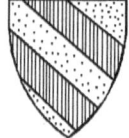   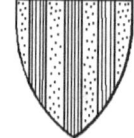

Beatrice of Rethel	Sibylla of Acerra	Irene	Constance of Sicily*	Constance of Aragon

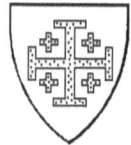    

Yolanda of Jerusalem	Bianca	Elisabeth of Bavaria	Beatrice of Savoy	Helena

TINCTURES - COLORS

Or *Gold*	Azure *Blue*	Gules *Red*	Vert *Green*	Sable *Black*	Argent *Silver*

*The Hauteville coat of arms is apocryphal

Blazons of Queens' Coats of Arms

Judith. Argent a fess gules in chief three torteaux (Evreux).

Adelaide. Argent a chief gules (Aleramids).

Eremburga, Joanna, Isabella. Gules two lions passant guardant or (Plantagenets).

Elvira, Margaret. Gules a cross, saltire and orle of linked chains or in fess point an emerald vert (Navarre).

Sibylla of Burgundy. Bendy or and azure a bordure gules.

Beatrice of Rethel. Gules a rake or (*rateau* canted for Rethel).

Sibylla of Acerra. Bendy or and gules.

Irene. A two-headed eagle crowned (Constantinople).

Constance of Sicily. Azure a bend checky argent and gules.

Constance of Aragon. Paly or and gules.

Yolanda. Argent a cross potent between four crosslets or.

Bianca Lancia. Argent a chief azure (Aleramids differenced).

Elisabeth of Bavaria. Fusilly in bend argent and azure.

Beatrice of Savoy. Gules a cross argent.

Helena. Argent a two-headed eagle sable (Constantinople).

Geoffrey of Anjou with his emblazoned shield

Chapter 5
SEXUALITY AND MARRIAGE

Certain biographical details involving our queens' power and identity, whether directly or indirectly, will always be cloaked in shade and shadow. This chapter is an attempt to elucidate these to the very limited extent that it will ever be possible. Here, where the sources provide us with only scant information, typically one or two fleeting comments, any evaluation necessarily involves a great degree of hypothesis and conjecture even where it is firmly rooted in social context and feminist theory. What is presented is a series of simple summaries with a few notes. The challenge confronting any biographer is that even though these topics concern things that were part of the queens' lives, perhaps in significant ways, most were intrinsically personal and private. In essence, we are attempting to find private information in public records.

A number of circumstances and conditions touching the queens and the Sicilian court involve sexuality, fertility, gender identity, spousal abuse, mental health and perhaps even sexual orientation. Not only are some of these intimate matters potentially quite complex, they are — perhaps infamously — ignored or minimized in the historical record and commentary because of what was typically reported, underreported or unreported in medieval chronicles and letters. Moreover, most of these things reflect phenomena and conditions which by their very nature were regarded as private, and therefore unlikely to be discussed by a woman with a chronicler (typically a monk) or expressed in a letter that might be seen by prying eyes.

With the exception of a few comments by, in particular, Hugh Falcandus, who is notorious for being obnoxious, whispers and rumors at the Sicilian court, understandably, were rarely recorded for posterity; even Falcandus mentions these cautiously and sparingly where the royal family is concerned, perhaps fearing the consequences for himself were his words exposed while he was living in Palermo. A few overt criticisms survive. In a letter to Walter, the royal tutor who became Archbishop of Palermo, Peter of Blois, who had also been the tutor of young William II but was then (in 1177) living in England, compared his former pupil unfavorably to Henry II.[1]

A few aspects of sexuality and marriage were addressed in the two principal legal codes of the Norman-Swabian era. These were the Assizes of Ariano and then, nearly a century later, the Constitutions of Melfi.

Because our knowledge of what is considered here will always be sketchy, what follow are not conclusions but descriptions and possibilities. The wider topic of women's medieval biography and feminism has been addressed thoroughly and eloquently elsewhere.[2]

Before considering the historiography and prosopography, let us cast an eye over the reasoning behind what, *per forza,* can be rather conjectural theses. Here these are viewed in a historiographical environment rather than a scientific, juridical or purely philosophical context. Even if those of us who have undertaken originative studies in history are (or should be) aware of these concepts, they are sometimes overlooked in the course of research, analysis and criticism.

We will never have all the answers, but only through careful reasoning and investigation can we ascertain, at the very least and not without equivocation, what the questions are.

Black Swans and Logical Fallacies

The "black swan fallacy," or — for our purposes — a historian's variation of it, is by definition a flawed line of reasoning that leads one to conclude that something must not, or can not, exist simply because it has not yet been seen, perhaps falling outside of a known norm. In other words, the historian may disregard a certain body of evidence supporting the existence of a thing because she, herself, has never seen an example of that thing. By way of analogy, if every swan she has ever seen is white, she may be inclined to refuse to acknowledge the possibility of the existence of a black swan, either now or in the future. Lying at an intersection of probability and philosophy, this idea governs what we should be willing to accept as being possible or plausible under specified conditions.[3]

A related idea is reflected in the familiar aphorism, favored by Carl Sagan (1934-1996), that "absence of evidence is not evidence of absence." We should not affirm that something does not exist simply because we have not seen the evidence for it. At best, we can state that there is no evidence for it *that we have seen*. Nevertheless, such an observation should be stated cautiously, especially when the biographer is writing about "proof." For example, the lack of *known* letters of Queen Margaret does not "prove" that none were ever written by her. Of course, we should remember that evidence and proof are two different things. This is not sophistry; it is fundamental epistemology.

Under many conditions involving historical events, these principles may reflect the burden of proof for a claim and the premise that we "cannot prove a negative." More precisely, it is usually impossible to demonstrate conclusively that something did *not* happen or did *not* exist. (This gave rise to a modern judicial standard requiring an accuser to prove the guilt of the accused rather than expecting the accused to prove her innocence, or that she did *not* commit a crime.)

We cannot prove beyond doubt that Queen Margaret did *not* meet her future *consuocera,* Eleanor of Aquitaine, when the latter arrived in Palermo in July 1149 (we do not know exactly when Margaret arrived in the city from Spain). Conversely, we cannot prove that the two women did indeed meet, as there is no known record of it, nor sufficient information to draw a solid conclusion. Viewed from either the negative or the affirmative, the case is circumstantial.

More generally, these concepts open the door to epistemological discussions far more sophisticated than need be addressed here. The point is that historians occasionally reach conclusions based on reasoning rooted in flawed or incomplete information.

Some reasoning is simply mathematical. If something is known to occur in human experience at a certain statistical frequency, then it is reasonable to presume it as a possibility corresponding to that level of probability. Let us say that a certain genetic physical condition occurs at around five percent in a specific population in a defined region. Knowing nothing of the genomes of every person in that population and place, it is logical to conclude that, as a group, they will conform to this probability, with, on average, one out of every twenty people having that trait. This principle comes into play with the genetic haplogroups present in the Sicilian population and such statistics as the number of Sicilians having red hair or blue eyes.

Bearing in mind that our example involves historiography and genetics, not theoretical physics and cosmology, we are not talking about, for example, a child born with green hair, horns and a forked tail, but with red hair, freckles and blue eyes, something in the natural realm of physical possibility.

Additional fallacies relevant to our discussion are the argument from ignorance (and the false dichotomy) and confirmation bias, among others. Such principles as the "law of parsimony" should also be borne in mind. These the author shall leave to the reader's exploration beyond the confines of this volume.

Let us travel into the realm of the unsaid.

Matilda's Marriage

Rare are instances of spousal abuse or mistreatment that are mentioned explicitly as occurring in the Sicilian royal family. The most evident case is that of Matilda Hauteville, who seems to have been born around 1191.[4]

Matilda, an elder sister of Roger II, wed Rainulf of Alife and Caiazzo, holder of a number of large estates in and around the Volturno Valley near Naples. His Drengot ancestors had ruled Capua until they were expelled by the city's Lombard residents, and under other circumstances this Norman house might have seriously challenged the Hautevilles for power.

Matilda is known to historians as the patron of Alexander of Telese, whom she commissioned to write about her younger brother, the king. Alexander's chronicle, effectively a biography, has little to say about Matilda except for her unhappy marriage. Clearly, the work is intended for the edification of her brother, not for her.

Nevertheless, it is remarkable that Matilda thought her unfortunate marital experience worth noting in a project over which she had some control. She thus exercised a degree of female "editorial" agency rare in her times. Matilda does not appear to have been excessively worried about her experience with Rainulf becoming known to posterity or even to contemporaries, nor it being held against her; here there was no "victim shaming." It may be that, sensing her story would be mentioned by any chronicler who became privy to it, she felt the need (through Alexander) to write her own narrative rather than have somebody else write it for her. Admittedly, the situation was likely to become known through gossip in court circles, where other women, and perhaps a few men, even not knowing any details, might speculate that there were only so many reasons for a noblewoman to leave her husband. This was Matilda's chance to "set the record straight." It is highly unlikely that she would have had such an opportunity were she not the king's sister.

Rainulf initially supported Roger as king. In 1131, at the king's command, he and his Drengot kinsman, Robert of Capua, led an expedition to Rome in a show of Norman force to impress Roger's strength upon the supporters of Pope Innocent II, the pontiff who opposed Roger's recent coronation by authority of Anacletus II, subsequently viewed as an antipope.

In the late spring of that year, in Rainulf's absence, Matilda, fled to her brother, leaving the castle of Alife for Salerno, taking her young son (and possibly her daughter) with her and explaining to Roger that she had been abused by her husband. Instigated by Pope Innocent, baronial unrest was growing in the region, but Matilda and her suite traveled to Salerno without incident because most of the lands they passed through were those of her husband.

Roger responded to his sister's lament by divesting Rainulf of some of these feudal lands, including manors held by his younger brother, Richard, notably the prosperous town of Avellino. Learning of this, and that Matilda had received protection and refuge from the king, Rainulf and Robert, along with their two hundred knights, left Rome to discuss matters with the sovereign. Initially at least, there was a serious effort at negotiation. When this deteriorated, both men came to oppose the king's rule. What followed was protracted warfare over the next eight years. Without ignoring the gravity of this situation, which came to involve other players, let us consider Matilda's predicament.

Matilda declared that she would not return to live with her husband unless her dower, the Caudine Valley, was returned to her. This territory included several towns and straddles what are now the provinces of Benevento and Avellino.

Three principal sources state that Matilda was mistreated by her husband. These are the chronicle of Falco of Benevento, the Ferraris Chronicle based partly on Falco's work, and the chronicle of Alexander of Telese commissioned by Matilda herself. Falco, whose family was of Lombard origin, was at least somewhat biased against the Normans, though not to the point of fabricating events. Alexander was a supporter of Roger. The author of the Ferraris Chronicle wrote long after the facts he described, but besides Falco's work he may have had access to additional information unknown to us. We must examine each account.

According to Alexander of Telese, Roger found his sister's complaints justified and permitted her to stay at court as long as she wished, seeing no other way to obtain justice for her except through royal intervention.

When Rainulf demanded, through messengers, that his wife, his son and his lands be returned, Roger responded that he, the king, was not forcing Matilda to stay with the traveling court. She was free to return to Rainulf, to whom Roger had arranged her betrothal years earlier, if and when she wished. However, the monarch chastised Rainulf for remaining silent when his brother, Richard, had refused to pay homage to the king at the coronation in Palermo. Now Rainulf himself refused to go to Salerno to pay homage and fealty to Roger, who returned to Sicily with Matilda and her young son.[5]

The historical record does not state or very convincingly imply that Rainulf assaulted his wife. Only with caution might we compare Matilda's predicament to that of her contemporary, Urraca "the Reckless" of Leon and Castile, elder half-sister of Roger's wife, Queen Elvira. Urraca accused her husband, Alfonso I "the Battler" of Aragon (who was also King of Pamplona), of physically abusing her. Elvira may well have heard of Urraca's treatment at the hands of Alfonso.[6]

Falco of Benevento states simply, and concisely, that Roger, who loved his sister, learned that Rainulf had humiliated Matilda in many ways. The king honorably received her, consoled her and sent her to Sicily. Being something of a critic of Roger, Falco goes on to explain Rainulf's grief, and his effort at intervention by Pope Anacletus.[7] Clearly, this chronicler pitied Rainulf, whom he saw as a victim.

Only the author of the Ferraris Chronicle mentions that Rainulf's chief affront to Matilda was adultery, writing that:

Roger's sister, Matilda, was the wife of Rainulf of Alife, who had taken a concubine. Matilda much lamented her husband's comportment. Learning of this situation, Roger rescued his sister, along with her son by Rainulf, from the unfaithful husband. For this reason, Rainulf was ever more indignant about the king and grew ever nearer Roger's adversaries. Robert of Capua, who Pope Anacletus had sent to Roger's coronation, was fearful that the king might use the same tactics with him that he used with Rainulf. With this in mind, and seeking allies, Robert solicited the Pisans and Genoans, offering them gifts. The citizens of these important mercantile cities then sent a large fleet of galleys to Naples against the King of Sicily.[8]

The significance of Matilda's impact on the events leading to a *de facto* civil war in the peninsular regions of Roger's kingdom has generally been overlooked by historians. As there were other factors in play, we cannot know for certain that her leaving her husband, to whom she returned in 1134, was the catalyst for what ensued. Clearly, however, it was a major cause as it provoked concrete reactions by the Drengots.

As events unfolded, Rainulf and his allies, supported by Pope Innocent and the emperors of east and west, prosecuted a largely successful campaign against Roger's forces across southern Italy over the next few years. Pope Innocent and the two emperors might well have invaded anyway, but the Drengots and other families of the realm probably would have supported the king had the incident with Matilda never transpired.

Rainulf died in 1139, the same year Pope Innocent finally recognized Roger. Proving ultimately successful in suppressing opposition, both foreign and domestic, in his realms, Roger promulgated the Assizes of Ariano in 1140 or shortly thereafter.

Rainulf, whose corpse Roger ordered exhumed from its tomb at Troia so that, according to Falco, he could drag it from his horse as he rode around the city, was survived by his two children, Robert and Adelisa. By then Matilda may already have been deceased.

Alexander's chronicle ends in 1136, about two years after Matilda returned to Rainulf, although the biographer lived on. This has suggested to some historians that Matilda died in that year.[9] Falco of Benevento does not mention her reacting to her husband's death in 1139.

The accounts differ slightly, yet all three allude to the mistreatment of Matilda by her husband, implying offense taken by Roger that his sister did not receive the respect she deserved.

It is tempting to speculate about why Matilda returned to her husband, apart from the question of her dower being restored to her. If Rainulf's only misdeed were conjugal betrayal, he may have promised not to repeat it. Much remains unknown, and neither Matilda or Rainulf lived very long after their separation.

Marital infidelity, particularly by men, was not terribly unusual. Perhaps Matilda felt especially humiliated because her husband took up with a woman of low birth. On the other hand, it may have been a woman she knew, such as a lady-in-waiting. However, there could have been other affronts she was forced to endure. Except for Ferraris, the surviving reports are rather vague about what Rainulf actually did. In the twelfth century, it was rare for any woman to leave her husband, and the "scandal" was arguably magnified when the woman was an aristocrat.

Few woman of lower birth than Matilda Hauteville would have had the possibility of leaving an abusive husband, for they would have been dependent on him socially and financially. This includes not only common women but most countesses and baronesses. Matilda's success in fleeing Rainulf was based on her exalted social status and her geographical proximity to her protective brother at a certain moment, as well as that brother's willingness to defend her.

Significantly, Roger's attention to Matilda's grievances is the first case of a King of Sicily using his authority to "arbitrate" a personal matter concerning a member of the royal family.

It seems unlikely, based on the statements about mistreatment made by the three chroniclers, that Matilda's actions were merely political, as if she separated from her husband because he was already conspiring against Roger. Despite the apparent dissonance of his younger brother, Richard, Rainulf himself does not seem to have expressed overt disapproval of Roger before the spring of 1131, and he attended the coronation with Matilda the previous year.

For his part, Roger's defense of Matilda does not seem to have been motivated by politics. With a pope, two emperors and a few unruly vassals already acting against him, it was hardly expedient to lose the Drengot contingent of his army. In the end, Rainulf only became one more thorn in the king's side, and a large one at that.

We must conclude that Matilda's grievances were real and painful. Their revelation contributed to the causes for the first war fought by a King of Sicily.

Joanna's Fertility

Joanna of England was not quite twelve years old when she wed William II of Sicily in February 1177, and it is probable that the couple did not actually live together for another year or two. Initially, Joanna and her ladies-in-waiting resided in the Zisa palace in Palermo's Genoard park while William lived at the Norman Palace, where he had a harem.[10]

There was never any doubt that Joanna's chief duty as queen consort was to give birth to an heir, and it would have been reasonable to expect her to be pregnant by 1181 when she was sixteen. So far as we know, this did not happen even though it was reported by Robert of Torigni, a chronicler in Normandy, that Joanna bore a son, Bohemond, around that time. It was said that this child died in infancy.[11]

Except for this, Joanna is barely noted by the chroniclers over the next few years. There is no record of her bearing children before her husband's death late in 1189, nor is there any record of a bastard child of William II.

Following the Third Crusade, when her brother tried to betroth her to Al-Adil ("Saphadin"), she returned to France, the land of her birth, where she wed Raymond VI, Count of Toulouse. Before long, Joanna was pregnant with what may have been her first child. She gave birth to a son, the future Raymond VII, in July 1197, followed by a daughter and another son.

This suggests that, although Joanna's rapport with her second husband may have been strained at times, the couple did not have any physical impediments to having children. There can be no doubt about Joanna's fertility.

Unless she did, in fact, bear a child by William, which remains doubtful, the causes for her lack of pregnancies during her first marriage would have been questioned and it is even possible that some kind of "treatment" was attempted, such as consuming herbs or other foods thought to aid fertility.

A few methods of diagnosis and treatment are mentioned in the *Trotula,* the treatise attributed in part to the enigmatic Trota of Salerno, a noteworthy gynecologist of the eleventh century.[12] Trota is deservedly praised, but that is not to say that every idea in the work was very enlightened, even if it must be considered in the context of its time.

For example, one form of analysis called for each spouse to urinate into a separate pot containing wheat bran, with infertility assumed if worms were thriving in it after nine or ten days.[13]

Virtually nothing is known of Trota herself, or whether she actually existed, and in recent historiography she is not always identified precisely with a figure who lived during a very specific period.[14] However, given her education at the Salerno medical school (or at least the formulation of the gynecological treatise there), it is reasonable to believe that her methods were known at the Sicilian court, where Romuald of Salerno, a later student of the same school, was present. Romuald's chronicle takes us only to 1178. He died three or four years later, and he did not live in Palermo during his last few years, so it is unlikely that he was ever consulted regarding the royal couple's infertility. There were, of course, other competent physicians at court.

Unlike many of her contemporaries, Trota, whoever she was, believed that failure to conceive could be attributed to the husband as much as the wife.[15] This belief was not altogether unknown, but during the twelfth century most physicians and churchmen still preferred to place the blame for infertility on the woman. In many places, this mentality actually survived into modern times.

We cannot know which fertility treatments Joanna was subjected to between 1182 and 1189, or which potions she had to consume. There are, however, a few distinct possibilities present in the *Trotula*.

If the couple wanted a son, the male was to consume the uterus and vagina of a hare, dried, powdered and mixed with wine. The woman should ingest a similar potion made from the testicles of a hare.[16] Other potions prescribed for the woman were made from the dried, powdered testicles and liver of a boar or pig.[17]

In modern times, these medieval therapies would be dismissed as folk cures or even witchcraft. An example employing a similar principle, though it is not mentioned in the *Trotula,* survived in Sicily into the twentieth century. This "cure" for male infidelity called for a wife to sprinkle some of her dried, powdered menstrual blood over some food, such as pasta, to be consumed by her unfaithful husband.[18]

As we have seen, although Joanna does not seem to have had any children by William, she later bore three by her second husband.

Lacking children or legitimate nephews, William eventually undertook to declare that his aunt, Constance, should succeed him as Sicily's ruler. Constance's fertility may also have been questioned for a few years, but eventually, at the age of forty, she gave birth to a son, Frederick II.

Constance's Choices

Born in November 1154 as the posthumous daughter of King Roger II, Constance of Sicily was raised by her widowed mother, Beatrice of Rethel, at the royal court and also at the Hauteville castle at San Marco d'Alunzio. As the younger half-sister of William I, she was the aunt of William II.[19]

With the death of Henry, the younger brother of William

II, in 1172, Constance became heiress presumptive to the Sicilian throne. She was about the same age as William II, who wed Joanna of England in 1177. As we have seen, Joanna did not give birth to any surviving children by William.

Whereas Joanna was not even a teenager when she married William II, Constance was twenty-two and still a maiden at the time of her nephew's nuptials in Palermo. By then, the Hautevilles had a dearth of legitimate heirs, and it was hoped that Joanna would give birth to one soon enough.

Constance, as a female, could not solve this problem, for a hypothetical son of hers would not be a Hauteville. Indeed, a marriage of Constance might take her far from her native Sicily because a husband of suitable rank would presumably be a king or the heir to an important kingdom. Nevertheless, it is remarkable that, in view of general practice, there was, so far as we know, no effort to betroth her by this time. In any case, the wedding of her nephew probably would have occasioned curiosity among courtiers and clergy as to why Constance was still unmarried.

The theory that she was living in a nunnery has generally been dismissed as unfounded because it was advanced during the fourteenth century by Guelphs in Tuscany. It is, however, quite possible that Constance was living in a convent near San Marco d'Alunzio, perhaps the one established by Queen Margaret, even if she had not taken vows.

That we are told virtually nothing about Constance's youth before marriage is not atypical; indeed it is normal in view of the attention, or lack of it, paid to royal maidens by most chroniclers. Yet, by 1177 she was William's nearest relative among his contemporaries, probably regarded more as a sister than an aunt. Of young Constance herself we know little except that she had red hair and may have been considered pretty. Later events would reveal her to have a keen intellect and an instinctual courage, complemented perhaps by headstrong independence and decisiveness, or at least a certain willingness to confront tasks.

Not only were the *familiares* (royal counsellors) undoubtedly aware of the problem posed by the lack of an heir, both the queen dowager (Beatrice of Rethel) and queen mother (Margaret of Navarre) must have understood its implications. As we have seen, it is quite possible that Joanna was even being treated for infertility.

Finally, in 1184, perhaps reluctantly but out of a sense of duty, Constance accepted a betrothal to Henry Hohenstaufen, who was King of Germany as the son of Frederick I "Barbarossa." This union pacified a longstanding conflict between the two dynasties but it was not the only such attempt; a few years earlier, Frederick had proposed that his daughter, Beatrice, marry William.

A decade Constance's junior, Henry was destined to become Holy Roman Emperor. By now, with no sons, William may already have been considering designating Constance his heir. If so, he and his advisors underestimated the possibility of the Sicilian crown ending up on the head of an emperor.

Constance went to live in Germany and eventually became empress as Henry's consort. Her marriage does not seem to have been especially felicitous, and she bore her first child in 1194 at the age of forty; we do not know if she had miscarriages before giving birth to her son.

The circumstances, which (considered together) make for an unusual "profile" for a woman of Constance's rank and era, prompt several questions to which we shall never have answers. Why was Constance betrothed so late? Did she, in fact, plan to become a nun? Why did she have only one child, and only after so many years of marriage?

These questions reflect medieval sensibilities and curiosities more than modern ones. Is it possible that Constance's choices were based on something more than what is known to us?

There are a number of possibilities, and to explore each in detail would take us further into the realm of conjecture than the evidence suggests that we need venture. A few come to mind.

Most obviously, it may be that Constance did not enjoy the company of men. Perhaps she preferred an intellectual life amongst women.

Could her choices — if such they were — have been rooted in a personal sexual orientation at variance to the norm?[20] This is somewhat complex because it is highly unlikely that such a thing would have been discussed, even among kin, let alone written.[21] Statistical probability alone argues for the possibility that the sexual orientation of some women, perhaps one in ten, did not conform to the "traditional" model, and in the twelfth century such deviation was severely condemned by the church, if less so for women than men.[22]

There is no particular woman with whom Constance seems to have been closely associated but, again, this is not likely to have been recorded for posterity in any event.

In the end, there is much about Constance's persona, both public and private, that we shall never know, and the nuances of her sexuality will remain an enigma. However, she was a devoted mother of her one child and a devout daughter of the church. As Queen of Sicily, she did not shirk from her duties. As queen regnant (or the nearest thing to it in the Kingdom of Sicily) and then queen regent, she was steadfast in her convictions.

Sicilians justifiably regard her as one of our greatest medieval queens. By any measure, Constance was an exceptional woman.

Isabella's Melancholy

Isabella "Plantagenet," a daughter of King John of England and his tempestuous wife, Isabella of Angoulême, was born in 1214 during a turbulent time in English history.[23] Following the death of her father in 1216 and, soon afterward, the flight of her mother to France, young Isabella and her siblings were raised in England by courtiers until her brother, Henry III, reached the age of majority.

Efforts were made to find a husband for Isabella. One of these plans, undertaken when the girl was eleven years old, would have seen her wed to a son of Frederick II, Holy Roman Emperor and King of Sicily. When this did not materialize, Henry seems to have set aside the idea of finding his sister an appropriate husband, at least for the immediate future.

The years passed, and by 1229 Isabella was living away from her family with her own little court. Incredibly, this situation was accepted, or chosen, over betrothing one of Europe's most eligible maidens to a continental king or prince. How could this be?

Like the marriage of Constance Hauteville, that of Isabella was "delayed," though not so much and probably for different reasons. Isabella, at twenty-one, was still quite young when she was betrothed to Frederick II in 1235. Like Constance's marriage to Henry VI, Isabella's marriage to Constance's son was a political union in its purest form. Even so, Frederick needed legitimate sons as heirs and Isabella was obviously young enough to provide at least one or two.

What makes Isabella's situation unusual is not the timing or objective of her marriage but certain circumstances which would have been considered unorthodox in the thirteenth century.

Isabella's establishment of her own household, at times some distance from her brother's royal court, is strange indeed. Still stranger is the fact that she was already living with her own suite at Marlborough when she was just fifteen years old. She sometimes lived at Gloucester, her birthplace.

Henry did not forget his sister; he often sent her letters and gifts.[24] By 1234, a year before her betrothal to Frederick II, she was living at the Tower of London. This was nearer her brother, who was then at Westminster except when his duties required his presence further afield. Earlier biographers have remarked on this unusual circumstance. Of note is the insightful commentary by Mary Anne Everett Green:

A considerable degree of mystery hangs over the residence of the princess in this fortress. It was very unusual for one who, as being the elder sister of the yet unmarried king, should have occupied a conspicuous station at court, to be thus kept aloof and so often alone, and the expression used by Matthew Paris, that she was "in vigilant custody," seems to imply more than a mere voluntary detention. No clue can however now be found to lead to a discovery of the reasons for this honorary imprisonment, if such it should be considered; it must remain in the obscurity in which ages have wrapped it.[25]

Matthew's phrase, *sub vigilanti servabatur*, is used in the context of Isabella being in the Tower of London when she was summoned to meet the emissaries of Frederick II in 1235.[26] Another interpretation would be "under vigilant guard." It could well be argued, depending on the chronicler's choice of words, that this referred merely to the fact of her being protected. In its simplest forms, *servare* means "to save" or "to guard."

More remarkable in this regard is Matthew's mention of the use of the Tower to confine Peter of Rievaulx in 1234, possibly at the same time Isabella was living there.[27] Even so, Peter was not a prisoner in the usual sense (and he was soon given his liberty), and it appears that King Henry himself occasionally stayed at the Tower.

What is more striking is the manner in which Frederick II is thought to have treated his wife. She often seems to have been secluded, or at least somewhat removed from court affairs, and at one point her brother, Henry, wrote to Frederick expressing dismay that she was rarely seen in public wearing her crown.

A cryptic entry by Matthew Paris in the year 1240 refers to "the rising hopes of Isabella."[28] This seems to imply that, until then, there had been some kind of problem between the queen and her husband. It is difficult to know what to make of this. A few years earlier, Matthew had claimed that on Isabella's wedding night Frederick spurned her company for that of a concubine.[29] Although, taken literally, this seems unlikely, and Matthew attributes it to the advice of Frederick's astrologers, it may reflect a perception of the marriage that was commonplace at the time.

Matthew also mentions that Isabella's attendants were sent back to England, leading biographers to infer that Frederick did not want his young wife to have the company of friends from her own country.[30]

When Isabella's brother, Richard of Cornwall, visited the traveling court in northern Italy in 1241, he had to make a formal request to Frederick to see her because, it seems, she was not permitted to attend the reception held upon his arrival.

Some of the ideas that have grown around this circumstance have been distorted beyond reason, for while Isabella may have been kept away from some of her husband's daily duties she did bear three or four of his children over the next five years.

Isabella died in childbirth in 1241. She was entombed in the cathedral of Andria, in Apulia, where Frederick's previous wife, Yolanda (Isabella) of Jerusalem, also rested. After several centuries the two queens' remains ended up in a common sarcophagus in the crypt for bishops and other important personages.

Anything that could be said about Isabella's personality or mental state is necessarily largely conjectural. She may have had a condition, such as depression, which affected her at some times but not at others; perhaps she was bipolar. There is, indeed, a broad range of conditions she may have had. It is quite possible that Isabella inherited the fickle, and often angry, temperament both her parents are reputed to have had. Perhaps Isabella's abandonment by her mother traumatized her in a way that left deep mental scars.

However, it seems rather unlikely that a peculiar condition was apparent to the ambassadors of Frederick II who visited (and inspected) her in London in the spring of 1235.

Much about Queen Isabella, and Frederick's treatment of her, will always be left to interpretation and speculation.

Isabella was, sadly, outlived by her mother, who died in 1246 after having given birth to fourteen surviving children by two husbands. Isabella's son, Henry, died in 1254 after serving as the governor of Sicily for his elder half-brother, Conrad. Her daughter, Margaret, gave birth to five children and lived until 1270.

Bianca's Single Motherhood

Bianca Lancia of Agliano is the only Queen of Sicily, though probably uncrowned, who gave birth to an heir outside marriage during the Norman-Swabian era. In the years between the death of his second wife, Yolanda of Jerusalem, in 1228, and his marriage to his third wife, Isabella of England, in 1235, Frederick II fathered two or three children with his beloved mistress, Bianca Lancia. The known children were named Constance and Manfred; the third (hypothetical) child was Yolanda.

Various reasons could be posited for Frederick not marrying Bianca until much later, around 1246, shortly before her death.[31] Most often, it is supposed that such a union with her dynasty, whose lands in northwestern Italy he already controlled as emperor, did not bring sufficient political advantages to Frederick to justify marriage.

Yolanda of Jerusalem was descended through her mother, Maria of Montferrat, from the same family as Bianca, namely the Aleramids. Indeed, we find the Aleramic dynasty elsewhere in Sicilian royal unions; Adelaide del Vasto, third wife of Roger I, comes to mind, and we may note the similarity of her family's coat of arms to that of Bianca (see the heraldry chapter).

Whether or not Bianca's dynastic political position was initially appreciated by the courtiers, it is a fact that her children by Frederick were born outside marriage. Unlike most of Frederick's many other bastards, however, Bianca's children were born when he, as a widower, was free to marry. Although Manfred seems not to have been "formally" identified (by chroniclers and scribes) as the emperor's son until Frederick wed Bianca, he is depicted in Frederick's falconry treatise, which was written at least a few years before this. Indeed, it seems that, at the time of Frederick's death in 1250, Manfred was his favorite son.

For better or worse, Bianca and her children have come to be identified historiographically by the fact of their not being part of Frederick's lawful royal (or imperial) family. However, it is highly probable that they lived at his court, at least much of the time.

The longstanding belief that Frederick gave Bianca estates in Sicily or elsewhere has never been proven. However, Manfred eventually enfeoffed some of his Lancia kinsmen, who strongly supported his efforts to defend the kingdom against papal ambitions after 1250; the Lanza family of Sicily is thought to be descended from them.

The concept of legitimacy has more complexity than many historians ascribe to it. There is much to be said for the thesis that illegitimacy of birth became a serious impediment to identity and succession only during the twelfth century.[32] This, of course, coincides with the emergence of the Kingdom of Sicily. By the thirteenth century, heirship, whether to a kingdom or a barony, was governed chiefly by legitimacy, and it is probably for that reason that Frederick sought to regularize the status of his children born outside marriage.

Only rarely is illegitimacy examined from the point of view of the medieval woman who gives birth to a child outside marriage. There is nothing to suggest that Bianca's motherhood, about which little is known, was much different from that of any other aristocratic mother in Italy during this era.[33]

In the Kingdom of Sicily, an obvious precedent reflecting the importance of legitimate birth is Tancred of Lecce, who became king in 1189 (or early in 1190) by baronial and ecclesiastical assent but not by lawful hereditary right. Constance of Sicily was correct when she brought this to his attention (see Chapter 2). However, Tancred's father, Roger of Apulia, was not actually a king but the eldest son and heir apparent of a king, Roger II, and the incentive for Tancred's coronation was that there was a dearth of legitimate Hauteville males by 1189. Simon of Taranto, who in 1161 conspired with Tancred and others to overthrow King William I (Simon's half-brother), was a bastard son of Roger II.[34]

Though the status of illegitimate children, even those of kings, was dictated by canon law, in practice we see a widely varying treatment of such children. Tancred inherited Lecce through his mother. Over time, he was rehabilitated to the point of becoming a general of William II, and perhaps even something of a confidant to the young king. Simon was despised by William I and divested of the wealthy city of Taranto granted him by Roger II (Frederick later gave Taranto to Manfred). Tancred became a king, while Simon died in obscurity beyond the kingdom's borders.

We may well debate whether Frederick's recognition of Manfred, as well as Enzo (for whom there was a formal decree of legitimization), his child by still another woman, actually legitimized them. So far as we know, the papacy did not consider them thereby legitimate for the purpose of heirship.[35]

In Manfred's case, unlike Enzo's, the marriage of his parents, though not sanctioned by the papacy as suitable for dynastic succession, changed his status and was sacramentally valid. In papal eyes, it made Bianca a wife but not a queen.

Recent scholarship has revisited the stereotype of the medieval bastard.[36] Yet there were always differences between aristocratic bastards and common ones, who were far worse off than their nobler counterparts. Whereas the bastard son of a farmer might (along with his mother) be disparaged and disowned, the out-of-wedlock son of a baron or knight would at least be cared for, presuming that his mother was the baron's mistress and not simply a woman with whom the man had engaged in a tryst. Women usually found themselves at a decided disadvantage in this predicament.

That begs the question, was it better to be the legitimate son of a serf or the bastard son of a king?

By the thirteenth century, coats of arms, which were hereditary, took into account (through the use of specific symbols) the fact that a knight was born outside marriage and was therefore a bastard.[37] In other words, he could use some form of his father's coat of arms, and could even be knighted, and though he might not inherit his father's lands it was possible for him to be granted a manor of his own during his father's lifetime, even if it were something less prosperous than Taranto.

Bastardy might sometimes be painless but it was rarely pleasant. In our very modern, mostly successful, effort to remove the social burdens placed upon children born outside wedlock, it is easy to forget how terrible the social stigma could be until quite recently. In Italy, where, according to the national statistical institute (ISTAT) thirty-one percent of children were born outside marriage in 2017, the law distinguishing between legitimate and "natural" children was abolished only in 2014. At the dawn of the twenty-first century, many here in Italy still entertained attitudes about illegitimacy that were known since the time of Frederick and Bianca.

How did Bianca's relationship with Frederick affect her status as the mother of his children?

Certainly, her status improved upon her marriage. Even if, sadly, she wed Frederick only on her death bed, she died with the knowledge that her children would henceforth be recognized as the children of a king and emperor.

Although Frederick's recognition of his children born outside marriage was not atypical of Christian monarchs, there was no uniform policy governing the treatment of royal bastards in the Kingdom of Sicily, nor, for that matter, in most European kingdoms. In rare circumstances even the identity of a royal child's mother might be placed in doubt; it was for that reason that Constance Hauteville ensured that plenty of dignitaries were present to witness her giving birth to Frederick II.

Were it not for Bianca's son, the Hauteville reign probably would have ended with Conrad's death in 1254 unless his son, Conradin, could have marshalled enough support to wrest back the kingdom from the Angevins or whoever was ruling it.

We know virtually nothing about any negative treatment of Manfred that can be attributed explicitly to the fact of his being born outside marriage. Like Tancred before him, he was viewed by the barons as the best hope for the preservation of the Kingdom of Sicily as they knew it. Accordingly, he was crowned in 1258

In 1282, the Sicilian baronage, seeking to legitimize their revolt against the Angevins, looked to Manfred's daughter, Constance, then married to the King of Aragon, as the lawful heiress of the Hohenstaufens. And so Bianca's legacy survived.

Harems

The harem was one of the many traditions that Sicily's Christian kings inherited from the Kalbids. We find several references to it by people familiar with the palace and its court. Hugh Falcandus mentions it during the time of William I.[38] This was in connection to the Bonello revolt, when some of the concubines were raped and others abducted. Later, the traveler ibn Jubayr notes it in his diary during the reign of William II.[39] He states, through hearsay, that Christian women converted to Islam and joined the harem.

In daily life, the women of the harem were silk weavers. Some may also have had other duties at court as artisans or cooks. We do not know how many concubines there were, but in the reign of Frederick II, the last king known to have maintained the harem, they traveled with him; Frederick also seems to have had a harem at Lucera, a Muslim city in Apulia.[40] Neither Tancred nor Manfred seems to have had harems, and Conrad spent very little of his short reign in Italy.

The harem in the palace may have been guarded by eunuchs, as was the practice in Tunisia, yet we have no specific record of Sicily's court eunuchs performing this task. Although it is quite possible that a concubine could have given birth to a child of one of our kings, no such children are known to us by name or otherwise mentioned.

The precise location of the palace harem is unknown. It was probably somewhat isolated on a high floor of one of the towers, though not the tower that housed the Palatine Chapel and Roger's chamber.

Our knowledge of medieval harems like the one in Sicily comes to us from Fatimid history, though much that has been written about the institution itself concerns its modern incarnations.[41] It could be argued that little is known of the Sicilian harem because medieval harems, by their very nature, were discreet.

Whether the king was the only person in the *Regnum Siciliae* permitted a harem is difficult to know, but he was probably the only Christian to enjoy such a privilege. Henry Aristippo (see Chapter 1) formed a small harem in his home in Palermo with some concubines he abducted from the palace during the Bonello revolt. This was plainly illegal as Henry was a man of the church, and for his insolence he paid with his life.

In the same city, some of the local leaders of the Muslim community, even during the Norman era, may have had small harems, which (for the purpose of this discussion) should not be confused with the habitation of four wives in the same large residence. Prominent among such men during the reign of William II was Abu'l Kasim (Bulcassis), who is mentioned by both Hugh Falcandus and ibn Jubayr, and his rival Caïd Siddiq (Sedictus), who Falcandus states was even wealthier than Abu'l Kasim and perhaps more respected among the Muslims.

Later, the Arab governors of Lucera, where Frederick II sent many Sicilian Muslims, may have had harems. Being isolated from the kingdom's major cities, these Luceran leaders lived like emirs until the Angevins suppressed them following the defeat of Manfred and Conradin.

Ibn Jubayr observed Christian women in Sicily who dressed like the Muslim women, in veils or scarves.[42] This was also true of the Jewish women. Except for being exceptionally beautiful and well-dressed, a girl of the harem, if permitted to walk about Palermo, perhaps in the nearby souk (which still exists as the Ballarò street market), would be indistinguishable from most other young women.

Whether the Sicilian concubines could be described as "slaves" is open to debate. Too little is known about the Sicilian royal harem to conclude much about this. Although the women were secluded most of the time, it is quite possible that, perhaps accompanied by guards, they could occasionally venture beyond the palace walls.

The right to have a harem is not considered in either the Assizes of Ariano of Roger II or the Constitutions of Melfi of Frederick II, though both legal codes address such matters as prostitution and rape whilst establishing a universal standard of justice for Christians, Muslims and Jews.

Much about the royal harem remains unknown. The palace has yet to reveal many of its secrets.

Eunuchs

Contrary to a popular belief implied by much literature, making boys into eunuchs was not a practice of Muslim Arab origin, nor even an official part of Islam. In fact, eunuchism was a practice known to the Byzantine Greeks, from whom the Muslims adopted it. There were eunuchs in antiquity.[43]

In the Middle Ages, part of the historical reasoning for appointing eunuchs to positions of trust was that they had no wives or children of their own, hence no conflicts of loyalty. This questionable logic endured in the Mediterranean region and some parts of Asia for many centuries.

Eunuchs were often charged with guarding harems but (as mentioned above) perhaps less so in Sicily than elsewhere. Most of the Sicilian eunuchs were slaves, at least initially, and most began their lives as Muslims. As the kingdom's Arab population gradually converted to Christianity, there were ever fewer eunuchs.

Questions of gender are unavoidable. To the modern mind, castration is usually viewed as a form of genital mutilation. In some societies, eunuchs constituted a "third gender." Castration affects sexual development, libido and even appetite.[44]

Several Sicilian eunuchs who converted to Christianity rose to become important, trusted court officers: Caïd Martin, Caïd Richard, Caïd Peter (Ahmed es-Sikeli), Philip of Mahdia.[45]

Besides men of such rank, there were a fair number of eunuchs at the court in the Norman era, for Hugh Falcandus mentions Norman rebels attempting to massacre many of them during a revolt in Palermo. Although it may not have been cited at the time, the tenuous Biblical pretext for such discrimination is found in Deuteronomy 23:1. The Koran does not mention eunuchs explicitly but Islamic law prohibits castration; the existence of eunuchism tells us that this proscription was not always put into practice.

Virtually nothing is known about Sicily's eunuchs as a group or community, and the only references made to them refer to those at court. We have no indication of the number that became Christian; it should be remembered that the vast majority of conversions were not to Greek Orthodoxy but to Roman Catholicism.

Too little is known to ascertain the precise motivations for the loyalty of most of Sicily's Muslims to the king, but it may be explained by the simple fact that the monarch was the guarantor of their safety. Not for nothing were most of the king's bodyguards and archers Muslims.

This loyalty extended to Sicily's female leaders as well. The regencies of Adelaide del Vasto and Margaret of Navarre are anomalous instances of medieval women ruling large populations of Muslims.

Another example, though by her reign the Muslim population was much diminished, was Constance Hauteville. When Henry VI arrived in the kingdom with Constance at the end of the twelfth century, he introduced Germans and other Catholics into the administration, and in many cases these men replaced Muslims and Arabs. However, Muslims from Lucera formed Europe's finest company of archers into the reign of Henry's grandson, King Manfred, who ruled until 1266.[46]

Except for trusting certain eunuchs, we know little about what the kings and queens thought of the practice itself. The queens seem to have accepted eunuchism as part of life in

Sicily, just as they accepted the reality of the royal harem. Unlike the other queens, Constance Hauteville, being raised in Sicily, would have known something of these practices since her youth.

Like the harem, the *diwan* (treasury), Arab cuisine and certain tenets of Maliki Law, eunuchism was something inherited from the Fatimids that did not immediately change.[47] It is one of many things that the Hautevilles left in place for a rather long time.

The Hohenstaufens, as we have seen, did not maintain this tradition. Frederick II may have spoken Arabic and appreciated Islamic culture, but Muslims were a rarity at his court.[48] When they disappeared, so did the eunuchs.

Women and the Law

In the Kingdom of Sicily, like most western European monarchies, the function of a queen was defined by practice, tradition and necessity rather than by specific legal statute.

More generally, a number of phenomena were known which reflect the true social status of most women. Here we shall very succinctly summarize a few which, though they did not touch the rank or status of queenhood itself, would have been known to our queens. Through their justiciars, the queens regent were sometimes called upon to address such matters.

Except for fleeting references to prostitutes by chroniclers or churchmen (and most chroniclers were churchmen), most of our information about prostitution in the Kingdom of Sicily comes from the Assizes of Ariano and the more sophisticated Constitutions of Melfi, which outlaw the promotion and facilitation of prostitution (pimping), such as mothers acting to prostitute their daughters, without making the sexual act itself illegal. This principle, which actually exists in Italy today, effectively decriminalizes a woman's use of her own body for the purpose of prostitution yet protects her from being forced into that profession.

The same law codes outlawed rape, though chiefly when the victims were nuns, virgins or widows, rather than married women. Raping a married woman seems not to have been viewed in the same light.[49] The Assizes (article 21 in the Vatican codex) state that raping a nun is illegal even if done for the intention of the rapist attempting to thereby use the act to justify a claim to forcibly marry the woman.

The statutes were uneven from an ethical point of view. Assaulting a prostitute was against the law, yet a man could kill his wife and her lover if he caught them in the act of adultery (sexual intercourse). Otherwise, if he did not kill his wife on that occasion, a husband might sue for divorce; that this was nearly impossible in practice could make homicide appear to be a simpler solution.

Few cases would have reached the sovereign for adjudication. Unless these involved prominent persons or special circumstances, they would be heard by justiciars or circuit judges. Under normal conditions, Sicily's queens regent would have referred such cases as divorce claims brought before them to the justiciars or the church. Unfortunately, we do not know how many cases of this kind there were, either among the nobility or the common folk, in the Kingdom of Sicily before 1266. By modern standards they were quite rare.

Most divorce procedures were decided based on religious jurisdiction. Although, strictly speaking, divorce, as we understand that term, was not sanctioned by Catholic canon law, it existed in Judaism and Islam. The crown did not usually involve itself directly in problems between spouses, even when they were aristocrats; Matilda's case was thus highly exceptional.

Queen Margaret referred a notorious divorce case to the church, which treated it as a marital annulment for adultery.

Both spouses were aristocrats.[50] In 1184, the Council of Verona, acting in response to the Cathar heresy, formally declared marriage to be a sacrament.

Sacramental or not, the decaying marriage of Matilda Hauteville, discussed earlier, did not reach the point of the spouses asking that the union be dissolved for adultery, and in such an event there is no certainty that the church would have granted an annulment solely on those grounds. However, unlike most women, Matilda was in an economic and social position to leave her husband.

Compared to the Judaic and Muslim procedures, the Catholic approach to the question of marital separations could be rather inconsistent. The first marriage of Eleanor of Aquitaine was annulled based on her kinship to her husband falling within the degrees of consanguinity permitted by canon law. Yet the canonicity of many such marriages was uncontested. In the Kingdom of Sicily, Yolanda of Jerusalem and Frederick II were third cousins, a degree of kinship permitted at that time.

Slavery existed, and the rape of a female slave might go unpunished. However, the Constitutions of Melfi make it illegal to assault a slave (book 3, article 34). As we have seen, the legal status of concubines in a harem was not addressed in civil law. These women do not seem to have been considered either prostitutes or slaves even though, arguably, they were both. We cannot know how many of these women would have chosen concubinage even if given the choice. Most knew no other status, having been committed to this way of life at a rather young age.

The Constitutions of Melfi also consider dowries and establish the rights of noblewomen to inherit manors from their fathers in the absence of male heirs, a principle likewise implemented in some form in Spain, France and Scotland. This "Sicilian Succession" was part of law into the nineteenth century.

In permitting female succession, Frederick's Constitutions confirmed a practice that, though not formally codified by his predecessors, was already known amongst Norman and Lombard barons. Frederick may simply have wanted to regulate it.

We have ample proof that female feudal tenure had already existed in some form since the earliest days of the kingdom. For example, Lucy of Cammarata (see Chapter 3), who was probably a niece or younger cousin of Roger I, is described as *castelli camarate dominatrix* from 1141. Over time, she ceded lands and serfs to the diocese of Cefalù.[51] In 1154, following the death of her son, Adam, without heirs the castle and barony of Cammarata reverted to the crown. The castle still stands guard over the town.

Clearly, certain laws were more enlightened than others, but it is worth placing some of these into a wider temporal context. As regards rape, in Italy the deplorable practice of forcing a young woman to marry the man who raped her (mentioned in the Assizes of Ariano in connection with men raping nuns in order to marry them) existed until a notorious case in 1966.[52]

The rape statute promulgated by Roger II fell into disuse in the modern era, to the point of Italian legislation making the crime a felony only in 1996.[53] Only in 1974 was divorce legalized, and in 1981 (with public law number 442/1981) the penalty for a man killing his wife (in an *omicidio e lesione personale a causa di onore* or "honor killing") if he caught her in the act of adultery was finally increased beyond a sentence of seven years (article 587 in the penal code of the Kingdom of Italy enacted by royal decree number 1398 in 1930) to be thenceforth defined as murder, with the attendant penalties; the law of 1930 was simply abrogated.

Conclusions

Much that is presented in this chapter is reasonably complex, perhaps more so than some scholars imagine. Yet the essential principles are fairly simple. It is this very human angle that allows us to view our queens, and all medieval women, as real people entitled to human dignity, and not simply objects of specialized study.

Excessive speculation about medieval sexualities is a slippery slope. The controversial theory about the sexual orientation of Richard I of England was first published only during the twentieth century.[54] We are not seeking controversy but humanity.

Justice should never be a privilege.

NOTES

1. Giles, John (editor), *Petri Blesensis Opera Omnia* (1847), volume 1, letter number 66, pages 192-197.

2. See Bennett, Judith, "Medievalism and Feminism," *Studying Medieval Women* (1993), pages 7-29; Murray, Jacqueline, "Historicizing Sex, Sexualizing History," *Writing Medieval History* (2005), pages 133-152; Partner, Nancy, "Preface," ibid, pages xi-xvi. These works contain useful bibliographies. Also see the papers and monographs cited below and in the notes of Chapter 11. More generally, see Brundage, James, *Law, Sex and Christian Society in Medieval Europe* (1987).

3. For some logic underpinning this, and its application to scientific fields, see Taleb, Nassim, *The Black Swan* (2007).

4. Not to be confused with her elder half-sister (daughter of Judith of Evreux), who wed Raymond IV of Toulouse in 1080, as noted in chapter 22 of Malaterra's chronicle, Matilda was probably a daughter of Adelaide del Vasto, the third wife of Roger I. There exists a hypothesis that she was born around 1087 as the daughter of Eremburga of Mortain, Roger's second wife. This seems somewhat less likely given the presumed year of birth of Rainulf of Alife around 1093 and Matilda bearing a child around 1125, but it is far from impossible.

5. From Alexander of Telese, book 2, chapters 14, 15, 17: *Verum comitissa Matilda, cuius iam longe superius mentio habita est, audiens Rogerium regem fratrem suum Salernum advenisse, de Alifis, absente et ignorante viro suo Ranulpho comite, ad eum profecta est, profitens se nulla ratione nullo ve pacto ad eius thorum ulterius redituram, nisi ei dotalia cuncta restituerentur, videlicet tota vallis Caudina cum eius omnibus infra manentibus oppidis. Cuius quidem iustam adventus causam cum Rex cognovisset, cupiens illi patrocinium impendere, eam apud se pro suo velle manere permisit. Videbatur enim iniustum omnino non esse quod ipsa poscebat, neque enim eam aliter suam posse optinere iustitiam arbitrabatur, nisi ei secum manendi ad tempus daretur facultas. Cumque comes Roma, quo ierat, reversus, uxorem suam recessisse, nec non Avellinum atque Merculianum sibi dempta reperisset, immenso animi merore concutitur, non tantum quod prefatas amiserat terras, quantum quod se a coniuge ita dimissum comperisset. Quam ob rem misit ad Montemfuscum, quo ipse erat, deprecans obnixius quatinus coniux eius sibi, simulque Avellinum nec non Merculianum restituerentur. At ille his qui missi fuerant respondens dicebat: "Ego quidem uxorem Comitis nec teneo, nec redire cogam, quoniam eam non abstuli; ipsius ergo requiratur voluntas, et si quidem revertendi habuerit animum, ego non contradicam, verum tamen quod querit, videtur iustum querere, nec esse utique sibi denegandum, quandoquidem sub horum que dicit condicione dotalium eam, me concedente, duxit uxorem. Avellinum autem et Merculianum, ea propter non reddere debeo, quoniam Ricardus frater eius, ipso audiente atque omnino tacente, fatebatur ea sibi ita esse propria ut neminem inde dominum super se cognoscere nec cuiquam famulari deberet. Si igitur, inquam, sui iuris, ut ipse asserit, erant, ut quid cum inde nullum se habere dominum Richardus, ipso audiente, testaretur, ea iuris sui esse non ore proprio notificabat? Est et aliud propter quod ei non sunt reddenda que querit: quoniam cum Panormi positus essem, et de eius superbia, quod nec mihi nec ulli alii ex his que tenere videbatur, subdi volebat, presente eodem, conquererer, ipse per omnia tacendo, potius fratris fallentis verbis, quam hiis que a me dicebantur, consentire videbatur. At tamen, veniat ipse*

SEXUALITY AND MARRIAGE

Salernum ad me cum proceribus, quos voluerit, suis; et quidquid a me recti exhigendum fuerit, libenter paratus ero eidem persoluturus; eo tamen interposito pacto, ut et ipse mihi, de quibus iuste eum causatus fuero, iustitiam faciat."

6. Reilly, Bernard, *The Kingdom of León-Castilla Under Queen Urraca* (1982). Alfonso's death in 1134 paved the way for Garcia Ramírez, father of Margaret of Navarre (destined to wed Roger's son, William I of Sicily), to become King of Pamplona (and Navarre).

7. From Falco of Benevento: *Eodem anno, rex prefatus deprehendens comitem ipsum Rainulphum convicia multa et afflictiones Matildi uxori suae inferre, eiusdem regis sorori, quam, ultra quam credi potest, diligebat, consilio habito, ipsam suam sororem vocari mandavit, quam honeste accipiens eam dulcibus colloquiis consolatur, et eam Siciliam mandavit. Hoc anno, rex ipse predictum principem et comitem Rainulphum cum ducentis militibus ad auxilium predicti Anacleti Romam delegavit; et eis euntibus, sicut predixi, uxorem iam dicti comitis, et filium et civitatem Abellinum ei abstulit. Cum autem princeps et comes Roma reverterentur, turbati animo et dolore immenso percussi mirabantur, qualiter rex ipse uxorem eius abstulisset. Precipue tamen comes Rainulphus, cuius uxor carissima, et filius, sic ablata fuisset, palam quandoque, privatim aliquando, lacrimis conquerebatur manantibus, iniuste coniugem et filium perdidisse; inde per se ipsos et amicos eorum predictum Anacletum rogaverunt, ut a rege Rogerio impetraret redi filium et uxorem. Anacletus igitur regem per nuntios deprecatur, ut uxorem comiti rederet, et filium; quod obtinere non potuit; unde comes ille dolore accensus ultionis tempora rogabat.*

8. Translation from Alio, Jacqueline, *The Ferraris Chronicle: Popes, Emperors, and Deeds in Apulia 1096-1228* (2017), pages 102-103.

9. Matilda's death is not mentioned in the *Necrologio del Liber Confratrum di San Matteo di Salerno.*

10. Broadhurst, Ronald (translator), *The Travels of Ibn Jubayr* (1952, 2008), page 341.

11. In the chronicler's words: *Audivimus a quibusdam quod Johanna uxor Guillelmi regis Siciliae, filia Henrici regis Anglorum, peperit ei filium primogenitum, quem vocaverunt Boamundum. Qui cum a baptismate reverteretur, pater investivit eum ducati Apuliae per aureum sceptrum, quod in manu gerebat.* See Howlett, Richard (translator), *The Chronicle of Robert of Torigni* (1889), page 303; also Stevenson, Joseph (translator), *The History of William of Newburgh and the Chronicles of Robert de Monte* in *The Church Historians of England: Pre-Reformation Period* (1856), volume 4, part 2, page 806.

12. See Hamilton, George, "Trotula," *Modern Philology,* volume 4, number 2 (October 1906), pages 377-380. Elizabeth Mason-Hohl's translation, *The Diseases of Women* (1940), was based on a 1547 print edition of the *Trotula*. The translation by Monica Green (see below) is based on manuscripts and includes the Latin texts. The *Trotula* is actually three works in one. These are dedicated to conditions, treatments and cosmetics; only the section on treatments is attributed to "Trota" herself.

13. Green, Monica (translation and notes), *The Trotula: A Medieval Compendium of Women's Medicine* (2001), pages 94-95.

14. This has given rise to questions of Trota's existence, or even whether she may have been a "composite" of two or more unnamed women. Over the centuries, most historians have contended that "Trota di Ruggero" probably lived in Salerno during the eleventh century.

15. Green, op. cit. supra, pages 112-115.

16. Ibid, pages 94-97.

17. Ibid.

18. An acquaintance of the author living in Palermo made use of this remedy around 1998; it was unsuccessful.

19. For the biographical details about Constance, see *Queens of Sicily,* pages 313-356, and the accompanying notes.

20. For introductory discussions of medieval sexuality generally, see Karras, Ruth Mazo, *Sexuality in Medieval Europe: Doing Unto Others* (2005); Lochrie, McCracken, Shultz (editors), *Constructing Medieval Sexuality* (1997); Schaus (editor), *Women and Gender in Medieval Europe* (2006), pages 745-748. For historiography: Skinner, Patricia, *Studying Gender in Medieval Europe: Historical Approaches* (2018).

21. Murray, Jacqueline, "Twice Marginal and Twice Invisible: Lesbians in the Middle Ages," *Handbook of Medieval Sexuality* (1996), chapter 8, pages 191-214; Lochrie, Karma, "Situating Same-Sex Female Love in the Middle Ages," *The Cambridge Companion to Lesbian Literature* (2015), pages 79-92. Also see the preceding note.

22. For some observations see Murray, Jacqueline, "Historicizing Sex, Sexualizing History," *Writing Medieval History* (2005), pages 133-152; Puff, Helmut, "Same-Sex Possibilities," *The Oxford Handbook of Women and Gender in Medieval Europe* (2013), chapter 24, pages 379-395; Partner, Nancy, "No Sex, No Gender," *Studying Medieval Women* (1993), pages 117-141.

23. For the biographical details about Isabella, see *Queens of Sicily,* pages 435-452, and the accompanying notes.

24. Idem.

25. Green, Mary Anne Everett, *Lives of the Princesses of England from the Norman Conquest* (1850), volume 2, page 8.

26. *Matthaei Parisiensis, Chronica Majora* (1877), edited by Henry Luard, volume 3, page 319.

27. Ibid, volume 3, page 294.

28. Ibid, volume 4, page 83, under the rubric *De spe orta per imperatricem Isabellam.*

SEXUALITY AND MARRIAGE

The text reads: *Temporibus quoque sub eisdem, coepit dominus imperator Anglos specialius caeteris nationibus diligere, gratia imperatricis Isabellae, sororis regis angliae, quae forma et moribus praecellens omnium favorem sibi comparavit. Insuper jam gravida augusto sponso suo spem uberioris fructus propagandae repromisit, sed sinistro sidere multo aliter quam sperabatur contigit, sicut sequens narratio prolixius declarabit.*

29. Ibid, volume 3, page 324, *Nocte vero prima qua concubuit imperator cum ea, noluit cam carnaliter cognoscere, donec competens hora abastrologis ei nunciaretur.* Nancy Goldstone repeats the defamatory (and anachronistic) rumor hatched later that Frederick kept Isabella in his harem; see her *Four Queens* (2007), page 44. This idea may be rooted in a passing statement by Matthew Paris, already noted, that on Isabella's wedding night Frederick preferred the company of a concubine to that of his bride.

30. *Matthaei Parisiensis,* op.cit. supra, volume 3, page 324.

31. See *Queens of Sicily,* pages 453-460.

32. See McDougall, Sarah, *Royal Bastards: The Birth of Illegitimacy 800-1230* (2016).

33. See Skinner, Patricia, "The Light of My Eyes: Medieval Motherhood in the Mediterranean," *Women's History Review,* volume 6, number 3 (1997), pages 391-410.

34. *Queens of Sicily,* page 489.

35. See McDougall, op.cit. supra, pages 233-235. Although this succinct exposition about Frederick II does not cover new ground, it is interesting that it is the subject of analysis.

36. Matthews, Helen, *The Legitimacy of Bastards: The Place of Illegitimate Children in Later Medieval England* (2019). Also McDougall, op.cit.

37. Fox-Davies, Arthur, *A Complete Guide to Heraldry* (1909), pages 508-522.

38. From Hugh Falcandus: *Nec deerant qui puellarum pulchritudinem crederent lucris omnibus praeferendam. Sic homines aetate, moribus genereque diversi, variis nichilominus dissonisque rerum studiis agebantur.* See also *Queens of Sicily,* page 192.

39. Broadhurst, op.cit. supra, page 341.

40. See Abulafia, David, *Frederick II: A Medieval Emperor* (1988), pages 81, 147, 397.

41. For a good general introduction, though its emphasis is Ottoman Turkey, see Croutier, Alev, *Harem: The World Behind the Veil* (1989).

42. Broadhurst, op.cit., page 350.

43. El-Azhari, Taef, *Queens, Eunuchs and Concubines in Islamic History 661-1257* (2019); Scholz, Piotr, *Eunuchs and Castrati: A Cultural History* (1999).

44. For the physical and psychological effects of castration, chiefly on adults, see Brett, Roberts, Johnson, Wasserug, "Eunuchs in Contemporary Society," *Journal of Sexual Medicine,* volume 4 (2007), pages 930-955.

45. For recent work see Catlos, Brian, "Who Was Philip of Mahdia and Why Did He Have to Die?" *Mediterranean Chronicle,* volume 1 (2011), pages 73-103; Birk, Joshua, *Norman Kings of Sicily and the Rise of the Anti-Islamic Critique: Baptized Sultans* (2017), pages 173-205.

46. Mendola, Louis (translator), *Frederick, Conrad and Manfred of Hohenstaufen, Kings of Sicily: The Chronicle of Nicholas of Jamsilla 1210-1258* (2016).

47. For a fine introduction to Sicily's Aghlabids, Fatimids and Kalbids, see Chiarelli, Leonard, *A History of Muslim Sicily,* second edition (2018).

48. This has been considered extensively by David Abulafia and others. More recently, see Dalli, Charles, "Contriving Coexistence: Muslims and Christians in the Unmaking of Norman Sicily," *Routines of Existence: Time, Life and After Life in Society and Religion* (2009), pages 30-43.

49. For both codices of the Assizes of Ariano, see *Queens of Sicily,* pages 509-531; for an English translation of the older codex, see Loud, Graham, *Roger II and the Creation of the Kingdom of Sicily* (2012), pages 314-328. For an English translation of the Constitutions of Melfi, see Powell, James, *The Liber Augustalis or Constitutions of Melfi* (1971).

50. See *Queens of Sicily,* pages 212-214.

51. See Garufi, Carlo Alberto, *I Documenti Inediti dell'Epoca Normanna in Sicilia,* document 27, pages 64-65.

52. For the infamous rape and kidnapping case involving Franca Viola, see Galli, Natalie, *The Girl Who Said No: A Search in Sicily* (2019). Article 544 of the penal code of 1930 absolved a rapist from prosecution and sentencing (minimal though this was) if he subsequently married his victim; this statute, the basis for the defense of the perpetrator in the case described by Natalie Galli, was finally abolished in 1981.

53. Van Cleave, Rachel, "Rape and Querela Law in Italy: False Protection of Victim Agency," *Michigan Journal of Gender and Law,* volume 13, January 2007 (Ann Arbor 2007), pages 273-310. From 1930 until 1996, rape was considered a minor offense "against public decency" rather than a felonious form of assault.

54. See Harvey, John, *The Plantagenets* (1948), pages 33-34. This theory had already been propounded in France by Alfred Richard in his *Histoire des Comtes de Poitou* (1903).

Chapter 6
QUEENLY CUISINE

What did our queens serve their guests? Aside from their personal preferences, which are unknown to us, these women, and the people visiting Sicily's royal court, indulged in culinary delights known through recipes present in the historical record.

Food could be symbolic, sometimes even representing power or privilege.[1]

Apart from what was served, hospitality toward guests was the hallmark of royal courts, baronial households and monasteries, and, here in Sicily, the homes of the emirs who came before them.

Some courts — certainly Sicily's — were wealthier than most others. The role of the queen as hostess likely came to the fore during the regencies of Margaret of Navarre and Constance Hauteville, though virtually nothing is known in the particulars with regard to feasts and the precise foods served at these events, or even such occasions as tournaments and festivals.[2]

Like literature (see Chapter 7), cuisine was an important part of the social milieu of the times, and a very significant aspect of identity (Chapter 10) often overlooked by otherwise thorough biographers.

The sociological aspects of medieval food and diets have been the subject of insightful study in recent times. Beyond such phenomena as halal and kosher observance, there were "prestige" foods and those considered more "common." There were also medicinal uses for certain foods, particularly herbs, thought to cure everything from headaches to infertility (Chapter 5). Preservation existed in a rudimentary but efficacious form. Drying and pickling were both commonplace; olives were conserved using either method. Fish was dried and salted. In a certain cultural sense as well as a nutritional one, we are what we eat.

It should be remembered that the ordinary person might consume two meals per day, in the late morning (or early afternoon) and in the evening after the sun had set. A third meal, or even a very large one, was a luxury; an actual breakfast was unusual. For the common folk, many meals were as simple as a piece of cheese with bread and perhaps a seasonal vegetable or a few nuts, and ordinary people consumed less meat than the aristocracy. The Italian word *pranzo* (lunch) comes to us directly from the Latin *prandium,* and *cena* is the same in both languages.

Such foods as roasted meat were typical of more formal meals. To graze and feed livestock was more costly than fishing, or raising chickens. Most fish and seafood has become far less abundant (and comparatively more expensive) in the Mediterranean than it was in centuries past, but in medieval times fish was normally more available or affordable than mutton or beef in cities and towns fairly near the coast. Whilst fasting, monks at monasteries near coastal areas might consume crustaceans, but crabs and shrimp, though widely consumed, were not prized as particularly "estimable" or desirable foods. At the court, an important guest was more likely to be served roasted meat than fried fish.

In the culinary hierarchy, hunted game such as deer, hare

and boar were more "noble" than the meat of domesticated sheep, goats, pigs and rabbits. Doves, pheasant, partridge, storks, starlings and peacocks outranked chickens and geese. Tuna and swordfish were prized, but smaller fish, along with such creatures as urchins, prawns, squid and cuttlefish, were considered "common."

Enough contemporaneous reporting exists for a good picture of Sicilian agriculture in Arab and Norman times. Mohammed ibn Hawqal, Abdullah al Idrisi, Mohammed bin Ahmad bin Jubayr al Kenani and Hugh Falcandus all left us ample descriptions. Much of Sicily's agriculture was greatly augmented during the Aghlabid and Fatimid eras, when sugar cane, mulberries, lemons, citrons and oranges were cultivated on a large scale. Wheat, almonds, olives, figs, artichokes, cardoons and other foods had been present since antiquity. We know of the Arabs' irrigation systems, the *kanats*.

The present is not always a clear window to the past. Some fruits and vegetables were more widely cultivated in Sicily during the Middle Ages than in later times. Here mulberries come to mind, as these trees were used in silk production, which essentially vanished by 1300. With the European colonization of the Americas, sugar cane production decreased in Italy. Over time, rice production also diminished.

Lacking in most of the colorful accounts left to us in Latin and Arabic are recipes or detailed descriptions of specific prepared dishes. There is no eye-witness account of a meal at court sufficient to conceive of a menu. Fortunately, enough is known of Arab cuisine elsewhere in the Fatimid world to form a picture of what was served.

Though some of our foreign-born queens may well have brought cooks or recipes to Sicily from their countries of birth, it is reasonable to believe that they partook of the local cuisine, which was diverse enough to accommodate most tastes.

SICILIAN QUEENSHIP

Context suggests that, as early as the eleventh century, the Normans adapted to the flavors and tastes present in the Italian lands they conquered. If anything, there was a greater variety of fruits and vegetables in southern Italy than what was available in Normandy. (Italy has a greater diversity of native flora than any other European country except Russia.) Early chroniclers, notably Amato of Montecassino, William of Apulia and Godfrey Malaterra, did not refer to cookery in explicit terms; at best, they alluded to terrain, agriculture and wine.

The delicious cuisine of the Sicilian court may be divided into several direct ethnic influences and two dynastic eras: Hauteville and Hohenstaufen.

The court's greatest kitchens were in the Norman Palace in Palermo, probably in one of the towers that is no longer standing. In addition to the large kitchens, there was probably a small kitchen in the Pisan Tower near Roger's Chamber, a suite the king used as a kind of "office" and throne room. (Even the Pisan Tower has been restructured so extensively that it is impossible to identify most of its original chambers and corridors very precisely.) In reality, the court traveled; it was wherever the king was, and some cooks traveled with their monarch. Some of our queens spent more time in the capital while their husbands were off besieging the kingdom's rebellious cities or disciplining barons.

Here our focus is Sicily. There were, of course, regional cuisines throughout the kingdom, with that of the mainland influenced more by the Lombards and Greeks than the Arabs.

The widowed Adelaide raised her children mostly in Messina and San Marco d'Alunzio, bringing them to Palermo when her sons neared the age of majority. Western Sicily was then more Fatimid than Greek, and the inception of a court cuisine was essentially an Arab development. Even the comital court of Roger II was impressive, but in 1130 it became a royal court to rival those elsewhere in Europe. The food had to be good.

The next nearest court, just north of the kingdom's border, was papal Rome, where the greatest similarity to Sicilian cuisine was to be found during the Hohenstaufen era, when we find the early evolution of what is now regarded as the quintessential "Italian" cookery, which itself varies from region to region. That a few Sicilian cooks or recipes ended up at the English court would be expected considering the ties between the two capitals.[3]

The first consort to reside in Palermo's palace most of the time was Elvira of Castile. The contact of her Jiménez dynasty with the Almoravids to the south of Castile probably fostered culinary influences that would have given her a foretaste of Sicilian cuisine. Elvira herself was something of an "outsider" as the first Sicilian consort born beyond the more "familiar" territories of Italy and Normandy. The exogenous marriages reflected the new-found power of the Hautevilles as rulers of what became an important kingdom, and to some degree this involved contact between different cultures.

Although the cooking was, for the most part, left to the palace cooks, it was part of a noblewoman's training to recognize good meat, vegetables and fruit, and to be able to prepare some dishes herself. Even if our queens spent little time in the kitchen except for supervising, they certainly knew their way around it.

There were two major markets near the palace. The Balarah souk, now the Ballarò street market, was Palermo's largest marketplace. The market now called *Capo* was chiefly a boucherie just beyond Old Saint Agatha's Gate near the church dedicated to this saint; this was right outside the city walls along what had once been the course of the Papyrus River, in the Sari al Kadi district. While the commerce of the Balarah souk was based on a great diversity of foods, spices and various products, the boucherie was chiefly a meat market. Each was just a short stroll from the palace. There were other markets, but the Vucciria, whose name recalls the Boqueria of Barcelona, was established later, after 1300, during Sicily's Aragonese period.

With the obvious exceptions of modern transatlantic introductions like tomatoes and avocados, most of the fruits and vegetables cultivated in southern Italy by 1900 were already present in the eleventh century, many introduced by the Byzantines or Arabs. Only a comparatively small number, such as the artichoke and certain broccoli varieties, were truly indigenous to Sicily and Calabria.

As we shall see, at least a few recipes that are popular today survive from the Norman-Swabian era.

Arab Cookery

When he arrived in Sicily during the reign of William II, probably late in 1184, the traveler bin Jubayr noted that the palace chef was a Muslim.[4] Arab cuisine was still dominant in most of Sicily at that point, even if the culinary traditions of the eastern third of the island probably ran more to the Greek. Some of the recipes were doubtless similar to many in the *Kitab al-Tabikh* (the Baghdad Cookery Book) and other compilations known to us, such as the earlier collection of ibn Sayyar al Warraq.[5] In Sicily, there were probably some subtle African influences, thanks to the Aghlabids' historical contact with the Berbers they ruled.

Many dishes were quite simple. Chicken or beef would be roasted and served with a sauce of walnuts, pistachios or hazelnuts. Lamb or goat might be stewed, served with rice or couscous. The Aghlabids of the ninth century introduced spices formerly unknown in Sicily, some from Asia.

They may also have introduced certain ovine and caprine varieties. The Girgentan goat, *capra girgentana*, with its spiralled horns, resembles the Asian markhor, *capra falconeri*. It may have been brought to southern Sicily by the Arabs or Berbers. Today, this breed is prized for its milk.

A typical recipe, *tardin*, calls for finely chopped, pounded lamb or goat meat to be mixed with onions and egg whites, with a bit of olive oil, flavored with powdered coriander, anise seed, cumin, cinnamon, grated galangal, murri (fermented barley paste) and mustard. This is then fried.

There were also simple broths. Olives and cucumbers were pickled in brine.

Al Idrisi, the court geographer of Roger II, mentions spaghetti being made in Trabia, outside Palermo, probably from a variety of durum wheat introduced by the Aghlabids, but we know virtually nothing about the sauces (if any) with which it was served before the thirteenth century.

Couscous is still popular in western Sicily, historically the island's most overwhelmingly Arab region, though the recipes have been altered a bit over time as such ingredients as potatoes and tomatoes came from the Americas during the sixteenth century.

Tuna might be roasted over an open flame. The *mattanza,* the practice of capturing tuna in huge nets, originated in Arab times and still exists off the coast around Trapani, where the head fisherman is still called the *rais.* Dried fish was also popular, as was *bottarga,* tuna roe. *Stemperata,* fried fish cooked in white wine or white vinegar and sugar, is an Arab recipe. It was the Aghlabids who introduced cane sugar on our island.

Dairy products included ricotta (from sheep's milk), yogurt and kamakh rijal. Sugared fruits were made, and sorbet. Almond paste biscuits, and baked cookies consisting of almonds and sugar ("brittle") are still made. It is quite likely that the sugary cheese cream used in *cassata* and *cannoli* was influenced by a recipe known to the Fatimids.

Cassata is an example of a recipe having vague Arab influences rather than a proven Arab pedigree. It is a tort of sweet ricotta cheese filling inside a thickly frosted crust topped by candied fruits. Every indication, including the candied fruits, points to it being a Fatimid creation, at least in some form, yet we have no precise evidence of it in the Arabic record.[6] Its name comes either from the Arabic *kas'at*, for a bowl, or *caseus*, the Latin for cheese. *Cassata,* as it has come down to us, seems to bear the mark not only of Arab cookery but, as well, the cuisine of northern Spain. This may be a culinary influence that arrived with Elvira's Jiménez dynasty. *Cassata* probably evolved over time; the sponge cake base used today may have begun as a simple crust similar to the crispy *cannolo* shell.

Although *gelo di melone,* watermelon gelatin, seems to be Arab in origin, there is no evidence of it in Sicilian medieval records.

The *sfince,* from the Arabic *isfang* (fried pastry), was made of a light dough of flour, eggs and butter, formed into a ball and quickly deep fried to a light, spongy, porous consistency. After it was removed from the oil, strained, and allowed to cool to room temperature, it was served with honey poured over it. The traditional folk recipes for the dough are far superior to what is used in Sicilian pastry shops nowadays, when sfinci are stuffed with ricotta cream (with no honey in sight) as if they were Neapolitan *zeppole.*

Almond nougat, called *turrón* in Spain and *torrone* in Italy, seems to be Arab in origin, though *cupedia,* a Roman confection, was similar. It is mentioned in a medical treatise, the *Book on the Simple Medicines,* written by Ibn Wafid Abul Mutarrif, a physician of Cordoba, and translated by Gerard of Cremona.

The *Kitab al Tabikh fi'l Maghrib wa'l Andalus*, a cookbook compiled in Andalusia during the thirteenth century, identifies a certain mutton recipe as Sicilian. This calls for varied pieces of mutton or lamb steamed with three times as much chopped onion. Once this meat is nearly cooked, one adds oil, pepper, cinnamon, spikenard, Chinese cinnamon and saffron, boiling down the liquid mixture into a gravy.

In his chronicle, Godfrey Malaterra mentions the Arabs of Troina getting drunk on wine: *Quamobrem hostes balnearum aes-*

tuationibus aestuari assueti, frigidori aura flante, dum vini potationibus naturalem calorem intra se excitare nituntur, sommo propter vinum, ut assolet, subsequente, tardiores ad excubias vigilarum urbis esse coeperunt.[7]

Few of the native grape varieties of Sicily survived the phylloxera epidemic of the nineteenth century, but Nero d'Avola, which seems to be indigenous to Sicily or Calabria, is still used to make a hearty red wine. Zibibbo, a grape of the muscat family, takes its name from the Arabic *zabib* (raisin), and it was the Arabs who introduced this grape on Pantelleria.

Though some of Sicily's Arabs consumed wine, it is unlikely that they were so lax regarding certain meats. The dearth of pork recipes in modern Sicilian cuisine is usually attributed to its proscription by Muslims and Jews. However, the boarish Nebrodian black swine may have been raised by the Greeks of northeastern Sicily, being isolated to that region.

There are recipes containing chickpeas and *tahini* that are similar to *hummus,* and aubergine (eggplant) salad recipes not unlike Sicilian *caponata.*

It is obvious enough that some recipes of Arab origin are, in one iteration or another, still present in Sicilian cuisine. It would not be unreasonable to ask what happened to the others. Some probably waned in popularity over time as others evolved. A good example is the *arancina.*

Rice Balls

The *arancina* is the stuffed rice ball, its Sicilian name (literally "small orange") coming to us from the Norman French *poume d'orange,* and the name of the fruit deriving from the Arabic *narang,* from the Sanskrit *naranga.* It has an orangish color. There was a trend in using saffron, a spice known in Sicily in antiquity, in medieval recipes.

The rice ball, which in eastern Sicily is conical rather than round, is coated with a light batter that forms an exterior crust when deep fried; commercially, a coloring agent is often used instead of saffron to flavor the rice. The traditional recipe calls for a filling of cooked, seasoned beef in a spicy gravy. The *arancina* is rather like a ball of *paella*. Its origins and development are parallel. Rice was introduced in Sicily by the Arabs, just as it was brought by them to Spain, though the chief variety cultivated was slightly different.

The *poume d'orange* introduced in England during the Norman period was a meat ball that did not contain rice or saffron, and the claim that an Arab cook from Sicily introduced it at the English court is unproven. The recipe is documented in an extant manuscript, written in Norman French, dating from the thirteenth century.[8]

Some historians believe that rice was imported into Sicily during the Fatimid period but not cultivated here. That theory is similar to others involving agricultural import-export at specific times; Sicily exported sugar. Rice was introduced into Piedmont, in what is now northern Italy, during the fifteenth century; this is the *arborio* used to make *risotto*.

Unfortunately, most medievalists are blissfully unaware of the fact that rice was, in truth, cultivated in Sicily into the nineteenth century, long after the Fatimid irrigation systems had faded from memory. A flood plain outside Ribera, in southern Sicily, provided the ideal environment. This was where the Verdura River neared the coast. The towns in this region were dominated by the Norman castle of Poggiodiana. The name Ribera, akin to *riviera*, may be translated from a Sicilian phrase meaning "river basin." Deforestation and climate change have sealed the stream's sad fate, and a golf resort named for it stands nearby.

In 1841, Ribera was the largest rice producer in Sicily, with five thousand quintals. When did it cease producing rice?

The town was the birthplace of the unificationist Francesco Crispi. In reprisal for a slight he suffered at Ribera during a visit following Italian unification, he convinced the crown to prohibit the cultivation of rice in that part of Sicily, thereby giving Piedmont, the home region of the ruling House of Savoy, a national monopoly henceforth, although a small amount of rice was still produced around Siracusa into the beginning of the twentieth century. (By way of comparison, cotton was still grown in Sicily, on some two thousand hectares, until 1982.) Rice has been reintroduced in Sicily in recent years, and Italy is Europe's largest producer of this grain.

What evidence is available suggests that the rice ball is one of the few "native" Sicilian recipes to survive from the Norman-Arab era.

There is debate about whether *panelle* (chickpea fritters), *caponata* and *cannoli* were conceived during this period or invented later. Nevertheless, a few surviving recipes seem to have been inspired by Arab cuisine, which has left us certain Sicilian words, such as *fastùka,* from the Arabic *fatùk,* for pistachio.

It is difficult to trace the exact origins of most modern Sicilian recipes, but historians postulate that many more are, in fact, of Arab creation than the few mentioned here.[9]

Another rice recipe, *tummàla,* was known after 1200 yet is thought to owe its name to an emir of Catania, Muhammed ibn Thummah, who lived during the eleventh century. This is a complex casserole, or *timbale,* of chopped chicken, livers, eggs, rice and cheese.

Turks' Heads

An interesting example that seems to survive from the Norman era is called *Testa di Turco.* It is difficult to know with certainty whether any of the recipes bearing this name actually derive from medieval ones, but a leading scholar of culinary history suggests that, at the very least, they are all similar in being filled pastries.[10]

There are distinct sweet pastry recipes called *Testa di Turco* at Scicli and Castelbuono; the former takes its name from the dough being swirled to resemble a turban, the latter is a layered cake filled with cream and berries.

Another recipe is a pastry filled with meat and cheese. This seems to be similar to recipes brought to Plantagenet England, perhaps through its contact with Sicily.[11] A kindred example of this "Turk's head" was a kind of pasta pie filled with rice, chicken (or even eel), flavored with spices and sugar, then roasted until browned, hence the name.

One might expect *Testa di Saraceno* to be more descriptive if the name referred to the Arabs of Sicily, who the Sicilian chroniclers called *Saracens*. The *Testa di Moro,* conversely, is not a food but a majolica pot shaped and painted to resemble the head of a Moor wearing a crown.

The origin of the *Testa di Moro* is as uncertain as the *Testa di Turco,* but an old folk tale traces it to the Norman era, when a beautiful maiden wed a Moorish trader. When she learned that he had a wife and children in his home country, to which he planned to return, she decided to kill him in his sleep. Thereafter, she used his head as a flower pot. In this way, he could never leave her. (The lesson of the story is that a man should never betray his Sicilian wife.)

Beyond the macabre, the tendency to disparage Muslims became popular during the fifteenth century. By then, with the Inquisition in full flower in some parts of western Europe, the Turks had taken Constantinople and invaded the Balkans, with Albanian Christian refugees eventually settling in Sicily, Puglia and Calabria. Not only was Sicily ruled from Spain during the bloody *Reconquista,* but Barbary corsairs were raiding the island's coasts.

Nevertheless, the name of the food may be a modern misnomer. By way of analogy, *Piazza Meschita,* in Palermo, was not the site of a mosque (here the majestic *Mezquita* of Cordoba comes to mind) but a synagogue. By the time the living memory of the conversions of 1493 had faded, so had the Sicilians' distinction between Muslims and Jews.

La Cuccagna

The Sicilian word *cuccagna* derives from the Medieval Latin *cocania,* "a country of abundance," from which the German *kuchen* (which now refers to a cake) may also come to us. In the Middle Ages, it connoted the game of climbing a greased or soaped pole, the *albero di cuccagna,* to snatch sweets or other tasty food attached at the high end as a prize; this survives as the Spanish *cucaña.* Details of this form of *cuccagna* in the Kingdom of Sicily are sparse before 1266, but it was an event popular across Europe.

Better known is a festival that came more than two centuries later, when Sicily's prosperity was on the wane. At this "cuccagna" a vast table of food was placed in a large square or field protected by guards and a cordon. At a signal, the crowd surrounding it was allowed to throng the table and eat the food that had been prepared. The sadistic aristocrats watching this spectacle found it entertaining to see the poor trample each other to reach the food. A King of Sicily would not countenance such a humiliation of his own people, but by 1415 the island was administered by viceroys representing kings in Spain.

European Cookery

As we have seen, there is no conclusive evidence to suggest that the Normans introduced any of their recipes in the Italian lands they conquered during the eleventh century. The cuisine of the urban centers, large and small, that they occupied in Apulia and Calabria was based on longstanding Greek culinary traditions. This was also true of oeniculture.

For the most part, the hunting culture was introduced, or

at least popularized, in Sicily by the Normans. On the mainland, it was already commonplace among the Lombards who ruled cities like Salerno. Deer, boar, partridge and hare thus made their way into Sicilian cookery, whereas the Arabs had consumed more goat, mutton, rabbit and chicken. The Christians used lard, pork fat and butter.

Despite such additions, the cuisine seems to have remained predominantly Arab in orientation into the reigns of William II and Tancred. The next step in its evolution occurred during the Swabian period. At least, this is when the greater number of "European" recipes known to us were recorded. These have come to be identified with Frederick II and his successors, particularly Manfred.

Although the Sicilian language that flourished during the Swabian era did not have a continued, long-lasting impact on Italian culture beyond Sicily and Calabria after Manfred's death in 1266 (see Chapter 7), the cuisine of southern Italy during this period survived and evolved to form the foundation for what exists in Italy today.

Spaghetti, as we have seen, was already being made in Sicily during the twelfth century. In the next century we find recipes for such things as ravioli. Risotto recipes have their origins in Piedmont during the fifteenth century, but rice was already cultivated in Sicily and other southern regions, and this may explain its introduction in the north.

This is not to suggest that every recipe known at the court of Frederick II originated south of Rome. Many were known in the northern Italian comunes that he ruled, and a few may have come from his German lands.

Because Frederick's court traveled often, almost constantly, not only throughout his dominions in northern Italy but into his Holy Roman Empire, some of these recipes were known in these regions. Therefore, by 1250, not every recipe was exclusively "Sicilian."

The chief sources for court recipes during the Swabian era come to us from several manuscripts copied early in the fourteenth century. The *Liber de Coquina* is conserved as two codices (Lat 7131 and Lat 9328) in the Bibliothèque Nationale in Paris. Its first section is usually called the *Tractatus,* which may be the work of a French copyist, and the second part, the *Liber de Coquina,* which was probably composed by an Italian. A reference to Frederick II suggests that the recipes probably date from his reign; in other places Manfred is mentioned. Specifically, we find such phrases as *secundum usum imperatoris* ("according to the emperor's preference") in the second recipe of the *Liber,* on the preparation of *caulles,* which may refer to either cabbage or to plants such as cauliflower (and broccoli), the latter being more likely, especially when stems are mentioned. Yes, certain words present in these medieval texts are open to interpretation based on etymology and context.

Another codex containing recipes from this era is called the *Meridionale* because it was written in Neapolitan.[12] (Presently, this manuscript is privately owned.) Many of these recipes first appeared in the *Liber.* Significantly, both the *Liber* and the *Meridionale* laid the groundwork for what became Italian cuisine.[13]

In general, the *Tractatus* has recipes for meat, poultry, fish, legumes and sauces, while the *Liber* concentrates on pastry as well as fish, poultry and vegetables. The *Meridionale* is rather general and highly informative. *The Forme of Cury* written in England (see note 5) was influenced by these works, which should not be confused with compilations of Neapolitan recipes that came later.[14] It is interesting to speculate that certain medieval recipes and cooking methods which came to be known in England and elsewhere in northern Europe originated in Italy and Spain.

There also exist other compilations including Sicilian recipes which, in some cases, may date from the end of the

Middle Ages, some recorded in monastic records during the early modern era.[15]

A number of recipes were extracted and translated (and in a few cases prepared) by the author; a few appear in more detailed form later in this chapter.

There was a great temptation to present "instructive" recipes accompanied by the precise method of preparation and quantities of ingredients. However, apart from the internationalization of units, this is challenging because there are few "canonical" recipes that include exact measurements in the original, leaving the preparation open to a certain degree of interpretation. Over the course of decades, the author has sampled or prepared the modern variations of recipes such as *maccu,* and some of these dishes are described in her book on this topic written with Francesca Lombardo.[16]

Let us consider some of the actual recipes.

A typical recipe is chicken with fennel sauce. Here chicken is cut into pieces, then cooked and browned in lard. The cooked meat is then removed from the lard and broth, to which is added finely chopped fennel leaves, a bit of chopped parsley and crushed almonds, along with water, olive oil, salt and spice (a mixture of ground cinnamon, pepper, saffron and cloves). This green sauce is either served over the chicken or the individual pieces of meat are coated with it. (A similar recipe follows below.)

It is interesting how "Arab" or "Spanish" some of these recipes seem.

A simple recipe called *laudo* in the *Meridionale* calls for broiling chicken, to which is added onions, wine, saffron and other ingredients.

Saffron was ubiquitous, present in many recipes of the Swabian era. Except for desserts, about one out of four recorded recipes called for it. We also find the liberal use of lard and butter.

The *Meridionale* brings us a number of curious recipes of Arab origin. *Eucabam,* its name a corruption of the Arabic *ukaybiya,* was chicken served in a sauce of milk, egg yolks, almonds and saffron, with bread. *Aaneth* was broiled mutton browned, then cooked in vinegar, flavored with spices, almonds, egg yolks, parsley and saffron. *Schinchinelli* was a kind of large raviolo filled with almond paste, dried fruit, perhaps preserved pears, and honey, then baked; its name derives from the Arabic *kuskenole.*

There are recipes for small birds such as doves and pigeons, and offal, such as stuffed pig's stomach.

There are several recipes for fava beans. The simplest is to boil and flavor the fresh beans. This is similar to *fritedda,* or *fritella*, a dish popular in spring which consists of whole, fresh fava beans, peas and pieces of fresh artichokes cooked together and flavored with salt and black pepper. Another recipe, *maccu,* is a thick soup which is usually made in the winter with dried beans. This contains beans without the skin, crushed, boiled, and flavored with some chopped onion, olive oil and finely chopped parsley, salt and pepper. The medieval recipe had a bit of honey in it.

There are a few very simple recipes for boiled, fresh, green fava beans. Indeed, many of the recipes in these collections are so strikingly elementary that they are really little more than very concise notes of instructions.

Among the seafood recipes was one for prawns in pastry (heavy batter) served with almonds or pine nuts, flavored with saffron. The prawns, of which there are several varieties, are cleaned and peeled except for the tails.

There are similar recipes for many fish and seafoods, including lamprey and trout. A very simple recipe for stuffed sardines is present in the *Liber,* and though it is not very similar to the modern *beccafico* it may have been an early inspiration.

We find numerous recipes for *frittate,* or omelets, made from eggs and various vegetables, such as chards and mushrooms, though not usually with more than one kind of vegetable. This was almost a genre unto itself. Some of these omelets, made with the addition of flour, were rather similar to quiche (which is baked). Not all these recipes called for cheese.

Cheeses, though not described extensively, have changed little over time based on the milk source, the culture used and the process of ageing. Many were made from the milk of sheep or goats, as were milk products such as *ricotta* (cottage cheese), curds without a culture. *Ricotta salata,* as its name implies, was salted, aged ricotta but without a culture.

One recipe that called for cheese was *lassanis* (the recipe appears in English below), the precursor of modern lasagna. It was a baked pie of flat pasta noodles layered with spices, eggs, cheese and bacon. In the original:

Si uis facere tortam de lassanis, pone lassanas, ova frissa uel lixa uel perduta et raviolos incisos uel integros, caseum pinguem grattatum uel incisum, lardum sufficientem, et hoc compone solaria faciendo, species apponendo. Et forma super istam de pasta unum serpentem preliantem cum columba, uel quecumque alia animalia uolueris. Deinde, accipe intestina implecta de bona impletura et ponatur in circuitu quasi murus. Tunc solaria coloretur pro uoluntate et ponantur in furno. Postea, portetur coram domino cum pompa.

The last sentence expresses the pride with which the lasagna was presented to the pleasure of the diners. In one form or another, lasagna remained popular at court into the nineteenth century; it was the favorite food of Francesco II of the Two Sicilies, who reigned until 1861, nicknamed "The Lasagna King" or simply *Lasa*.

In the Neapolitan of the *Meridionale* we find this description of a simple sauce for flavoring fried fish: *Affare sapore per pescie fricto tolli salsa verdi che è scricta desopra et suco de citranguli o agresta et gecta sopre.*

Another dish, the *torta de montano,* was similar to a roasted "meat pie," while *torta defoliata* was more like a meat loaf.

In the *Libro di Cucina* of the "Anonimo Veneziano" compiled in northern Italy late in the fourteenth century we find two pie recipes, one for chicken livers with bacon (number 111) and the other for fava beans with bacon (number 109), favored by King Manfred and bearing his name.

Some recipes are virtually unchanged in hundreds of years. Today, pork sausage with fennel seeds is based on the same simple preparation as that described in the *Meridionale*.[17] Another form of sausage was stuffed with fish.

There is a recipe for a sauce made from black cuttlefish ink. A very similar sauce is still used for spaghetti.

Frederick II favored *scapece,* which could be conserved in a jar. known as *askipecia* or *scapetia* in Latin, the word *scapece* ultimately derives from the Arabic *sikbaj,* aubergines marinated in vinegar. Frederick's version was made of fried eggplant (alternatively zucchini), anchovies preserved (or cooked) in vinegar, some mint, a bit of garlic and pepper, and perhaps a touch of saffron.[18] This was prepared during Frederick's travels by his chef, Bernard. It brings to mind the caponata and stemperata mentioned earlier; like these, it was influenced by Arab cuisine. Interestingly a variation on the original *scapece* recipe has survived in Puglia into our time.

We find a number of Sicilian names for prepared foods of the Norman era. *Itria* (vermicelli), *cubaita* (sesame brittle) and *cuscusu* (couscous) come to mind. Although Angelo Senisio's *Declarus*, a Sicilian dictionary written around 1350, refers to some foods that may have been known a century earlier, it is not intended as a description of recipes.

Crespelle, which are still made in our times, are extremely thin, crispy, fried "cookies" made with white flour and eggs, flavored with sugar or honey. Known as *chiacchiere* in Sicily, these are described below.

Ricettariu di lu Regnu di Sichilia

It seemed appropriate to present a sampling of recipes from the two earliest written collections known in the kingdom.

Though the surviving copies of both works were written in the fourteenth century, many recipes in the *Liber* are also present in the *Meridionale,* where we encounter a few linguistic subtleties. In the Latin of the *Liber* the word *lardum* is usually bacon, whereas in the Neapolitan of the *Meridionale* the term *lardo* may sometimes be simple fat (lard) from pork. Because certain ingredients, such as pomegranate wine, could be difficult to find, substitutions were sometimes indicated. The *vernaccia* mentioned was probably a slightly fortified wine from Liguria rather than the white table wine made today; *Greco* was a Neapolitan white wine that may have aged to a light amber. The Latin *cavli* may refer to either cauliflower (or broccoli) or, less often in southern Italy, cabbage. "Fennel" is not always true fennel, *foeniculum vulgare,* but anise (Florence fennel), *pimpinella anisum,* which has a large white bulb. Even in Modern Sicilian diction often varies; around Palermo *sparacelli* refers to broccoli while in central Sicily the same word refers to asparagus.

It is possible that certain recipes calling for "bread crumbs" actually require a small amount of whole-grain durum flour as a thickening agent.

Some recipes were seasonal. Broccoli had a long season, from October through March, while fava beans were harvested in the spring but could be dried. Nuts, grains, olive oil, honey, sugar and spices were easily conserved. Although fish could be dried and salted, most recipes call for using it fresh. The comparatively cooler climate of the Middle Ages facilitated the natural preservation of many ingredients. Bread was usually made from whole-grain wheat; it had a thick crust and, if placed in a cool, dry place, might last for several days. Grain and other products were stored within thick walls, in places similar to the crypts of churches.

Certain ingredients were a bit different in times past. Almond milk, for example, was somewhat viscous and unsweetened; it is made by soaking almonds in water for ten or twelve hours, then removing the skin and crushing the soft nuts into a juicy puree to which more water might be added. The term "bitter herbs" may refer to such things as arugula.

If there were a cryptic element in a recipe, it was most likely ingredients such as the specific spices used. This makes some of the recipes recorded in the *Liber de Coquina* rather difficult to replicate precisely today. Generic references to "spices" are enigmatic and these will vary by recipe. In the absence of more detailed information, an imperfect general solution is a mix of these powdered spices: cloves, saffron, cinnamon, pepper, ginger. For desserts: cinnamon, cloves, ginger. For a stronger flavor: cloves, black pepper, nutmeg.

A potential problem is posed by the fact that quantities are not indicated, though experienced modern cooks have sometimes resolved this through experimentation. In fact, the descriptions recorded for many recipes were imprecise even by medieval standards.

Visitors to Sicily sometimes wonder why so few restaurants serve chicken except for the small establishments that sell it skewered (rotisserie). In modern times, the Sicilians have come to regard chicken as something "informal" to be prepared and consumed in a family setting, much like turkey on American Thanksgiving. Roasted chicken is sometimes made in homes, and the most common Sicilian recipe for stuffing (bread crumbs, eggs, grated cheese, minced onions and chopped parsley) may well be medieval in origin.

Actual restaurants, as opposed to simple trattorias frequented by travelers, were quite rare in Sicily until the twentieth century except for a few establishments in a few cities.

What follow are a few simple recipes, most published here in English for the first time, present in both codices; sometimes there are variations in ingredients and cooking method between the same recipe in the *Liber* and the *Meridionale*. As the recipes presented here are intended to be suitable to modern tables, such delicacies as peacock, stork and dove, though included in both books, were not considered. Likewise, lamprey is usually difficult to find.

Poultry Sauce: Add powdered marjoram and cardamom to a puree of chicken livers cooked in olive oil with pomegranate wine. If you have no such wine, use Greek wine with a touch of vinegar. (This gravy is suitable for chicken that is simply grilled or fried and not otherwise flavored.)

Fennel Chicken: Fry chicken pieces in olive oil until they are almost completely cooked. Then add some water, finely chopped chicken liver, finely chopped wild fennel leaves (not anise) and parsley. Add spices to taste and cook the mixture. (This varies slightly from the similar recipe noted earlier.)

Lemon Chicken: Cook chicken pieces in lard and onions. Add (unskinned) almonds and some water to the mixture, which should be thickened by the addition of a beaten egg yolk. When fully cooked, sprinkle liberally with lemon juice and serve.

Fruity Chicken: Fry chicken pieces in lard until mostly cooked. Then add water and saffron to cook completely. After a few minutes, add to this mixture sugared (pitted) dates, (pitted) plums or prunes, raisins and almonds. Allow to simmer another few minutes before serving.

Stuffed Chicken: Into the cavity of a clean, dressed chicken, place a mixture of ground pork (or bacon), chopped chicken liver, chopped leeks, chopped parsley, spices, saffron, eggs and grated cheese. Roast the stuffed chicken (on a spit) until brown and fully cooked.

Partridge: Cut the dressed birds into pieces and cook these in lard with chopped onions. When they are cooked and browned, let simmer in pomegranate wine with sugar and add vernaccia wine. (This recipe is equally suitable for pheasant, quail or other birds.)

German Chicken Soup: Boil chicken pieces until cooked. Set aside broth. Remove bones and chop the chicken meat finely. Add meat to the broth with chopped parsley, mint, marjoram and rosemary, sage and a bit of saffron. Bring this to a boil. Salt to taste.

Saracen Chicken Soup: Broil small pieces of chicken and chopped liver in lard until partially cooked. Add wine and spices and continue cooking. Add water as necessary. Finally, add pitted dates, raisins, and sugar. Serve with crumbled, dried bread. (This a typical Arab sweet-and-sour recipe. The recommendation for the use of pork lard in the text probably reflects later usage.)

Imperial Soup: Boil chopped green broccoli (the florets but not the stems or leaves) with a small quantity of very finely-chopped whole fennel (anise), including the bulb as well as the leaves. Add beef or chicken broth, a bit of olive oil, and salt to taste. (This vegetable soup was a favorite of Frederick II.)

Ceci Soup: Boil ceci (chickpeas) until soft. Remove ceci from water and mash, adding a touch of olive oil, with spices and powdered white pepper. Place the mashed ceci mixture back in the remaining water adding some chopped parsley and a few chopped, roasted chestnuts. Bring to a boil. Serve hot.

White Meat Broth: To the broth of lamb or kid add finely-chopped, skinned almonds and grated white ginger. Boil. Add salt and white pepper to taste. (For modern cooks chicken broth is a good substitute for the broth of lamb or kid.)

Creamy Chicken Rice: Cook white rice and allow it to cool. In another pan, cook some boned chicken chopped into small pieces. Then combine the two, adding sheep's milk, and bring the mixture to a boil. Add sugar and spices before serving. (The more recent recipe calls for the further addition of pieces of fried bacon.)

Poultry Innards: Clean and chop livers and gizzards. Mix together with eggs and cheese and form into flat cakes. Fry or deep fry in oil and lard.

Mamonia: Prepare boned, chopped mutton or goat meat. Boil this with whole-grain white rice in bitter almond milk and spices. When cooked, add honey. (This was a variation of the Arab *mamunya,* of which there were other, very distinct, forms in Syria and England.)

Ravioli Pork Filling: Chop and boil pork meat until most of the liquid has evaporated. Remove from heat and let it cool. Then chop it very finely. Add grated cheese, eggs, spices and salt. (For a modern approach, grind the pork before cooking.)

Herring in Broth: Boil Greek wine in a pan. Add fresh, cleaned, boned sardines without overcooking. There should be just enough wine to cover the fish. Add pepper, saffron and sugar. Then add oil and let the mixture thicken. (This is similar to stemperata.)

Tench: Steam very briefly so the fish is just tender enough to cut and clean easily without breaking the backbone. Sprinkle the inside with almond milk and stuff with marjoram, parsley and mint. Then fry the fish in olive oil to cook it. Serve with green sauce. (Tench is a freshwater fish but this recipe is equally suitable for saltwater fish of this size having white flesh.)

Fish Sausage: Clean the fish, then steam it just enough to easily remove the scales and bones. Next, chop it finely, adding chopped grassy herbs with the desired spices. Stuff it into goat or sheep intestines and fry it. Alternatively, form it into a cylinder wrapped in a sheet of thin, clean linen, remove it and then boil it in oil until cooked.

Roasted Squid: Clean the squid, leaving the tentacles attached to the body, which should be slit along its length to form an open butterfly shape when cooked. Roast over an open flame until cooked. Flavor with lemon or citron juice, or rose water.

Simple Shrimp: Place live shrimp in boiling water. Do not overcook. Remove, strain, and sprinkle with verjuice or red vinegar. Salt to taste. (Verjuice is preferable to vinegar.)

Cuttlefish and Octopus Broth: Clean both, setting aside the ink gland of the cuttlefish. Cut these into pieces and sauté in chopped onion and olive oil until cooked. Gradually add just enough water to cover this mixture, adding marjoram and chopped parsley. As soon as this comes to a boil, add some crumbled bread crust. Then add more water with spices, saffron, chopped almonds and the cuttlefish ink. If a sweet-and-sour flavor is desired, add citron juice and sugar.

Cuttlefish: Thoroughly clean the cuttlefish, removing the ink and bone. Fry it in olive oil. Add salt and pepper. Serve it with a green sauce (see below).

Green Sauce: Finely chop parsley leaves, adding (in a lesser quantity) chopped mint leaves. Flavor with powdered nutmeg, cloves, cardamom and ginger. Add bread crumbs and oil, mixing the ingredients thoroughly. Then add salt and a small amount of vinegar to taste.

Wild Mushrooms: Boil mushrooms until cooked. Drain. Cut into pieces if necessary. Sauté with finely chopped onion in olive oil or pork lard. Flavor with spices or chopped, grassy herbs such as chives.

Mushroom Tart: Add steamed chopped mushrooms to eggs and Comino pecorino cheese (made from sheep's milk in Abruzzi) with spices. Bake in a greased pan. (This may be cooked as an omelet or poured into a pie crust like a quiche.)

Lentils: Boil the lentils with aromatic herbs (such as chives), olive oil, salt and saffron. When cooked and soft, almost a paste, mix into the lentils a beaten egg and grated cheese before serving.

Lentils and Pork: Boil lentils with fresh, boned pork, without adding eggs or cheese.

Fried Spinach: Clean spinach thoroughly, then boil for a few minutes until partly cooked. Remove from water with a fork and press to strain well. Next, sauté chopped onion in olive oil, then adding bitter spices and saffron. Salt to taste, sprinkling with lemon juice if desired. (This is a variation of the *isfanak muttajan* known in Arab cookery.)

Green Soup: To meat broth add chopped swiss chard (the main ingredient) and a lesser quantity of chopped escarole (or spinach). Let this boil until cooked, then add a bit of chopped mint and chopped parsley just before serving. Salt and pepper to taste.

Gnocchi: Mix white flour with eggs, water and a small quantity of white bread crumbs. Form into small balls. To cook, place these into water that is already boiling. Remove after a few minutes. Serve with butter and grated cheese.

Lasagna: Roll pasta (see the gnocchi recipe) into thin sheets cut into rectangles. In a shallow, flat, greased pan, form these into three or four layers between a mixture of chopped hard-boiled eggs, chopped bacon, spices (which may include finely-chopped chives and parsley), grated or chopped cheese and small pieces of boiled pork sausage. The sheets of pasta should be soft (freshly-made). Bake.

Pancakes: Add egg whites to white flour with water and some chopped, fresh flower blossoms such as lavender. Add salt or sugar to taste. Mix, but do not whip, to a smooth, pasty consistency. Fry in butter or lard. Serve with honey or a sauce.

Fried Cheese: Coat chunks of soft, slightly-aged sheep's cheese with a mixture of beaten eggs and green herbs dredged in bread crumbs. Fry in oil or lard until a crust is formed.

Stuffed Figs: Fill large, fresh figs with small pieces of skinned apples and pears, adding pieces of walnut and ground cinnamon.

Crespelle: Mix white flour with water, egg and saffron, and very little yeast. When it has risen, roll the paste into a very thin layer and cut into long, narrow strips. Deep fry in oil with lard until cooked and crispy but not browned. Set the cookies on a cloth to drain the oil. When cool, coat with sugar or honey and serve. These are the *frittelle ubaldini* mentioned in the *Meridionale,* so-called because they were preferred by Ubaldino della Pila, brother of the cardinal Ottaviano degli Ubaldini, a contemporary of Frederick II. (The recipe mentioned earlier is identical but without the eggs or saffron, and the strips are cooked in oil without lard.)

Candied Violets: Gently rinse edible blue violets, holding the delicate flowers by their stems, and allow to dry. Heat cane sugar in a pan with a little water as needed until the mixture is melted and liquid. Remove from heat. Carefully dip the flowers into the liquid and set to dry on a lightly oiled cutting board or other surface. (These were said to be a favorite of Frederick II.)

Biancomangiare: Slowly heat milk and cream in a pot with cane sugar and a bit of chopped, crushed vanilla bean. Permit the sugar to dissolve but do not boil the mixture. Then stir in a bit of liquefied *amidon* (wheat starch) and let the whole mixture thicken before removing it from the heat and pouring it into small bowls to let it cool in the coldest part of the cellar. Sprinkle ground cinnamon or crushed almonds over the top. (This is just one variation on this recipe popular in France and Spain, and nowadays cornstarch can be substituted for wheat starch.)

Wren Pie: Bake a large, bowl-shaped pastry shell and let it cool to room temperature. Then use a knife to make an opening at the bottom of it. At the top or along the side, fashion a series of rectangular holes to resemble the bars of a cage. Shortly before serving place a few live birds into the pastry via the hole in the bottom and set the pie upon a heavy plate. Present it to a diner with a knife to carve into the top and free the birds. (It is not suggested that any reader attempt to prepare this, but it is a fine example of what was sometimes made for royalty.)

Courtly Dining

What was a formal meal like at the Sicilian court? It should be remembered that, unlike the courts of many parts of Europe, Sicily's was influenced initially to a great degree by Byzantine and Arab culinary traditions, which in certain ways were more refined and sophisticated than those known in England, France, Germany and some parts of Italy.

Fragments of medieval plates of the Norman-Swabian era survive that were discovered in the royal palace in Palermo; some of this pottery is decorated with Fatimid or Byzantine motifs. These items were somewhat similar to majolica but without the white glaze undercoating that characterized that medium.

The use of knives and wooden spoons was normal at court. Indeed, it is even possible that simple forks (with two tines) were used at court meals in Sicily before this was common practice in most of Europe. At her wedding feast in 1004, Maria Argyropoulina, the niece of Basil II of Constantinople, scandalized many of the Venetian guests present when she ate her meat with a fork, and a golden one at that, but over time the utensil came to be viewed as slightly less eccentric.[19] The story about the Byzantine princess is rather significant because it informs us of one of the first public uses of what became the modern fork, and the church's view of the dining utensil as a sinful luxury. Yet it is difficult to imagine any of the Hautevilles or their spouses worrying about offending the clergy by using a fork to eat food.

Another detail worth remembering is that spaghetti was known in Sicily as early as the reign of Roger II, and this food is sometimes mentioned as a reason for Italians' early use of the fork, albeit some time later. Even so, this suggests that forks may have been used in Sicily before the rest of Italy.[20]

Nevertheless, guests would eat some foods with their hands, and finger bowls and linen napkins were provided.

Though a guest might bring his own knife and cup to dinner at a comparatively humble baronial castle, this was less necessary at a royal palace, where it was usually presumed that these things would be provided.

We do not know exactly which service tradition prevailed at which time, and it is quite possible that particular practices continued from one reign into another. The Arabs might place several different dishes on the table simultaneously, whereas the Greeks and Normans might prefer sequential courses. Naturally, the king and queen could dictate their preferences not only for the food served but for the mode of service. Elvira may have preferred one approach, Margaret another. Whatever the case, by the Hohenstaufen era, service probably began to conform more to the prevailing European norm.

Where were the meals served? So extensively have the major medieval palaces been restructured or destroyed that it is impossible to determine where a "great hall" was located in most of them. Little remains of the Favara (in Palermo's Brancaccio district) or the royal palace at Monreale. The palace at Messina is long gone. Some royal residences, like Arechi Castle in Salerno, have been extensively modified since 1266, though Castel del Monte, Frederick's Apulian hunting lodge, survives unscathed. There were, in fact, many other castles where the traveling court stayed occasionally, particularly during the Swabian era, such as the imposing fortresses still standing in Bari and Catania. (See Appendix 1.)

The Barons' Hall in Palazzo Steri, overlooking Piazza Marina in Palermo, though built later (it was completed by 1307), offers a glimpse of what a Sicilian royal dining hall looked like. It is spacious, its wooden ceiling painted with typical medieval figures, scenes and coats of arms. This was larger than the great hall of the typical baronial castle, and the edifice was eventually used as the royal palace of Palermo.

The great hall at San Marco d'Alunzio, the first castle

erected by the Hautevilles in Sicily, was certainly smaller than this. Like the castle at Mileto, in Calabria, it has fallen victim to earthquakes. The castle at Melfi is in better condition, while that at Ariano has been largely reconstructed.

A few of our queens sometimes had what were, in effect, their own castles and households. We thus find Adelaide at San Marco d'Alunzio and later (following her marriage to the King of Jerusalem) at Patti, and Joanna at the Zisa in Palermo. Would that we knew more about the dinners served in these residences. Each cook doubtless had his own specialties, each woman her own food preferences.

Because the court traveled often, in warmer weather some important meals were certainly served in the royal presence under a large tent-like pavilion. It was beneath such a pavilion that Constance gave birth to Frederick in a public square along the route of her journey into Apulia.

As to feasts and tournaments in the capital, the *Fiera Vecchia,* located outside the walls of the Norman city in the area that is now Via Garibaldi, was a jousting ground and then, beginning in the fourteenth century, a fair that later became a street market. Today there is little evidence of either.

Entertainment at formal court dinners and royal feasts would be provided by minstrels and troubadours (see Chapter 7), who were ever more present beginning with the reign of William II and the influence of his wife, Joanna of England. Even before then, there were fine musicians in Sicily, and the painted Fatimid muqarnas ceiling of Palermo's Palatine Chapel depicts them playing lutes and harps.

The meal served at midday or in the early afternoon was the chief meal of the day (until recent times this was still true in Italy). Formal royal meals were more likely to be served at this time than in the evening, even if a major banquet lasted until dusk. There was a general sense of order, with meat dishes following lighter foods such as soups. Menus, and even the scheduling of a banquet, were planned around Christian feasts, which might entail fasting, and days on which it was customary to refrain from consuming either meat or fish; into modern times fish was popular on Fridays during Lent. Some clergy eschewed meat generally.

Halal and kosher requirements were easily accommodated given the nature of most recipes and the possibility of substituting olive oil for pork lard. Historians disagree about the reasons for the increasing use of lard, and even butter, by the thirteenth century; the thesis that olive oil was somehow scarce or particularly costly in regions such as Sicily, Calabria or Puglia is questionable. Much of the salt used was extracted from sea water; there are still salt evaporation ponds near Trapani.

Almost everybody of note who visited the court in Palermo probably dined with the king or queen at some point, even if some of these dinners were less formal than others. This included Eleanor of Aquitaine during the reign of Roger II and the nephews of Thomas Becket during the reign of William II. More so than most European medieval kings, Sicily's monarchs were likely to invite intellectuals to court.

Often, formal dinners were distinguished not only by the Sicilian court's polycultural cuisine but by the company itself. At times, there may have been a diversity of guests present. Travelers arrived from the Arab and Byzantine lands of the Mediterranean, naturally, and the Plantagenet dominions in France and England. Beginning with the marriage of Roger II to Elvira of Castile, there was increasing contact with northern Spain. The Staufen reign brought with it greater contact with Germany. This was also an opportunity for the sharing of recipes.

During the Norman era, there were initially certain differences between the food served at the royal court, with its Arab cooks, and the cuisine at the castle of a typical Norman or Lombard baron in the hinterland in Campania or Basilicata.

Yet a heretofore unfamiliar cuisine could be introduced more rapidly than a language or faith because it was intrinsically easier to learn a new recipe than a new tongue or ideology. When the barons and their companies attended meals at court, either in Sicily or during the king's travels around the peninsular part of the kingdom, they would have a chance to sample this cuisine. Little effort was required for a baron to present the recipe to his wife and cook once he returned to his own lands. This is likely how *scapece* became known in Apulia and other regions that Frederick II visited often. Other recipes of Arab or Byzantine origin were likely introduced as a consequence of contact with the eastern Mediterranean during the crusades and the Normans' incursions into regions such as Greece.

Obviously enough, a great celebration like the banquet at a wedding or coronation was much more complex and impressive than a "routine" dinner for a visiting diplomat. Some wedding celebrations lasted for days.

Though certain banquets and feasts in the Kingdom of Sicily, such as the wedding of William II and Joanna of England in 1177, stand out for their grandeur, virtually nothing is known about the menu or the quantity of food served.[21] We know that the wedding celebrations of Frederick II and Isabella of England in Germany in 1235 lasted at least four days but we have only sparse details about the food. For a general idea of this we may look to the magnificent feasts known elsewhere in western Europe during that era.[22]

For the wedding on the day after Christmas in 1251 of Margaret, the daughter of Henry III, to Alexander III, the young King of Scotland, the festivities lasted a week, and Matthew Paris tells us that sixty bulls constituted the first and main course.[23] Whether, as the chronicler claims, more than a thousand knights attended with their spouses and esquires, is debatable. Even so, it is reported that the guests consumed seventy pigs, almost two thousand hens, sixteen hundred partridges, three hundred rabbits, and a large number of peacocks, pheasants and of course swans, along with plenty of fish. Nearly seventy thousand loaves of bread were baked. In fact, the planning and preparation began months before the wedding in York. The detail with which the feast was described was rather exceptional for its time because it reflected a personal account; Matthew seems to have been present.

Bovine livestock was rarer in Sicily, but it is reasonable to presume that the amounts of other kinds of protein served at some celebrations held in the *Regnum Siciliae* rivalled those known in England and France.

It was during this era, and probably just a few years after Isabella's wedding to Frederick at Worms, that Bartholomew the Englishmen, while living in Magdeburg, wrote his encyclopedic *De Proprietatibus Rerum,* which describes, among many other things, the character of society. Here he considers aristocratic dining etiquette, stating that bread is served first, followed by wine and meat, and then fruit:

Meat and drink is ordained and convenient to dinners and to feasts, for at feasts first meat is prepared and made in a readiness, guests be called together, forms and stools be set in the hall, and tables, cloths and towels be ordained, disposed, and made ready. Guests be set with the lord in the chief place of the board, and they sit not down at the board before the guests wash their hands. Children be set in their place, and servants at a table by themselves. First knives, spoons and salts be set on the board, and then bread and drink, and many diverse messes, household servants busily help each other to do everything diligently and talk merrily together. The guests be gladded with lutes and harps. Now wine and now messes of meat be brought forth and divided. At the last cometh fruit and spices, and when they have eaten, board, cloths, and relief be borne away, and guests wash and wipe their hands again.

Then grace is said, and guests thank the lord. Then for gladness and comfort drink is brought yet again. When all this is done at meat, men take their leave, and some go to bed and sleep, and some go home to their own lodgings.[24]

Here, incidentally, we find the origin of the phrase "set the table" rooted in the practice of laying a board across a trestle, then covering it with a linen cloth.

While Bartholomew was writing his "encyclopedia," another Englishman, John of Garland, was working on his *Morale Scolarium,* which considered, among many other things, table manners.

Medieval eating could be a messy affair, especially without the use of forks, and one imagines noble ladies taking care not to splatter gravy on their elegant silken gowns.

The significance of the medieval precursor of what nowadays would be termed a "state dinner" cannot be understated. This was a chance for a sovereign to impress upon his guests that he and his kingdom were truly important. Everything, from the food to the entertainment to the palace itself, enhanced this impression.

As we have seen, the court was wherever the monarch was. Frederick II, as emperor, had to travel constantly; indeed, he spent very little of his reign in Palermo. In truth, his imperial status spoke for itself. Even a meal under a tent could not diminish the prestige of a man so powerful and so intelligent.

For the Hautevilles, Palermo itself was impressive enough. During the reign of William II, the city and its environs likely had well over a hundred thousand residents; in Europe only Constantinople, straddling two continents, boasted a notably larger population, though Cordoba likely rivalled the Sicilian capital. Certainly, a number of European palaces and fortresses were larger than Palermo's royal residence. What distinguished the Palermo palace was not its size but its sumptuousness. Its position on high ground was also impressive. On one side was the vast city of domed churches and mosques and the sea; on the other were impressive mountains beyond the royal park and hunting ground, with Monreale's cathedral and an imposing castle visible. Surrounding the city was the *Conca d'Oro,* the "golden conch," so named for its seemingly endless orchards of orange and lemon trees. Palermo's souks were more alluring than most European fairs; only Spain offered anything comparable. London, Paris and Milan were destined for greatness, but this was Palermo's moment.

One thing about Palermo's royal residences was especially helpful in the preparation of food. Unlike many European castles and palaces of its era, Palermo's royal palace had rudimentary plumbing, with water supplied by the kanats running to the city from the rivers and springs near Monreale and Baida. (Such a kanat connected to the Kemonia River fed the mikveh of the great synagogue near the Balarah souk.) This meant that water for cooking did not have to be carried from a river or well. Some of the springs, such as the Sorgente del Gabriele, which feeds a kanat near Via Nave and the Scibene palace, still supply Palermo with water.

Guests might be entertained at one of the smaller royal palaces around the city, especially during warmer months. The Zisa, the Cuba, the Favara and the Scibene, all surrounded by gardens, were also provided water through kanats. These palaces had ponds or pools similar to those of the Alhambra in Andalusia.

A case could be made that Sicilian cuisine was superior to what was served in most of Europe. Some would say that it still is.

Conclusions

The court cuisine of Sicily evolved greatly from the foundation of the kingdom in 1130 until the fall of our second royal dynasty in 1266. The gradual culinary changes shadowed those in other areas of society, particularly its Latinization and the diminishing influence of Islam and Arab culture generally. Moreover, many of the foundations of the Sicilian cookery that survived over the centuries paralleled trends in other areas, such as language.

Through all of this, the queens of Sicily ensured that their guests enjoyed the pleasures of the table derived from the fusion of Mediterranean and European culinary traditions.

NOTES

1. It is not the author's intent to minimize this idea. See Bynum, Caroline, "Fast, Feast and Flesh: The Religious Significance of Food to Medieval Women," *Representations*, number 11 (summer 1985), pages 1-25.

2. The problem in the Kingdom of Sicily is that we have very few household accounts from these reigns that indicate exactly what was being served, either at the royal court or at baronial castles. There is some foreign literature that may be consulted for comparison. See, for example, Kjaer, Lars, "Food, Drink and Ritualized Communication in the Household of Eleanor of Montfort, February to August 1265," *Journal of Medieval History*, volume 37, number 1 (2011), pages 75-89; also Mead, William, *The English Medieval Feast* (1931).

3. Hieatt, Constance, "How Arabic Traditions Travelled to England," *Food on the Move: Proceedings of the Oxford Symposium on Food and Cookery 1996* (1997), pages 120-126. For some insights see Salloum, Habeeb, "Medieval and Renaissance Italy: Sicily," in *Regional Cuisines of Medieval Europe: A Book of Essays* (2002), pages 113-123.

4. Broadhurst, Ronald, *The Travels of Ibn Jubayr* (1952, 2008), page 340. This also mentions some crops raised, such as pears, apples, hazelnuts.

5. Zaouali, Lilia, *Medieval Cuisine of the Islamic World: A concise history with 174 Recipes* (2007); this is the *Kitab al-Tabikh*. Nasrallah, Nawal, *Annals of the Caliph's Kitchens: Ibn Sayyar al-Warraq's Tenth-Century Baghdadi Cookbook* (2007). For some modern adaptations of some of these recipes, see Salloum, Habeeb, *Scheherazade's Feasts: Foods of the Medieval Arab World* (2013).

6. Martellotti, Anna, *La Cassata Siciliana: Un Dolce Arabo e la Sua Fortuna in Occidente* (2012).

7. This was early in 1062, reported in the chronicle of Godfrey of Malaterra, book 30; the author's translation: "The Normans' adversaries, being accustomed to the warm waters of summer, began to feel the coldness of the air and tried to warm themselves by drinking wine. This, however, made them drowsy. Thus they began to neglect their vigilance of the city during the nights."

8. Hieatt, Constance, and Jones, Robin, "Two Anglo-Norman Culinary Collections Edited from British Library Manuscripts Additional 32085 and Royal 12,C.xii," *Speculum*, volume 61, number 4 (October 1996), pages 859-882. Another example is Pegge, Samuel, *The Forme of Cury* (1780), page 106; this is a collection of recipes from the court of Richard II of England around 1390.

9. For some observations see Anderson, Melitta Weiss, *Food in Medieval Times* (2004), pages 130-121. This is an excellent summary but whether certain introductions, such as pistachios, should be attributed to the Arabs, is debatable as some were also cultivated by the Byzantine Greeks.

10. Hieatt, Constance, "How Arabic Traditions Travelled to England," op.cit. supra, page 123, page 126n31.

11. Ibid.

12. For the complete text of the *Liber de Coquina* and the *Meridionale* see Martellotti, Anna (editor), *I Ricettari di Federico II: Dal Meridionale al Liber de Coquina* (2005). For the *Meridionale* see Boström, Ingemar (editor), *Due Libri di Cucina: Anonimo Meridionale* (1985).

13. Some recipes influenced by these early compilations are included in *De Arte Coquinaria* by Martin of Como, written in the fifteenth century, for which see the translation by Jeremy Parzen, et al., published in 2005 as *The Art of Cooking*.

14. Scully, Terence, *The Neapolitan Recipe Collection* (2000).

15. Musso, Pasquale, et al., "Il 'Ricettario di Cucina' di San Martino delle Scale," *Bollettino del Centro di Studi Filologici e Linguistici Siciliani*, volume 21 (2007), pages 243-321.

16. *Sicilian Food and Wine: The Cognoscente's Guide* (2015). Another fine work, which includes many historical Sicilian recipes, is Mary Taylor Simeti's *Pomp and Sustenance: Twenty-Five Centuries of Sicilian Food* (1989), later released under another title. More generally, see Scully, Terence, *The Art of Cookery in the Middle Ages* (1995); Montanari, Massimo, *Medieval Tastes: Food, Cooking and the Table* (2012).

17. Martellotti, Anna, op. cit. See also Möhren, Frankwalt, *Il Libro de la Cocina: Un Ricettario fra Oriente e Occidente* (2016).

18. The source for this is a charter of Frederick II given at Foggia in March 1240 ordering Richard of Policoro to procure wine and the ingredients for *scapece* for Berardo (sic), the emperor's cook. See Huillard-Bréholles, Jean (editor), *Historia Diplomatica Friderici Secundi,* volume 5, part 2, pages 861-862. This was not an isolated request; two months later, Frederick ordered that some Sicilian livestock herds (cows, sheep, goats) be sent to the mainland to supply the meat he preferred (ibid., pages 943-945).

19. The incident was reported much later by Peter Damian, who states that Maria's food was cut into pieces by eunuchs before she ate it with this two-pronged golden fork, *fuscinulis aureis atque bidentibus*. This was cited as divine justification for Maria's death from the plague not long after her wedding to John Orseolo, son of the Doge of Venice. See Migne, Jacques (editor), "Opuscula Varia," in *Patrologiae Cursus Completus* (1853), series 2, book 145, column 744. For Maria's marriage and death see the chronicle of John Sagorino the Deacon in Zanetti, Girolamo Francesco (editor), *Chronicon Venetum* (1765), pages 113-119. For more about the history of the fork, see Wilson, Bee, *Consider the Fork: A History of How We Cook and Eat* (2012).

20. No dining forks are known to exist from Norman Sicily. However, such forks might well have been fashioned of silver, and their absence should be considered

in light of the general lack of survival of gold and silver objects, or even steel swords or knives, of the Norman-Swabian period of Sicilian history. Only one reginal crown (shown on this book's cover) has been preserved *in toto,* along with a few queens' rings and the pendant reliquary given to Queen Margaret.

21. See *Queens of Sicily,* pages 537-543.

22. Barber, Richard, *The Prince in Splendour: Court Festivals in Medieval Europe* (2017).

23. *Matthaei Parisiensis,* Luard, Henry *(editor), Chronica Majora* (1877) volume 2, page 470.

24. Batman, Stephen (editor), *De Proprietatibus Rerum* (1585), page 81, chapters 23 ("On Dinner and Fasting") and 24 ("On the Supper") of book 6 ("De State Hominis"). This is the translation by John Trevisa and except for a few spellings it is extracted directly. Bartholomew, who later became minister of Austria and Bohemia, may have met Frederick II.

Chapter 7
POETRY FOR QUEENS

An important part of courtly culture was its literature, including its poetry. Which poems did our queens hear?

Although we can never know if certain queens listened to troubadours or minstrels recite specific verses, a corpus of the poetry of the Sicilian School survives. Composed in Sicilian, it is the earliest known literature of any of the Italian languages. Its geographical focus was Palermo, where the sonnet was born as part of this movement.[1]

Though Dante and his contemporaries knew of Sicilian, it did not directly influence Tuscan or Umbrian, which developed on their own from Latin.

Until around 1200, most of the poetry heard in Sicily was written, and recited, in Siculo Arabic[2] or in Norman French.[3] We know something of the Arabic works, such as the *qasidas* of Abd al-Jabbar ibn Hamdis, but virtually nothing of those composed in French save for one significant example.

Set largely in Calabria, the *Chanson d'Aspremont,* part of the Charlemagne Cycle, is an epic of over ten thousand lines composed in southern Italy, probably in Calabria or Sicily, shortly before 1190. The author himself seems not to have been from

Italy. The poem became popular in England and Italy, later copies of the work reflecting English or Italian linguistic influences. The romance seems to have been written for Richard Lionheart and his dynasty. Prominent amongst its themes is the story, or backstory, of *Durendal,* a mystical sword obtained from a Muslim owner in the context of a tale that is an allegory for the forthcoming Third Crusade.

Not all poetry known in Sicily before the thirteenth century was, strictly speaking, *court* poetry, which is part of the courtly tradition that began to flourish in the Norman era during the reign of William II. William's time on the throne coincided with the introduction of Provençal culture and art (notably the carved capitals in Monreale's abbey), tournaments, heraldry and what, in common parlance, has come to be called "chivalry." It also coincided with the arrival, in 1177, of Joanna of England, whose mother was a great patroness of the troubadour tradition.

To place this into perspective, we must cast a glance backward. Throughout the first half of the twelfth century, most Sicilians spoke Greek, Arabic or both. Indeed, chroniclers identified the Sicilians by the languages they spoke. Referring to the plight of Roger Hauteville and his wife, Judith, when besieged at Troina during an unusually cold winter in the first phase of the conquest of Sicily, Godfrey Malaterra states that, *Graeci vero et Sarraceni, quibus omnis patria favens pro libito patebat, plurima replebantur abundantia.* "Instead, the Greeks and Saracens received provisions from the entire region and were supplied abundantly."[4] The Normans spoke French among themselves, and this became the court language. Many Sicilians were bilingual or trilingual. Charters were issued in some combination of Greek, Arabic or Latin.

Although Sicilian began its evolution as a vernacular language during the last decades of the twelfth century, the surviving examples of actual poems can be dated accurately only to the majority of Frederick II. Constance of Aragon heard this tongue, but we cannot be absolutely certain that Margaret ever did, nor that the evolving Sicilian language was even much appreciated in royal circles before Frederick's time. It was, however, a result of the gradual Latinization of Sicily and Calabria since the arrival of the Normans.

Classified as "Italo-Dalmatian," the earliest Sicilian was a Romance language having French, Arabic, Greek and even German influences. It was influenced by Catalan after 1282, when Sicily, but not the peninsular part of the kingdom, was ruled by the royal house of Aragon. A distinction may be drawn between the medieval (or "Middle") Sicilian spoken and written into the fourteenth century and the modern form of the language sometimes heard today.

During Frederick's reign, Sicilian was spoken across Sicily and in southern Calabria and in a few parts of Apulia, such as Taranto and Lecce. In other regions of the kingdom the people spoke early forms of Neapolitan, Pugliese and Calabrian.

The Sicilian Tongue

Interesting as the language is, it is no longer spoken as it was in Frederick's time. This is not the suitable venue for a philological treatise on the intricacies of Sicilian and its survival. Nevertheless, a few observations are in order.

Succinctly, we may note that it is a slightly guttural tongue, sounding vaguely like Catalan, lacking a true future tense or (historically) a standard orthography. The long "u" is often used in words similar to Italian ones which use the long "o." We find *picciottu* instead of *giovanotto* (young man), *chiddu* for *esso* (it), *chistu* for *questo* (this), *iddu* for *egli* (he) and *idda* for *ella* (she), and so forth. Its verb forms make Sicilian as distinct from Italian as it is from Spanish. Certain nouns and adjectives are rather peculiar: *parrinu* instead of *prete* (priest), *beddu* for *bello* (beautiful).

SICILIAN QUEENSHIP

The Sicilian word *tascio,* which means "tacky," falsely sophisticated or lacking in good taste, is understandably offensive in fashion-conscious Italy, though to refer to somebody as *vastaso,* "uncouth," is far more insulting. Certain Sicilian phrases seem appropriate sometimes. *Ammunì* sounds much more persuasive than the Italian *Andiamo* ("Let's go").

Some words come directly from Arabic: *babbaluci* (also the Greek *boubalàkion*) for *lumache* (snails), *dammusu* for ceiling, *saia* (from *saqiya*) for "canal," *gébbia* for "reservoir," and *azzizare* ("to make beautiful") from a*ziz*. Other words rooted in Arabic: *favara* (a well), *mischinu* (an unfortunate person), *zagara* (orange blossom), *zammù* (anise), *balata* (stone), *cafisu* (a liquid measure, from *qafiz*), *tarì* (a gold coin).

A number of Sicilian words derive from Norman French: *buatta* (jar, from *boîte*), *custureri* (tailor, from *coustrier*), *largasia* (largesse), *racìna* (grape), *vuccèri* (butcher, from *boucher*), *accattari* (to buy, from *acater,* modern *acheter*), *cavallu* and *cavaddu* (horse, from *cheval*).

From Medieval Greek we find: *carusu* (boy, from *kouros*), *cona* (icon, from *eikona*), *crastu* (ram, from *krastos*), *pistiari* (to eat, from *apestiein*), *naca* (cradle, from *nakè*), *bucali* (pitcher, from *baukalion*), *grasta* (a terracotta vase, from the classical *gastra*).

Among words from Middle High German are: *arbitrari* (to work, from *arbeit*), *vardari* (to wait or watch, from *warten*), *sparagnari* (to save money, from *sparen*), *guastari* and *vastari* (to waste, from *wastjan*).

Provençal has made a few contributions, notably: *lascu* (thin or sparse, from *lasc*), *addumari* (to light, from *allumar*), *aggrifari* (to kidnap, from *grifar*).

There are, of course, many words from Latin and Catalan.

On a more hypothetical note, the Indo-European etymologies of a few Sicilian words may be connected to the language of the Sikels who already populated the island's eastern region when the Greeks arrived in antiquity. Two oft-cited examples are: *dudda* (various red berries, akin to the Welsh *rhudd* meaning "pink" and the Romanian *dudà*), *scrozzu* ("short" or "undeveloped," similar to Germanic *scurz* and Lithuanian *su-skurdes*).

Contrary to a common notion here in Italy, Sicilian is not a "dialect" of Italian. That idea was advanced with notable zeal after 1860, when unificationists discouraged the use of Italianate tongues other than Tuscan Italian; later, the Fascists even banned the teaching of English in public schools. Recent years have seen a renewed interest in Italy's regional languages.[5]

The Sicilian School

The best known of the poets of the Sicilian School are Giacomo of Lentini, by profession a notary, and Cielo of Alcamo. Although Cielo's *Contrasto* is the longest surviving poem, and the most popular among Sicilians, Giacomo's known body of work surpasses that of his peers in quantity.

Amongst the other poets are the Abbot of Tivoli (whatever his name), Roger d'Amici, Otto delle Colonne, Guy delle Colonne, Rinaldo of Aquino, Stephen the Pronotary, Mazzeo of Ricco, Jacopo Mostacci, Percival Doria, Giacomino the Apulian, Tommaso of Sasso and Arrigo Testa of Lentini.

Those boasting important court connections include Peter della Vigna, onetime chancellor of Frederick II, John of Brienne, Frederick's father-in-law, Enzo (or Enzio), one of Frederick's illegitimate sons, and Manfred, the son of Frederick who became King of Sicily.[6]

The only female poet mentioned in connection with the Sicilian School is "Nina of Messina," whose exact name is unknown (see Appendix 2).

Frederick himself composed a number of poems, and five surviving works are usually attributed to him, but did any of our queens ever write such a thing? We may never know, yet it is a distinct possibility that one or two of the queens of the

Swabian era did indeed write something in Sicilian, and that, in an earlier time, Judith or Margaret wrote a verse or two in Norman French that has not been preserved. The French and Provençal influences on the Sicilian School are obvious; Cielo's *Contrasto* is a Sicilian adaptation of *Le Roman de la Rose*.

We may theorize that, had any queens of the Swabian era composed poetry in Sicilian, it most likely would have resembled the poetry attributed to Nina, reflecting a woman's point of view.

When did Sicilian become the principal court language? This, again, is difficult to estimate precisely, but during the regency of Constance, the mother of Frederick II, both German and French were the predominant spoken languages at court, while there were ever fewer speakers of Arabic and Greek at the palace.

Sicilian developed, in the first instance, as the spoken language of the ordinary people as they became "Sicilian" rather than remaining identifiably Arab, Norman or Greek. It is a product of the gradual amalgamation of cultures and the eventual dominance of Latin in liturgy, chronicles and charters, along with the conversion of Muslims to Christianity and, however insidiously, the Byzantine Greeks to Catholicism.

Most of the poems translated from Sicilian into English into the middle of the twentieth century were rendered in a slightly "Victorian" style that attempted to maintain their rhyme and prosody. Frede Jensen led a new wave of scholars who sought to translate this work in a more "realistic" manner.

The translations in this chapter are almost literal, with no attempt at rhyme or poetic style, as the original words should, in a sense, speak for themselves.

The work selected for this chapter is the poetry generally attributed to Frederick II. Some of this has already been translated for publication elsewhere. However, what follow are the author's original translations, effected without reference to any others. As the poems of Frederick presented here were slightly "tuscanized" by copyists, they are not available in "pure" Sicilian. Apart from that, the orthography of the poems as they were copied in the earliest known codices differs somewhat from the texts presented here; for an example of this phenomenon see the original text of *Tapina me che amava uno sparviero* following the translation in Appendix 2.

The principal source for Frederick's poems, and those of most of the other poets, are the manuscripts *Codex Vaticanus Latinus 3793* and *Codex Urbinas Latinus 697,* housed in the Vatican Apostolic Library. These are the work of copyists working late in the thirteenth century; earlier copies of the poems of the Sicilian School are virtually unknown. (Other manuscripts containing poems of the Sicilian School are the *Banco Rari 217,* formerly *Palatino 418*, and the *Laurenziano Rediano 9,* both in Florence; the former may be the oldest of all.) Some of the orthography varies slightly between manuscripts, and in some instances it is more typically Sicilian, with more frequent use of the "k" and the "u" as well as "j" in place of "i."

Frederick himself presents us with some complexities. His falconry treatise reflects an unusual proclivity for scholarship by a monarch of his era. This was probably dictated to scribes, who wrote it in Latin. His poems, on the other hand, were probably his own words, even if they were dictated. That is the simpler aspect of any study of his poetry.

For whom did Frederick write these poems, and when? His rapport with his first wife, Constance of Aragon, was a good one, likewise that with his last wife, his former mistress Bianca Lancia. However, it is difficult to imagine Frederick writing poems for his other wives, Yolanda of Jerusalem and Isabella of England, with whom he does not seem to have had very good relationships. Of course, he had other mistresses besides Bianca.

To the modern mind, it may seem paradoxical that a king, or any man, would compose a love poem for a wife whom he was betraying, especially if the poem itself spoke of love and loyalty. Yet that seems to be the case here.

Constance of Aragon is a most interesting case, as she brought troubadours and musicians with her from Spain to Sicily and is reputed to have cultivated an interest in these arts, something which, one imagines, would have made her appreciative of the nascent Sicilian School. However, Constance died in 1222, and it is generally believed that the surviving work of the Sicilian School was written after that time; this would include Frederick's poems.

As the court traveled with Frederick around Italy, into Germany and as far as Palestine, we cannot know precisely which poems were composed in Sicily.

We have no direct evidence, such as a specific example, of any Sicilian queen writing poetry or personally sponsoring the efforts of the court poets who wrote in Sicilian.

In another chapter, the author has speculated that, when speaking to Tancred late in 1191, Constance of Sicily may have spoken to him in a very early form of Sicilian. This is based on the fact that both she and Tancred were raised in the *Regnum Siciliae* and had much contact with its baronage and populace. For the most part, Constance spoke French and, when necessary, German, and in any case the Sicilian School emerged two decades after her death.

Significantly, many poems of the Sicilian School were intended to be recited rather than sung to an instrumental accompaniment. Frederick's *Dolze Meo Drudo* is an exception, but its musical accompaniment was written long after the poem itself was composed.[7] The song-like, lyrical *canzone* (from the Provençal *canso*) was suitable to be sung; this form gave rise to the sonnet. The poems of the Sicilian School are broadly divided into these two categories.

The ephemeral Sicilian School dissipated and disappeared upon the death of its last royal patron, King Manfred, who was felled at the Battle of Benevento in 1266. It has been suggested that, had the Staufen dynasty survived and prospered, ruling the Kingdom of Sicily and the northern Italian comunes for a few more generations, perhaps even into the fifteenth century, Sicilian, rather than Tuscan, might have emerged as the principal Italian vernacular. Like his father, Manfred was an avid patron of the arts and sciences.

The lengthiest original work composed in Middle Sicilian before the widespread emergence of Tuscan as Italy's literary language is a prose chronicle, the *Rebellamentu di Sichilia contra Re Carlu*. Thought to be the memoir of John of Procida, this narrative recounts the history of the War of the Sicilian Vespers of 1282 from the Ghibelline point of view. It was probably written a few years before John's death in 1298. The work is significant because, unlike most of the existing texts of the poems of the Sicilian School, its language has not been tuscanized. It is, in fact, the earliest known narrative of substantial length written in one of the Italian languages.[8]

In reality, the surviving texts of most of the poems are problematical because, being transcribed from around 1280 onward, apparently by speakers of Tuscan, they do not accurately reflect Sicilian as it was actually spoken.

Apart from its orthography, it is obvious that the language of the following text from the sixty-fourth chapter of the *Rebellamentu*, based on the *Spinelli Codex,* the oldest known manuscript (consulted by the author at the Sicilian Regional Library in Palermo), is quite different from the poetry we find in *Codex Vaticanus Latinus 3793* and *Codex Urbinas Latinus 697,* with their words altered by Tuscan influences. This is a Sicilian nearer to what the poets actually spoke and wrote:

Quandu lu re di aragona audiu quisti palorj, sì appj grandi dubitanza, audendu chi lu re carlu avia tantu putirj. Et incontinenti mandau currerj per l'isula di sichilia, chi si re carlu vinissi inver palermu. Et in quilla nocti vinni unu notaru inbaxaturi di parti di lu comunj di missina, e quillu missaiu dissi a lu re di aragona comu in missina non avia vidanda exceptu per octu iorni et non per chuj e kj "vuj nj dijati dari ayutu e ssiccursu di gentj e di victuagli, chi per nixunu modu nuj non putimu pluj resistirj dananti di lu re carlu, sì kj nuj nj rindirimu ad ipsu, kj nuj non putimu altru farj." [9]

Any fluent speaker of Modern Sicilian would recognize most of the words written in this tongue. (The author had no difficulty translating the text on a first reading.) It is safe to say that, in their original form, the poems of Frederick II and the other poets of the Sicilian School probably sounded more like this than what appears below and in Appendix 2.

Analogies are rarely precise, but we may view the older ("Medieval" or "Middle") Sicilian spoken before 1300 the way that native speakers of English regard the language of Chaucer, and the more modern Sicilian, influenced by Catalan, as the language of Shakespeare.

By the time John of Procida died, a monoculture, at once Italian and Spanish in almost every discernible way, had enveloped Sicily, where the Jews remained as the only identifiable religious or ethnic minority. Socially, the Aragonese Kingdom of Sicily was virtually indistinguishable from the Angevin Kingdom of Naples of the mainland.

A good reference — though not the only one — is the *Declarus* of Angelo Senisio, composed during the middle of the fourteenth century as what may be considered the first "dictionary" of the Sicilian language as it existed at that time, marked by Catalan influences.[10]

Although Sicilian continued to be spoken, evolving with time, it was no longer the important literary language it had once been. By 1500, official documents such as the *riveli* (a tax census) were recorded in what was essentially Tuscan with a few Sicilian phrases and usages. Yet most Sicilians still spoke Sicilian into the early years of the twentieth century.

Sicilian is part of the *Sicilianità* considered in Chapter 10. It is inseparable from the place and its culture.

These five works constitute the entire "Frederican Canon" of the emperor's poems, of which much has been written.[11] Wherever possible, words were preferred in the manuscript texts which reflect the Sicilian language of Frederick's era over the more tuscanized versions. The first work is a sonnet.

Misura, Providenzia e Meritanza

Misura, providenzia e meritanza
fanno l'uomo eser sagio e conoscente
e'n ogni nobeltà l'uom se n'avanza
e ciascuna riccheza fa prudente.

> Judgment, consideration and merit
> make a man wise and knowledgeable
> propagating every sign of nobility,
> and every wealth earned makes him prudent.

Nè di riccheze aver grande audanza
faria l'omo ch'è ville esser valente,
ma della ordinata costumanza
discende gentileza fra le gente.

> A man lacking wealth in great measure,
> even if lowborn, will be seen as worthy,
> by consistently behaving honorably,
> and he'll be esteemed by the folk as a gentleman.

Omo ch'è posto in alto signoragio
e in riccheze abunda, tosto scende,
credendo fermo stare in signoria.

> Instead, a man who enjoys aristocratic rank
> and abundant wealth quickly loses status
> by thinking himself better than others.

Unde non salti troppo omo ch'è sagio,
per grande alteza che ventura prende,
ma tutt'ora mantegna cortesia.

> Contrarily, a wise man who is discreet in manners,
> confronting his every destiny with dignity,
> will always remain courteous to all.

SICILIAN QUEENSHIP

Poi Ch'a Voi Piace Amore

Poi ch'a voi piace, amore,
che eo degia trovare,
faronde mia possanza
ch'io vegna a compimento.
Dat'agio lo meo core
in voi, madonna, amare,
e tutta mia speranza
in vostro piagimento;
ed eo non mi partiragio
da voi, donna valente,
ch'eo v'amo dolzemente,
e piace a voi ch'eo agia intendimento.
Valimento — mi date, donna fina,
chè lo meo core adesso a voi s'inchina.

> Since it pleases you, my love
> That I should write poems
> I will do everything I can
> To succeed in bringing you joy.
> My heart is devoted
> To loving you, milady,
> And all I hope for
> Is for your appreciation;
> I will not leave you, worthy lady.
> Because I love you sweetly
> And my aspiration pleases you.
> Give me strength, perfect woman,
> Because my heart now bows to you.

S'eo inchino, rason agio
di sì amoroso bene,
ch'eu spero, in voi sperando
ch' ancora creio avire
allegro meo coragio;
e tutta la mia spene,
ch'ò data in voi amando
ed in vostro piacire
ca veio li sembianti
di voi, chiarita spera,
ca spero gioia intera

ed ò fidanza ne lo meo servire
a piacire — di voi che siete fiore
sor l'altre donn'e avete più valore.

> If I bow down to you, it is with reason,
> Before such a loving woman
> That I await and hope for,
> And that I still have to achieve,
> But joyful is my courage.
> And all my hope
> Was devoted to loving you
> And pleasing you
> And I see your face, oh bright star,
> For I desire complete happiness
> And I trust in my ability to serve you in love,
> And to please you, who are much more beautiful
> Above all other women and you are more worthy than them.

Valor sor l'altre avete
e tutta caunoscenza,
ca null'omo porria
vostro pregio contare,
che tanto bella sete!
Secondo mia credenza
non è donna che sia
alta, sì bella, pare,
nè c'agia insegnamento
'nver voi, donna sovrana.
La vostra ciera umana
mi dà conforto e facemi alegrare:
s'eo pregiare — vi posso, donna mia,
più conto mi ne tegno tuttavia.

> You have more virtue than any other woman
> And you are full of wisdom,
> So much so that no man can
> Grasp the depth of it,
> Because you are so beautiful!
> I believe there is no other woman
> who equals you in beauty,
> nor anyone as intelligent
> compared to you, regal woman.
> Your kind human face

> Comforts me and makes me happy;
> If I were to praise you, oh perfect woman,
> I could always boast and be proud of it.

A tutt'or vegio e sento,
ed ònne gran ragione,
ch' amore mi consenti
voi, gentil criatura.
Già mai non n'ò abento,
vostra bella fazone
cotant' à valimenti.
Per vo'son fresco ognura;
a lo sole riguardo
lo vostro bello viso,
che m'à d'amore priso,
e tegnolomi in gran bonaventura.
Spreio à tuttura — chi al buon segnore crede
però son dato a la vostra merzede.

> I always see and feel,
> And with good reason,
> That Love makes me feel in touch
> With you, oh gentle woman.
> I am never at peace,
> Because of the strong virtue
> Emanating from your beautiful face.
> I am always calm for you:
> In the sunlight I see your beautiful face,
> Which has made me fall in love,
> And I keep it as a sign of good luck.
> He who trusts in a good lord is always hopeful:
> This is the reason why I trust in your mercy.

Merzé pietosa agiate
di meve, gentil cosa,
chè tutto il mio disio
e certo ben sacciate,
alente più che rosa,
che ciò ch'io più golio
è voi veder sovente,
la vostra dolze vista,
a cui sono ublicato,
core e corp' ò donato.

Allora ch'io vi vidi primamente,
mantenente — fui in vostro podere,
che altra donna mai non voglio avere.

> Have mercy
> on me, oh gentle lady,
> Because of all my desire.
> And you know very well,
> More fragrant than a rose,
> That what I most desire
> Is to see you often:
> It is for the sweet vision of you
> Before which I fade,
> That I have given up my heart and body.
> From the very first moment I saw you
> I suddenly fell under your power,
> for I don't ever wish to have another woman but you.

De la Mia Disïanza

De la mia disïanza
ch'ò penato ad avere,
mi fa sbaldire, poi ch'ì n'ò ragione,
chè m'à data fermanza
com'io possa compire lu meu placire,
senza ogne cagione,
a la stagione, ch'io l'averò 'n possanza.
Senza fallanza, voglion le persone,
per cui cagione, facciamò membranza.

> The object of my desire,
> For which I suffered to conquer,
> Makes me joyful now that I have reason to be so
> Because it assures me that I can carry out my pleasure
> Without any deceptive obstacle
> During the time I will have her in my power.
> Without any delay I want the person
> Of whom for now I dream about.

A tuttt'or membrando
de lo dolze diletto
ched'io aspetto, sonne alegro e gaudente.
Vaio tanto tardando,

chè'n paura mi metto
ed ò sospetto, de la mala gente,
che per neiente, vanno disturbando
e rampognando, chi ama lealemente;
und'io sovente, vado sospirando.

> I am constantly contemplating
> The sweet delight
> That awaits me. I am happy and content.
> If I continue to delay
> It is only because I am fearful
> And suspicious of those evil people,
> Who without any reason disturb
> And criticize those who truly love;
> And this often makes me suffer.

Sospiro e sto 'n rancura;
ch'io son sì disioso
e pauroso, mi fate penare.
M'a tanto m'asicura
lo suo viso amoroso,
e lo gioioso, riso e lo sguardare
e lo parlare, di quella criatura,
che per paura, mi face penare
e dimorare, tant'è fine e pura.

> I suffer and feel afflicted
> For having this strong desire
> And with fear they make me suffer.
> But that is when I find reassurance
> Thanks to her loving face,
> And the joyous laughter and the way she looks at me
> And the manner of speech of that good woman,
> Thus I am afraid to suffer and to be doubtful
> And to delay; she is so perfect and pure.

Tanto è sagia e cortise,
no credo che pensasse,
nè distornasse, di ciò che m'à impromiso.
Da la ria gente aprise
da lor non si stornasse,
che mi tornasse, a danno chi gli ò ofiso,
e ben mi à miso
in foco, ciò m'è aviso,

che lo bel viso, lo cor m'adivise.

> She is so wise and courteous,
> That I cannot even contemplate her changing her mind
> Nor pulling back from what she promised me.
> Evil people's behavior has made her understand
> Not to be lured by their ideas,
> As to avoid being hurt by those who I offended,
> And this has made me happy,
> On fire, it seems to me,
> That her lovely face has divided my heart.

Diviso m'à lo core
e lo corpo à 'n balia,
e tienmi e mi lia, forte incatenato.
La fiore d'ogne fiore
prego per cortesia,
che più non sia, lo suo detto fallato,
nè disturbato, per inizadore,
nè suo valore, non sia menovato,
nè rabassato, per altro amadore.

> My heart is divided
> And my body has power over it,
> It holds me and bonds me tightly in chains.
> The most beautiful flower above all others
> I pray, in all kindness,
> That her words will never again be lies,
> Nor that they will ever again be disturbed
> By those who sow discord,
> Nor that her worthiness will ever be lost,
> Or diminished by another lover.

Dolze Meo Drudo, e Vatène

Dolze meo drudo, e vatène!
Meo sire, a Dio t'acomano,
ché ti diparti da mene
ed eo tapina rimanno.

> My sweet lover, begone!
> Milord, I entrust you to God
> from the moment you leave me
> and I, in misery, remain here.

SICILIAN QUEENSHIP

Lassa, la vita m'è noia,
dolze la morte a vedere,
ch'io non penso mai guerire
membrandome fuor di gioia.
Membrandome che te'n vai,

> Oh, life for me is misery,
> death seems a liberation,
> for I believe there is no cure for me
> as I think of myself deprived of joy,

Lo cor mi mena gran guerra;
di ciò che più disïai
mi tolle lontana terra.
Or se ne va lo mio amore
ch'io sovra gli altri l'amava.

> Just thinking of you leaving me
> makes my heart fight against me.
> A faraway land deprives
> me of what I most desire.
> The love I cherished
> above all others has abandoned me.

Biasmomi de la Toscana,
ch'è mi diparte lo core.
Dolce mia donna, lo gire
non è per mia volontate,
ché mi convene ubidire
quelli che m'ha'n potestate.

> I curse Tuscany,
> who has stolen my heart.
> My sweet lady, my departure
> is not by my own choice,
> but I must obey
> who has power over me.

Or ti conforta s'io vado,
e già non ti dismagare,
ca per null'altra d'amare,
amor, te non falseraggio.

> Now be brave even as we part,
> and don't lose faith,
> for I shall never betray you,
> my love, for another.

Lo vostro amore mi tene
ed hami in sua segnoria,
ca lealmente m'avene
d'amar voi sanza falsìa.
Di me vi sia rimembranza,

> Your love holds me
> under your dominance,
> and keeps me faithful to love
> you without deceit.
> Remember me.

E non mi aggiate 'n obria,
c'avete in vostra balia
tutta la mia disïanza.
Dolze mia donna, 'l commiato
domando sanza tenore,

> And don't forget me,
> for you have in your power
> all of my desires.
> My sweet lady, I pray
> that you bid me farewell
> without further delay,

che vi sia racomandato,
ché con voi riman mio core.
Cotal è la 'namoranza
degli amorosi piaceri,
che non mi posso partire
da voi, mia donna, in lleanza.

> as I commend to you my heart
> so that it remains with you.
> So pleasing is the memory
> of our time together that in perfect faith,
> I cannot truly leave you, my lady.

Per la Fera Membranza

Per la fera membranza,
de lo mio gran disio
malamente fallio
che mi fece partire e dipartire
la gran gioia ch'avea;

SICILIAN QUEENSHIP

ma senza dubitanza
lo meo signor sentio,
alorché mi partio
del mio pregio gradire
che fallire, non vol né non porea;
e non comportaria
la mia pena sapesse,
che tanto mi stringesse
quanto temesse, de la vita mia.
Per che si converria
che tal gioia si desse,
che, s'altri l'aprendesse,
dir no 'l potesse, ch'eli sofferia.

> For the tormented memory
> Of my intense desire
> A grave error was made
> That made me leave
> And separate from the intense joy that I felt;
> But without a doubt, when I left
> I felt that my lord
> Appreciated my worthiness
> As he would never and could never be mistaken;
> And he would not allow
> Me to suffer if he knew
> That this saddens me so much
> As to fear for my life.
> So it may be better
> For someone to give me such joy,
> So that if someone were to learn of it
> They would not mention it due to envy.

Farò come l'ausello
quand'altre lo distene,
che vive ne la spene
la quale à ne lo core,
e no more, sperando di campare;
e aspettando quello
viveraggio con pene,
ch'io non credo aver bene
tant'è lo fino amore
e lo grande ardore, ch'aggio di tornare

a voi, donn' ad amare
di tutte giò compita,
ch'avete la mia vita
di giò partita, e da ralegranza;
e mille anni mi pare
che fu la dipartita,
e parmi la redita
quasi fallita, per la disïanza.

> I will be like a bird
> Held as a prisoner,
> Living for the sole hope
> That it keeps in its heart.
> It does not die hoping to survive;
> And anticipating
> That way of living whilst suffering,
> But I don't believe I have a like virtue.
> For my love is so precious
> And my desire to return to you is so strong,
> Oh loving woman, endowed with joy,
> You have taken away from my life
> Joy and happiness;
> And it seems to me that a thousand years
> Have passed since I left,
> And it seems to me that my return
> Has failed because of my desire.

NOTES

1. This chapter is merely an introduction with a few essential translations. A great deal has been written about the Sicilian School and the role of Frederick II as its patron. As a starting point, the reader is referred to the following: Jensen, Frede, *The Poetry of the Sicilian School* (1986); Langley, Ernest, *The Poetry of Giacomo da Lentini* (1915); Lansing, Richard, *The Complete Poetry of Giacomo da Lentini* (2018); Mallette, Karla, *The Kingdom of Sicily 1100-1250: A Literary History* (2005); Mangieri, Cono Antonio, *Il Contrasto di Cielo d'Alcamo: Introduzione, testo manoscritto e diplomatico, testo critico-congetturale, traduzione e note* (2005); Panvini, Bruno, *Le Rime della Scuola Siciliana,* volume 1 (1962); Di Girolamo, Costanzo, et al., *Poeti della Corte di Federico II,* volume 2 in the series *I Poeti della Scuola Siciliana* (2008). The *Contrasto* of Cielo of Alcamo appears with a translation in *Queens of Sicily,* pages 549-565. See also note 11.

2. This language survives in its modern form as Maltese. See Agius, Dionisius, *Siculo Arabic* (1996).

3. For the development of Norman French, see Jones, Mari, *Variation and Change in Mainland and Insular Norman* (2014). For its use in England, see Ingham, Richard, et al., *The Anglo-Norman Language and its Contexts* (2010).

4. Reported in the chronicle of Godfrey Malaterra, chapter 29; translation by the author.

5. The Sicilian language is another topic about which much has been written in recent decades, albeit mostly in Italian. For Medieval ("Middle") Sicilian: Sottile, Roberto, *L'Atlante Linguistico della Sicilia* (2019); Sucato, Ignazio, *La Lingua Siciliana: Origine e Storia* (1975). For Modern Sicilian: Bellestri, Joseph, *English-Sicilian Dictionary* (1988); Bonner, Kirk, and Cipolla, Gaetano, *Introduction to Sicilian Grammar* (2001); Cipolla, Gaetano, *Learn Sicilian* (2013); Varvaro, Alberto, *Vocabolario Storico-Etimologico del Siciliano* (2014).

6. For a good discussion see Maggiorella, Antonia, *Il Principe Poeta: Manfredi di Svevia* (2005).

7. For a fine commentary on this poem, see Mallette, Karla, op.cit., pages 90-91, 177-178.

8. For the Sicilian text with an English translation and notes, see Mendola, Louis, *Sicily's Rebellion against King Charles: The Story of the Sicilian Vespers* (2015).

9. Ibid, pages 128, 205.

10. The manuscript (IV.H.14) is conserved in the Sicilian Regional Library in Palermo; see also Marinoni, Augusto, *Dal Declarus di Angelo Senisio: I Vocaboli Siciliani* (1955).

11. For a detailed analaysis of the poems of Frederick II, citing the contributions

of various scholars, see *I Poeti della Scuola Siciliana* (op.cit. supra), volume 2, chapter 14 (by Stefano Rapisarda), pages 439-494. There have been many papers and opinions published on the topic over the last century; see, for example, Thornton, Hermann, "The Poems Ascribed to Frederick II 'Rex Fredericis' and King Enzio," *Speculum,* volume 2, number 4 (October 1927), pages 463-469, and "The Poems Ascribed to Frederick II and Rex Fredericis," *Speculum,* volume 1, number 1 (January 1926), pages 87-100.

Poetry in the manuscript indicating Frederick II as the author of a poem on this folio

Courtesy Vatican Apostolic Library

Livauṣi misser palmeri abbati & dissi
signuri Re laudatu sia deu & ben
chi esti vinutu e ffactu n'tu intendimentu
p'vostra bontati e quilla di misser iohanni
di prochita sipo v'plaza chi quista cosa
asa bon mezu e boniu fini si comu a'vuitu
boniu in comezamentu ma ben virtia ki
omi fussimu vinutu cum plui genti ch
silu Re carlu di pon son p'tucta la ysola di
sichilia luquali ani ben gradichi milia
homini accavallu seki nui auitimu t'p'pu
affari accumbactiri cum ipsu et sipero mi
pari ki penzamu di vinciri plui agenti di
quali partikamiri sindi p'utissi sipo eu
cosyu ki missima sia p'duta tantu ora
ristricta et in succareu di vidanda.

Quandu lu Re di aragona audiu q'sti
paroli si appi grandi dubitanza
audendu ch lu Re carlu amia tantu pu
titi et in continenti madau dicen p'
li sula di sichilia ch si R carlu vinissi

Rivelo che fa M.ro Vincenzo Cipriano figlio delli quondam M.ro Oragio e Giovanna di questa Terra di Petralia Sott.na nell'Officio del Mag.co Cont.e D. Gasparre Gatto, giusto in.a di bando promulgato, oggi li 7 Marzo 1756

Anime

M: C: M.ro Vincenzo Cipriano d'anni 43 —
F: Serafina moglie
M: Antonino figlio d'anni 17

Beni Stabili

Possiede una casa in questa Terra e g.ta del Casale consistente d'una stanza solam.te confine la casa di D. Carmelo Calascibetta e la casa di Jacob Ferrara, Stefano che troviamo la rela.ne dell'Esperti e valutata ~~per tarì duodeci ann. che al sette~~ ~~cento donano il Capitale d'onze cinque et un tarì uno~~   10 — 21 —

Esiste in d.a Casa un magazeno che secondo la rela.ne dell'Esperti è valutato per tarì due ann: che al sette per cento importano tarì uno otto   — 28 —

Beni Stab. Innur.ti   6 — 19 —

          10 : 28

Beni Mobili

Tiene sud.o un Cavallo Merlino che secondo l'esti= mo dell'Esperti è valutato per onze cinque   5 —

Più Terre seminate in Trum.o tumuli tre nel feudo di Mandanici sovrani di questo Stato che valutato a ragione d'onze sei ultima secondo la rela.ne ingon= ta onza una, e tarì quattro   1 — 4 —

Beni Mobili Innur.ti   6 — 4

Rivelo (tax census) of 1756 recorded in Sicilian and Tuscan

Chapter 8
MARGARET'S MATRONAGE

What moves a woman to build a cathedral?

In medieval Europe, her motivation was rooted in the concept of royal patronage, one of the phenomena that, in a much later age, gave rise to the principle of *noblesse oblige*. By definition, royal patronage was the establishment, endowment or explicit protection of abbeys, monasteries or other religious communities. Much land, and a significant segment of the populace, fell under the more-or-less direct domain of the church, and this is a vast topic about which entire volumes have been written.[1] In southern Italy during the Norman period, the very concept of patronage was concerned principally with Latin foundations, even if our counts and kings occasionally lent their support to Greek churches, whilst protecting Jewish communities and their synagogues. At Lucera, an entire town founded, arguably, on the principle of royal patronage, Frederick II was the protector of the kingdom's last Muslims.

In all of this, it should not be forgotten that places of worship embody the power of God and the identity of a people.

While royal patronage might help to pave a monarch's path to heaven, in the earthly realm it was, more immediately, a sign of power. Battlefield victories may be forgotten; cathedrals were meant to last forever. Life was ephemeral; souls were eternal.

We find ladies mentioned in connection with churches from the very beginning of the Norman era, though not always as patrons. The name of Sichelgaita of Salerno appears in the inscription dedicating the church of Saint Peter *la Bagnara* near Palermo's sea castle in 1081 not because she was its benefactor (who was a Greek priest named Nicholas) but because she was the consort of Robert Guiscard. (Though this church, formerly Saints Peter and Paul, was destroyed during the Allied bombings of 1943, the Greek inscription, shown at the end of Chapter 3, was restored and is conserved in the regional art museum at Palazzo Abatellis in Palermo.)

While our queens — as needs be — might be called upon by circumstance to remove an adversary (see Chapter 1) or suppress a few unruly barons, a duty that fell upon the shoulders of the widowed Adelaide as countess regent, none ever declared an actual war.[2] Reginal patronage reflected their use of "soft" power.

Adelaide's early efforts overshadowed those of the other women. As regent for her young sons for a decade from 1101, she famously lent her patronage (or matronage) to a number of abbeys in Sicily and Calabria.[3] Adelaide, who rests at Patti, where she endowed an abbey, was the third wife of Roger I and the mother of Roger II. After Roger I died, leaving two sons, namely Simon (who died in 1105) and the future King Roger II, she effectively ruled Sicily until around 1111.

Other countesses and queens of Sicily also supported abbeys and churches. To cite just a few specific examples, Judith of Evreux endowed her brother's abbey at Saint Euphemia in Calabria and Constance Hauteville founded Saint John's Abbey at Fiore in the Sila Mountains, later endowed by her daughter-in-law, Constance of Aragon. Sibylla of Acerra and her consort, Tancred, were patrons of Saints Nicholas and

Catald at Lecce. Elisabeth of Bavaria endowed Saint Mary (a Carmelite basilica) in Naples in memory of her fallen son, Conradin, and, with her second husband, the Cistercian monastery at Stams in Tyrol.

Many of these foundations no longer exist even in name, having fallen to ruin centuries ago; a fair number have been destroyed by earthquakes.[4] Even the most important abbeys in the kingdom, such as Cava, though under papal jurisdiction, might benefit from royal largesse from time to time. Yet neither Cava nor Cassino was founded by a monarch but by a saintly abbot, namely Alferio of Salerno and, in the case of the latter, by Benedict himself.

Each religious order had its moment of glory, and for the Benedictines it would prove to be a rather long moment in the Sicilian sun. By the time Margaret became regent upon the death of her husband, the kingdom was dotted with Benedictine abbeys, including Saint John of the Hermits, just a few steps from the royal palace in Palermo.

If we seek a singular, imposing benefice that epitomizes the favor of a medieval Sicilian queen, it is Monreale Abbey. Indeed, one might go so far as to suggest that familiarity with this place is a necessary key to understanding the intricate social, juridical and cultural rapport amongst the Sicilian monarchs, their subjects, and the papacy. Nothing in chronicles, letters and charters can prepare any scholar for what confronts her in this unique monastic complex, where Komnenian, Norman, Fatimid and Provençal art come together in a syncretic moment that transcends any single work or movement. It is here that one encounters the quintessential spirit of Sicily's greatest medieval queen.

Invisible Hand

The planning and construction of Monreale's church and

cloister began not long after the end of Margaret's tumultuous regency of William II. This period found her efforts directed toward the abbey at Maniace and a nunnery outside San Marco d'Alunzio.

Such objectives were hardly unique to our Sicilian queens during this period. Sancha of Castile founded Santa María de Sigena in Aragon in 1183, and her daughter, Constance, resided there before marrying Frederick II. Although she did not herself found Fontevrault, Eleanor of Aquitaine was a notable benefactress and, in death, so was her daughter, Joanna, widow of William II of Sicily and then wife of Raymond VI of Toulouse. Joanna's sister, Leonor (Eleanor) of England, founded Santa María la Real de las Huelgas with her husband, Alfonso VIII of Castile, in 1187. To the east, Melisende of Jerusalem, who was descended from the same dynasty as Beatrice of Rethel, the third wife of Roger II, founded and endowed the Benedictine convent of Saints Mary and Martha at Bethany (now Al-Eizariya) near the tomb of Saint Lazarus; she died there in 1161.[5] Margaret's Jiménez kinswoman, Urraca "the Reckless" of León and Castile, was a patron of the Basilica of San Isidore in León. Margaret thus stood in good company.[6]

Her most personal model, albeit a woman she barely knew, was her own mother, Margaret of l'Aigle, whose name appears in a charter of 1135 confirming certain privileges to the Diocese of Pamplona.[7] As Queen of Pamplona, the elder Margaret may also have been involved with the initial reconstruction of its castle, of which little remains (it is now an archive), a necessary effort as the structure was dilapidated when she and her husband arrived there with their three young children. Under Sancho VI of Navarre there was a further expansion (see the photograph).

We know of our Margaret referring to her mother on only one public occasion, when Stephen of Perche arrived at court (see Chapter 2).

It is interesting to speculate that Margaret and her son may have contemplated Monreale before the young king reached the age of majority. If, indeed, Monreale reflected, amongst nobler motives, William's rebellion against the yoke of Archbishop Walter of Palermo, his onetime tutor, either the king or his mother may have already been thinking about it. Certainly, Walter's machinations, first against William I during the Bonello revolt and then against Margaret's cousin Stephen of Perche, could not have endeared the archbishop to her.

Wiley Walter wanted a new cathedral in Palermo. The petulant prelate was destined to get what he desired, but only over Margaret's dead body.[8]

In the years after her regency, we find Margaret issuing decrees in her own name relative to foundations at Maniace and elsewhere in northeastern Sicily.[9] By that time, she was sometimes using San Marco d'Alunzio, the Hauteville castle from whence Adelaide, as regent, had occasionally issued charters, as her base, perhaps during the warmer months of some years. There, and at Palermo, she was likely in close contact with another queen, the widowed Beatrice of Rethel, but we have no explicit records to provide us with exact details of this relationship.

In this connection, it is remarkable that, by 1177, there were four once-and-future queens living in Sicily. Margaret, formerly regent, was now queen mother. Beatrice was queen dowager. Joanna was queen consort. Constance was destined to become queen regnant (or the nearest thing to such a queen in Sicily). It was a unique moment for queenhood in the medieval history of the *Regnum Siciliae*.

Little is known of these four strong women at that specific moment, but their presence represented a reginal nexus virtually unknown in Europe during this decade, for while three or four queens might occasionally be present in one place, it was rare to find them residing in the same place, and possibly in the same city, for years.

By the time he wed Joanna, William had no surviving brothers, and though his bastard kinsman, Tancred of Lecce, had been rehabilitated, there was a dearth of Hauteville men at court.

Margaret's name is not given as the issuer of any known decree involving the building of Monreale or establishment of its Benedictine community. This is reasonable, both socially and juridically, for while Maniace, though an abbey (rather than a simple monastery), was small and geographically isolated, Monreale, from the outset, was to be large and very visible, literally standing guard over Palermo. There was a garrisoned castle dedicated to Saint Benedict, now called *Castellaccio*, on the mountain overlooking Monreale itself (the fortress is visible from the Porta Felice gate near the Palermitan coast), to remind the Muslims on the other side that the erstwhile emirate was now a Christian kingdom. The abbey itself, visible from the city below, was surrounded by walls with embattled towers, and the church had two stout, crenelated towers of its own. Here was the ultimate symbol of royal power and patronage, but, apart from its obvious purpose as a religious community, it was not meant to show the personal power of the queen mother. Rather, this was intended as a symbol of the authority and independence of Sicily's third king, the son whom Margaret had raised, and whose birthright she had adamantly defended for five years.

It was more than a gesture.

What was Margaret's precise role in the development of Monreale? William II reached the age of majority at the very end of 1171, and Margaret founded the abbey at Maniace the next year. That her name does not appear in any charters relevant to Monreale is not unusual; even certain charters issued in her son's name during his minority do not mention her. Therefore, the simple answer is that we do not know the exact details of her involvement besides her encouragement.

The architecture and art of Monreale were actually very different from Maniace, and altogether more complex. It is, however, quite similar to Cefalù's cathedral and cloister, which were erected four decades earlier, in 1131, as a sign of the power of Margaret's father-in-law, Roger II. Indeed, his grandfather's foundation of Cefalù's cathedral may well have inspired William II to make his own mark.

Unlike most foundations, Monreale had a second queenly patron, Joanna of England. Although Thomas Becket was already widely venerated before Joanna's arrival in Palermo early in 1177, it may have been her devotion that prompted the "writing" of a mosaic icon of him in the church's apse. Significantly, he is the only saint represented here who is not also venerated in the Orthodox Church.

The mosaics were not the only Byzantine touch. The Greek mosaicists also created an iconostasis, whilst the architects ensured that the apse faced east in the Greek manner even though the long nave was essentially Latin in design. The exterior of the apse was decorated in typical Fatimid geometry reflecting Islamic spirituality.

If Monreale was an exercise in defiance against nasty Archbishop Walter, that was hardly its only statement. While the burgeoning Gothic movement was redefining ecclesial architecture across western Europe, Monreale's cathedral was conceived as an expression of the cultures of the Kingdom of Sicily consecrated to the glory of the Divine Maker in one place. Here, in one of Europe's most important realms, was proof that the Romanesque was not dead. Gargoyles and grotesques would have to content themselves in other dominions.

The erection of Monreale begs comparison to other churches in southern Italy. Architecturally, Cefalù's cathedral and abbey are very similar. There an early benefactress was another woman connected to the royal family, Lucy of Cammarata, whom we met in Chapter 3. More generally, it was not unusual for a baron and his wife to support a local church or monastery.

Monreale was not only an abbey and church but the manifestation of identity and power, both Margaret's and William's. For several centuries before the equally impressive (but far smaller) Palatine Chapel was open to the public, Monreale stood as a tangible reminder to Sicilians of our Byzantine, Norman and Fatimid heritage in the face of the onslaught by Baroque and Rococo architecture.

Upon its completion, it became the largest cathedral, and one of the largest monastic communities, in the Kingdom of Sicily (it should be remembered that Cassino was on the other side of the border in papal territory). By 1190, with both Margaret and William gone, Palermo's new cathedral supplanted Monreale as the largest church in the kingdom, eclipsing it in size but never in sophistication. It had no cloister, and over the centuries its interior was gutted and modified while Monreale was untouched and unscathed except for the fire that destroyed its original ceiling and, sadly, Margaret's original tomb. Monreale's monks are gone, and their refectory is now a museum.

Details

One of the peaks overlooking the Genoard park to the immediate south of Palermo has come to be called *Mount Caputo*. Except perhaps for a tiny Arab village, the mountain seems to have been uninhabited until 1172.[10] Favored for its hunting, it afforded the visitor a commanding view of the city, the royal hunting grounds and the Genoard park. The site was known for its springs.

Margaret loved such places so much that she was already undertaking the construction of an abbey at Maniace (already mentioned) on the site of a dilapidated Greek monastery.[11]

With royal involvement, the place was renamed, appropriately enough, *Mons Regalis,* "Royal Mountain." It soon came to be called *Monreale*. Mother and son planned to erect Sicily's most beautiful church on this spot, along with the island's largest monastery and a walled town.[12] An imposing castle (noted earlier) was already being built on the rocky summit overlooking the church.

The planning of such a project could not be kept secret for very long. Walter, the Archbishop of Palermo, was much chagrined to hear about it.[13] In a time when tangible symbols were the most salient, Monreale was a royal reproach, a sign that Walter's power was on the wane.

Writing long afterward, the chronicler Richard of San Germano believed that the construction of the abbey church at Monreale was suggested to the king by Matthew of Aiello. He tells us that Matthew despised Walter, and vice versa, yet the two *familiares* behaved amicably toward each other in public. He goes on to report that Monreale reflected a certain diminution of Walter's effective power.[14] Not surprisingly, the chronicler overlooks Margaret's influence and, for that matter, William's role.[15]

Yet Peter of Blois, another former tutor of the young king, seems to have surmised William's intention to distance himself from Walter upon reaching the age of majority, if not earlier. This the monarch did by interrupting his formal studies as soon as he could.

Peter later exploited this fact to compare William II of Sicily unfavorably to a much older Henry II of England: "Although your king has studied well, ours is far more learned. In fact, I have had the chance to assess the practical education of both monarchs. As you know, the King of Sicily was my pupil for a year, having already studied with you to acquire a knowledge of general studies and literature. He was able to benefit from my special efforts to motivate him, but as soon as I departed from the kingdom he fell into the habit of reading frivolous books and enjoying royal pleasures."[16]

There may be some truth in this. Few sovereigns were as erudite as Henry. However, Peter may have overlooked, or chosen not to see, William's quest for autonomy.

Although the King of Sicily and his guests could stay at the castle above Monreale, there would also be a comfortable palace on the north side of the church's apse (what remains of this edifice is now part of the city hall). From the highest floor of the palace, the royal family could see Palermo, just a short ride away, yet enjoy the privilege of being, quite literally, above the fray whose petty intrigues infested the court in the city far below. Margaret appreciated this, and so did William, who had been raised amidst a succession of troublesome plots.

From the outset, Monreale Abbey, officially "New Saint Mary's," was intended to be part of a vast monastic complex of the Benedictines, far larger than Saint John of the Hermits. The monks of Cava, near Salerno, were happy to oblige the king by sending some of their number to Monreale.

By longstanding tradition, major Benedictine abbeys like Cassino and Cava were autonomous, answering, through their order's hierarchy, to the pope himself. Local diocesan bishops had little say in monastic administration. Pope Alexander III (Roland of Siena) granted Monreale's Benedictines a similar privilege.[17] This meant that they were outside Walter's jurisdiction. All he could do was watch as the new church took shape.

King William endowed the monastery with extensive lands and towns populated largely by Arabs: Corleone, Jato, Partinico, Battallario, Calatrasi.[18] The Arabs' villages bore names like *Rahal Algalid* and *Menzil Zarsun*. This was a vast, fertile territory bordering the Archdiocese of Palermo. No wonder Walter was distressed.

In aggregating these estates for the Benedictines and removing Monreale from Palermo's ecclesiastical authority, was the hand of Margaret at work, snatching power from Walter's grasp just as he had tried to wrest it from hers? The possibility cannot be ruled out. If not vindictive, the queen was certainly shrewd. It was a trait acquired through her experience with jackals.

With papal and royal approval, the abbot of Monreale gradually obtained authority over numerous monastic estates in Sicily, such as those Margaret founded around Maniace, and some in regions as far afield as Apulia.

The construction of the town, the hilltop castle, the royal palace and the walls encircling the abbey seems to have been initiated in 1172, but two years were to pass before work began on the church and monastery following papal approval for the project.

The greater part of the church's stout superstructure was completed by 1180. Although a Gothic cathedral of comparable size might take decades to build, a church like Monreale's could be completed in less time so long as the work went uninterrupted and there were enough men assigned to the project.

It would be another few years before the mosaics in the church and the columns in the cloister were completed.

Building such a monument required a monumental effort. What follows is a very concise overview (maps follow the text of this chapter).

The Church

Whether one refers to it as a basilica, *duomo* or cathedral, the church around which Monreale was built is impressive. The layout is a classic cross plan with a transept. The two massive towers were meant to serve as fortifications. The floor area measures slightly over four thousand square meters (more than forty thousand square feet), the nave being just over a hundred meters (at three hundred thirty feet) in length.

The nave is positioned generally, though not precisely, on an east-west axis *ad orientem,* with the apse toward the east. This tradition dates from the early centuries of the church in Greece and elsewhere in Europe. In former times, the celebrant faced the altar and apse during liturgy; this is still true in Orthodoxy, and it was the case in Catholicism until the twentieth century, when altars were positioned so that the priest faced the congregants.

There was initially a Byzantine *templon,* essentially a low iconostasis (icon screen), separating the sanctuary from the nave.

Inside the church is a wide central aisle between two narrower ones, for a total nave width of forty meters. Eighteen columns support the arches. These pillars were not built for the church; they were taken from a temple in Rome, and many of their capitals bear the likeness of Roma, one of that city's deities.[19] Most of the columns are made of syenite, an igneous rock very similar to granite but bereft of more than rare traces of quartz. It takes its name from Syene (Aswan) on the Nile, where the Romans quarried it.

The church's wooden roof replaces the one destroyed by fire in 1811. The original ceiling had muqarnas "stalactites" similar to those of the chapel in the palace in Palermo.

An interesting detail is the occasional use of *strata* of timber between some of the large stones of which the thick walls are constructed; this serves as a soft buffer to absorb seismic shock that creates fissures during earthquakes.

Among the distinctively Arab features are the geometric motifs of the exterior of the three apses, typical of Fatimid designs.

The Mosaics

What most strikes the visitor are the walls covered with

mosaics set upon an endless field of gold tesserae. At six thousand three hundred and forty square meters (nearly seventy thousand square feet), thus eclipsing the wall area of the mosaics of Saint Mark's in Venice by around thirty percent, this is the largest medieval display of its kind in Italy. It was inspired by the mosaics of the Palatine Chapel in Palermo.

Many figures are icons, while others are Biblical scenes. The Old Testament is depicted on the walls of the central aisle. The mosaics of the lateral aisles and those above the sanctuary depict the New Testament. Some are accompanied by inscriptions in Latin or Greek.

As stated earlier, all the saints but one are venerated in the Orthodox church. The lone exception is Thomas Becket, depicted in the central apse; this is the earliest public image of Saint Thomas of Canterbury.

Overlooking the royal thrones in the presbytery, one mosaic shows King William II offering the church to the Virgin Mary, while another shows the same king being crowned by Christ, recalling the mosaic in Palermo's Martorana depicting Roger II receiving the crown from Jesus; here the symbols on his robe are clearly crosses (see the heraldry chapter). The two lions *passant guardant* facing each other in the triangular mosaic immediately above the royal throne on the north wall resemble the heraldic beasts in the royal coat of arms of England (displayed by English kings beginning with Richard Lionheart) and the lions flanking the royal throne dais in the Palatine Chapel in Palermo's Norman Palace, repeated in a motif of the exterior of the apse of that city's cathedral.

Dominating everything is the imposing icon of Christ Pantocrator, "Ruler of All," looking down from high in the central apse above the main altar. At thirteen meters wide and seven meters high, this is thought to be the largest medieval image of the Pantocrator to survive. Indeed, the extent of Monreale's mosaics dwarfs that of any similar display that survives from the Middle Ages in what was once the Byzantine world. Beneath the Pantocrator is the Theotokos, the Mother of God; below this is a window of fine Fatimid design.

Begun in 1180, the mosaic work took about a decade to complete.

The Cloister

If Monreale's mosaics leave an impression, so does its large cloister. The colonnade is formed of two hundred twenty-eight pillars, most in pairs.

The Fatimid fountain in one corner is very similar to the one in Palazzo Falson in Mdina, Malta. The water spouts from the faces of men and lions carved in relief into a sphere set upon a column of zigzag motifs. When the water spurts out, the fountain's ensemble gives the appearance of a palm tree, representing life. The fountain was probably intended to be placed in the center of the cloister in representation of the spring of eternal life in the garden of paradise of all three Abrahamic faiths.

Most of the cloister and its decoration are essentially Provençal in style. Some of the same artisans carved similar capitals at Maniace and elsewhere. The columns and capitals in Cefalù's cloister are quite similar.

The columns were carved by a number of sculptors working under a few masters who seem to have been Provençal, Greek, Norman and Lombard (northern Italian). This explains the widely varying styles, themes and symbolism, from Biblical and mythological scenes and figures to representations of kings, Norman knights and Arab warriors.

There are archers, lions, mermen, boars, and Norman knights bearing long shields devoid of heraldic devices.[20] The Arab warriors are depicted holding round shields. Also present are owls with monks' heads representing vigilance. There are grapes representing autumn and even the depiction of blowing leaves. One scene shows lions devouring men and stags. The double-tailed mermaid sitting among the evangelists and their symbols is Melusina, whose legend was popular in northern Europe. Along the eastern colonnade is a capital showing William II offering the cathedral to the Blessed Virgin Mary and Baby Jesus.

A few capitals are particularly informative about aristocratic life. Though we have no written record detailing tournaments involving participation of a "Sicilian William Marshal," the jousting knights suggest that such things existed here in the Kingdom of Sicily, as in England and France.

The columns themselves vary in design superficially. Some bear sculpted motifs while others are decorated in patterns with mosaic tiles. The alternating pairing of smooth and decorated columns was meant to create a subliminal sense of endless movement linked to the infinity of God or Allah.

Bordering the cloister are a refectory and dormitory. Beyond these is a large courtyard, the *belvedere,* from which the entire Gulf of Palermo is visible, as well as the mountains to the south where the smallholdings of the Arabs were located.

The Royal Tombs

Queen Margaret and two of her sons, Roger and Henry, whose remains were transferred from Mary Magdalene in Palermo, rest in the north semitransept. In the opposite (south) semitransept are the two Williams.[21]

Margaret's original sarcophagus was porphyry, which preserved her body remarkably well until 1811, when lightning struck the cathedral's wooden roof, setting off a fire. Fed by the resinous Nebrodian fir (a timber harvested in Sicily) of which the ceiling was constructed, the flames severely damaged her tomb and those of her sons Roger and Henry. The queen's remains were subsequently placed into a sarcophagus constructed in 1846 modelled on the original one but made of marble. An epitaph in mosaic (see the photograph) appears in the wall above the tomb.

A curious detail is the altar near Margaret's tomb dedicated to King Louis IX of France, who died whilst crusading in Tunisia. A reliquary preserves his heart and viscera, translated here in 1270 by his brother, Charles, who was then King of Sicily, as part of an effort to gain favor with the Sicilians just a few years after defeating Manfred and Conradin, who had enjoyed the islanders' support.[22] This is an example of royal patronage by the dynasty that succeeded the Hohenstaufens.

Bronze Doors

Two impressive sets of bronze double doors bearing panels depicting biblical scenes grace the church. Forged in 1186, the doors beneath the main portico at the end of the nave are by Bonanno "Pisano" of Pisa, architect of his city's leaning tower. The pair of Byzantine design under the north portico is the work of Barisano of Trani. Similar bronze doors designed by both sculptors are conserved in churches elsewhere in Italy.

What one finds at Monreale transcends any single work of art. Here Margaret and her son fashioned part of the Kingdom of Sicily into a piece of the Kingdom of Heaven.

Matronage Beyond Monreale

By early 1178, a number of Margaret's projects were nearing completion. An impressive church, dedicated to the Holy Spirit, was being erected outside Palermo's city walls near the Oreto River.[23] It was given to the Cistercians[24] but assigned to the episcopal jurisdiction of Archbishop Walter, perhaps as something of a consolation to him for the lack of a new cathedral in Palermo. Indeed, Walter was showing himself to be uncharacteristically cooperative in order that he might obtain royal support for the grand church he envisaged; he even conceded some additional rights to Monreale's abbot.[25]

In addition to recent foundations, the crown supported a number of existing monasteries. Amongst the Benedictine abbeys outside local episcopal jurisdiction was one in Calabria where the poet William of Blois[26] had once been the abbot.[27] Unlike his brother, the royal tutor Peter of Blois, he had decided to remain in the kingdom for some time following the departure of Stephen of Perche. At his brother's urging, William finally returned to his native France. Peter eventually ended up in the service of Eleanor of Aquitaine.

By 1178, Maniace boasted a thriving religious community. Besides Maniace, Margaret patronized the abbey of Saint Philip of Fragalà, near Frazzanò. Like Maniace, it was built on the site of a Greek monastery.

Legacy

Would that more were known of the details of Margaret's role in the foundation of Monreale. No relevant correspondence of hers survives that elucidates the matter further than what we know. Presuming her frequent presence in the capital, such letters might not even be necessary, for she could easily meet with her son and his architects when needed. She may have chosen to reside at Monreale, rather than Palermo or San Marco d'Alunzio, for long periods after 1172.

Margaret's involvement is readily deduced by the conditions affecting her son and his dynasty. By 1174, with work on the complex beginning, William had no close kin to speak of except for his mother and his aunt, Constance. It is logical that he would still turn for counsel to Margaret, who, amongst other efforts, was trying to arrange a marriage for him.

Even though he probably looked to his counsellors and his mother for advice, William, at twenty, was no longer a mere boy. Much as we may ascribe many of the efforts at Monreale to Margaret, we must not overlook the king's role. Nevertheless, monarchical rule was "collective" in significant ways, and excluding the queen and courtiers from any consideration of it would be inappropriate.[28]

Work on the mosaics continued after Margaret's death in 1183, when her daughter-in-law, Joanna, may have assumed a greater role in the project, thus encouraging the creation of the icon of Thomas Becket. The fact of Margaret's sepulture at Monreale is itself emblematic of the connection the queen felt to this church.

Much remains shrouded in mystery. Though three of Margaret's sons rest with her in Monreale, the fate of several other royal tombs once housed in the church of Mary Magdalene, near Palermo's royal palace, is unknown. This includes the tomb of Beatrice of Rethel, who died in 1185, though her remains may have been transferred to the church's crypt; this edifice was much altered over the centuries.

Nor do we know much of the rapport between Margaret and her husband, William I, who is entombed at Monreale. Was it her decision to bring him there?

Romuald of Salerno and his fellow Salernitan, Matthew of Aiello, who seem to have shared Margaret's suspicion of Archbishop Walter, may well have encouraged the foundation of Monreale. Both were benefactors of their own projects. Matthew famously constructed the church of the Magione for the Cistercians, who interred Tancred of Lecce and his son there, though both tombs were later cast out by Henry VI and Constance Hauteville.[29] The remains, as well as the sarcophagi, were most likely destroyed; there is no record of their discovery near the Magione or elsewhere in the city in subsequent centuries, when numerous excavations were undertaken to construct buildings.

Not much beyond likely political considerations can be surmised for the reasoning behind the presence of three distinct royal "pantheons" in and near the capital. At Monreale, as we have said, we find Margaret, her husband and three of her sons. In Palermo's cathedral are Roger II, Frederick II, Constance Hauteville and Constance of Aragon. At the Magione were Tancred and Roger III; here Sibylla of Acerra, as regent in 1194, may have been a benefactress.

Had Margaret not refused the request of the canons of Cefalù to transfer the remains of Roger II and William I to that church, there would be four places of royal sepulture in this part of Sicily.[30] It seems likely that Beatrice of Rethel never left Mary Magdalene, where her remains presumably ended up in the crypt; there is no ready explanation for Constance Hauteville leaving her mother's tomb in this small church instead of transferring it to the newly-erected cathedral nearby, though she may have done so had she lived longer. Adelaide, of course, is entombed at Patti.

In retrospect, and while we should be wary of generalities, the Norman-Swabian era may be viewed as a golden age of reginal patronage in southern Italy because of the substantial benefaction involved, some resulting in the foundations of churches and abbeys of major importance. Much of this was the result of sponsoring these projects in the many places where there had previously been mosques or Byzantine churches; the foundations and endowments were part of the Latinization of Sicily, Calabria and parts of Apulia. By 1200, there were parallel social developments, such as emergence of the Sicilian language (see the poetry chapter), which likewise reflected Latinization in these regions.

Considered in that context, Monreale is an exceptional metaphor for a wider movement, and an impressive example from a physical and political point of view. It is certainly the largest and most important complex supported by any of our queens but, as we have seen, it was by no means the only one.

The Vespers rebellion of 1282 left the island of Sicily separated dynastically and politically from the peninsular part of the kingdom for centuries despite close geographical contact and occasional marriages between the Aragonese and Angevins. Some of the differences between these dynasties were vaguely "Spanish" and "French," yet both houses were very Catholic. Royal patronage continued, but it was arguably somewhat less significant in a land that was already Roman Catholic, where it often reflected petty rivalries between religious orders.

As we have seen, some medieval churches and abbeys founded through reginal benefaction no longer exist. Patronage is not a place. It is an idea and an action. Even so, the places are important. They make it easier for the mind, whether medieval or modern, to capture the spirit of queenly patronage.

For most visitors, the queen and kings who rest in Monreale are not its chief attractions. Royal tombs and beautiful cloisters can be seen across western Europe. At Monreale, most of the students, tourists and culture vultures come to see the mosaics more than anything else. The recent publication of the long-awaited first biography of Queen Margaret made it easier for these visitors to learn something about her before coming (see Chapter 11).

The places, as well as the stories, teach us something about the women. It is an effective combination.

NOTES

1. See White, Lynn Townsend, *Latin Monasticism in Norman Sicily* (1938); a good supplement to this is Loud, Graham, *The Latin Church in Norman Italy* (2007).

2. It could be argued that the incursions of Constance Hauteville and her husband, Henry VI, into southern Italy to dislodge Tancred of Lecce were effectively "wars." However, these were not wars declared by a foreign enemy, nor were they prosecuted for the purpose of expansion or conquest but to claim Constance's birthright as the heir of William II.

3. Adelaide sponsored, amongst many others, Holy Spirit Monastery (Caltanissetta), Santa Maria delle Scale (near Messina), Saint Philip of Fragalà, and later Saint Anne of Galath (in Jerusalem). In the diplomatic record, see also the following charters retained at the Archive of State (Catena division) in Palermo: Tabulario dei Monasteri di San Filippo di Fragalà e di Santa Maria di Maniace, 1, 2, 3, 4, 5, 6 (decrees issued early in the twelfth century by Adelaide in the name of her son Roger II chartering the monastery and granting it privileges); 7, 11, 12 (decrees made into 1112 endowing the monastery on Adelaide's initiative). For a good study see von Falkenhausen, Vera. "Zur Regentschaft der Gräfin Adelasia del Vasto in Kalabrien und Sizilien 1101-1112," *AETOS: Studies in Honor of Cyril Mango Presented to Him on April 14, 1998* (Stuttgart 1998), pages 87-115.

4. This was the case of the Benedictines' Holy Trinity Abbey at Mileto, erected in 1080. There were major earthquakes affecting southern Calabria and eastern Sicily in 1125, 1169, 1202, 1295, 1509, 1542, 1638, 1693, 1783, 1894 and, most infamously, 1908.

5. This structure was largely destroyed and later replaced by a mosque. However, a psalter written and illuminated (in the Byzantine style) for Melisende survives; this is *Egerton Manuscript 1139* in the British Library. See also Folda, Jaroslav, "Melisende of Jerusalem: Queen and Patron of Art and Architecture in the Crusader Kingdom," *Reassessing the Roles of Women as Makers of Medieval Art and Architecture* (2012), pages 427-477. For the complexities of Melisende's reign, see Jordan, Erin, "Corporate Monarchy in the Twelfth-Century Kingdom of Jerusalem," *Royal Studies Journal*, volume 6, number 1 (2019), pages 1-15.

6. Walker, Rose, "Leonor of England, Plantagenet Queen of Alfonso VIII of Castile, and Her Foundation of the Cistercian Abbey of Las Huelgas. In Imitation of Fontevraud?" *Journal of Medieval History*, volume 31, number 4 (2005), pages 346-368. Martin, Therese, *Queen as King: Politics and Architectural Propaganda in Twelfth-Century Spain* (2006).

7. The charter is conserved in the Gran Cartulario de la Catedral de Pamplona; *El Libro Redondo*, folio 61 recto. For a transcription see *Colección Diplomática de la Catedral de Pamplona* (edited by José Goñi Gaztambide, 1997), volume 1, page 173.

8. In fact, the construction of Palermo's Norman cathedral began following Margaret's death in 1183. Part of this chapter is drawn from two of the author's ealier books, *Margaret, Queen of Sicily* and *Norman-Arab-Byzantine Palermo, Monreale and Cefalù*.

9. Archivio di Stato di Palermo, Tabulario dei Monasteri di San Filippo di Fragalà e di Santa Maria di Maniace: Manuscript 17 (TSFF17), 27 November 1171. The charter (figure H in Chapter 3) is unsealed, probably a copy of an original, sealed charter; recorded in Greek and Latin, confirming privileges of Roger II protecting said monasteries, exempting them from the obligation to provide timber and livestock, lodge men-at-arms, and so forth, effectively exempting them from local civic authority.

10. That an Arab village near the site of Monreale Abbey was called *Ba'lat* or *Ba'lara* is open to question. The oft-repeated claim that a Greek Orthodox chapel was already located on the site of Monreale's *duomo* is based on an erroneous interpretation of the phrase *super sanctam Kuriacam*, properly "the place overlooking" an existing church (not literally "on top of" it) in William's charter of August 1176. See Garufi, Carlo Alberto (editor), *Catalogo Illustrato del Tabulario di Santa Maria Nuova in Monreale* (1902), page 11, footnote number 1.

11. Interestingly, the foundation date of Maniace (1172) is given in the *Annales Siculi*, in *Rerum Italicarum Scriptores*, volume 5 (edited by Muratori, Lodovico, 1774, reprint Bologna 1928), page 116. See also *Catalogo Illustrato* (op.cit), page 7. For a detailed summary of sources, see White, op.cit., pages 145-148. See also Radici, Benedetto, "Il Casale e l'Abbazia di Santa Maria di Maniace," *Archivio Storico Siciliano* (Palermo 1909), pages 1-104.

12. Numerous records attest to the details of the foundation of this monastery and diocese and its subsequent status. See, for example, *Italia Pontificia* (compilation by Kehr, Paul), volume 10, pages 272-281; also *Catalogo Illustrato* (op.cit.), pages 6-32. For a list of additional original sources, see White, op.cit, pages 132-145.

13. The chief source for Walter's reaction is the prologue of the chronicle of Richard of San Germano. Although this was written some sixteen years after the fact, it does seem to reflect a perception held by many during the first few years of William's majority.

14. From the chronicle of Richard of San Germano: *Quod idem archiepiscopus ad instinctum ipsius cancellarii factum intelligens (nam odio se habebant ad invicem, quamquam se in publico diligere viderentur, et per invidiam detrahentes libenter unus alteri in occulto) hanc suam injuriam et capitis diminutionem patienter portavit ad tempus. Qui tandem processu temporis cum non posset quod factum fuerat per ecclesiam revocare, hoc fieri subdole procuravit.*

15. Regardless of what Richard of San Germano and other chroniclers state, or refrain from mentioning, charters confirm that Margaret sponsored or endowed a number of other monastic churches in Sicily. Her support of the project at Monreale, just a few miles from Palermo (indeed visible from the Pisan tower), is consistent with these other projects, to which she could dedicate more time now that she was no longer regent.

16. The letter was written to Archbishop Walter of Palermo in 1177: *Nam quum rex vester bene litteras noverit, rex noster longe litteratior est. Ego enim in litterali scientia facultatus utriusque cognovi. Scitis, quod dominus rex siciliae per annum discipulus meus fuit, et qui*

a vobis versificatoriae artis primitias habuerat, per industriam et sollicitudinem meam beneficium scientiae plenioris obtinuit. For the entire letter, see number 66 in *Petri Blesensis Opera Omnia* (edited by Giles, John, 1847), volume 1, pages 192-197.

17. This privilege was granted in late 1174 and repeatedly confirmed over the next few years; see *Catalogo Illustrato* (op.cit.), pages 7-13. Monreale was eventually erected into an archdiocese. Reference is made to it in several subsequent Papal bulls and royal decrees.

18. This area is still part of the Archdiocese of Monreale. For an example of some Arab smallholdings in each fortified locality (Jato, Corleone, Calatrasi, Battallario) see *Catalogo Illustrato* (op.cit.), pages 18-20.

19. Located in the forum near the Colosseum, the site of temples dedicated to Roma and Venus is easily identified by the remains of capitals nearly identical to those installed at Monreale.

20. That the escutcheons, which resemble those of the Bayeux Tapestry commemorating the Battle of Hastings (1066), are not embellished with heraldic insignia suggests that armorial heraldry was introduced in the Kingdom of Sicily after 1180. See Mendola, Louis, "English and Italian Legacy of the Norman Knight Figures of Monreale," *The Coat of Arms,* journal of The Heraldry Society, London, edited by John P. Brooke-Little, Norroy and Ulster King of Arms; NS Volume X, Number 166 (London 1994), pages 245-254; also Chapter 4 in this volume.

21. Carved from a porphyry column, the sarcophagus of King William I was transferred to Monreale in 1182 and still survives. The sarcophagus of Frederick II in Palermo's cathedral is very similar.

22. Though venerated since his death, King Louis IX was canonized in 1297. Following the destruction (by revolutionaries) of most of his remains at Saint-Denis, more of his bodily relics may have been conserved at Monreale than anyplace else. The small chest of Catalonian manufacture that formerly contained the king's heart and viscera is kept in Monreale's diocesan museum. Geoffroy of Beaulieu, long the king's confessor, was present in September 1270 when the relics were translated to Monreale, for which see *Recueil des Historiens des Gaules et de la France* (1840), volume 20, page 24 (sections XLVI and XLVII). Geoffroy's "Life of Louis IX" is considered at some length in De Wailly, Natalis, "Examen Critique de la *Vie de Saint Louis* par Geoffroi de Beaulieu," in *Bibliothèque de l'École des Chartes* (1844), volume 5, pages 205-231. French scholars have long questioned whether anything more than the saint's viscera and (perhaps) two fingers was ever present at Monreale. For a review of the analysis of the remains of the relics in 1843, see Letronne, Antoine, *Examen Critique de la Découverte du Prétendu Coeur de Saint Louis* (1844); more recently, Charlier, Philippe, et al., "Schistosomiasis in the Mummified Viscera of Saint Louis (1270 AD)," *Forensic Science, Medicine and Pathology,* volume 12, number 1 (March 2016), pages 113-114. Further observations appear in Bourassé, Jean Jacques, *Dictionnaire d'Épigraphie Chrétienne* (1852), volume 1, columns 908-912; the Monreale entry ends with column 939 following extensive historiography regarding the heart of France's patron saint.

23. This church, restored to its original state, stands amidst what is now a large cemetery. It is known as the site of the Vespers uprising in 1282. For some observations regarding its foundation and Margaret's known role, see White, op.cit. supra, pages 169-170.

24. Founded in France in 1098 as a splinter from the Benedictines, the Cistercians were growing in importance. To some degree, the establishment of a major Cistercian church in Palermo, in the shadow of the rival Benedictines, probably reflected Walter's attempt to assert his own influence in the monastic environment. At all events, as Primate of Sicily Walter was still the senior prelate of the *Regnum*. His brother, Bartholomew, was now Archbishop of Agrigento (see the following note).

25. For the charter of March 1177 exchanging the tithes of the churches of Corleone for episcopal jurisdiction over Baida, a village on the southern edge of the Genoard, see *Catalogo Illustrato* (op.cit.), page 13. Since 1171, Walter's brother, Bartholomew, had been Archbishop of Agrigento, for which see, *exempli gratia*, the charter in *Catalogo Illustrato* (op.cit.), pages 20-21.

26. Not to be confused with the Bishop of Lincoln who died in 1209 (see also the next note).

27. The talented William of Blois was the abbot of the monastery of Santa Maria della Matina at San Marco Argentano in Calabria. See Conti, Emanuele, "L'Abbazia della Matina," *Archivio Storico per la Calabria*, volume 35 (Rome 1967), pages 11-30. He was once considered for the bishopric of Catania, an appointment which went to John of Aiello. This rejection probably saved William's life, for John perished in the earthquake of 1169. Despite what some modern historians have written, there is no contemporary evidence that William of Blois was ever the abbot of Maniace; charters issued in 1177 and 1178 refer to the abbot of that monastery as "Timothy" (see *Catalogo Illustrato*, pages 14-16). The confusion probably results from poor interpretation of a phrase in letters from William's brother, Peter, *abbas matinensis*, "abbot of Matina," as if it were *abbas maniacensis*, "abbot of Maniace."

28. William II was probably born in December 1153. For insights into accurate historiography regarding the role of queens, see Earenfight, Theresa, "Without the Persona of the Prince: Kings, Queens and the Idea of Monarchy in Late Medieval Europe," *Gender and History*, volume 19, number 1 (April 2007), pages 1-21.

29. Though this is not stated explicitly by the Sicilian chroniclers, Roger of Howden mentions it, perhaps based on information he obtained from persons in the Kingdom of Sicily; it is consistent with the policy of Henry and Constance toward the deposed royal family. See *The Annals of Roger de Hoveden* (translated by Riley, Henry, 1853), volume 2, page 341.

30. In 1169, the canons, addressing William II, "together with the most clement Queen Margaret his mother," requested the privilege of entombment of both Roger II and William I in their church. See *I Documenti Inediti dell'Epoca Normanna in Sicilia* (edited by Garufi, Carlo Alberto, 1899), document 46, pages 106-109.

+ HIC REGINA IACES REGALIB
EDITA CVNIS: MARGARITA TIBI
NOMEN·QVOD MORIBVS VNIS:
REGIA PROGENIES PER REGES
DVCTA PROPAGO: VXOR REGIS
ERAS: ET NOBILITATIS IMAGO:
SIC ACERM QVIBVS IPSA RE-
PLES PRECONIA MVNDV: REGE
W. SATIS E PEPERISSE SECVNDV̄
+ VND ETES CENTV·DECIES VIIETU
BVS ANNIS: POST hOMINEM XPM·
MIGRAS NECIS ERVTA DAMPNIS:
LVX EA QVA POPVLIS DANT PETRI
FESTA CATENE: hIS TE DE NEBVL
TVLIT AD LOCA LVCIS AMENE

Margaret's mosaic epitaph and marble sarcophagus

SICILIAN QUEENSHIP

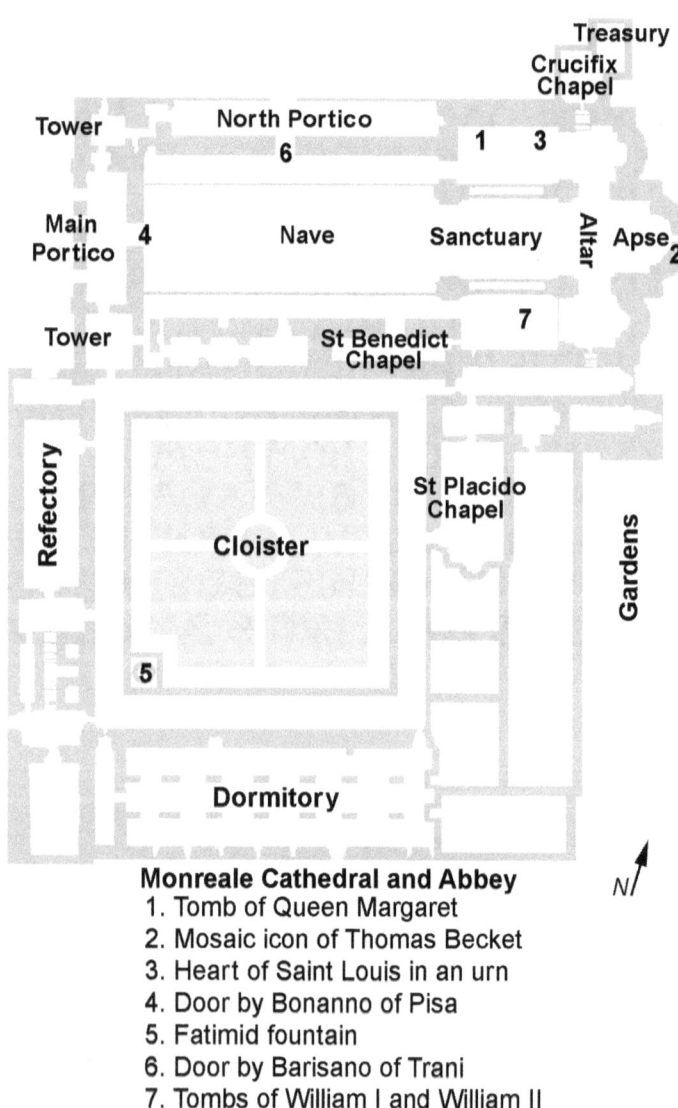

Monreale Cathedral and Abbey
1. Tomb of Queen Margaret
2. Mosaic icon of Thomas Becket
3. Heart of Saint Louis in an urn
4. Door by Bonanno of Pisa
5. Fatimid fountain
6. Door by Barisano of Trani
7. Tombs of William I and William II

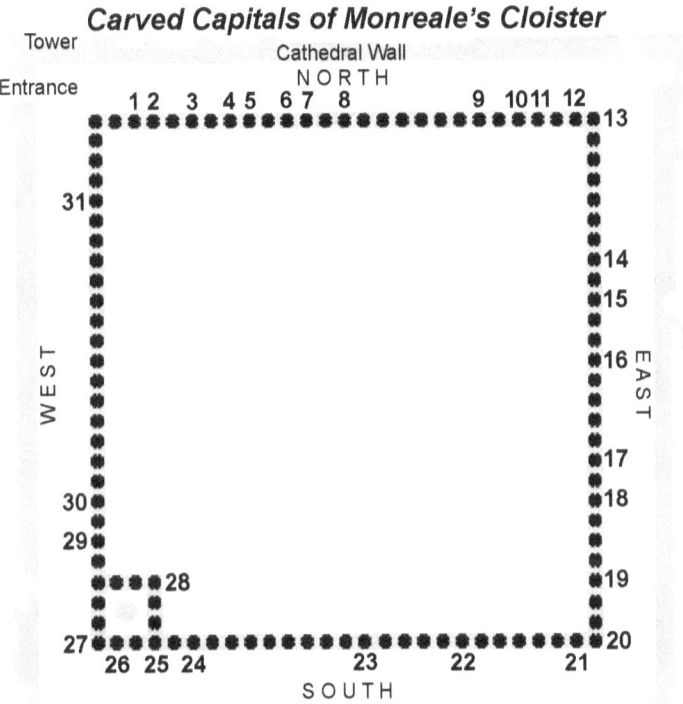

Carved Capitals of Monreale's Cloister

1. Arab archer and swordsman
2. Lions and other beasts
3. Merman (triton) and knights
4. Parable of Lazarus
5. Knights and Saracens
6. Windswept leaves
7. Men killing beasts
8. Life of John the Baptist
9. Story of Samson
10. Norman knights
11. Massacre of the Innocents
12. Evangelists and mermaids
13. Magi, Annunciation, etc.
14. Men supporting capitals
15. Vigilant owls, harpies
16. Men, beasts, lizards
17. Joseph of Old Testament
18. Abraham sacrifices Isaac
19. Resurrection of Jesus
20. Willam and Margaret (?)
21. Lions devour men and stags
22. Acrobats
23. Eagles supporting capital
24. Arab killing sheep or goat
25. Mounted Norman knights
26. Harvesting of grapes
27. Apostles, Flight into Egypt
28. Wine barrels, seasons
29. Prophets and angels
30. William II offers cathedral to Virgin
31. Lion slaughters pig as Norman knight and Saracen warrior watch

SICILIAN QUEENSHIP

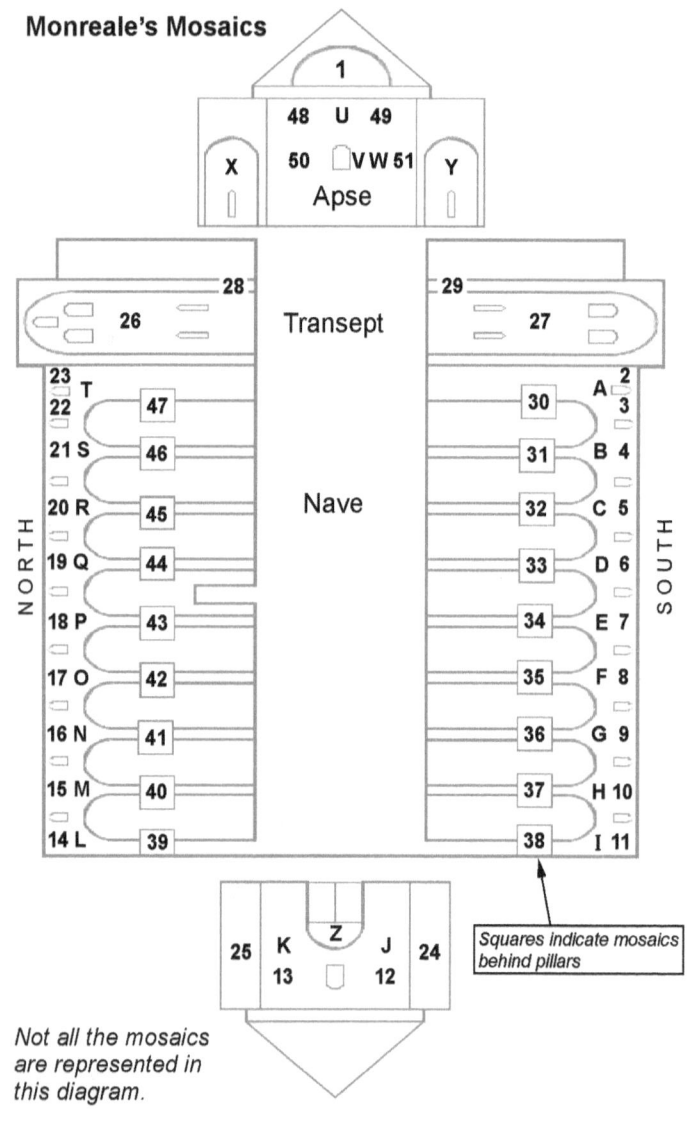

Key to Numeration of Principal Mosaics in Monreale Cathedral

1. Christ Pantocrator (ruler of all)
2. God creates Heaven and Earth
3. God divides light from dark
4. God divides waters
5. God separates lands from seas
6. Creation of sun, moon, stars
7. Creation of birds and fish
8. Creation of Adam and animals
9. God rests
10. Adam placed in Garden of Eden
11. Adam dwells in Eden alone
12. God creates Eve
13. Eve presented to Adam
14. Eve tempted by serpent
15. Forbidden fruit consumed
16. God confronts Adam and Eve
17. Expulsion from Eden
18. Adam and Eve toiling
19. Sacrifice of Cain and Abel
20. Cain kills Abel
21. God confronts Cain
22. Lamech kills Cain
23. Noah commanded to build ark
24. Miracle of loaves and fishes
25. Healing of crooked woman
26. Events from life of Jesus
27. Miracles of Jesus
28. William crowned by Christ
29. William dedicates church to Mary
30. Possessed woman healed
31. Healing of leper
32. Healing of lame man
33. Peter rescued from water
34. Raising of widow's son
35. Healing of woman's hemorrhage
36. Raising of Jairus' daughter
37. Peter's mother-in-law healed
38. Loaves and fishes (also 24)
39. Crooked woman healed (also 25)
40. Man suffering edema healed
41. Healing of ten lepers
42. Healing of two blind men
43. Money changers expelled
44. Jesus saves adulteress
45. Paralyzed man healed
46. Healing of lame and blind
47. Magdalene washes Jesus' feet
A. Noah constructs ark
B. Animals board Noah's ark
C. Dove arrives
D. Animals exit ark
E. Rainbow signifies God's covenant
F. Drunken Noah in vineyard
G. Tower of Babel constructed
H. Abraham meets angels at Sodom
I. Abraham's hospitality
J. Lot protects angels
K. Lot flees destruction of Sodom
L. God commands sacrifice of Isaac
M. Angel stops sacrifice of Isaac
N. Rebecca offers water to servant
O. Rebecca journeys to meet Isaac
P. Isaac with sons Esau and Jacob
Q. Isaac blesses Jacob
R. Jacob flees Esau
S. Jacob dreams of ladder
T. Jacob wrestles with angel
U. Theotokos and Jesus enthroned
V. Saint Sylvester
W. Saint Thomas Becket
X. Saint Paul enthroned
Y. Saint Peter enthroned
Z. Theotokos and Infant Jesus

48. John, Philip, Bartholomew, Luke, James, Peter, Archangel Michael
49. Angel Gabriel, Paul, Andrew, Mark, Thomas, Simon, Matthew
50. Martin, Agatha, Anthony, Blaise, Stephen, Peter of Alexandria, Clement
51. Lawrence, Hilarion, Benedict, Mary Magdalene, Nicholas

SICILIAN QUEENSHIP

The facade and porticos

Fatimid geometric motifs of the apses

Apse viewed from the roof

The roof with the castle visible on the mountain at the upper right

Cloister from cathedral roof

Tower of the cathedral viewed from the cloister

Fatimid fountain in the cloister

The nave and apse

View of the Fatimid fountain

SICILIAN QUEENSHIP

These Norman knights on a capital in the cloister are just one example of what awaits the visitor.

Deer hunting, knight fighting lion, Arabs with shields and scimitars, knight, lion devouring boar, Arab

Jousting knights

The nave

The sanctuary and Pantocrator

Pantocrator overlooking other mosaic icons in the apse of Monreale Abbey. The second figure from the right of the Fatimid lattice window is Thomas Becket.

Royal dais beneath mosaic of King William II crowned by Christ

Bronze door by Bonanno of Pisa

St George on bronze door panel and mosaic detail on wall

Though built some forty years earlier, the cloister of Cefalù, erected on the orders of King Roger II, is strikingly similar to Monreale's in layout and design.

Holy Spirit, Margaret's other major monastic foundation in the environs of Palermo

Apse and tower of Walter's cathedral in Palermo

Except for this wall and crypt, little remains of the royal palace built by Margaret's brother near Pamplona's cathedral. The site now houses the Archivo Real y General de Navarra.

Chapter 9
QUEENS DUBBING KNIGHTS

The very idea of a Sicilian countess or queen raising a young man to knighthood has generally been ignored by historians. This can be partly attributed to sexist attitudes prevailing in Italian historiography into recent times, though in truth its subtext may be nothing more pernicious than simple oversight or the lack of much supporting source information, as what little exists is more implicit than explicit.

As we shall see, the only one of these women known with reasonable certainty to have knighted her son is Adelaide. First, let us consider context in view not only of Norman and Swabian usage but what was actually practiced here in Sicily, which for the most part has become common knowledge among historians. This begins with a few generalities.

Background

In the Kingdom of Sicily there were two broad classes of knights.

The greater number were enfeoffed ("feudal") knights who held land in exchange for military service to the king.

The other class, the "military-religious" knightly orders founded in the Holy Land after the First Crusade, were eventually represented in the *Regnum Siciliae* by priories, commanderies and preceptories, particularly in Apulia and Sicily. However, only the Hospitallers, founded in 1099, existed when Roger II was knighted, the Templars being founded in 1119, and neither order was yet present in Sicily or Calabria, his two dominions.

Birth into the landed caste was a prerequisite for entering either category of knighthood even if, at a certain moment, a young knight might lack much property of his own.[1]

Into the twelfth century, the making of knights was chiefly a feudal affair. Outside the knightly orders (in the Kingdom of Sicily the Hospitallers, Templars and later the Teutonic Knights), knights were dubbed by other knights, usually at around the age of twenty, following an esquireship of five or six years. The *Catalogus Baronum* and other early records list feudal (manorial) tenure and the number of knights each baron was to provide. In the Norman-Swabian period, titled nobles, men of the landed class, were firstly knights, their counties or baronies reflecting the holding of towns or large territories (such as Molise). A barony might consist of several manors, each, in turn, held by an enfeoffed knight.

Dubbing of a feudal knight entailed the man's fealty and homage to the sovereign as a vassal and, more immediately, to the count or baron he served. Although most knights held land, dubbing should not be confused with feudal investiture, a further step which involved infeudation (enfeoffment), the holding of land "in fee" in exchange for military service.

Knighthood in the military-religious orders presupposed the postulants' religious devotion, at least in some measure, but they were not monks in the traditional sense and prayer was not their only vocation; as knights these men were often called upon to kill in the name of God, typically in crusades.

Most of the men in these orders were the younger sons of barons or enfeoffed knights and therefore excluded from feudal succession by the laws of primogeniture but not necessarily inclined to become clerics.

In the feudal environment, the dubbing of a knight signalled not only his coming of age as a man-at-arms but his status as the legal heir to his own father's position (as a baron, enfeoffed knight or other lord) and potential inheritance of an ancestral estate. Most knights were the legitimate sons of such nobles, and for this reason historians speak of an exclusive "knightly class." A bastard could be knighted if recognized by his father; it was less likely that the same bastard would inherit a major estate if he had a legitimate half-brother to inherit it, but he could be granted other lands and enfeoffed *ex novo,* though this might require royal assent.

In the Kingdom of Sicily, knights enjoyed certain privileges and prerogatives set forth in the Assizes of Ariano (1140) and then the Constitutions of Melfi (1231). Indeed, the twelfth century was a time of great evolution in the norms governing the rank and status of knighthood. It saw landed warriors become respected nobles.

Amongst the rarest exceptions in the manorial (or feudal) system were the women who, through inheritance, succeeded in their own rights to counties or baronies, a practice that existed in the Kingdom of Sicily right into the nineteenth century.

A woman, like Clementia of Catanzaro who infamously seduced Matthew Bonello and (arguably) instigated his rebellion against King William I, might well inherit a feudal territory, a birthright of heiresses later codified in the Constitutions of Melfi, but she would still have to provide a certain number of knights. (Scutage, the payment of money in lieu of a knight's military service, did not yet exist, nor did the kings of Sicily make great use of mercenaries.)

Clementia and her ilk were not alone. Knights were known to take orders from Judith of Evreux and Sichelgaita of Salerno, even if neither woman was actually a warrior in the manner of Empress Maude, who made a name for herself in England during the Anarchy. Nevertheless, Constance Hauteville commanded knights when besieged in Salerno during her campaign against Tancred, and as Countess of Toulouse Joanna led knights whilst besieging a castle in France.

The case of Clementia as a countess in her own right prompts consideration of a principle both legal and (in a certain arcane sense) even metaphysical, namely that knighthood and kinghood, though complementary, were two different things where the hereditary ruling class was concerned. Oddly enough (at least to the modern mind), there were cases wherein a boy of the ruling family became a king or duke before becoming a knight. Notably, the two eldest sons of Roger II were invested with crown lands in Apulia before being knighted, even though they had already accompanied their father on military campaigns (see note 16).

When the kingdom was founded, dubbing knights was not yet an exclusively royal prerogative. However, it was nevertheless predicated upon nobility of birth. A statute in the Assizes of Ariano states that "no man who is not the son of a knight may be dubbed a knight except by royal authority."[2]

The dubbing ceremony itself was not yet standardized across realms; investiture into a knightly order was a religious rite, whereas the dubbing of an enfeoffed knight was based on longstanding lay practice within the warrior class. In either case, it was a public act before witnesses, followed by festivities as a significant rite of passage.

Varied though they were, the knightings of the sons of kings, dukes and counts shared a few universal characteristics. The simple ceremonies were public and they were usually held on recurring feasts, with at least a few other knights present as witnesses. An older person, usually the king or duke himself, dubbed a younger one. Some kind of arming was involved, be it placing a helm upon the new knight's head, girding him with a sword belt or placing a sword in his hand. Knighting signalled, or coincided with, the young man coming of age, typically at around twenty for the son of a baron or *seigneur* (manorial lord) but usually a few years earlier for the son of a sovereign leader. Whether in Italy, France or England, the knightings of the twelfth century were simple and frequent enough, and their formal procedure known so well, that chroniclers did not find it necessary to describe the actual ceremonies in great detail.

Outside knightly orders such as the Hospitallers, dubbing knights was still a secular affair. Some Catholic abbots controlling large estates were, in effect, feudal lords required to provide their sovereign a certain number of knights, just as a baron or other vassal would have to do. Yet the seventeenth canon issued at the Council of London of 1102 forbade such abbots to dub knights, and it would not be unreasonable to presume the application of a similar principle in Sicily during this era. Indeed, in view of the apostolic legateship granted to the Hautevilles for the island in 1098 (some modern scholars have questioned the historicity and effect of this papal policy), Adelaide may well have exercised more control over the Latin church in Sicily than King Henry I enjoyed in England.

Where royalty or "quasi-royalty" was concerned, the latter referring to sovereign ruling families such as the Hautevilles before foundation of the kingdom in 1130, it was normally presumed that a young prince (though that term was not yet in common use), as his father's heir, would be knighted before succeeding him. A king's son might thus be knighted at around the age of fifteen or sixteen.

Instructive examples will be found in the other great Norman kingdom. In 1086, William the Conqueror knighted his son, the future Henry I of England, who was then seventeen or eighteen years old.[3] A century later, Henry II of England knighted his son, John, before sending him to Ireland as his governor or "viceroy" at the age of eighteen.[4]

A young heir's knighting could be delayed by his father's untimely death. Roger I, William I and Henry VI (and Constance Hauteville as Queen of Sicily) all died before their heirs, respectively Roger II, William II and Frederick II, reached the age of majority.

The practice of a young son being crowned during his father's lifetime ensured that the succession was not subsequently contested by churchmen or rebellious barons; Constance sagely had Frederick II crowned shortly before her death from what seems to have been a long illness.

Exceptionally but fairly frequently, a boy who had not yet reached the age of majority might become a king, albeit reigning under a regent or guardian, without yet having been knighted. This was the case of Frederick.

That predicament might not have presented itself if Frederick's parents had lived to see him reach adulthood. A good comparison is Henry the Young King, the eldest son of Henry II of England, who was knighted just prior to being crowned *rex filius* at the age of fifteen in 1170.[5] As Henry the Young King predeceased his father, he never ascended the throne to rule in his own name, but the idea of the young man being knighted before being crowned made sense.

Not that the circumstances of each example are identical to those of every other, but amongst queens those of at least two from this era come to mind. Urraca "the Reckless" of León and Castile was a queen regnant who endeavored to ensure the rights of her young son, Alfonso VII. Melisende of Jerusalem did the same for her son, the young Baldwin III. Both women were successful, as were our own Adelaide, Margaret and Constance.

The royal age of majority varied somewhat depending upon necessity. It was about seventeen for Roger II and William II, but fourteen for Frederick II.

No record exists to indicate precisely when William II and Frederick II were knighted, or by whom. The former would seem to have been knighted by his father, William I, the latter by his guardian, Walter of Capparone.

Adelaide was not the only widowed consort of a Siculo-Norman ruler to exercise the bestowal of knighthood early in the twelfth century. In June 1119, Cecilia, daughter of King Philip I of France and widow of Roger's kinsman Tancred of Antioch, knighted Gervase of Dol and some other squires on the eve of the Battle of Sarmada against Muslim forces. Roger of Salerno, another Hauteville cousin, was killed in the subsequent fighting.[6]

It must be remembered that all European monarchs except women and popes were assumed to be knighted. This was not merely a formality. It was presumed that a king or duke might be called upon to lead troops into combat to defend his rights and his people. He need not be the most capable warrior in the realm, but at the very least he had to be marginally competent as a battlefield commander. Even if we presuppose that young William II was knighted at the age of twelve, just before his father's death, he certainly received martial training before he began to rule on his own five years later. Even heirs having physical disabilities, such as Charles II "the Lame" of Naples, son of the Charles who defeated Manfred at Benevento, were expected to achieve an essential mastery of riding skills and swordsmanship.

The mere possession of a sword was viewed as a knight's prerogative. Eventually, laws were enacted proscribing the bearing of arms by most people.[7]

Though some swords borne by kings had names, in most cases these were ascribed apocryphally by legend; here Charlemagne's *Durendal* comes to mind. Little is known of the *Mikalis* said to have belonged to Roger I; there seems to be no contemporaneous reference to it, yet the idea of a mystical sword likely came to the Normans from the *Tyrfing* of their Norse forebears. This practice was confirmed by later Norman literature. *Durendal,* mentioned in the *Chanson d'Aspremont* (as a sword appropriated from its original Muslim owner), an epic set in Calabria and performed at Messina for Richard I of England in 1190, may have inspired a gesture on the part of the English king.

The chronicler Roger of Howden, who was present, mentions that, while at Catania early the next year, Richard gave Tancred of Lecce, the King of Sicily, a sword called *Excalibur,* as if it were the mythical weapon of King Arthur, to reciprocate the Sicilian monarch's generosity in providing some twenty ships for the voyage to Palestine for the Third Crusade. Another influence upon Lionheart may have been the literature of Geoffrey of Monmouth (about which more below), with its Arthurian details.

The later legend of *Mikalis* seems to have been based upon *Durendal* or *Excalibur* (or both), but it is not accompanied by similar literature.

Turning our attention from swords to shields, the origin of the coat of arms later attributed to the Hautevilles (see Chapter 4) is equally ambiguous. It was added in mosaic over the royal throne platform in Monreale's *duomo* some years after the death of William II.

Nevertheless, much is known of the culture that came to be called *chivalry,* reflected in literature and art (see the chapters on poetry and matronage). The well-documented lives of El Cid (Rodrigo Díaz de Vivar) and, in a later time, William Marshal, offer insights into the nexus of knightly and courtly culture. Although the *Historium Regum Britanniae* of Geoffrey of Monmouth, written around 1136, is essentially fiction, its

Arthurian passages, though clearly idealized, reflect the details typical of the twelfth century where perceptions of knighthood are concerned.

That we find queens regent and regnant performing virtually every other duty of a king, including the infeudation of barons, suggests that it was perfectly normal for such a queen, as *fons honorum pro tempore,* to elevate a man to knighthood, including her own son. It would be ridiculous for such a regent to be obligated to seek out a baron to knight her son, as if she had the power to do everything but that; moreover, it would permit the baronage, which could be quite wicked, to control her by withholding approval for her son to be elevated to knighthood.

It was a fundamental precept that only the sovereign, or his regent, could change a man's inherent legal status. Dubbing or enfeoffing him were rudimentary examples of the use of such power. Another example was legitimization, for while a baron who fathered a bastard could recognize him as his own son, only the monarch could actually legitimize such a child in law.

These matters were essentially the exercise of a leader's legal authority but, like many observances involving the Catholic church, which was gradually making rites of chivalric investiture into quasi-sacramental rituals such as coronation, adoubement became endowed with a certain mystique, as if it were a transcendent, almost magical, act. Knights were no longer the simple mounted warriors of yore but an elite hereditary class entitled to special rights, something explicated in the Assizes of Ariano (as already noted) and other legal codes promulgated by sovereigns around Europe during the twelfth century. Indeed, the Hautevilles were among the first monarchs to codify this principle formally.

It is difficult to date precisely the metamorphosis of knighthood from a military status and rite of passage into something more. Most of the lore associated with knighthood accrued to it after Adelaide's time. Chivalric ideals developed as literary themes between the time *The Song of Roland* was written, around 1100 (if not somewhat earlier), and *Parzival* a century afterward, the former based on actual events and the latter on Arthurian legend, itself the inspiration for certain romanticized tropes. As the perception of knighthood became aggrandized in this way, Saint George, long a patron of the mounted soldier, came to be identified as a knight, almost as if he were a medieval personage.

In the popular mind, the affluence of the county, and then kingdom, of Sicily may have enhanced the impact of public ceremonies such as knightings, especially where the person doing the dubbing was not a lowly baron in a rustic castle but the sovereign in a magnificent capital city. Whereas the knighting of a young man in a remote barony might be attended by his family, peers, local folk and perhaps a friar or two, the dubbing of a ruler's son could be a grand event.

Adelaide

When Roger I, Count of Sicily, died in 1101, he was survived by his wife, Adelaide, two sons, Simon (born in 1093) and Roger (born in 1095), and a daughter, Maximilla (born in 1097). Whether an older child, Matilda, was the daughter of Adelaide or an earlier wife is debated (see Chapter 5). At his death, Roger had a number of legitimate children from his three wives, as well as a few born outside marriage. He had designated as his heir a bastard son, Jordan, who served as regent (governor) while Roger was away subduing Malta, but died in 1092 after marrying one of Adelaide's first cousins.

Apart from Sicily and Malta, Adelaide's two sons were heirs to most of Calabria. She raised them there, at Mileto, but also at Messina and San Marco d'Alunzio. Simon's death in 1105 left Roger as Count of Sicily under Adelaide's regency. Henceforth, his name appears alongside hers, usually as *comes* (count).

Young Roger's succession to the county was automatic upon the death of his elder brother. Although Adelaide had to undertake to defend his patrimony from usurpers, either half-siblings or Hauteville cousins in Apulia, no formal ceremony was necessary to invest him with Sicily and Calabria.

When was Roger II knighted?

He and his brother may have first been knighted as early as 1105, possibly at a public ceremony in Messina. However, very little is known about this. What is known with greater certainty is that Roger was knighted at Palermo, probably early in 1112. The fact of the dubbing, but not its details, is mentioned in passing by the Calabrian chronicler Alexander of Telese.[8] Repeating such a ceremony, or even a coronation, was not extremely unusual when it was deemed necessary to demonstrate its fact to the baronage or populace (Frederick II was famously crowned King of the Germans in Mainz and then in Aachen).

The perfunctory simplicity of Alexander's comment about this occasion is typical of the brief descriptions by chroniclers of that time, such as Orderic Vitalis, but it should also be remembered that he wrote his *Ystoria Rogerii Regis Sicilie, Calabrie atque Apulie* at least twenty years after an event at which he was not present. His information about it probably came from Matilda (whom we met in Chapter 5), the sister of Roger II, who may well have been present to see her brother knighted.

Adelaide had good reasons for knighting Roger in a very visible manner. She had only recently transferred the court to Palermo, probably the most populous city in Italy. Whereas the populations of Calabria and northeastern Sicily were predominantly Greek, Palermo's population was mostly Arab. This was not, in itself, problematic. The Arabs respected Adelaide's authority and position enough to accord her the same appellation that they had used for her late husband, "great leader," though *malik* and *malikah* are also "king" and "queen" (see Chapter 3). Indeed, at this moment Adelaide probably ruled a larger Muslim population, of at least a few hundred thousand, than any other woman. If anything, she enjoyed more loyalty from the Arabs than from the unruly Norman barons whose dissent she sometimes had to suppress.

As Roger was a count but not yet a king, there would be no coronation, but knighting him was a clear sign that now, at sixteen, he had reached the age of majority and was ready to rule in his own name and on his own sovereign authority. It also served to introduce him, in a very public way, to his Palermitan subjects. Henceforth, beginning with charters issued in 1112, Roger is styled in such terms as *iam miles iam comes*.[9]

The boy was now a man, but his inheritance still had to be protected. Adelaide's husband was survived by kinsmen and other rivals who would more than gladly usurp Sicily and Calabria as their own if they could. Not for nothing did Adelaide's support network consist, in the first instance, of her own family, led by her brother Henry, along with some loyal Greeks.

In Apulia, young William had just succeeded his father, the late Roger Borsa, the son of Robert Guiscard and Sichelgaita of Salerno, thus inheriting most of the Hauteville dominions in southern peninsular Italy. William of Apulia was the same age as Adelaide's son and just as ambitious.

Henry, Adelaide's brother and counsellor, may well have assisted in planning the dubbing ceremony. We do not know where the brief event took place or precisely which form it took. Perhaps Adelaide literally placed a sword into her son's hand as she stood beside him and raised his arm in unison with hers. It seems less likely that she struck his face, but it is possible that he was girded with a sword by high-ranking nobles; there is little doubt that numerous barons were present to witness the event.

Perhaps Adelaide also placed a helm upon Roger's head. A well-known image of such an act appears in the Bayeux Tapestry, which depicts William the Conqueror arming Harold

Godwinson (see the figure at the end of this chapter). As Harold, who was then over forty years old, had already been knighted many years earlier, this may be nothing more than the simple "delivery of arms" rather than a dubbing, but it does show a similar gesture.

While knighting was frequently mentioned by Norman chroniclers, surprisingly little of the ceremony itself was described by them in Adelaide's era, and (as we have seen) across Europe there were localized usages. In fact, Alexander of Telese tells us no more about this ceremony than he reveals about a later one (see note 16).

Even though the brief ritual was not actually a religious rite, it is quite likely that a prelate attending Roger's knighting came forth to perform a benediction immediately following the simple dubbing ceremony, and we can hypothesize about who this was. Archbishop Alcherio died in 1110, soon succeeded by a certain Walter, probably a Norman (not to be confused with the Walter consecrated during Margaret's regency). In that connection, it should be remembered that in Sicily, unlike other Hauteville dominions such as Calabria and Apulia, the ruler enjoyed the legatine powers (noted earlier) supposedly granted by Pope Urban II in 1098 to approve episcopal appointments or even to suggest them.

To envisage a prelate blessing Roger's sword, helmet or spurs would be pure speculation. However, the twelfth century did see such practices become more commonplace, and blessing objects was not unusual.

Whilst it could well be argued that blessing the young knight, if not his sword, conferred a certain religious relevance, or ecclesiastical approval, upon the event, postulating a significance beyond this might not bear scrutiny were we to compare this Norman knighting to those at England's Norman court, described above.

In fact, benedictions accompanied many events, and there

is nothing known to posterity to suggest that the dubbing of Roger II took place in a church.

Though we may theorize about the existence and importance of the ceremony's details, there is at least some relevance in the fact that the sons of Robert Guiscard and Roger I were part of the first generation of Hautevilles to be born and raised in Italy. This is the generation that came of age at the dawn of the twelfth century. Unlike their fathers, these men inherited important lands which they did not have to obtain through conquest. Although they continued to seek territorial acquisitions, particularly in the central and eastern Mediterranean, the Hauteville men were no longer destined by necessity to be mere mercenaries in search of ever-greener pastures but legitimate rulers of sovereign territory. By the time Roger II was knighted, the Normans had been in Italy for nearly a century, and a branch of the Hauteville family was ruling a piece of the Holy Land.

As a knight dubbed in such an environment, Adelaide's son was more than a warrior. How much more remains open to debate, except for the obvious fact of his inheriting Sicily and Calabria.

Another factor in dubbing a young heir such as Roger during this period was the concept of the knight as a crusader rather than (or in addition to) a warrior or feudal vassal. Here we refer not only to the crusading Templars and Hospitallers but to knights in general. True, there were isolated crusading movements against "infidels" even before the First Crusade, and the Norman invasion of Sicily was itself viewed by the papacy as something of a "crusade" against Islam, but by 1112 this activity had been formalized.[10] It was now presumed that, at least in the abstract, there was an implicitly Christian side to feudal knighthood; even in multiconfessional Sicily a Muslim was unlikely to ever be knighted.

Here an obvious complexity confronting the young count

was that in Sicily many of his subjects, perhaps the majority, were still Muslims, who in the years to come would provide his corps of loyal bodyguards and archers; the Arabs' *furusiyya* was somewhat similar to knighthood in its warrior code. The Muslims' smallholdings gradually came under Norman feudal control; many rural Arabs were enserfed and, decade by decade, most converted to Christianity.

Where in the vast city was the ceremony performed?

The royal palace near Palermo's cathedral was still being built over the Arab (and Punic) citadels whose traces are today seen crowning the Halkah district overlooking the Kasr, but it is quite possible that Roger II was knighted there or even at one of the other Arab palaces, such as the Favara. There is, however, another possibility, and it seems more likely in view of its geographic centrality.

Until now, the Hautevilles had held few ceremonies in Palermo except for such events as the funeral of Odo of Bayeux in February 1097, mentioned by Orderic Vitalis.[11] Except for a few walls, the cathedral, where Odo was entombed, was not the present structure but an older edifice, erected as a basilica, that had been used as a mosque for two centuries before the Normans' conquest of the city.

Next to it stands a chapel erected in Byzantine times at the corner of what are now Via Incoronazione and the inappropriately-named Via Matteo Bonello. For a time, this edifice too had been used as a mosque, but the Normans had restored it as a church. Attached to it is a dais (see the photograph at the end of this chapter).

The longstanding belief that the small church itself was the site of coronations may be dismissed as mere supposition. However, the dais could well have been a convenient place to present the newly-crowned queens and kings to the people. Though much altered over time, its height and dimensions are essentially unchanged since the eleventh century.

It is highly possible that Adelaide knighted her son on this spot in 1112. Even inclement weather would not have dissuaded the people from witnessing such an event, and the dais could easily have been covered by a canopy if necessary. As stated earlier, a prelate may well have attended.[12]

Roger's ascent up to the dais was nothing less than an ascent to power.

The dubbing seems to have effectively marked the end of Adelaide's influence at court as queen mother. She soon sailed for the Holy Land to wed King Baldwin I of Jerusalem and became his queen. The marriage did not end well.[13]

Yet Adelaide kept Roger's interests in mind, stipulating that he would succeed as King of Jerusalem in the event that she bore Baldwin no sons. This never came to pass.

In Adelaide's absence her brother, Henry, assisted Roger as counsellor and confidant. Rather little is known of the precise extent of his influence, and he was not always in Sicily.[14] However, Alexander of Telese went so far as to write that it was Henry who later suggested that his nephew be crowned King of Sicily.

Conclusion

The Kingdom of Sicily flourished for over seven hundred years, until 1860. The fact that its first king was knighted by a woman has generally gone unnoticed. Likewise, the fact that this singular Christian woman, destined to be crowned Queen of Jerusalem, governed a large Muslim population in Sicily, has often been overlooked.

Much has been written about knighthood and the dubbing of knights.[15] As we have seen, knighthood was in a gradual (but barely evident) state of change by the early decades of the twelfth century, with the simple martial training and rudimentary warrior code slowly evolving into something vaguely resembling what has come to be called *chivalry*. Yet in 1112 it still had a long way to go. Tournaments were not the elaborate affairs they were destined to become by the end of the century, and in Norman Italy there were few, if indeed any, knights like William Marshal who made tourneying an activity akin to a lifestyle, as if they were professional athletes.

Adelaide could not have foreseen such developments when she dubbed Roger. This was a serious, pragmatic affair.

Alexander of Telese tells us that at Bari in 1135, when Roger II, by now King of Sicily, knighted two of his sons, Roger and Tancred, he also knighted forty other young men.[16] In this way he conferred the status upon others that had been bestowed upon him twenty-three years earlier. Here was the continuity of tradition.

Did Adelaide ever dub anybody besides her son? We do not know.

What we know about Adelaide herself is somewhat less than what is known of Queen Margaret, but no less impressive. Although she was not a queen of Sicily, she was the first of our sovereign ladies to be crowned a queen.

Not only did she raise Roger II to knighthood, as his mother she raised him to manhood. Through Adelaide's efforts, Sicily became a dominion fit for a queen, and that is what her daughter-in-law, Elvira, came to be.

NOTES

1. For good overviews see Cuozzo, Errico, *La Cavalleria nel Regno Normanno di Sicilia* (2008) and of course Seward, Desmond, *The Monks of War: The Military Religious Orders* (1972). See also the works mentioned in note 5 below. For the status of landless knights see: *The Historical Works of Ralph de Diceto, Dean of London*, volume 2, pages lxxx and lxxxi; *The Annals of Roger de Hoveden*, volume 2, page 339; *Chronicles of the Reigns of Stephen, Henry II and Richard I*, volume 2, pages 422-423 (William of Newburgh).

2. Article 19 in the Vatican codex, article 31 in the Cassino codex, published in *Queens of Sicily*, pages 516 and 528.

3. Riley, Henry (translator), *The Annals of Roger de Hoveden* (1853), volume 1, page 168. This is likewise reported in Giles, John (translator), *The Anglo-Saxon Chronicle* (1914), page 157.

4. Ibid, volume 2, page 50. For analysis of this see Boulton, D'Arcy Jonathan, "Classic Knighthood as Nobiliary Dignity: The Knighting of Counts and Kings' Sons in England 1066-1272," *Medieval Knighthood V: Papers from the Sixth Strawberry Hill Conference 1994* (1995), pages 41-100.

5. From the letters of Thomas Becket: *Transacta Dominica, rex apud Londonias filium suum cingolo militiae donavit, eundemque statim Eboracensis in regem inunxit.* Robertson, James (editor), *Materials for the History of Thomas Becket, Archbishop of Canterbury* (1885), volume 7, *Epistolae* number 476, page 316. For a recent view see Weiler, Björn, "Knighting, Homage and the Meaning of Ritual: The Kings of England and their Neighbors in the Thirteenth Century," *Viator*, volume 37 (2006), pages 276-299. A fine general reference is Barber, Richard, *The Knight and Chivalry* (revised edition, 2000). For a sober analysis see Keen, Maurice, *Chivalry* (1984). See also Crouch, David, *William Marshal: Knighthood, War and Chivalry 1147-1219* (2002). A good general introduction to knighthood and the dubbing ceremony in Norman England will be found in Chapter 4 ("The Aristocracy") of Bartlett, Robert, *England under the Norman and Angevin Kings 1075-1225* (2000).

6. Forester, Thomas (translator), *The Ecclesiastical History of England and Normandy*, the *Historia Ecclesiastica* of Orderic Vitalis (1854), volume 3, page 392.

7. For the English laws during the reign of Henry II see Riley, op.cit., volume 2, pages 9-11.

8. In the chronicle of Alexander of Telese, book 1, chapter 4: *Cum autem adolevisset, factusque miles...*

9. Historians usually determine the date by references to Roger as *miles* (knight), rather than simply *comes* (count), in certain Latin charters. Unlike the hereditary status of count, based on automatic succession upon the death of his brother, knighthood had to be conferred *ad personam*. For a charter of June 1112 see Brühl, Carlrichard

(editor) *Rogerii II Regis Diplomata Latina (Codex Diplomaticus Regni Siciliae), Diplomata Regum et Principum e Gente Normannorum,* series 1 (1987), pages 7-9, number 3; see also the manuscripts transcribed in Cusa's *I Diplomi Greci ed Arabi* consulted at the Palermo Archive of State (Catena division), namely Tabulario dei Monasteri di San Filippo di Fragalà e di Santa Maria di Maniace, Manuscript 6 (decree issued on parchment before 1113, probably *circa* 1111, by Adelaide in the name of her son Roger II renewing to the monastery privileges granted by her late husband replacing the previous decree written on paper); Tabulario dei Monasteri di San Filippo di Fragalà e di Santa Maria di Maniace, Manuscripts 7, 11, 12 (decrees made into 1112 endowing the monastery on Adelaide's initiative); Manuscript 10 (reissue in 1109 of former decree of Roger I delimiting territory of abbey of Saint Barbarus). Another indicator may be Adelaide's release of some serfs in San Marco d'Alunzio to a nearby abbey in 1112, ostensibly in gratitude for her son's recovery from an illness more than a decade earlier but coincidental to him reaching majority.

10. Whether the Christian campaigns against the Muslims in Iberia during this period should be defined as "crusades" is open to question. However, this chapter is not a treatise on the crusades, a topic that has elicited much eclectic scholarship in recent decades; for a solid introduction see Riley-Smith, Jonathan, *The First Crusade and the Idea of Crusading* (1986) and *The Crusades: A History* (third edition, 2013).

11. See Forester, Thomas (translator), *The Ecclesiastical History of England and Normandy,* the *Historia Ecclesiastica* of Orderic Vitalis (1854), volume 3, page 206.

12. The fact that a prelate might, in some way, be involved with a secular knighting, had certain precedents among the Normans. For example, we are told by Orderic Vitalis that the future Henry I of England was knighted by Lanfranc, Archbishop of Canterbury, who "armed him for the defence of the kingdom, clothing him with a breastplate, putting a helmet on his head, and giving him the belt of knighthood, in the name of the Lord, as the king's son, and born on the steps of the throne." See Forester, Thomas (translator), *The Ecclesiastical History of England and Normandy,* the *Historia Ecclesiastica* of Orderic Vitalis (1854), volume 2, page 431, where footnote 3 clarifies that young Henry was, in fact, knighted by his father a year prior to this (as mentioned earlier in this chapter and at note 3 above), and perhaps Orderic, writing some time after the fact and not having been a witness to the event, intended to say that Lanfranc ceremonially *presented* Henry to be knighted by the king. In any case, the passage clearly implies that, despite the lack of a formal religious rite at this early date, when knighting was still a secular affair, the participation and benediction by a bishop was not altogether unusual. Orderic and his brother monks at Saint Evroul, where Robert, the half-brother of Judith of Evreux, was once the abbot (see *Queens of Sicily,* pages 86-88), had frequent contact with the Normans of southern Italy and the *Historia Ecclesiastica* makes occasional reference to them.

13. See *Queens of Sicily,* pages 118-121.

14. See Garufi, Carlo Alberto, "Gli Aleramici e i Normanni in Sicilia e nelle Puglie," *Centenario della Nascita di Michele Amari: Documenti e Ricerche,* volume 1 (1910), pages 47-83.

15. Besides Barber, op. cit. supra, see its supplement, *The Reign of Chivalry* (1980), and also Keen, op. cit. For armor and details see Funken, Liliane and Fred, *Arms and Uniforms: The Age of Chivalry,* part 1, (1977). So ingrained did knighthood and its ritual become in European culture during the twelfth century that a chronicler writing about the Third Crusade even claimed that Saladin was knighted according to Christian usage; this appears in the *Itinerarium Peregrinorum et Gesta Regis Ricardi* (book 1, chapter 3) in Stubbs, William, *Chronicles and Memorials of the Reign of Richard I,* volume 1, page 9.

16. This appears at the very end of Alexander's chronicle, book 4, chapter 5: *Ipse autem rex, natalis dominici subsequentis die adveniente, duos liberos suos ad militiam promovit, Rogerium scilicet ducem, et Tancredum barensem principem, ad quorum videlicet laudem, et honorem quadraginta equites cum eisdem ipsis militari cingulo decoravit.* It was at this ceremony that the king's sons were knighted, though they had already been invested as Duke of Apulia (Roger) and Prince of Bari (Tancred). This example is cited by Keen, op.cit. supra, page 69, who also notes a similar knighting of thirty knights at Rouen in 1127 to mark the marriage of Geoffrey of Anjou and Matilda of England (Empress Maude), parents of Henry II of England, an event chronicled by John of Marmoutier.

Beginning with Roger and Elvira, kings and queens were acclaimed on this coronation dais next to Palermo's cathedral. It was probably on such a dais that young Roger was knighted publicly by Adelaide.

Rulers were often depicted as knights. This is Roger I on a copper follaris coin struck in Messina.

William the Conqueror arms or dubs Harold Godwinson before the Battle of Hastings (Bayeux Tapestry)

Chapter 10
QUEENS AND SICILIANITÀ

The study of queenhood is of general interest, or should be. But why are the queens of Sicily especially important to those having roots in southern Italy? It's because they are an integral part of our heritage and identity as Sicilians. We would be much the lesser without them. Our early countesses and queens have much to do with what we have inherited from the medieval past. This phenomenon is not unique to Sicily or Sicilians, but little has ever been written about it, even in Italian, and it is worth contemplating when we reflect upon the legacy of the queens of Sicily.

Sicilianità. The Italian word for things pertaining to the social and ethnic culture of Sicily is, arguably, a misnomer if we consider that the Kingdom of Sicily, as it existed from 1130 to 1282, included not only the island of Sicily but most of the Italian peninsula south of Rome. For the purposes of this chapter, however, the term shall be used to encompass, as well, the Neapolitan, Salernitan, Apulian, Lucanian and Calabrian cultures as these flourished until around 1282, the year that these peninsular regions were politically separated from Sicily by the War of the Vespers. For the periods after 1282, the word

Sicilianità, as it is used here, pertains exclusively to the island. The term is analogous to *Italianità.*

Sicilianità should not be confused with *Sicilianismo* (Sicilianism), which usually refers to an intentional effort to affect what are perceived to be Sicilian mannerisms and tastes, or to support "Sicilianist" movements such as separatism. This chapter's focus is history and culture, not modern political movements or subjective literary perceptions. *Sicilianità* is not an ideology or philosophy but a very general concept of what it is that makes Sicilians and Sicily "Sicilian." It is a sense of identity that is usually more instinctive than conscious, with little formal pedagogy. The Palermitans celebrating the feast of Saint Rosalie may not all know that the saint's mythos is rooted in her identity as an archetypal Norman princess, but that doesn't change the reality of the social culture expressed through her legend.

None of this is very surprising. Where would we expect to find the influence of Sicilian queenhood if not in Sicily?

Queens and Countries

Geography is not the only complexity implied by a word like *Sicilianità,* for most of the kingdom's earliest queens were foreign-born, exogenous marriages being the norm among our first kings. These women did not begin their lives being "Sicilian" but, in a sense, became so through marriage. The obvious exceptions were Constance Hauteville, who was born in Palermo, Sybilla of Acerra, and perhaps Bianca Lancia.

Queenhood is an important part of the social history and culture of monarchies.[1] Without our countesses and queens, there would have been no *Regnum Siciliae,* a state which survived, in some form, for seven centuries.

More precisely, the peninsular region, which eventually came to be known as the *Kingdom of Naples,* was a separate realm beginning with the War of the Vespers in 1282, although its Angevin kings still claimed the island of Sicily and therefore insisted on calling their peninsular state the "Kingdom of Sicily." Later, the two kingdoms were occasionally ruled by the same monarch in a "personal union" (notably 1442-1458 and 1735-1815) but they were formally constituted as a unitary state, the *Kingdom of the Two Sicilies,* only in 1815.

Sicily's last queen, Maria Sophia of Bavaria, consort of King Francesco II of the Two Sicilies, wore her crown until 1861 and died in 1925. More so than most of her predecessors, she became a symbol of the place and its people.

Interestingly, she descended from the same Wittelsbach dynasty as Elisabeth, consort of King Conrad who succeeded Frederick II in 1250. Some genealogical links are more tenuous than this because not every Queen of Sicily has direct descendants. Margaret, for example, had no grandchildren who survived to provide descents to posterity.

It is obvious enough that modern queens regnant, such as Britain's long-reigning Victoria and Elizabeth II, are guarantors of continuity and law as heads of state. The same could be said of medieval queens regent like Constance, the mother of Frederick II, in an age long before the advent of constitutional monarchies. Beyond these considerations, important as they may be, are questions of a queen's place in regional, national or ethnic identity.

Italo-Norman Culture

After a century of assimilation and amalgamation in southern in Italy, most of the knightly families from Normandy, which had begun arriving around 1015, were not exclusively Norman culturally any more than the "Lombard" families of Salerno and various feudal localities, after living for centuries in Campania, Basilicata and Abruzzo, were truly Longobardic. In the case of the Normans, rather few women from Normandy came to Italy; most of the Normans and French arriving on the peninsula were knights, clerics and other men. With few exceptions, the knights married local women.

Most of the kings of Sicily of the Norman-Swabian era were born in the *Regnum Siciliae,* as were a few of their consorts. The mothers of the greatest kings, the Italian-born lawmakers Roger II and Frederick II, were born and raised in Italy.

It is difficult to quantify this ethnicity as "Sicilian" in very precise terms; it was a precursor. *Sicilianità* itself was evolving from the mix of diverse cultures present in the south of Italy. Here there are many complexities.

Granted that the geographic origins of the nobility of this period might be reflected in genetic haplogroups, this cannot be tested very generally or reliably at this distance of time (few remains of the persons in these families even survive). Rather, most of our considerations are vaguely sociological and cultural.

A precise dating of the "disappearance" of Norman culture in Italy is necessarily somewhat conjectural. Clearly, the Norman French language was used at court as long as the Hautevilles ruled. However, it was seldom written; we find records in Latin, Greek and Arabic but only very rarely in French (see chapters 2, 3 and 7). Language is not the only determinant of origins or ethnic culture (by way of example, the author of these English words has no ancestral connection to England, nor was she born or raised in Britain).

The best way to gauge the degree to which the Kingdom of Sicily was still "Norman" by the time Constance of Sicily was crowned in 1194 would be to compare her realm to Normandy and perhaps England during the same period to ascertain similarities and differences with the mother culture. Without literally traveling back in time, however, it is not possible to know how many people in southern Italy, or even at court, still spoke Norman French or identified themselves as "Norman" by the time Constance died in 1198. By then, under the influence of Constance's husband, there was an influx of Germans at court, and it is likely that the new language, Sicilian, was already being spoken in some parts of the kingdom.

Like most historians of the last five or six centuries, we may be inclined to regard the Hautevilles as a "Sicilian" dynasty even whilst identifying them as "Norman." Certainly, they became sovereign rulers not in Normandy but in southern Italy and then in Antioch. Sicily was their Land of Opportunity. The cliché that sometimes painted them as foreigners come to subjugate Sicily is a simplification favored by a few historians of the nineteenth century in their Risorgimentalist desire to oust the Neapolitan Bourbons in favor of the Piedmontese Savoys; such ideas have been questioned. (In 2011, the sesquicentennial of Italian unification saw the publication of a plethora of books and articles, along with academic conferences and national television programs, casting serious doubt upon the historiography, propaganda and effects of unification; since the official commemorative events held in Sicily were all but ignored by the populace, a formal boycott wasn't even necessary.)

Interestingly, though a few nineteenth-century historians viewed the Neapolitan Bourbons and their Capetian forebears, the Angevins, as "colonialists," the same historians generally regarded the Norman and Swabian dynasties that ruled until 1266 not as conquerors but as natives interested in prosperity and development rather than exploitation.

Questions of ethnicity and social identity do not always yield very clear answers. Ethnology is nothing if not complex. What is beyond cavil is the identity of the Hautevilles as our first royal dynasty and the founders of the Kingdom of Sicily.

Identity

The origins of *Sicilianità,* in its most rudimentary form, are sometimes debated. In antiquity, Sicily was divided among the Sicanians (the island's oldest civilization), the Sikels and the Elymians. Neither the Punics nor the Greeks united the island or its inhabitants, though the latter lent a certain identity to *Sikelia* and its *Sikeliotes*. Under the Romans, Byzantines and Arabs, Sicily was a small part of large empires. Not for nothing do we Sicilians look to 1130, the year Roger II founded his kingdom, as the beginning of an era that saw the naissance of a true national identity.

Subjective descriptions of a perceived "Sicilian character" or collective personality are occasionally found in chronicles and letters of the Norman era. In a letter written by Peter of Blois to Richard Palmer around 1173, the former is critical of Sicily and its "nasty" Sicilians. This missive is relevant to us not for Peter's specific criticisms but for the fact that he seems convinced that stereotypes exist to an extent that justifies generalizations of this kind regarding the people of Sicily, to whom he refers as a population rather than identifying Normans, Arabs or Greeks. This may suggest that, at least in Peter's mind, the Sicilians were already a single people despite their cacophony of tongues. Our Sicilian forebears were not his only targets; two decades later, after having returned from the Holy Land, Peter penned an infamous diatribe against Jews, a like reference to an entire ethnic group.[2]

The Sicilian vernacular emerged by around 1200 (see Chapter 7), but medieval *Sicilianità* transcended language. A national identity need not be zealously ethnocentric; it can be multicultural as well as multiconfessional, and part of Queen Margaret's task as regent was the defense of the kingdom's ethnic and religious minorities against the zealous baronage.

There can be little doubt that the lives and reigns of Sicily's first kings and queens were closely intertwined with the development of a distinctive *Sicilianità*. The realm of Roger II may have extended its tentacles to the Balkans and northern Africa, but its nucleus was never presumed to be anything other than southern Italy, with Palermo as its capital. Even cuisine (see Chapter 6) is part of a Sicilian identity.

The Sicilian (and southern Italian) cultural identity that exists today was shaped by the cultures of the Arabs, Byzantines, Lombards and Normans, and then the Swabians, Angevins and Aragonese, to form something distinctive. By 1300, it was essentially a monolithic, Latin monoculture except for the presence of the Jews.[3]

During the fifteenth century, four pillars that once belonged to a mosque were utilized to support the Gothic portico added to Palermo's cathedral. One bears a Koranic verse, yet it is unlikely that anybody living in the city at that time knew enough Arabic to read it.

If little has been published about Sicily's Latin monoculture from an explicitly anthropological perspective, it is because, in many respects, this was fundamentally the same Sicilian social culture that existed into the nineteenth century, when the folklorist Giuseppe Pitrè wrote about it. Pitrè dedicated much of his life to the preservation of literature written in Sicilian, leaving Arabic studies to scholars like Michele Amari.

Sicilianità need not be argued from a historicist point of view, and we need not find a latter-day Margaret Mead to study and evaluate social norms that have been quite apparent since the Middle Ages. On the other hand, it is not possible to know the exact role played by every nuance of history in the formation of a society's culture over time. At best, we can examine these details, events and trends to see their aggregate effects over the course of centuries. Much medieval knowledge has been lost.

The Sicilians' sense of uniqueness or "separateness" is based on more than the fact of the region being an island, though (like the case of Ireland) it is related to that reality, and it is not an abstract concept. Indeed, there is a modern point of reference for it.

During the War of the Vespers of 1282, Angevin forces abandoned Sicily, an integral part of the kingdom, retreating to Calabria and leaving the island to the invading Aragonese. History repeated itself in the summer of 1943 when the poorly-motivated Italian army did the same thing, abandoning Sicily and her people to the Allied forces, thereby relinquishing sovereign territory. In both cases the invaders enjoyed wide support from the Sicilians themselves. In connection with the latter, it should be remembered that the Kingdom of Italy did not change alliance until September of 1943, meaning that Sicily, unlike the peninsular regions of the country, was not only liberated but literally conquered from the decrepit Savoy monarchy. Covering more territory than Piedmont, Sicily is the largest of Italy's twenty political regions.

We cannot know with precision the degree to which the majority of subjects mourned the deaths of our earliest queens or venerated their memories thereafter. With some justification, certain queens are sometimes described as "forgotten," mostly because rather little has been written about them by modern biographers.[4] Some of us may be reluctant to adopt such a characterization because it can be misleading to readers.

Over the centuries, Sicily's Norman roots have not always been so remote in the collective memory as one might be given to conclude from reading certain commentaries by foreign historians over the last sixty or seventy years. In 1625, when Saint Rosalie, for whom there is only dubious historicity, became the principal patroness of Palermo, she was claimed to have been a Norman damsel, perhaps even a granddaughter of Robert Guiscard. She was famously depicted by Antoon van Dyck with a light complexion and reddish hair, as if she were a sister of Constance Hauteville.[5] Ecclesiastical censorship meant that this imaginative iconography was rarely questioned. Before long, Rosalie eclipsed the city's other patronesses (Ninfa, Oliva, Cristina, Agatha) and its patron, Benedict the Moor.

Though Rosalie is probably an apocryphal figure, hers was not a novel legend. As a virgin maiden, she may have been venerated in several localities before the seventeenth century, and was believed to have been a lady-in-waiting of Sybilla of Burgundy or Margaret of Navarre. A popular tradition identifies her as the daughter of a Norman baron and a woman thought to be a daughter of Robert Guiscard. Real or not, Rosalie was emblematic of the Norman noblewomen of medieval Sicily. In that respect, her legend may have been inspired by twelfth-century queens or even by women such as Lucy of Cammarata, discussed elsewhere in this volume. She could well be considered a latter-day metaphor for these ladies.

It is important to understand that even though the concept of *Sicilianità* has an overwhelmingly geographic and cultural component, it is not, strictly speaking, about bloodlines, nor is it necessarily Siculocentric.[6] In some of Palermo's neighborhoods today one encounters the young children of immigrants from Nigeria, Bangladesh and elsewhere in Africa and Asia speaking Sicilian as well as Italian and their ancestral language. Clearly, this is not a question of monarchism, as Italy has no monarchy, nor do today's Italians (compared to Japanese or Americans) have a very profound sense of nationalism. More often, Italians' cultural identity is found in regionalism, and many speak "regional" (formerly national) languages like Neapolitan and Sicilian in addition to Italian (Tuscan). This dovetails with such distinctive "regionalisms" as cuisine and folk customs.

It is easy to overlook the myriad of things that constitute the identity of a culture in a specific place. As an example, outsiders may not realize that southern Italy even has several of its own breeds of dog, notably the *cirneco* (Sicilian hound), Neapolitan mastiff and Sicilian sheepdog, known during the Middle Ages. Into the twelfth century the aristocrats bred a local variety of the Norman deerhound, used to hunt the deer that populated much of the kingdom.

The recognition of Sicily as an autonomous region of the Kingdom of Italy reflected broad ideals of cultural identity.[7] For comparison, we may look to the culture, identity and political status of Catalonia.[8]

Queenhood is part of ethnosymbolism, which predates modern concepts of nationalism and supports the historical and cultural basis for an *ethnie* (identifiable ethnic group). This is true whether an individual, or a segment of society, knows it or not.[9]

Visually, Sicily's "national" symbol dates from antiquity. This is the triskelion, or *trinacria,* three conjoined legs (shown in the map at the end of this chapter). Representing the triangular island's three geographical points, it has no special connection to queens or kings except that in the fourteenth century the Angevin rulers of Naples, who wanted to continue being called kings of *Sicily,* wished for their Aragonese counterparts in Palermo to be called kings of *Trinacria.* This is the origin of the phrase *Two Sicilies* popularized when both kingdoms were united in a personal union (in 1735) by Charles III and a political one (in 1815) by his son, Ferdinand I.

Sicilian History by Sicilians

Significantly, much of Sicily's medieval and modern history is taught very differently here in Sicily than it is outside Italy. This is not due to blind nativism, but the way history is learned in most of the postcolonial world, by people living in the place that experienced the events over the centuries. In other words, it is a case of people writing their own history.

A noteworthy scholar who advanced this kind of historiographical perspective in writing about his own homeland was Rosario Gregorio, whose six-volume *Considerazioni sopra la Storia di Sicilia dai Tempi Normanni sino ai Presenti* (1816) reflects the views that existed for centuries until that time, some since the era of Thomas Fazello, whose history of Sicily was a post-incunable work published in 1558 and is still consulted by those of us who study Sicilian historiography, along with the *Sicanicarum Rerum Compendium* published by Francesco Maurolico in 1662.

Rosario Gregorio was born in Palermo in 1753 and educated in this city during the Bourbon era. Significantly, his tome about the Kingdom of Sicily is not tainted by the slanted Risorgimentalist (unificationist) and nativist (Italianist) perspectives that emerged later.

That was a major flaw in the subsequent writings of Michele Amari (1806-1889), a rabid unificationist who sought to compare the War of the Vespers of 1282 to the Piedmontese invasion of 1860. It should be noted, however, that Amari's work as an Arabist was highly competent, on a par with that of Salvadore Moreso (1766-1828), and in our times the contributions of both are occasionally overlooked.

One of the post-Fascist historians who contributed the most constructive ideas about the nature of a Sicilian identity was the late Santi Correnti (1924-2009), whom we met in the Introduction. He is distinguished for advocating, in a post-Fascist environment, the concept of a history of the Sicilian people rather than the history of Sicily as a place ruled by conquering civilizations and dynasties. This was based on our island's complex historical ethnography and the nature of the kingdom as it existed by 1300 in view of Norman, Swabian, Angevin and Aragonese influences.

Correnti's *Storia di Sicilia come Storia del Popolo Siciliano,* first published in 1956, is not too different from works by contemporary historians of Catalonia, Ireland, Bavaria and other parts of Europe, or the Jewish diaspora.[10] It is, however, the general history of Sicily most read by Sicilians, and for a half-century following the establishment of the Italian Republic it was the only Sicilian history read by most of the island's adults. Correnti, a professor at the University of Catania, was critical of the historiography advocated by his contemporary, Denis Mack Smith (1920-2017), whose cynical ideas sometimes facilitated bizarre conclusions.[11] Those debates need not concern us at length, but although the Englishman was viewed as something of a revisionist, Correnti had many sober, accurate words about things like Nino Bixio's execution of civilians at Bronte in 1860.[12] Indeed, he was one of the first Italian historians to write accurately about many events of the unification era, and he recognized the reign of Charles III (from 1735 to 1759) as a turning point that truly, finally freed Sicily from the mentality that had dominated the island since the end of the Middle Ages.

His ideas about the medieval historiography of Sicily should be read by anybody who hopes to write a biography of a Sicilian medieval queen, even if one questions his characterization of Hugh Falcandus, the chief source for the regency of Queen Margaret, as "the Tacitus of the Middle Ages."[13] Anglophone scholars are entitled to their own views, but to understand the Sicilians' views of our Middle Ages it is important to know something about the way Sicilians have been writing history for the last seven hundred years.

On the other side of Sicily, in Palermo, another historian of note who wrote about the concept of Sicilian identity was Virgilio Titone (1905-1989). In 1943, the Allied military government appointed him to a professorship so that he could expurgate Fascist propaganda from the university curricula that had corrupted young minds for the better part of a generation.

Many Sicilians have a greater sense of history than may seem apparent. Certainly, the antiquity of the island's history is evident in its ancient Greek temples and theatres. Beyond this, many families, even those not descended from the aristocracy, can actually trace their lineages, documenting their ancestry not in a vague manner but generation by generation, with names and dates, into the fifteenth century. Elsewhere in Europe the records do not exist that make this possible for most ordinary families.[14]

Legacy

It is sometimes said that if you don't write your story, somebody else will write it for you. Ironically, we don't know for certain who first said this, but the idea was embraced by Julius Caesar. More than a memoir, his commentaries about his conquests in Gaul were meant to influence opinion back in Rome, hopefully in his favor.

History, in the first instance, is written, or passed down orally, by the people of the society that is its subject. A modern criticism in certain quarters is the risk of a history thereby becoming too Eurocentric, Anglocentric, Siculocentric and so forth, because it is self-interested.

One may well postulate that history written by "outsiders" is more "objective" than that authored by those within the society about which they are writing, but what of Thucydides, Sima Chian, Diodorus Siculus, Tacitus, Bede, Anna Comnena, David Hume and Winston Churchill? Whatever their biases, was their familiarity with the place, its people and its culture not a decided advantage? Were they not, in some way, writing about themselves, much as a memoirist might? Were their histories parochial?

Sir John Malcolm's history of Persia, published in 1815 and soon translated into French and German, is a good example of a work intended to introduce foreigners to the history of a country with which few Europeans or Americans were then familiar, but it was not written with the aim of educating the Persians themselves, as they had their own history books. Nor do we have any indication that Malcolm, as a xenophile, was attempting to usurp or appropriate the culture of the Persians or their heritage. Problems arise when a society has not published much about its history.[15]

Malcolm's work was based on the diaries and notes he wrote while in Persia, augmented by his reading of its history in the original. Similarly, Marco Polo's account of his travels was a first-person "history." Yet the Silk Road was already well-traveled, with Muslim dominions ranging from Portugal to Pakistan, fostering European contact with China. In 1241, Batu Khan had made it as far westward as central Europe, even dispatching a letter to Frederick II.

The perceptions of outsiders can be contentious. In 2015, a general history of Sicily written by the late John Julius Norwich was released in Britain with the title *Sicily: A Short History, from the Greeks to Cosa Nostra*. In the United States, the title was changed to *Sicily: An Island at the Crossroads of History*. Presumably (and understandably), the association of Sicily with organized crime, a phenomenon rooted not in antiquity or the Middle Ages but the eighteenth century, would offend readers, including Sicilian descendants who otherwise might consider purchasing the book. Why should such a fine work be disparaged because of its title, which may not even have been chosen by its author?

The relationship of cultural identity to collective identity and nationhood is nothing if not complex.[16]

As noted in the Introduction, it is not altogether unusual for Britons, or anybody outside the place they write about, to present one image whilst the "natives" present another. Be that as it may, it is hardly "identity politics" to suggest that people should be permitted to write their own history. Just as we could reasonably expect the first biography of a certain Queen of England, such as Elizabeth I, to be written by somebody having roots in England, it makes sense that the first biography of a Queen of Sicily, such as Margaret, would be written by a

Sicilian. (Here, by way of comparison, the author is reminded of rather uninspired Sicilian-born professors at the University of Palermo teaching equally uninspired courses in American history and law.)

This is not an apologia for the exclusion of curious foreigners from the conversation about the history or culture of this or that place. As regards the Kingdom of Sicily, the matter of such scholars' viewpoints as "outsiders" has, in fact, been addressed by non-Italian professors of Siculo-Norman history. Professor Donald Matthew wrote that: "If we became aware of foreign authors regularly selecting a chunk of English history, such as the Civil War, and not bothering with what came before or after, I think we would likely feel entitled to point out the importance of studying problems in their proper context. We might also, as Englishmen, I think, rather wonder at, even resent, perhaps, foreigners meddling with our history and wonder about their motives for doing so."[17]

Until very recently, Sicily had nothing like Agnes Strickland's *Lives of the Queens of England,* completed in 1848. If the dearth of Sicilian historians who have written biographies of our queens based on original sources was lamentable, the reluctance of presses to publish these was nothing less than egregious.

Be it agreed that queens, especially those of a kingdom, like Sicily, where these women came from various places, may well be perceived as part of an elite sisterhood firstly and part of a specific country secondly, the place where they lived — and perhaps ruled — cannot be overlooked. Neither can its people.

The abbey built under a queen's patronage is as relevant to her legacy as surviving regalia.[18] Recent decades have seen authors writing about queenship consider that kind of thing.

The souk — now a street market — that a queen visited near her residence is another aspect of her daily life in Sicily.

We are extremely fortunate that such things as Ballarò, in central Palermo, have existed continuously in the same place, and arguably with something of their original ambience, for a thousand years; consider that, by comparison Barcelona's Boqueria is much changed over time. Such details as Ballarò should not be overlooked.

While *Sicilianità* is not explicitly monarchist, and has flourished quite well in the absence of a monarchy, that tradition was one of the greatest influences upon it over the centuries.

There is a temptation — perhaps instinctive — to dismiss the impact of monarchy in a country, like Italy, where one has been lacking for a few generations. Leaving aside the more general reasons for Italians' lack of nostalgia for the dystopia that was the modern Kingdom of Italy, institutional vestiges of the Norman era were part of Sicilian life until quite recently. Feudalism, as a system of manorial land ownership, was abolished by the ephemeral constitution of 1812, which is itself quite recent in historical terms, but the *latifondi,* the large, formerly-feudal estates that survived the abolition of feudalism by King Ferdinando I of the Two Sicilies, were dissolved only in 1949.

Ethos

It is the past that shapes present concepts of group identity. Sicilian history would be much the lesser without our first few queens, who epitomize a collective historical experience. Could we present a complete view of Sicilian history without them?

Even if a Sicilian living today did not consciously recognize the significance of these women, they are an integral part of the foundations, the very underpinnings, of our history. If only because monarchy survived in Sicily for so long, and until so recently, the early queens could be said to be more immediately significant and meaningful than, for example, certain figures of the classical age, such as the tyrants of Greek Syracuse.

Like forms of government, practices connected to monarchy evolve over time.[19] That the symbolic or cultural importance of Sicily's medieval kings and queens has outlived monarchy itself is not atypical. Many European republics embrace their monarchical past as an important element in their heritage. Unlike the modern sovereigns who ruled Italy until 1946, the medieval monarchs are untainted by the ills of modern politics.[20]

The fact that forms of government change has not negated the significance of figures such as Charlemagne and Louis IX or (in southern Italy) Roger II and Frederick II. Indeed, recent decades have seen much published about Roger and Frederick here in Italy, not only academic titles but books of general interest.

Another fact to consider is that Sicily's countesses and queens were the first female leaders, or consorts of leaders, resident in Sicily during the Middle Ages about whom much is known. The emperor Constans II was in Syracuse in 663, but we do not know for certain that his wife, Fausta, was with him, and virtually nothing is known about the specific wives of Sicily's emirs.

This contrasts sharply with the history of England and certain other parts of Europe, where the names and lives of many women in this position (the consort of a monarch) before the eleventh century are known to us.

The site of a queen's tomb in a cathedral is an obvious place of commemoration, or even pilgrimage. Not many of the medieval queens' tombs in the former *Regnum* can be visited or even clearly identified. The remains of Yolanda and Isabella at Andria, for example, are in an ossuary (with others) in the crypt and unmarked. The remains of the queens of the Aragonese era who rest in Catania's cathedral are housed in sarcophagi, effectively ossuaries, containing the bones of several kings and kin.

We find, however, the tomb of Adelaide at Patti, near Messina. Margaret rests in Monreale. The tombs of Constance Hauteville and Constance of Aragon are in Palermo's cathedral.

Queenhood itself has religious connections, not only to archetypes but to theology. In Catholicism, perhaps more overtly than in Eastern Orthodoxy, Mary, the mother of Jesus, is revered as the Queen of Heaven (the feast of the Queenship of Mary is observed in August). This is one way in which the existence of queens facilitated Catholic belief as the Latinization of Sicily was achieved during the twelfth century. More relevant to Sicily's current social culture is the fact that queenhood is perfectly consistent with the concept of Heaven long espoused by the Catholic Church. Not surprisingly, many of the statues of Mary displayed in religious processions are adorned with crowns.

The only medieval monarch whose life is regularly celebrated in Sicily is a saint, Louis IX of France. His heart is preserved at Monreale, where his feast is celebrated annually on the twenty-fifth of August. Louis was the brother of Charles I of Naples.

No serious effort was ever made to canonize any of Sicily's early queens. For comparison, we look to Margaret of Scotland, who died in 1093. The consort of King Malcolm III, Margaret was canonized in 1250 by Pope Innocent IV.[21]

Nothing in Italy's eclectic political environment, from extreme left to extreme right, has altered certain fundamentally ecclesiastical (religious) aspects of its culture.

There is, however, a particularly "southern" social orientation to it south of Rome. This may be explained by the fact that, into the nineteenth century, the southern kingdom was a centralized state, whereas Lombardy, Tuscany and Veneto were built upon the tradition of the *commune* or "city state" and, at that time, ruled by the Austrian dynasty.[22] This may partly explain why the unificationist and Fascist rhetoric received so well in northern and central Italy never entirely convinced the southerners. Nevertheless, the fact that southerners voted overwhelmingly for the monarchy in 1946 may reflect traditionalist attitudes that transcend modern political movements.

The degree to which Sicilian identity, or that of the other populations of Italy's twenty political regions, is "Italian" is open to debate because the nation was unified so recently, and (unlike Germany) was not united throughout the Middle Ages.

If, after death, none of our early queens was openly glorified over the centuries, were any overtly vilified in a public way? There are three notorious cases.

Most obviously, Constance of Sicily, the last Hauteville, was explicitly disparaged by Giovanni Boccaccio, a Guelph, in his *De Claris Mulieribus* composed around 1361.[23] The pretext for this entry, which was inaccurate in some of its details, was that Constance was the mother of Frederick II, who was despised in many of the communes of northern Italy, particularly by the Guelphs.

Adelaide, the Countess of Sicily who was later Queen of Jerusalem, was derided by Orderic Vitalis, who never met her, as "old and wrinkled" when she died at the age of forty.[24]

In his chronicle, Hugh Falcandus claimed that Margaret was occasionally referred to by malcontent barons as "the Spanish woman." Yet the general populace praised her.[25]

Very few Sicilians could have read these unflattering descriptions over time, and there is no evidence that defamatory remarks influenced modern opinions as they exist today. Although much is said, both positive and negative, about Eleanor of Aquitaine as Queen of England, the situation regarding Sicily's queens is very different. Tourists visiting the tombs of Margaret (at Monreale) or the two Constances (in Palermo) are not told that these were "bad" queens.

Monreale is visited by around a million tourists each year. In 2018, some five million, mostly foreigners, visited Palermo's

Norman Palace, the most important medieval royal site in southern Italy. Some of these visitors have a personal interest in Sicilian culture, being the descendants of Sicilians; they are proud of their cultural heritage.

Several universities outside Italy, particularly in the United States and China, teach introductory (undergraduate) courses in Sicilian Studies which mention our queens.

Conclusion

Sicilianità, like other examples of cultural and ethnic identity, can elude a precise definition. Yet, unlike the subtly shifting boundaries of a region such as Swabia or Kurdistan, an island and its islanders are defined in fairly accurate terms by geography.

On its face, *Sicilianità,* or any paradigm of ethnic identity formed over many centuries, may seem susceptible to the "ship of Theseus theory," which is an appropriate analogy in view of the connection of the history of our region to the ancient Greeks. In a popular version of this exercise in metaphysical thought, if part of the ship were refitted or replaced at every port during the travels of the hero Theseus around the Aegean, would it still be the same ship when it returned to Athens? By the same token, most of the substance of Sicilian identity, despite its many varied strata, has evolved over three millennia of history, yet it is still distinctively Sicilian.

Cultural (or social) identity may seem rather amorphous when compared to legal or political identity. It isn't something indicated under "nationality" on a passport and it is not something one actively chooses. It is largely a matter of attitude, tradition and self-perception. It seeks tangible expressions of intangible ideas, past or present.

Without it, there would be no "Sicilians" as an identifiable group, nor would there be other ethnicities in Europe or elsewhere.[26]

QUEENS AND SICILIANITÀ

Cultural identity is more than a vague idea or social meme, and a Queen of Sicily was more than a woman who just happened to be married to a certain king. She was a symbol to her people, and part of their culture.

In a more personal sense, some of these queens may be seen as heroines, if not "role models," especially for girls. Except for saints, this gender-linked social identity was something generally lacking from the social fabric of Sicilian society until recent times.[27]

The problem was that although the queens were at least mentioned in some books, by the end of the Middle Ages very few Italians could read what was published. At the unification of Italy in 1860, the national literacy level was perhaps twenty percent. Indeed, a larger percentage of Sicilians were literate in 1200 than in 1800.

Queenhood is an indelible part of history that should never be overlooked. Like Sicily's first kings, our queens are an intrinsic element in the heritage of southern Italians.

In some ways, folk culture has conserved something of Sicily's medieval past. Here marionette art comes to mind; although it emerged in its present form during the eighteenth century, most of the craft's figures, characters and plays come to us from the Middle Ages or are profoundly inspired by that era. Mosaicry is a direct reflection of our Byzantine heritage. Majolica likewise has medieval origins.

There is nothing inappropriate in a Siculophile historian who was not educated here in southern Italy writing about a medieval Queen of Sicily; indeed, such efforts should be encouraged. However, it is important for a biographer to understand the place and its people if she is to comprehend much about the life lived by a queen, or any woman, in southern Italy. As much as our world changes day by day, many aspects of Sicilian social culture are rooted in the Middle Ages, and they are subtly different from what one encounters in Tuscany,

Veneto and Piedmont, which did not have large, centralized monarchies of their own when the Hautevilles and Hohenstaufens ruled much of Italy. Indeed, it is likely that certain fundamental differences between the mentalities of Italy's northerners and southerners are rooted in the medieval era.[28]

Nowadays some of those differences, particularly social practices concerning families, are rather subtle. As a contemporary example, the 2017 report by ISTAT, Italy's national statistical institute, informs us that although births outside marriage account for thirty-one percent of the country's total, they comprise nearly forty percent in the regions north of Rome and closer to twenty percent in regions, such as Sicily and Puglia, south of the capital, where weddings are still comparatively lavish events.

Queens — both medieval and modern — evoke a certain mystique as uncommon women at the apex of society. As we have seen, they are much more than that.

One need only visit a few fascinating places to see their legacy (see Chapter 8 and Appendix 1), and even some words and flavors of their bygone era survive (chapters 2, 6 and 7).

Although their medieval legacy is not exclusively monarchical, one or two esoteric, ceremonial traditions redolent of monarchies have found their way into our times.

Following the fall of the Sicilian monarchy, the people did not forget their dynasty, and neither did kindred royalty.[29] The arcane legal right of the sovereign as *fons honorum* survived the end of the kingdom, permitting the heirs of the kings of the Two Sicilies to maintain a familial tradition by bestowing honors in several dynastic orders of chivalry which today support charitable activities throughout Italy and abroad.[30] Amongst these, the Constantinian Order of Saint George stands out for the scope of its projects. Beginning in 1787, this order's commandery in Sicily was the Magione, which, centuries earlier, during the regency of Constance

Hauteville for her young son, Frederick II, was held by the Teutonic Knights.

Unlike the monarchy, *Sicilianità* never entirely disappeared, nor was it forgotten; it was merely censored publicly in Italy for about eighty-six years. That's because the Kingdom of Sicily was more than a polity; it was the cornerstone of something greater than itself.

Part of it is the "diaspora" of *Sicilianità* one finds in the Americas and elsewhere beyond Italy, where certain customs, traditions and historical truths were preserved undisturbed by the vicissitudes that shaped life in Italy during the Fascist era.

Democracy brought forth a resurgence of the open expression of *Sicilianità* in Sicily after 1943, just as Catalonia experienced increasingly overt manifestations of Catalan identity and culture following the fall of fascism in Spain.

Certain aspects of medieval Sicilian culture have undergone actual revival. An example is the recent re-establishment of Palermo's Jewish community, with a synagogue at the site of the temple that was confiscated in 1493.[31] Several mosques have been founded in the city following an absence of Islam for seven long centuries.

A few years before his death, John Julius Norwich wrote that, "No non-Sicilian, I suspect, will ever be able to penetrate the island's mysteries altogether."[32]

Deciphering Sicily's complex identity can be challenging even for an islander. In learning more about our queens we unravel a mystery or two about Sicily and Sicilians.

NOTES

1. Here, as in the Introduction, the author suggests that in more nuanced discussions we might consider distinguishing between *queenhood* (the state of being a queen) and *queenship* (the exercise of reginal power). By way of analogy, a rather similar distinction is found in the terms *Hellenic* and *Hellenistic*.

2. Giles, John, *Petri Blesensis Opera Omnia* (1847): volume 1, pages 138-141 (letter 46 to Richard of Syracuse); volume 3, pages 62-130 ("Contra Perfidiam Judaeorum").

3. This is relevant because the outlines of the Siculo-Neapolitan culture, as it has come to exist over the last six centuries, became evident around 1300 with the suppression of Italy's last Muslim communities at places like Lucera in Apulia. Under Spanish rule, the Kingdom of Sicily suppressed its Jewish communities in 1493, with the neighboring Kingdom of Naples following suit a few decades later; whether some of the Italian Christians now converting to Judaism are, as is sometimes claimed, the descendants of *anusim* (the *conversos* of Spain or *neofiti* of Italy) is open to debate. Despite an influx of Albanian refugees, the population remained essentially monocultural for the next four centuries, bringing us the Latin culture with which the southern Italians are identified today. For insightful overviews of the European trends during this era, see Elliott, John, "A Europe of Composite Monarchies," *Past and Present,* volume 137, number 1 (November 1992), pages 48-71; Leyser, Karl, "Concepts of Europe in the Early and High Middle Ages," ibid, pages 25-47; Dunbabin, Jean, *France in the Making 843-1180* (1985, 2009); Ruddick, Andrea, *English Identity and Political Culture in the Fourteenth Century* (2013).

4. See *Forgotten Queens in Medieval and Early Modern Europe: Political Agency, Mythmaking and Patronage* (2018), edited by Valerie Schutte and Estelle Paranque.

5. This was sometimes justified, or rationalized, by historians based on the supposition that chroniclers were not likely to have mentioned a daughter of the king unless she married, and Rosalie was said to have become a nun.

6. This imprecise preconception is fostered in part by consumer DNA testing that informs customers they are descended from certain ethnic groups by percentage.

7. Contrary to popular belief, this was promulgated not by the Italian Republic but during the short reign of Umberto II, who issued the decree in May 1946 a few weeks before the referendum establishing the republic, and it can be said to have contradicted the spirit of the Savoys' effort to unify Italy during the nineteenth century.

8. Llobera, Josep, *Foundations of National Identity: From Catalonia to Europe* (2004); Balcells, Albert, *El Nacionalismo Catalán* (1991); Lledó-Guillem, Vicente, *The Making of Catalan Linguistic Identity in Medieval and Early Modern Times* (2018).

9. Much has been written about these concepts. See, for example, Armstrong, John, *Nations Before Nationalism* (1982); also Davies, Norman, *Vanished Kingdoms* (2012).

QUEENS AND SICILIANITÀ

10. Correnti, Santi, *Storia di Sicilia come Storia del Popolo Siciliano* (seventh edition, Catania, 1995), pages 17-22.

11. Denis Mack Smith infamously permitted one of his students to submit a dissertation asserting that the Mafia did not exist as an organization, something unlikely to be accepted by a professor in an Italian university. This bizarre idea eventually made its way into a condensed, revised edition of his history of Sicily published after the Italian government had recognized in law that the Mafia is indeed an organization. See *A History of Sicily* (1987), page 214: "The mafia has always been more widespread in fantasy than in fact." In fact, from my house in the outskirts of Palermo I heard the explosion of the bomb that killed Judge Paolo Borsellino on 19 July 1992.

12. Correnti, Santi, op. cit., page 245.

13. Ibid, pages 23-28.

14. See Mendola, Louis, *Sicilian Genealogy and Heraldry* (2013).

15. Despite what a few historians working outside Italy would have us believe, a substantial amount has been written about our Norman-Swabian history by earlier Sicilian scholars like Amari, Fazello, Garufi, La Lumia, Moreso, Siragusa and others. What was often deficient in this work was the study of Sicily's medieval women.

16. A fair amount has been written about this. An interesting discussion will be found in Strayer, Joseph, *On the Medieval Origins of the Modern State* (1970). For a more recent view of Europe, see Grimson, Alejandro, "Culture and Identity: Two Different Notions," *Social Identities,* volume 16, number 1 (2010), pages 61-77. Other relevant studies are Williams, Lynn, "National Identity and the Nation State: Construction, Reconstruction and Contradiction," *National Identity* (1999), pages 7-18; Smith, Anthony, "Chosen Peoples: Why ethnic groups survive," *Ethnic and Racial Studies,* volume 15, number 3 (1992), pages 436-456.

17. Matthew, Donald, "Modern Study of the Norman Kingdom of Sicily," *Reading Medieval Studies,* volume 18 (1992), pages 34-56 (the citation is from page 37). For similar commentary on the practice see Schulman, Sarah, "White Writer," *The New Yorker* (21 October 2016); de Waal, Kit, "Don't dip your pen in someone else's blood: Writers and 'the other,'" *The Irish Times* (30 June 2018); Balakrishnan, Anjana, and Cleveland, Mark, "Appreciating versus Venerating Cultural Outgroups: The Psychology of Cosmopolitanism and Xenocentrism," *International Marketing Review,* volume 36, number 3 (May 2019), pages 416-444.

18. For surviving objects see *Queens of Sicily,* pages 533-536, 545-547. For an interesting general commentary see Gosden, Chris, and Marshall, Yvonne, "The Cultural Biography of Objects," *World Archaeology,* volume 31, number 2 (October 1999), pages 169-178.

19. Mount, Harry, "How the Queen fused the medieval traditions of the Coronation with the modern world," *The Telegraph* (London), 31 May 2019.

20. Monarchism *per se* is not very popular in Italy today. The Neo-Bourbon movement in the south does not seek to restore a monarchy but to defend the history of the Kingdom of the Two Sicilies largely negated from 1860 until 1946. See Guerri, Giordano Bruno, *Il Sangue del Sud: Antistoria del Risorgimento e del Brigantaggio* (2010); Oliva, Gianni, *Un Regno Che è Stato Grande: La Storia Negata dei Borboni di Napoli e Sicilia* (2011). For the Savoy monarchy and Italian unification, see Smith, Denis Mack, *Italy and Its Monarchy* (1989); Katz, Robert, *The Fall of the House of Savoy* (1972); Gilmour, David, *The Pursuit of Italy: A History of a Land, Its Regions, and Their Peoples* (2011). More generally, see Kavanagh, Dennis, and Rose, Richard, "The Monarchy in Contemporary Political Culture," *Comparative Politics,* volume 8, number 4 (July 1976), pages 548-576.

21. See Keene, Catherine, *Saint Margaret, Queen of the Scots: A Life in Perspective* (2013).

22. See Gilmour, op.cit. supra; also Putnam, Robert, *Making Democracy Work: Civic Traditions in Modern Italy* (1993).

23. Though he was probably parroting Dante, his recent predecessor, Giovanni Boccaccio's laconic, superficial commentary may be considered the first "biography" of Constance. As a manuscript composed around 1361, *De Claris Mulieribus* ("On Distinguished Women") was widely copied, to be published as an incunable in 1473. The narrative reflects the jaundiced Guelphic (and anti-Ghibelline) view of the Hohenstaufen dynasty that colored Italian historiography for centuries. What is more, Boccaccio errs in identifying Constance's father as William I (rather than Roger II), and overstating the queen's age at the time of her pregnancy. For a fine English translation see Virginia Brown's *Giovanni Boccaccio: Famous Women*, pages 221-223.

24. In Orderic Vitalis we find blunt defamation of a kind divorced from fact and logic. From Forester's translation of the *Ecclesiastical History,* book 13, chapter 15 (volume 4, page 137 in the 1856 edition), one reads that Adelaide, "having collected money from all sources after her husband's death, amassed a great treasure. Baldwin the younger, King of Jerusalem, hearing this, coveted her wealth and sent noble proxies to demand her hand in marriage. Adelais (sic), insatiably greedy of pride, of rank, and honour, accepted the proposals of the illustrious suitors, and went to Jerusalem with a large retinue and a vast treasure. King Baldwin was pleased enough to receive her money, which he lavished on the stipendiaries who fought in the name of Christ against the pagans; but he repudiated the woman who was wrinkled with age, and had rendered herself infamous by many crimes. In consequence, the old woman returned to Sicily in confusion at her failure, and spent her declining years in general contempt."

25. *Queens of Sicily,* page 243.

26. For an insightful analysis of the concept of a continuum from the Middle Ages, see Davies, Rees, "Nations and National Identities in the Medieval World: An Apologia," *Belgisch Tijdschrift voor Nieuwste Geschiedenis: Revue belge d'historie contemporaine,* volume 34, number 4 (2004), pages 567-577. See also the Introduction and essays in Jensen, Lotte (editor), *The Roots of Nationalism: Identity Formation in Early Modern Europe 1600-1815* (2016).

27. See Alio, Jacqueline, *Women of Sicily: Saints, Queens and Rebels* (2014). One of the problems confronted in Italy generally is that since the establishment of the republic, and under the Fascist regime before that, the nation's rabid political divisions have precluded the universal recognition of many women in public life as heroines, and many of the greatest scientific minds leave the country in search of greater opportunities abroad. Hence there is no Italian Amelia Earhart or Grace Hopper.

28. Putnam, Robert, op.cit. supra.

29. Writing from Buckingham Palace on 12 February 1973, Her Majesty Queen Elizabeth II conveyed to Prince Ferdinando (1926-2008) her condolences upon the recent death of his father, Prince Ranieri (1883-1973), a nephew of Maria Sophia's husband, King Francesco II of the Two Sicilies. This was personal correspondence; Queen Elizabeth was writing privately (signing, "I am, Your Highness's good cousin, Elizabeth R") as head of her dynasty, not as head of state. (The author has examined this letter, now conserved in the private family archive of the Royal House of Bourbon of the Two Sicilies with documents that are not made available for consultation by the general public.)

30. These include the Constantinian Order of Saint George, the Order of Saint Januarius and the Order of Francis I, recognized by the Holy See and the Italian government. The work of these knights and dames is similar to that of the Sovereign Military Order of Malta based in Rome.

31. See Povoledo, Elisabetta, "Jews Find a New Home in Sicily 500 Years After They Were Forced Out," *The New York Times* (25 April 2017), Section A (city edition), page 4.

32. Norwich, John Julius, *Sicily: A Short History, from the Greeks to Cosa Nostra* (2015), page 6.

Historical Context: Segesta's Greek temple and the Norman castle at Erice (Mount San Giuliano)

Medieval Magione church in Palermo seen through portal displaying the emblem of the Constantinian Order

Maria Sophia of Bavaria, the last Queen of Sicily, died in exile in Germany in 1925

The Italian states in 1859

Knightly Orders of the Kingdom of the Two Sicilies

St Januarius

Francis I

St Ferdinand

St Charles

Constantinian Order

Chapter 11
A SICILIAN BIOGRAPHER'S NOTES

There are as many ways to write a biography as there are biographers. In its most essential form, a biography is simply a chronological account of a person's life written by somebody else. As a literary genre, biography takes many shapes and sizes. There is no one "correct" way to write a biography, and no universal model for the "perfect" one. Here beauty is in the eye of the beholder.

That's why several people reading the same biography will appreciate it, or not, in different ways. It is not unusual for one reader to love the biography that another hates. In telling the story of an individual, the art of biography has a way of touching our emotions that is unlike that of most other genres. An effective, memorable biography strikes a personal chord with the reader.

Even two biographies of the same person will differ in emphasis, detail and tone. One biography may be sympathetic to its subject while another is critical. Some biographies are more emotive, others more contemplative.

In 1950, two "modern" biographies of Eleanor of Aquitaine, by Amy Kelly and Curtis Howe Walker, were published within months of each other. Like the three major biographies written during the twentieth century about Frederick II (about which more below), they were quite different from each other in style and tone. Yet biographies can complement each other even when they contradict each other.

Many of us would agree that a biography should inform, but the best biographies also inspire. It is important to understand that there is no universal template for writing the biography of a medieval queen, and no single authority to define how this task should be accomplished. However, a number of historians have addressed this question over the last few decades, providing us with some very general ideas about the strategies that seem to be most effective most of the time.[1]

Biography exists at an intersection of two evolving areas, namely historiography and publishing. The biographer should never lose sight of the essential epistemology concisely outlined under "Black Swans" in Chapter 5.

What follows makes special reference to Sicilian queenhood during the Norman-Swabian era.

This chapter is intended not as a "guide," which would be an exercise in presumption, but as a "menu" of facts, observations and ruminations from which a few ideas may be selected, tested, ignored, appreciated or discarded. (Useful works are listed in the endnotes.) If anything stated here seems pedestrian or reductive, it is because this chapter is meant to be pragmatic. However, the following information is not intended as legal advice, for which the reader should consult a competent expert in her own geographic jurisdiction.

Formats

In our times, the biographer must decide which kind of biography to write. Opinions abound; no biography pleases everybody. For clarity, it should be remembered that there are several types of medieval biography, which may be categorized, albeit succinctly and imperfectly, in the following manner.

General, "conventional," popular or "trade" biographies were the norm into the end of the twentieth century and still constitute the lion's share of the market today. They may contain the same scholarly apparatus of notes and bibliography found in "social" biographies (the next category) but their emphasis is traditional, linear history. Some of these works reflect research in original sources and may be peer-reviewed, perhaps presenting heretofore unpublished information. However, their greatest appeal is to a general readership. Being somewhat more "commercial" than "social" biographies, these books are designed to be readable and attractive, printed in the thousands and sold at competitive prices. Their authors are sometimes promoted through book signings and interviews. There may be a photograph of the book's author on the back cover or an inside flap of the volume's dust jacket. It is not unusual for these biographies to have many pages of useful maps, genealogical tables and photographs. The print in these books is usually legible for both its point size and typeface. The prose is usually quite clear, perhaps even eloquent.

Social, or academic, biographies are the norm for consultation by scholars. These may focus more on queenship or the social aspects of a queen's life than what is presented in a conventional biography intended for a general readership. Some of this information may reflect originative theories about a queen's life, times and experiences. These biographies are likely to be peer-reviewed prior to publication, but some major academic presses also release titles for the general market. Though there are exceptions, these academic biographies, being intended for scholars, are not necessarily written in a very appealing style and their design is sparse, lacking much in the way of attractive graphics. An author's photograph is not usually included. These books are normally printed in the hundreds and typically cost more than trade biographies. Academic presses are infamously parsimonious with maps and other graphics, sometimes limiting these to just a few pages. Based on standard templates, these books may have rather small type. Even though they present the same essential facts and chronology as general biographies, these social biographies are more likely to be written in jargon-filled academese.

The distinctions between these two approaches concern the method of presenting history more than the history itself, though only vaguely corresponding to the differences between "political" and "social" historiography. Conventional biographies are sometimes criticized for being too "literary" in style, while some social biographies seek to shape the historical narrative to an author's preconceived thesis about the subject.

Some biographies do not fit very well into a specific category.

Crossover biographies, a rather small classification, may appeal to more than one readership, but are also likely to elicit criticism from purists in both camps. The only way to satisfy both factions would be for an author to write *two* books, one for academics and one for the general public. It is appropriate for the *first* biography of a medieval queen to focus more on essential fact than theory because this will be the first reference that readers find after an encyclopedia entry or general history.

Of course, these three forms are not the only way to classify biographies; historians propose other classifications.[2] A few variations should be mentioned as well.

Compendia compile several biographies or biographical studies in one or more volumes and may be intended as reference works. Examples are Rosalind Marshall's *Scottish Queens 1034-1714* and Alison Weir's *Queens of the Conquest*. These are sometimes edited as collections, with each chapter written by a different author, such as *Icons of the Middle Ages*, edited by the late Lister Matheson.

What might be called "thematic" biographies present information about several queens integrated into one volume. Nancy Goldstone's *Four Queens* follows the general (trade) model, and is priced accordingly, while Colette Bowie's book, *The Daughters of Henry II and Eleanor of Aquitaine,* is a social (academic) study of queenship biographically. Both of these books deal with sisters. Weir's *Six Tudor Queens* is a multi-volume series.

There are also analytical publications which consider one or another period or aspect of a queen's reign. Such works are broadly biographical.

Other genres exist. Mary Taylor Simeti's *Travels With a Medieval Queen* is a biographical travelogue. Significantly, it includes, albeit interspersed with other information, the first biography of Constance Hauteville published in English. Like *Margaret, Queen of Sicily,* it established a new subject category in libraries.

Some biographies are "situational," bringing us information about the lives of two or more genealogically unrelated figures at a certain nexus of history. In *The Maid and the Queen: The Secret History of Joan of Arc,* Nancy Goldstone tells us the story of Joan of Arc and Yolande of Aragon. This is a good example of a work in English following significant biographies in the language of the kingdom where a woman was queen; published in 2012, Goldstone's book trailed those about Yolande by Arnaud des Roches de Chassay in 2006 and Gérard de Senneville in 2008. Although there were already many books available about Joan of Arc, *The Maid and the Queen* formed the basis for a new subject category about Yolande in many libraries that did not have the earlier works in French.

Each publishing model and biographical form has its complexities. This includes pricing, as trade publishers usually offer lower prices than academic presses. As a typical example, let's first consider two biographies of the same queen, Mary Tudor, written around the same time by historians holding doctorates in history. In hardback, Linda Porter's *Mary Tudor, The First Queen* (Little, Brown), at 464 pages, has a retail list price of (US) 28 dollars; Judith Richards' *Mary Tudor* (Routledge), at 296 pages, lists at 120 dollars, or 90 pounds.

Let's look southward. Published in 2009, Nancy Goldstone's *Joanna: The Notorious Queen of Naples, Sicily and Jerusalem* (Walker), at 378 pages, lists for 27 dollars in hardcover; following this by a few years, Elizabeth Casteen's *From She-Wolf to Martyr: The Reign and Disputed Reputation of Johanna I of Naples* (Cornell), at 312 pages, retails for 50 dollars. Published in 1893, the first monographic English biography of Joanna was *Queen Joanna I of Naples, Sicily and Jerusalem,* the detailed, 380-page work of Welbore Saint Clair Baddeley, an Englishman who spent some years in southern Italy and came to know Joanna's realm intimately, to the point of becoming reasonably proficient in her Neapolitan tongue. There were, of course, numerous Italian biographies of this singular queen, to whom a certain body of Neapolitan folklore, and even Tuscan literature, was dedicated; a fine example is Matteo Camera's *Elucubrazioni Storico-Diplomatiche su Giovanna I Regina di Napoli e Carlo III di Durazzo,* published in Salerno in 1889, which includes the texts of important source documents. Indeed, Joanna stands apart from other medieval queens of southern Italy's twin kingdoms for the sheer number of biographies written about her before the twentieth century, which provided abundant material for her more recent biographers.

The research necessary to write a biography can be costly, and each publishing model has its own financing method. Academic publishers are less likely than their counterparts in trade publishing to pay an author an advance against future earnings; in academia the research costs may be defrayed by a university or government. Where subventions are not available, an author may have to cover her own research expenses, which can be substantial.

"Open access," simply defined, is a method for making published work, such as monographs and papers (articles), available to readers free of charge, in either print or digital form, where these can readily be read (especially via the internet). This already exists, in a sense, in public libraries, but the open access models currently advanced would extend this to the download of recent works still in copyright. For publishing houses, the key challenge of open access is that the costs of research, editing and publishing must be defrayed by somebody, and even academic publishers seek to make a profit. Presently, some scholarly work in social science and humanities is published through open access if that is a prior condition of the public funding that paid for the cost of its research and production. This makes sense where, for example, a public university, the European Union or the Italian education ministry funds research on the Normans of Italy. Without open access to the resulting work, some readers pay for it twice, firstly (through taxes) at the financing stage and then upon purchase of the monograph or journal that presents the results of the research.

Only rarely do publishers reveal their sales statistics to outsiders, but the significant success of bestselling titles like those of Alison Weir and Nancy Goldstone is obvious. In law, an author becomes a "public figure" if her books and articles are read by a large number of people and she receives media attention such as interviews for documentaries about her subject. The more a biography sells, the more readers want to know about its author; she will be lauded by fans and reviled by rivals. Popularity leads some biographers to do lectures based on their work.

Whether a biography gets published depends on several factors, ranging from politics to economics. We expect the first biography of a queen to be published in the country where she was crowned. One would not normally presume the first biography of Elizabeth I of England to be written by a xenocentric Italian woman in Rome and published in Italian in Turin. Indeed, William Camden was already writing about Elizabeth shortly after her death. The concept of "Sicilian-ness" and its relevance to biography was considered in the previous chapter.

Apart from the reluctance of publishers, it was censorship and its after-effects that delayed the publication of substantive monographic biographies of Sicily's first queens into the twenty-first century here in Italy. As the sluggish decades passed, there was a very real possibility that a woman would walk on the moon before these biographies were published!

Out of the Shadows

While each author has her own reasons for writing a queen's biography, there are some stories that demand to be written.

For more than two decades, I thought about the life of Margaret of Navarre almost every time I visited the *duomo* of Monreale, where she is entombed. That was quite often, as I sometimes lectured groups of tourists or students in the church or cloister. Many times in those twenty-odd years, I was asked by these visitors if there was a book with further information on Margaret.[3] A biography along the lines of Marjorie Chibnall's book about Empress Matilda.

There was not. Except for John Julius Norwich's general history of the Normans in Italy, which had little to say about Margaret, the only thing available in English came along in 1998; this was a translation of the chronicle of Hugh Falcandus that dealt with most of Margaret's regency of William II but not her childhood or her later accomplishments, such as patronage of the monasteries at Maniace and Monreale.[4] In fact, there was no biography of Margaret in *any* language. After waiting in vain, year after year, for somebody else to write the biography, it became clear that I would have to write it myself if I was not to go to my own grave still wishing that it had been written.

A temporary solution, beginning in 2002, was to publish a few articles about Margaret and our other queens on a popular travel website, a Sicily destination guide (online since 1999) that was read by more than two million visitors annually; my unsigned article on Monreale was particularly popular. This online presence resulted in these articles, considered collectively, being read by several million site visitors over the course of a decade. A few of the site's readers asked that the queens' biographies be expanded for publication as monographs. Margaret's biography had thus generated interest, and a potential market, years before the book was published.

The historian writing the biography of a queen about whom many books have been published enjoys a certain latitude in choosing her format. However, because this was the *first* monographic biography of Queen Margaret, it had to appeal to various readerships rather than just one segment of the market. Thanks to the chroniclers Hugh Falcandus and Romuald of Salerno, much was known about Margaret's life in Sicily. Her story even had a natural "narrative arc," something of a rarity in the biographies of medieval queens. The resulting volume, based on archival research in Spain and England as well as Italy, was over five hundred pages long, with ten informative appendices. As the first detailed biographical monograph of this queen, it necessitated the formation of a historiographical framework of original sources such as chronicles, letters and decrees, whereas recent biographies of queens such as Joanna of Naples or Eleanor of Aquitaine could benefit from prior research undertaken over the course of centuries.

Most readers – in Italy and abroad – praised this effort, and the book sold well enough to go to a second printing within a year of its publication. It was distributed internationally and sold in a bookshop in Monreale attached to the church. Public and university libraries around the world acquired it and students cited it. A screenwriter in California expressed an interest in writing a motion picture script based on the book.

Another woman, even one outside Sicily, might well share my passion for this singular queen, but for me it was more than that. It was not only academic and intellectual but personal; Margaret's biography is part of the Sicilianità, the heritage of Sicilians, described in the previous chapter. At its heart, this was the story of a woman in medieval Sicily, and a story that had to be told as something more than shreds and fragments. People besides me wanted to know about Margaret.

The fact that no other biography of her has been published since that book was released suggests (though it does not prove) that nobody else was working on anything similar at the same time, and that, if I had not written the book when I did, I would still be waiting for it to appear. Indeed, *Margaret,* like *Queens of Sicily* published two years later, has been purchased by a number of Italians who speak English as a second language because nothing comparable has yet been published in Italian.

To reiterate a principle mentioned earlier: *The duty and responsibility of writing a medieval queen's first biography falls to the historians of the country where she was crowned.* One does not presume to delegate this task to foreigners any more than we would expect foreigners to intervene in Italian politics or formulate superior recipes for *pasta con le sarde alla palermitana.*

Margaret was not the only queen to be generally overlooked. There was no consultative reference dedicated to the other queens, about whom I sometimes spoke during lectures at Palermo's cathedral (where the two Constances are entombed) and Norman Palace (the occasional setting for royal weddings). These women also sparked much interest, and so did court poetry written in Sicilian. By 2000, Frede Jensen's fine translation of the *Contrasto* of Cielo of Alcamo, a poet of the Sicilian School, was no longer in print, and in my lectures I had been using my own translation, so it seemed appropriate to include this in the book of biographies about our queens, as one or two of them may have heard this poem recited or sung. This poetry, being composed in Sicilian, has a direct relationship to the *Sicilianità* defined in the previous chapter. The English text of the *Contrasto,* published as Appendix 5 in *Queens of Sicily,* is a work of essential translation; detailed analyses are available elsewhere.

It must never be forgotten that a biography's chief purpose is to inform. Most readers seek an essential chronology and facts.

The pedantic criticisms of the many biographies of, for example, Mary Tudor focus more on style than substance because the essential facts of her life are so well known to us that new information is sought. For Sicily's queens, we are unlikely to meet with a legitimate debate about fundamental biographical facts.[5]

Who reads queens' biographies? The reading preferences of many devout reginaphiles seem to be national or dynastic in orientation. Feedback indicates that most readers of the author's books about Sicily's queens are firstly Siculophiles, among whom there are many men. These readers have a keen curiosity about queens and country. A good number have roots in southern Italy. Here is a typical example:

I was visiting the cloisters at Monreale Cathedral outside Palermo and rambled into the bookstore to find *Margaret, Queen of Sicily*. Being a huge Sicilian history buff, I couldn't wait to read it and was enormously surprised at how wonderfully written it is. I was particularly interested in the woman's perspective, as every other book I'd read about Sicily has been written by men. In this respect, the author did not lecture or pontificate; she beautifully wove into the narrative how women were expected to behave, and then how they were deftly able to control without a heavy hand — of course unless needed. It was great to read in the story about other ruling queens at the time, which inspired me to read further. I very strongly recommend this book, not only for the historical perspective, but also for the strong narrative and attention to detail.

A professor reviewing it for the *Medieval Feminist Forum* recognized the book as a seminal work:

Margaret, Queen of Sicily should easily become the first point of reference for scholars of Margaret working in English and for general readers interested in Margaret and her world.

These reviews were published in 2019.[6] By then, the book was beginning to inspire work such as dissertations and theses by junior scholars. The first biography of this long-ignored queen had thus started a trend in new scholarship.

This contrasts sharply with recent biographical studies of Joanna of Naples (discussed above), about whom a great deal had already been published.

Biographers

Most queenly biographies are written by women. That was not always the case, even though the phenomenon of European women writing about women is not new. Cristina da Pizzano (Christine de Pizan), who was born in Venice in 1364, wrote such works in French. With some justification, she could even be considered a "proto-feminist" author. Cristina famously challenged the merit of Jean de Meun's *Romance of the Rose,* the inspiration for the *Contrasto* of Cielo of Alcamo.

Is the study of medieval women a subfield of women's (or gender) studies or is it a specialty within medieval historical studies? One could argue that it should be considered part of both of these areas and others. Yet one awaits the day when there will no longer be a need to treat women's studies as something separate from those of the general population.[7]

When it comes to historiography, the author is a traditionalist, embracing conventional methods augmented by a few newer ones brought to us through the marvels of modern science.

Although the modern scholarly study of medieval queens by women found its greatest impetus during the second half of the twentieth century, we find an early trend in the oft-overlooked work of Agnes Strickland (1796-1874) and her contemporary, Mary Anne Everett Green (1818-1895); the latter wrote biographies of two of Sicily's queens, Isabella and Joanna. Some of today's more cynical critics are inclined to dismiss the efforts of such nineteenth-century historians as "romantic" or "Victorian." In fact, these women wrote sophisticated biographies based on original sources and the best scholarship of their era, laying the groundwork for later biographers.[8]

Here in Italy, where women were not even given the vote until 1945 (voting the next year), the advent of more than a few examples of literature written by women about women is a more recent development linked directly to the belated arrival of freedom of expression. Among the few exceptions in the Kingdom of Italy were the Sicilian essayists Elvira Mancuso (1867-1958) and Maria Messina (1887-1944), best known as novelists.

Not every significant biographical work about a Sicilian queen has been written by a woman. An early entry in the field was authored in 1791 by Domenico Forges Davanzati. His *Dissertazione sulla Seconda Moglie del Re Manfredi e sù Loro Figliuoli* also reproduced a number of source documents that had not yet been catalogued or published.

Initially, the new freedom led to very few biographies of the queens of the Norman-Swabian era; instead, there was a certain amount of effort directed toward those of the Aragonese period, which began in 1282.[9] This later period has bequeathed us much more source information (chiefly in archives in Palermo and Barcelona) than what remains for the earlier queens.

Aragonese rule led to Sicily, politically separated from the Angevins' peninsular Kingdom of Naples (still confusingly called the "Kingdom of Sicily" for many decades), becoming, in effect, part of the thalassocracy known as the "Crown of Aragon" ruled from Zaragoza and Barcelona. It is this "dynastic intersectionality" in a personal union (several distinct dominions ruled concurrently by a single monarch) that one encounters in writing about most of the Sicilian queens of the Aragonese era.[10]

There was some precedent for this. Beginning with Constance Hauteville, Sicily's queens were wed to the Staufen sovereigns who ruled lands beyond the Kingdom of Sicily: Henry VI, Frederick II, Conrad, Manfred.

Identification

The last two decades have seen a fair amount published regarding the process of evaluating the lives of medieval queens, some of it highly insightful.[11] Much of this scholarship regards "queenship" rather than traditional biography. As explained in this book's preface, queenship encompasses the study of female agency, diplomacy, the use of power, and various analytical considerations, whereas biography, in its most essential form, is a chronological story of one's life and experiences. The two areas often (and should) overlap, of course, and queenship studies necessarily rely upon biographical facts.

A great deal has also been written about the historiography of Sicily centering on the Norman-Swabian period, and particularly its multicultural side.[12]

The study of Sicilian queens benefits from more general scholarship.[13] Yet Constance of Sicily is mentioned only perfunctorily in recent reference works, where Margaret, perhaps Sicily's greatest medieval queen, is ignored.[14] Theresa Earenfight, however, mentions Constance and her daughter-in-law, Constance of Aragon, in her fine study, *Queenship in Medieval Europe* (see note 13).

Sicily's first queens are generally overlooked altogether in such works, although a few have been the subject of study in specialized monographs and papers.[15] There is also increasing interest in the aristocratic women of southern Italy during this period.[16]

There is nothing to suggest that a man cannot write a sympathetic biography of a woman, but we have come to expect a female point of view in the biography of a historical queen. Recent decades have seen the emergence of prevailing, well-defined ideas about women's biography and its importance in the field of women's studies and in society generally. Much has been published about this.[17] It comes as no great revelation that reginal biography is one of the few areas of history publishing where women authors are in the majority.[18]

An underlying challenge in writing about medieval women of any social class is the degree of inference from context necessary to garner information sufficient for a biography. We need not necessarily view this against the backdrop of movements like postmodernism. It is more a question of sources and the way we interpret, or reinterpret, them.

Except for especially powerful medieval queens, typically regents such as Margaret, there usually is not as much source information available as there is for a king.[19] This is logical, for why would there be as much documentation for the life of

Elvira of Castile, a queen consort, as there is for the reign of her husband, King Roger II? This principle has sometimes been cited to explain why our study of historical women is especially challenging, and why it must complement that of men without attempting to supplant it.[20]

In southern Italy before 1266, only a few women rival the queens for the quantity of information known about them. Trota and Sichelgaita, both of Salerno, are the most obvious examples.

As we see elsewhere in this volume, exploring the details of a medieval queen's private life usually proves difficult. How much must we know? "Do we really have to know of some famous person that he wet his pants at six and practiced oral sex at sixty?" asked Barbara Tuchman.[21]

No matter how much we search medieval history for more, and louder, female voices, they may always be more difficult to identify in the eternal din than those of their male contemporaries, exceptions notwithstanding. Therefore, despite exceptions such as Anna Comnena, considered the first European woman to write a history, and Sichelgaita of Salerno (consort of Robert Guiscard), who trained as a physician and led troops into battle, the search for women as intellectuals and leaders will not reveal many in chronicles and other records except for queens and prominent abbesses like Hildegard of Bingen. Most often, the role of queens is complementary to that of kings.[22] In the chronicle of Jamsilla, Beatrice of Savoy, Queen of Sicily, consort of Manfred, is mentioned exactly once, and then only in connection with her daughter's proposed betrothal.

Published in 1981, Barbara Tuchman's *Practicing History* is still a useful guide to many aspects of writing biography (other views about historiography are noted below). The first part of the book, titled "The Craft," is especially informative. It is facile to dismiss Tuchman as a modernist. Yet her landmark work *A Distant Mirror: The Calamitous Fourteenth Century* (1978) is based on original sources such as Froissart's chronicles of the Hundred Years' War, while its focus on a specific individual, Enguerrand de Coucy, lends it the perspective of a quasi-biography. Running to 678 pages in paperback, the volume has 596 informative endnotes — usually preferable to footnotes because they permit greater length and detail — and considers events around the Mediterranean as well as Europe.

Details are important. Considering the general dearth of sources before 1300 (compared to later centuries), every gesture is relevant, perhaps more so than it would be otherwise. If a certain chronicler is the only one known to have recorded a particular event or detail, there is little choice but to consider his words unless, for some reason, they completely lack credibility. Corroboration between sources is preferable but not always possible. Many incidents mentioned by the cynical chronicler Hugh Falcandus for the regency of Queen Margaret are not attested elsewhere.

Some queens are the beneficiaries of dozens of biographies. A seminal biography, like a first history, is merely a starting point, a basis for further research. Later critics sometimes forget that Thomas Fazello's *De Rebus Siculus* (1558-1560), the first published history of Sicily, was a cornerstone of its field. It is futile to criticize it today.

Sources

In medieval reginal biography, contemporaneous "primary" sources are the framework upon which everything must be built. They are the lifeblood of this literary form.[23] These are chiefly chronicles, annals, charters and letters.

Chronicles, if copied, might be distributed throughout a fairly wide geographic area over time; thus the surviving manuscript of the Ferraris chronicle, though written at a monastery near Naples, ended up in Bologna. One expects most of the relevant charters, if conserved, to be found where a woman lived; in Joanna's case this means England and France as well as Italy. It should be noted that, unlike England, which boasts archives such as the one at Kew, Italy, owing to the fact of it having been several states until 1861, lacks a single major "national" archive. Rather, it is a network. For the Kingdom of Sicily before 1266, the chief repositories are Cava, the Vatican, Montecassino, and the state and diocesan archives at Naples, Palermo, Salerno and Bari. Most of the relevant charters once housed in Messina were taken to Spain and are now at Toledo.

A review of the existing secondary literature is important (my personal library has more monographs and journals pertaining to Sicilian medieval history than most university libraries), but it is the contemporary, or near-contemporary, sources from which the chronology and details must be drawn. This is especially true where there is not much prior research, as was the case of several of Sicily's queens.

"The facts in a secondary source have already been pre-selected, so that in using them one misses the opportunity of selecting one's own."[24]

The biographer should keep in mind that, unlike a dissertation, thesis, paper or certain other forms of study, a biography does not exist to "prove" a theory, although it may present one. One of the potential pitfalls intrinsic in excessive reliance upon secondary literature of an analytical kind is that each successive monograph presumably builds upon what came before it, citing the beliefs of earlier historians in support of a certain premise. Since a chain is only as strong as its weakest link, the result can be a fallacious concept of, for example, the personality of a queen that is not rooted purely in fact because it has been obscured by successive layers of the dense patina of time. History is not historiography, and a biographer should not burden her reader with inaccuracies simply because these have been published elsewhere.

An obvious exception to this rule would be a fact, mentioned in a secondary work, that refers to an original source (such as a charter or letter) that has since been destroyed or otherwise lost. Let us say, for example, that a monograph published in 1650 quotes from a charter of 1150 that existed in the seventeenth century but is no longer conserved even as a transcription, nor listed in a chartulary. This is how the author established the location of the residence of the exiled nephews of Thomas Becket in Palermo.

Some secondary literature is hardly worth citing, much less relying upon, in a biography that seeks accuracy. For example, Isidoro La Lumia, whose biography of William II of Sicily presents a narrative about the regency of Margaret of Navarre that merely parroted the chronicles of Hugh Falcandus and Romuald of Salerno, described the queen's physical condition at the age of thirty-eight (she was actually about thirty-one) as "still beautiful, slender and proud."[25] The problem is that La Lumia had no way of knowing anything about Margaret's physical condition or appearance, unmentioned by these local chroniclers. Margaret was around forty-eight when she died. The remains in her tomb had been destroyed before La Lumia was born, and the reliquary pendant bearing what may (or may not) be an accurate likeness of her was, as yet, undiscovered. Repeating one of La Lumia's numerous errors, John Julius Norwich likewise reports Margaret's birth date inaccurately, at around 1128.[26] Another error appears in the necrology of Saint Matthew, published in 1922, where Carlo Alberto Garufi makes an unconvincing argument for the date of Margaret's death based on the citation of inaccurate information and his mistaken belief that her mosaic epitaph at Monreale (see Chapter 8) was completed four decades, rather than four years, after her death.

In *Margaret, Queen of Sicily* there was no compelling reason to rebut the opinions of these historians or draw attention to their errors. Such a decision was based on pragmatism and concern for the reader rather than any personal bias. (In the interest of full disclosure, it should be mentioned that I met Lord Norwich here in Palermo almost a decade before his passing, when I lectured a group he led on a tour of Sicily.) It seemed important, however, to place the queen's year of birth more accurately at *circa* 1135, something no preceding historian seems to have done.

Norwich's perception of Margaret as somehow ineffectual was not consistent with my own research, which revealed her to be something of a "she-wolf" (see Chapter 1) prepared to cast enemies, or perceived enemies, into prison and order the deaths of her husband's adversaries. This seemed to be accurate even when the principal source was the notoriously nasty Hugh Falcandus. Evelyn Jamison's view of Margaret as regent was generally favorable but somewhat problematical in certain details. In retrospect, and at the distance of many centuries of time, some of Margaret's decisions may have been ill-advised, but they cannot be said to indicate incompetence, nor were they atypical of their era.

Speaking generally, it has not been necessary to present very much "revisionist" information about the lives of Sicily's queens because, in reality, the body of biographical work about them is rather meagre.

At all events, it is not the purpose of a biography to present the reader with every erroneous idea ever hatched about the subject. The objective of a biography is to make available to the reader an accurate, informative (perhaps even interesting) account of the chronology and details of a life.

Often, it is simply unnecessary to critique the work of fellow historians, especially when the criticism concerns comparatively minor, banal details. This pedantic form of criticism can sometimes be perceived as an *ad hominem* attack. In the third edition of his *magnum opus* detailing the Norman conquest of England, Edward Freeman, who later wrote a history of Sicily, undertook to respond to subjective criticisms voiced by an envious colleague.[27]

Some affirmations are too bizarre to merit a response that merely serves to dignify their supposed legitimacy. This was the case of the unsupported claim by a non-Italian professor of medieval history (employed at a university outside Italy) that the roots of the Mafia could be found in Palermo during the reign of William I.

Though it is important to review the existing literature, an unfortunate result of dignifying every factual error or misconceived theory with a reply or rebuttal is that the biographer's own work comes to be defined "dialectically," in a Hegelian manner, by an earlier publication which may itself be flawed. We have seen this, to some degree, in the biographies of Frederick II written in the wake of Ernst Kantorowicz's *Friedrich der Zweite,* published in 1927 as the first "modern" biography of the emperor who was also King of Sicily. In 1972 and 1988, competent scholars writing lengthy biographies of Frederick felt called upon to expend much effort in rebutting some of the earlier biographer's claims and theses.[28]

This they did in the main (narrative) text, whereas a few footnotes, a concise paragraph in the introduction or perhaps a succinct appendix would have been more than sufficient for the task. That was the approach taken by Sir Steven Runciman in *The Sicilian Vespers,* published in 1958, in responding to the propagandistic history of Michele Amari, who had sought to compare Italy's *Risorgimento* movement to the popular rebellion of 1282.

The thesis-antithesis dyad is not restricted to biographical monographs. It sometimes appears in papers, articles, lectures, book reviews and other work when the writing of an author is predicated upon, even defined by, that of another to whom she is seen to be responding.

If enough information exists, the ideal format for a reginal biography is a monograph. This presupposes a volume containing the usual scholarly apparatus, not only an index but notes, charts, maps and a bibliography, as well as photographs.

It is the author's firm conviction that bibliographies should list only those works that are actually useful in a biographer's research. These works may not, in every case, be cited directly (as notes), but irrelevant monographs and papers need not be listed simply to "prove" to the reader that they were consulted by the author unless there is a compelling reason for mentioning them. The chief purpose of a biography is to support the biographer's account, not to address every "alternate" theory ever conceived about her subject. Admittedly, this stratagem is more easily applied to the story of a queen like our Margaret, about whom little was written, than to her *consuocera* Eleanor of Aquitaine.

Is it our objective to write an accurate, informative medieval biography based on the original sources, or an outline predicated largely on prior theses and opinions?

This query brings us to the next point.

Views

Historians entertain eclectic views about famous figures. The writing of history necessarily involves choices about what to tell and how to tell it. That was true in the time of Anna Comnena and it is still true today.

There are various schools of thought about the writing of biography. Disagreements are thus unavoidable. Peer review in the humanities and social science has become complex; it can also be sluggish. According to Patricia Skinner, "many activists in the field are no longer willing to submit to the power politics of academia's anonymous peer review, and then wait nearly a year to see their papers in print."[29]

Biography, like any other literary form, even translation, depends upon expertise and judgment. The most important element in biography is its accuracy, namely its names, dates, places and events.

Certain biographies are intended to be more analytical than others. In recent times we have seen books and papers which seek to evaluate, in a detailed manner, such phenomena as the marriages of medieval queens. Some of this work is useful even if, taken as a whole, its quality may be rather uneven.

The facts should not be presented "selectively" (or out of context) to support a preconceived thesis. In the sage words of Barbara Tuchman, "the material must precede the thesis."[30] The biographer must seek to avoid possible confirmation bias.

None of this is to imply that hypothesis has no place in biographical studies — there is a fair amount of it in this volume — but a distinction should be drawn between the biography of a queen and a theory about a particular aspect of her life.

Tossed into this mix is the "social history" that has largely supplanted "political history" in historical studies as these are taught in academia most of the time. The biography of a queen should incorporate both.

The parallel debate of structuralism versus post-structuralism tends to focus somewhat more on literature and the arts than history.[31] Although translation and interpretation necessarily entail judgment based on usage and social context, no serious medievalist presupposes that the words, however flowery and figurative, in a work such as the chronicle of Peter of Eboli were intended to be somehow "subjective," as if they were an exercise in semiotics. More realistically, it is the interpretation of historical facts in the context of social history that sparks many debates.

It must be remembered that consensus does not, in itself, determine what is accurate or true. If conventions never evolved with the introduction of original ideas, we would still believe that the sun orbits the earth.

No book is perfect, but the quality of editing and proofreading has suffered in recent times. Recently, I noticed several errors — including the obvious misspelling of the name of an Italian city and misidentification of a medieval chronicler — in a paper written by a tenured professor published as the chapter of an edited collection in a book of over six hundred pages released in English by a prestigious university press in Europe. This occurred in the first few paragraphs of a paper dealing with medieval women. It was not entirely the professor's fault; an author should have a reasonable expectation that this kind of thing is noticed, and duly corrected, before the volume goes to print. One of the many challenges facing the field of academic publishing is that most editors and proofreaders are "outsourced," while most expert reviewers are unpaid. Some academic presses even outsource the indexing of monograph texts, charging the authors for this "extra" service.

Despite the proliferation of new historical journals in recent years, in history studies a scholar's more important, original work is sometimes published as a monograph rather than an article in a journal or a chapter in an edited collection. Clearly, the information available on certain queens is insufficient for a biography presented as an entire volume.

Publishing is a competitive business and some books are potentially profitable. Even an academic press may discourage the biographer from submitting too much original work intended for the biography to journals for publication before the book is published. This is especially true in the ever-rarer case of the very first biography of a particular queen, which may have a commercial market. Peer review of a text prior to publication presupposes that the reviewers (readers or referees) will not share the biographer's work with outsiders; this may necessitate a non-disclosure and non-compete agreement which, admittedly, is not easy to enforce after an idea has been poached since an author cannot copyright a historical thesis, however original, the way an engineer can patent an invention. Prepublication confidentiality should include the book's concept and subject as well as its content.

Copyright is a rather complex topic best left to law experts. Here it may simply be noted that, at least in theory, copyright protects a completed work in fixed form, even before publication, and presently only one nation, the United States, offers formal copyright registration (certification) and even pre-registration, whereas China does not recognize all intellectual property rights and Italy has rather lax enforcement. Nowadays, many academic presses will accept a contractual copyright license in lieu of an outright transfer of the author's publishing rights.

Multidisciplinary Methodology

The use of the diplomatic and epistolary record is straightforward enough. Most of the more important charters have been published or at least catalogued. The more significant chronicles and poems of this era have been transcribed and published. Indeed, most have been translated into English from Latin, Arabic, Middle Sicilian or Norman French.

As the author has often stated, history is not religion; history has experts but no authorities. The only dogma of the biographer is factual, accurate history. This should be arrived at through research based on sound epistemology and solid investigative methods. Fortunately, these methods are increasingly multidisciplinary. They may involve such fields as genetic (DNA) research and climatology.

Very few historians writing about Italy's Norman-Swabian

history have even mentioned these fields, much less utilized them.[32] This omission may be attributed, at least in part, to the fact that so few historians who write in English about southern Italy have spent much time here, not in just a few localities but traveling around this region. The *Regnum* wasn't just Palermo, Bari and Salerno but Enna, Potenza and Brindisi.

Even without referring to actual genetic studies, one observes the numerous blue-eyed and red-haired Italians in Campania, Puglia, Calabria and Sicily; in Palermo children with red hair are actually called *Normanni* and women with black hair are called *More,* not as derogatory terms but as simple descriptions.

Global climate change is no secret, but those who live here in Sicily actually experience it acutely. The winters are ever shorter and milder while the summers are increasingly longer and hotter; bananas and mangoes are now grown in Sicily.

How is this relevant?

The genetic record identifying haplogroups, which are linked to specific populations, serves to enlighten historians who might otherwise consider the "disappearance" of Sicily's Muslims an "enigma."[33] Though Islam disappeared the Arabs themselves did not "vanish" but, for the most part, simply converted. We Sicilians are the descendants of our island's historical Arabs, Greeks, Phoenicians, Romans, Normans, Swabians, Angevins, Catalans and Jews.

Genetic testing also serves a forensic purpose. It can identify remains, such as those of the two queens in a tomb in the crypt of Andria's cathedral. Paleopathology can inform us about physiological details such as the possibility than Henry (1211-1242), the eldest son of Frederick II, probably suffered from the effects of leprosy.[34]

A consideration of climate change, specifically global warming, is necessary if we wish to accurately gauge the accounts of certain events, such as the Normans' experience at the Nebrodian town of Troina in the early months of 1062, for which a chronicler (in this case Godfrey Malaterra) cannot provide a precise indication of the temperatures beyond mentioning that it was colder than most recent winters and there was much snow.[35] Here in Sicily, today's concept of "much snow" certainly differs from that of the eleventh century.

This is an example of the influence of context on biography, and on historiography in general.

As we have said, travel is important because, even if a biographer need not consult archival records in a certain locality, it is beneficial to explore the places themselves. This includes places of birth but also the castles where the queens lived before being crowned. For Sicily's queens this meant everyplace from the Tower of London and Winchester to Pamplona and Zaragoza, to San Marco d'Alunzio and other towns here in Italy. To the modern eye, Margaret's greatest lasting achievement was Monreale's abbey; it must be seen to be appreciated.

In writing about the Bonello revolt that claimed the life of Queen Margaret's son, it was necessary to trace every step of the uprising based on the episode as it was recounted by Hugh Falcandus. Parts of the medieval city of Palermo mentioned in that chronicle and other sources are barely recognizable today. For example, a city gate, the Arabs' *Sant'agat,* that once stood near the paleo-Christian church of Saint Agatha, is long gone, and should not be confused for another "Saint Agatha's Gate" still standing in the Norman wall that shadows Corso Tukory at the eastern end of the Ballarò street market. It was at the former, near the cathedral, that Matthew Bonello and his accomplices killed Maio of Bari in November 1160. The church remains, and a street follows the path that once led to the gate, but the gate itself, along with the medieval wall, is gone, though a segment of the city's ancient Punic wall survives nearby. The site (shown in a photograph at the end of this chapter) is not much to see, and this exemplifies the condition of certain castles and other edifices mentioned in this book's first appendix. The author has thousands of photographs of this kind that are more useful for reference than for publication (and is willing to share these with fellow researchers).

In studying about the more noteworthy among the experiences of the other countesses and queens, it was equally necessary to explore Messina, Bari, Brindisi and Salerno, where, fortunately, it is still possible to identify certain places mentioned in chronicles and other sources.

In connection with the later revolt that led to the expulsion of Stephen of Perche, Falcandus mentions the riots ending as the sun set beyond the high mountain, Mount Cuccio (from the Arabic *Kuz* for its conical summit), to the south of Palermo. For this, one need only observe that the sun disappears beyond that mountain about a half-hour before dusk. In the Middle Ages, before there were lights lining the road (now Corso Calatafimi) to Monreale, this meant that darkness enveloped the city's older districts rather early.

Arguably, these may not be determining details in a reginal biography any more than knowing the room of Winchester Castle in which Isabella of England was born would shed much light on her life as a queen. However, even if the results of such research are not reported explicitly in the narrative or notes of the biography, they facilitate the biographer's understanding of her subject.

We can know more about a queen if we know more about her environment.

Although it may at first seem insignificant in the biography of a woman who died before 1300, a study of the kingdoms of Naples and Sicily into the first half of the fourteenth century is relevant because some of the developments of that period, reflected in royal charters and other records, are based on events, policies and legislation of the Norman-Swabian era that ended at Benevento and Tagliacozzo. By way of example, a useful work, though it comprises but a fraction of the relevant material that must be consulted, is the *Codice Diplomatico dei Re Aragonesi di Sicilia 1282-1355* of Giuseppe La Mantia, published in 1918.

Just as the cathedral of Siracusa was erected upon a Greek temple, whose pillars can still be seen, much of the social fabric of Angevin-Aragonese Italy was built during the Norman-Swabian era.

While the potential problem has, for the most part, been obviated by the publishing of important records and the redundant availability of work in libraries and on the internet, the loss of significant information can be a factor in writing biography. In many instances, we shall never know what we do not know because some sources, like Margaret's letters, were lost at an early date, perhaps before the advent of the printing press. This obviously involves not only the diplomatic record — some charters at the Naples Archive of State were infamously destroyed by German troops in 1943 — but vestiges of artistic or architectural patrimony. Fortunately, Joanna's funerary epitaph was published before its destruction during the French Revolution.[36] This principle also concerns the preservation of human remains for scientific analysis.

The importance of local knowledge is not to be underestimated. A potential problem arises when a biographer is not sufficiently familiar with the social culture of the place where a queen lived. For our purposes, this is southern Italy. One of this book's chapters considers the language, Sicilian, of the court known to the queens of the Swabian era. Another deals with cuisine. Among the many other significant topics are medicine and law, along with local feudal practices.

Political structures involving feudalism, the church and the law are well known. For the Kingdom of Sicily, the legal framework of society was rooted in the two major law codes, namely the Assizes of Ariano and then the Constitutions of Melfi, augmented by Catholic canon law. Based on the Code of Justinian, these laws were not tantamount to a constitution, whether written or unwritten, nor were they comparable to such milestones as England's *Magna Carta,* but they were the nearest thing to it in the Kingdom of Sicily. Though the Assizes of Ariano were not a foundation charter, they were promulgated just a decade after the establishment of the Kingdom of Sicily, following a few years of strife during which the king consolidated his power (see the section on Matilda in Chapter 5).

Feminism

An area of particular complexity concerns feminism and the integration of the modern principles of feminist (and gender) theory into the writing of biography. To what degree should reginal biography be feminist? That depends on how we define feminism. According to its simplest definition, feminism is an essential paradigm of equality between men and women. In medieval biography, it presupposes that we treat queens and kings equally historiographically.

Other connotations, influenced by specific schools of feminist thought, have led some scholars to question whether certain reginal biographies are sufficiently feminist.[37] Some female scholars expect queens' biographies to focus on queenship and feminism, and criticize those that do not, yet Hubert Houben's fine biography of Roger II is not criticized for its conventional format as the chronology of a king's life.

Arguably, we may be arriving at a place where nearly all female historians, and most of their male colleagues, are implicitly feminist. It could be argued further that most reginal biographies written in our times are intrinsically feminist by their very nature, perhaps by the simple fact of their being written.

The term, and the phenomenon it represents, may be more

necessary in some countries than others; a certain lack of feminism (or female equality) in Italy partly accounts for the dearth of reginal biographies in this country until quite recently.[38] Nevertheless, it is still the case that feminism, expressed through women's studies, is occasionally considered something of a "niche" in medieval studies.[39]

Out of discomfiture, an Italian *professoressa* might express "denial" to her foreign colleagues about the state of women in Italian society, yet journalist Lilli Gruber wrote a bestselling book about it, *Streghe: La Riscossa delle Donne d'Italia,* a decade ago.[40]

Part of more recent feminist theory is the concept of intersectionality mentioned earlier in another context.[41] In the case of a medieval queen, this means we would regard her status based on her position (queen regnant, regent or consort), or perceptions of her, as leader, wife, mother, peacemaker, warrior, judge, patron, protector, or perhaps even executioner (see Chapter 1).

The introduction of feminist principles in biography may prompt historical revision as we consider, or reconsider, the importance of certain queens based on modern insight and prosopography.

Each woman's story is dictated to some extent by what can be known about her from the historical record. Amongst our Sicilian queens, we find a vast difference in the available sources between Margaret of Navarre and Beatrice of Savoy.

No single solution is suitable to every biography. An overview of strategy in the study of medieval women is encapsulated by Patricia Skinner, who has researched in Italy, in her *Studying Gender in Medieval Europe: Historical Approaches.*

Revisionism and Changing Perspectives

Like *multiculturalism,* the term *revisionism* is often viewed negatively. Yet *corrective* revisionism is sometimes necessary if we are to arrive at an accurate account and perception of history.

History itself does not change but our knowledge and perceptions of it certainly do. Some corrective revisionism is rooted in social, scientific and intellectual evolution. Often, it simply broadens and deepens our view about things like legitimacy of birth.[42]

Since around 1960, historiography and the historical method have been shaped by a number of evolving if conflicting ideas, some quite complex, about what history should be and how it should be written. Barbara Tuchman was hardly alone, and here the budding biographer may wish to cast an eye over the work of Edward Carr, Geoffrey Elton, Arthur Marwick, John Tosh, Keith Jenkins, Alun Munslow, C. Behan McCullagh, Richard Evans, David Cannadine and Ian Mortimer. (For their books see note 11 in the Introduction.) The insights of Tuchman and Mortimer, as medievalists, may be particularly interesting to those writing medieval biography.

Specialized studies of queenship focus on medieval women and their social environment. This offers us information on some topics that, in certain cases, had not yet been explored in great detail, such as marital life, religious patronage, medicine, clothing, court culture, poetry and cuisine.[43]

Into the early decades of the twentieth century, phenomena such as mental health, spousal abuse and sexual orientation were relegated to the realm of the unspoken and unwritten, particularly when these deviated from the perceived, accepted norm. It is therefore logical to expect a biography of a certain queen written in 2020 to be somewhat different in sociological perspective from one written in 1920. In the past, before computers and instant communication, several centuries might pass before historians recognized that certain details about medieval royalty should be revised in biography.

The new paradigm has spawned the concept of the "modern" biography of medieval figures. This development is generally beneficial so long as we do not seek to ascribe modern views to a medieval person. The "new" approach to biography is consistent with multidisciplinary research and such ideas as intersectionality and feminism. In general, this is to be applauded.

Localized social change sometimes prompts revisionism. The fall of the Soviet Union permitted corrective history to be published in Russia and the fall of Francisco Franco's regime allowed revisionism to take root in Spain.

Here in Italy, the forced demise of the Fascist dictatorship, and with it the House of Savoy, facilitated freedom of expression. Not only did this allow for the publication and dissemination of balanced histories of the Kingdom of the Two Sicilies and the other pre-unitary Italian states that existed until 1860, it permitted the publication of lengthy biographies of important kings like Roger II and his grandson, Frederick II. The censorship that flourished from 1860 until Sicily's liberation by the Allies in 1943 discouraged the wide distribution of biographies of these monarchs because the subject might remind us southerners that our region was once a prosperous sovereign kingdom.

Conclusion

It is difficult to find fault with Barbara Tuchman's bold affirmation that biography is the prism of history, through which we can see much more than the life of the woman we are writing about.[44]

Writing biography can be a challenge even for a seasoned historian.[45] Whatever form it takes, the biography of a medieval queen must bring us the facts and, to the extent it is possible, something of the woman's personality.

Queenly biography, as it is written today, is usually seen to be intrinsically feminist. Whether this makes the biographer an ideologue is an open question.

Madeleine Albright has famously declared that, "There is a special place in hell for women who do not help other women." The writing and diffusion of medieval reginal biography does more than meet the academic standard of "adding something new to the body of knowledge." It opens an entirely new conversation that informs and benefits everybody.

NOTES

1. See, for example, the essays in *Writing Medieval Biography 750-1250: Essays in Honour of Frank Barlow,* (2006). See also note 13 below.

2. See, for example, Riall, Lucy, "The Shallow End of History? The Substance and Future of Political Biography," *Journal of Interdisciplinary History,* volume 40, number 3 (Winter 2010), pages 375-397; also Prestwich, Michael, "Medieval Biography," ibid, pages 325-346.

3. In 2018, for example, the author lectured around five thousand foreign visitors in Sicily. This exceeds the number of students taught in a typical undergraduate course by a history professor or the number of attendees at a lecture given at an academic conference. Among the organized groups were members of YPO, which recognized her as a "resource" (lecturer), and various university classes.

4. Norwich, John Julius, *The Kingdom in the Sun 1130-1194* (1970); Loud, Graham, and Wiedemann, Thomas, *The History of the Tyrants of Sicily by 'Hugo Falcandus' 1154-1169* (1998).

5. See, for example, Mortimer, Ian, and Vincent, Nicholas, "Was Edward II Really Murdered," *BBC History Magazine,* January 2016, pages 44-47.

6. The review by Professor James E. Purpura of Columbia University, New York, was published on Amazon.Com, 31 August 2019. The review by Professor Misty Urban was published in the *Medieval Feminist Forum: A Journal of Gender and Sexuality,* volume 55, issue number 1 (summer 2019), pages 319-321.

7. For an early overview, see *Women in Medieval History and Historiography* (1987), edited by Susan Mosher Stuard, and the same author's *Women in Medieval Society* (1976). For a fine essay reflecting a more recent perspective, see Goldstone, Nancy, "I'm a Historian, and I Think Women's History Month is a Mistake," *Time* (in HistoryBooks), 23 March 2018. Also Bennett, Judith, *History Matters: Patriarchy and the Challenge of Feminism* (2006).

8. See Krueger, Christine, "Why She Lived at the Public Records Office: Mary Anne Everett Green and the Profession of History," *Journal of British Studies,* volume 42 (January 2003), pages 65-90.

9. It is not the author's intent to evaluate this work, but it resulted in more papers than monographs. For an example see Sciascia, Laura, "Bianca di Navarra, l'ultima regina: Storia al femminile della monarchia siciliana," in *Principe de Viana,* volume 60 (1999), pages 293-309; also Fodale, Salvatore, "Blanca de Navarra y el gobierno de Sicilia," ibid, pages 311-322.

10. The Sicilian baronage initially (in 1295) resisted this by ensuring that the same son of Peter III of Aragon was not the king of both Aragon and Sicily, but in later times this principle was not rigorously respected, and in any case the Sicilian

monarch was, at the very least, a cadet of Aragon's dynasty. See: Testa, Francesco, *De Vita et Rebus Gestis Federici II* (1775); De Stefano, Antonino, *Federico III d'Aragona Re di Sicilia 1296-1337* (1937); Epstein, Stephan, *An Island for Itself: Economic Development and Social Change in Late Medieval Sicily* (2003); Backman, Clifford, *The Decline and Fall of Medieval Sicily: Politics, Religion and Economy in the Reign of Frederick III, 1296-1337* (1995). For the Aragonese Empire, see Davies, Norman, *Vanished Kingdoms* (2012). For queens specifically: Earenfight, Theresa, "Absent Kings: Queens as Political Partners in the Medieval Crown of Aragon," *Queenship and Political Power in Medieval and Early Modern Spain* (2005), pages 33-54; Woodacre, Elena, "Blanca, Queen of Sicily and Queen of Navarre: Connecting the Pyrenees and the Mediterranean via an Aragonese Alliance," *Queenship in the Mediterranean: Negotiating the Role of the Queen in the Medieval and Early Modern Eras* (2013), pages 207-227.

11. For some observations, with bibliographic references to numerous other works, see Huneycutt, Lois, "Queenship Studies Comes of Age," *Medieval Feminist Forum,* volume 51, number 2 (2015), pages 9-16; Earenfight, Theresa, "Where Do We Go From Here? Some Thoughts on Power and Gender in the Middle Ages," ibid, pages 116-121. Also: Walker, Gina Luria, *The Invention of Female Biography* (2017); Woodacre, Elena (editor), *Queenship in the Mediterranean: Negotiating the Role of the Queen in the Medieval and Early Modern Eras* (2013); Weikert, Katherine, and Woodacre, Elena, "Gender and Status in the Medieval World," *Historical Reflections,* volume 2, issue 1, (2016), pages 1-7; Erler, Mary C, and Kowaleski, Maryanne (editors) *Gendering the Master Narrative: Women and Gender in the Middle Ages* (2003); Stafford, Pauline (editor), *Gendering the Middle Ages* (2001). See also note 13.

12. For observations, and bibliographic references to other works, see Davis-Secord, Sarah, "Medieval Sicily and Southern Italy in Recent Historiographical Perspective, *History Compass,* volume 8, number 1 (2010), pages 61-87; also Mandalà, Giuseppe, "The Sicilian Questions," *Journal of Transcultural Medieval Studies,* volume 3, issues 1-2 (2016), pages 3-31.

13. Of note are Stafford, Pauline, "Writing the Biography of Eleventh-Century Queens," *Writing Medieval Biography 750-1250: Essays in Honour of Frank Barlow* (2006), pages 99-110; Chibnall, Marjorie, "The Empress Matilda as a Subject for Biography," ibid, pages 185-194; Parsons, John (editor), *Medieval Queenship* (1993). For reference: *The Oxford Handbook of Women and Gender in Medieval Europe* (2013); *Women and Gender in Medieval Europe: An Encyclopedia* (2006). See also Duggan, Anne (editor), *Queens and Queenship in Medieval Europe: Proceedings of a Conference Held at King's College, London, April 1995* (1997); Johns, Susan, *Noblewomen, Aristocracy and Power in the Twelfth-Century Anglo-Norman Realm* (2003); Rubenstein, Jay, "Biography and Autobiography in the Middle Ages," *Writing Medieval History* (2005), pages 22-41. More generally, see Leyser, Henrietta, *Medieval Women: A Social History of Women in England 450-1500* (1995); Lucas, Angela, *Women in the Middle Ages: Religion, Marriage and Letters* (1983); Stenton, Doris, *The English Woman in History* (1957); Robertson, Elizabeth, "Medieval Feminism in Middle English Studies: A Retrospective," *Tulsa Studies in Women's Literature,* volume 26, number 1 (2007), pages 67-79; Earenfight, Theresa, *Queenship in Medieval Europe* (2013); Benz, Lisa and Rohr, Zita (editors), *Queenship, Gender and Reputation in the Medieval and Early Modern West 1060-1600* (2016); Skinner,

A SICILIAN BIOGRAPHER'S NOTES

Patricia, *Studying Gender in Medieval Europe: Historical Approaches* (2018). Sauer, Michelle, *Gender in Medieval Culture* (2015). See also note 11 and this volume's bibliography.

14. See Fösser, Amalie, "The Political Traditions of Female Rulership in Medieval Europe," *The Oxford Handbook of Women and Gender in Medieval Europe,* pages 75-76, 79; also the concise entry on pages 165-166 of *Women and Gender in Medieval Europe: An Encyclopedia.* Constance Hauteville is mentioned in passing in Skinner, Patricia, *Women in Medieval Italian Society 500-1200* (2001), page 161.

15. For example: Bowie, Colette, "To Have and Have Not: The Dower of Joanna Plantagenet, Queen of Sicily," *Queenship in the Mediterranean: Negotiating the Role of the Queen in the Medieval and Early Modern Eras* (2013), pages 27-50; Eads, Valerie, "Sichelgaita of Salerno: Amazon or Trophy Wife?" *Journal of Medieval Military History,* volume 3 (2005), pages 72-87; von Falkenhausen, Vera, "Zur Regentschaft der Gräfin Adelasia del Vasto in Kalabrien und Sizilien 1101-1112," *AETOS: Studies in Honor of Cyril Mango Presented to Him on April 14, 1998* (Stuttgart 1998), pages 87-115; Mumelter, Maria Luise, *Irene von Byzanz* (Innsbruck 1936); Runde, Ingo, "Konstanze von Aragon," *Die Kaiserinnen des Mittelalters* (2011), pages 232-248; Storey, Gabrielle, "Berengaria of Navarre and Joanna of Sicily as Crusading Queens: Manipulation, Reputation and Agency," *Forgotten Queens in Medieval and Early Modern Europe: Political Agency, Myth-Making and Patronage* (2019), pages 41-59. Several chapters in *Medieval Italy, Medieval and Early Modern Women: Essays in Honour of Christine Meek,* a collection edited by Conor Kosick published in 2010, mention Sicily in connection with other topics but without dealing with our queens.

16. A good entry in this field is Drell, Joanna, *Kinship and Conquest: Family Strategies in the Principality of Salerno during the Norman Period 1077-1194* (2002).

17. A few works: Chassen-Lopez, Francie, "Biografiando mujeres: ¿qué es la diferencia?" *Secuencia,* number 100 (Jan-Apr 2018), pages 133-162; Chevigny, Bell Gale, "Daughters Writing: Toward a Theory of Women's Biography," *Feminist Studies,* volume 9, number 1 (Spring 1983), pages 79-102; Damousi, Joy, "Feminist Biography," *Hecate,* volume 15, number 1 (May 1989); Downs, Laura, *Writing Gender History,* second edition (2004); Heilbrun, Carolyn, *Writing a Woman's Life* (1988); Painter, Nell, "Writing Biographies of Women," *Journal of Women's History,* volume 9, number 2 (1997), pages 154-163; Wagner-Martin, Linda, *Telling Women's Lives: The New Biography* (1994); Ware, Susan, "Writing Women's Lives: One Historian's Perspective," *Journal of Interdisciplinary History,* volume 40, number 3 (Winter 2010), pages 413-435.

18. Flood, Alison, "Popular history writing remains a male preserve, publishing study finds," *The Guardian* (11 January 2016).

19. This is hardly an original idea. For a good exposition see Stafford, Pauline, "Writing the Biography of Eleventh-Century Queens," *Writing Medieval Biography 750-1250: Essays in Honour of Frank Barlow,* pages 99-109. A fine essay is Earenfight, Theresa, "Highly Visible, Often Obscured: The Difficulty of Seeing Queens and Noble Women," *Medieval Feminist Forum,* volume 44, issue 1 (2008), pages 86-90.

See also the comments in Mitchell, Linda, *Joan de Valence: The Life and Influence of a Thirteenth-Century Noblewoman* (2016), pages 1-7.

20. See the preceding note.

21. Tuchman, Barbara, *Practicing History: Selected Essays* (1981), page 90.

22. See Earenfight, Theresa, "Without the Persona of the Prince: Kings, Queens and the Idea of Monarchy in Late Medieval Europe," *Gender and History,* volume 19, number 1 (April 2007), pages 1-21. See also Paglia, Camille, *Free Women, Free Men: Sex, Gender, Feminism* (2017); Rosin, Dowd, Moran, Paglia, *Are Men Obsolete? The Munk Debate on Gender* (2014). The author does not necessarily share the nuances of Professor Paglia's view, expressed in her *Sexual Personae* (1990) and quoted in the Munk debate and elsewhere (she has famously stated "there is no female Mozart because there is no female Jack the Ripper"), that it is biological destiny for women to cluster statistically away from intellectual and emotional extremes. However, it is an observable reality that throughout most of history women were not generally afforded the same opportunities as men; it is therefore unsurprising that we would find fewer women than men mentioned as important physicians, artists and thinkers.

23. For some insight into the interpretation of chronicles and annals, see Foot, Sarah, "Finding the Meaning of Form: Narrative in Annals and Chronicles," *Writing Medieval History* (2005), pages 88-108.

24. Tuchman, Barbara, op.cit., page 19. She also states, on page 42: "If I were a teacher, I would disqualify anyone who was content to cite a secondary source as a reference for a fact."

25. "Bella ancora, superba, leggiera." La Lumia, Isidoro, *Storia della Sicilia sotto Guglielmo il Buono* (1867), page 55.

26. Norwich, John Julius: *The Kingdom in the Sun* (1970), page 300; *Sicily: A Short History, from the Greeks to Cosa Nostra* (2015), page 98.

27. Freeman, Edward, *The History of the Norman Conquest of England,* third edition (1877), volume 1, pages vi-ix. For the phenomenon of envy in a professional environment see: Leahy, Robert, *Emotional Schema Therapy* (2015), pages 246-248; Menon, Tanya, and Thompson, Leigh, "Envy at Work," *Harvard Business Review,* April 2010, pages 3-7; Smith, Richard, et al., *Envy at Work and in Organizations* (2016); Friedman, Bonita, "Envy: The Writer's Disease," *New York Times* (26 November 1989).

28. Van Cleve, Thomas Curtis, *The Emperor Frederick II of Hohenstaufen, Immutator Mundi* (1972); Abulafia, David, *Frederick II: A Medieval Emperor* (1988).

29. Skinner, Patricia, *Studying Gender in Medieval Europe: Historical Approaches* (2018), page 18. More generally: Hechinger, Fred, "Peer Review in Social Fields is Faulted,"

New York Times (30 September 1986); "Peer Review: The challenges for humanities and social sciences," *British Academy Report* (2007); Thomas, Sandra, "Current Controversies Regarding Peer Review in Scholarly Journals," *Issues in Mental Health Nursing*, volume 39, number 2 (2018), pages 99-101; Lee, Carole, et al., "Bias in Peer Review," *Journal of the American Society for Information Science and Technology*, volume 64, number 1 (January 2013), pages 2-17; Martin, Brian, "Jealousy, Happiness and the Quest for Status and Salaries," *Campus Review* (Australia), 23-29 October 1996, page 9. See also *Outlandish Knight: The Byzantine Life of Steven Runciman* (2016), where Runciman's biographer, Minoo Dinshaw, refers to the possible motive for comments by Helene Wieruszowski in *Speculum*, volume 34 (1959), number 2, pages 323-326, despite her work being cited on page 338 of the first edition of *The Sicilian Vespers* (1958). In a lighter vein, Professor Rebecca Schuman wrote: "Think of your meanest high school mean girl at her most gleefully, underminingly vicious. Now give her a doctorate in your discipline, and a modicum of power over your future. That's peer review." She notes that criticisms are often "hidden amidst the venting of petty vendettas and pettier agendas." See Schuman, Rebecca, "Revise and Resubmit!" *Slate*, 15 July 2014 (slate.com/human-interest/2014/07/the-easy-way-to-fix-peer-review-require-submitters-to-review-first.html, retrieved in September 2019). See also note 27 above.

30. Tuchman, op. cit., page 9.

31. See Stein, Robert, "Literary Criticism and the Evidence for History," *Writing Medieval History* (2005), pages 67-87.

32. The author herself has noted these in *Queens of Sicily* and *The Peoples of Sicily*, amongst other works. See also Louis Mendola's *Sicilian Genealogy and Heraldry*. In *A History of Muslim Sicily*, the Arabist Leonard Chiarelli mentions studies of genetic haplogroups attesting to the presence of the Arabs on our island.

33. For the haplogroups see *Queens of Sicily*, page 599, note 31.

34. This is relevant because it may be one of the reasons, unstated by chroniclers, for Frederick removing his son from power, as King of Germany, in 1135. This was reported by Gino Fornaciari, Francesco Mallegni and Pietro De Leo in "The Leprosy of Henry VII: Incarceration or Isolation?" published in *The Lancet*, volume 353 (27 February 1999), page 758.

35. *Queens of Sicily*, page 93.

36. Ibid, page 650.

37. See: Bennett, Judith, "Medievalism and Feminism," *Speculum*, volume 68, number 2 (spring 1993), pages 309-331; Pierson, Ruth, and Prentice, Alison, "Feminism and the Writing and Teaching of History," *Atlantis*, volume 7, number 2 (1982), pages 37-46; Skinner, Patricia, op.cit. supra; Lerner, Gerda, *The Creation of Feminist Consciousness: From the Middle Ages to 1870* (1994).

38. See note 5 in this book's introduction.

39. For example, the Society for Medieval Feminist Scholarship is dedicated to studies in this field, publishing the *Medieval Feminist Forum,* formerly the *Medieval Feminist Newsletter.*

40. A comedy, *Tuttoapposto,* filmed in Catania and released in 2019, accurately portrays the sexism, nepotism and corruption that characterizes Italy's public universities; it is rather difficult to imagine a film depicting student life at Oxford or Harvard in the same way. Very few universities in this country have implemented effective procedures to address complaints of sexual harassment (Cà Foscari in Venice is an exception), and Italian labor law makes it all but impossible to discipline or dismiss a lecherous male professor in a public university who harasses his female students. It is unsurprising that very little formal (statistical) research has been conducted in Italy on this subject but see note 5 in the Introduction, also: Bastiani, Federica, et al., "Mental Distress and Sexual Harassment in Italian University Students," *Archives of Women's Mental Health,* volume 22, number 2 (April 2019), pages 229-236; Romito, Patrizia, et al., "Sexual Harassment and Menstrual Disorders Among Italian University Women: A Cross-sectional Observational Study," *Scandinavian Journal of Public Health,* volume 45, number 5 (May 2017), pages 528-535; Marzano, Flavia, "Le Dinamiche di Reclutamento e di Carriera delle Donne nel Sistema Universitario Italiano," *Rassegna ASTRID,* number 77 (12 September 2008), year 4, number 15; Balloni, Bisi, Sette, *Gender-Based Violence, Stalking and Fear of Crime: EU Country Report for Italy* (University of Bologna 2012). An increasing number of cases have been reported in the press in the last few years, such as Campicelli, Lino, "'Vuoi laurearti? Resta nuda sotto la toga': nei guai un professore universitario," *Il Messaggero* (9 May 2019); Foschini, Giuliano, "Bari: Docente universitario accusato di violenza resta in servizio," *La Repubblica* (25 May 2019); Vigne, Aurora, "Abusi sessuali su studentesse a La Sapienza: Indagato un professore," *Il Giornale* (29 May 2019).

41. Bennett, op.cit. supra. See also Partner, Nancy, "The Post-Traditional Middle Ages: The Distant Past Through Contemporary Eyes," *Writing Medieval History* (2005), pages xi-xvi.

42. A good example of this is Sara McDougall's book, *Royal Bastards: The Birth of Illegitimacy 800-1230,* published in 2016. It could be argued, however, that medievalists were already reasonably familiar with most of the concepts presented in that work. See also Armstrong-Partida, Michelle, "Concubinage, Illegitimacy and Fatherhood: Urban Masculinity in Late-Medieval Barcelona," *Gender and History,* volume 31, number 1 (March 2019), pages 195-219. Two of Sicily's monarchs of the Norman-Swabian era were born outside marriage, namely Tancred and Manfred, each the last regnant king of his dynasty.

43. For some information on medieval Sicilian cuisine, see Chapter 6.

44. Tuchman, op. cit., pages 80-90. This part of her book should be required reading for aspiring biographers.

45. Fraser, Antonia, "Step Back in Time," *The Guardian* (24 September 2008); Banner, Lois, "Biography as History," *The American Historical Review,* volume 114, number 3 (June 2009), pages 579-586. See also Winstead, Karen, *The Oxford History of Life-Writing, Volume 1, The Middle Ages* (2018).

On-site Research: The Latin-Greek-Arabic inscription commemorating King Roger's water clock in the Norman Palace and Mussomeli's castle

Site where Maio of Bari was murdered in 1160

A biography can establish a new subject category and correct details such as a queen's year of birth

CONSTITUTIONUM
REGNI SICILIARUM
L I B R I   III.

Cum Commentariis Veterum Jurifconfultorum

ACCEDIT NUNC PRIMUM

DOMINICI ALFENI VARII J. C.
COMMENTARIUS

A D

F R I D E R I C I   II.
IMPERATORIS ET REGIS CONSTITUTIONEM

De Rebus non alienandis Ecclefiis.

EDITIO ABSOLUTISSIMA.

N E A P O L I   MDCCLXXIII.
SUMPTIBUS ANTONII CERVONII.

The Constitutions of Melfi of 1231 published in 1773

Chapter 12
QUEENSHIP STUDIES

The following works focus on the countesses or queens of Sicily, or topics related to the women of southern Italy more generally, before 1266. There are others, but these were selected for presenting the subjects in some detail and, in most cases, for relying upon original (medieval) sources. Although the author does not agree with every affirmation, conclusion or thesis presented in these works, this was not deemed an appropriate venue for critiques or rebuttals. It is hoped that this informal canon will be useful not only to scholars but to general readers. Some of the papers, and a few of the books that are no longer in print, may be available in electronic format for download from the internet. Most of the items listed have been published in a "formal" way, whether digitally or on paper, but others may be present on websites as "unpublished" papers, theses or dissertations.

Anna Comnena. *Alexiad*. Translated by Sewter, Edgar Robert Ashton (1969).

Bordone, Renata (editor). *Bianca Lancia d'Agliano: Fra il Piemonte e il Regno di Sicilia* (1992).

Bowie, Colette. *The Daughters of Henry II and Eleanor of Aquitaine: A Comparative Study of Twelfth-century Women* (2014).

Bowie, Colette. "To Have and Have Not: The Dower of Joanna Plantagenet, Queen of Sicily," *Queenship in the Mediterranean: Negotiating the Role of the Queen in the Medieval and Early Modern Eras* (2013), pages 27-50.

Davanzati, Domenico Forges. *Dissertazione sulla Seconda Moglie del Re Manfredi e sù Loro Figliuoli* (1791).

Del Giudice, Giuseppe. *La Famiglia di Re Manfredi* (1896).

Drell, Joanna. *Kinship and Conquest: Family Strategies in the Principality of Salerno during the Norman Period 1077-1194* (2002).

Eads, Valerie. "Sichelgaita of Salerno: Amazon or Trophy Wife?" *Journal of Medieval Military History,* volume 3 (2005), pages 72-87.

Elze, Reinhard. "Tre Ordines per l'Incoronazione di un Re e di una Regina del Regno Normanno in Sicilia," *Atti del Congresso Internazionale di Studi sulla Sicilia Normanna* (1974), pages 438-459.

von Falkenhausen, Vera. "Zur Regentschaft der Gräfin Adelasia del Vasto in Kalabrien und Sizilien 1101-1112," *AETOS: Studies in Honor of Cyril Mango Presented to Him on April 14, 1998* (1998), pages 87-115.

Frascadore, Angela. "Le Badesse del Monastero di San Giovanni Evangelista di Lecce," *Tancredi Conte di Lecce Re di Sicilia* (2004), pages 233-286.

Fröhlich, Walter. "The Marriage of Henry VI and Constance of Sicily: Prelude and Consequences," *Anglo Norman Studies 15* (1993), pages 99-125.

Green, Mary Anne Everett. *Lives of the Princesses of England from the Norman Conquest* (1850), volume 1, pages 308-403 (Joanna Plantagenet).

Green, Mary Anne Everett. *Lives of the Princesses of England from the Norman Conquest* (1850), volume 2, pages 1-47 (Isabella Plantagenet).

Green, Monica (editor). *The Trotula: A Medieval Compendium of Women's Medicine* (2001).

Hood, Gwenyth (translator). *Book in Honor of Augustus by Pietro da Eboli* (2012).

Houben, Hubert. "Adelaide 'del Vasto' nella Storia del Regno di Sicilia," *Itinerari di Ricerca Storica,* number 4 (1990), pages 9-40.

Hoving, Thomas. "A Newly Discovered Reliquary of St Thomas Becket," *Gesta,* volume 4, spring 1965 (1965), pages 28-30.

Jamison, Evelyn. "Judex Tarentinus: The Career of Judex Tarentinus *Magne Curie Justiciarius* and the Emergence of the Sicilian *Regalis Magna Curia* under William I and the Regency of Margaret of Navarre, 1156-72," *Proceedings of the British Academy,* volume I, iii (1968), pages 289-344.

Jensen, Frede. *The Poetry of the Sicilian School* (1986).

Johns, Jeremy. "Parchment versus Paper: Countess Adelaide's

Bilingual Mandate of 1109," *Documenting Multiculturalism* (November 2018).

Kölzer, Theo. *Urkunden und Kanzlei der Kaiserin Konstanze, Königin von Sizilien 1195-1198,* in *Monumenta Germaniae Historica,* volume 6, part 3 (1983).

La Grua, Gregorio. *La Corona di Costanza di Aragona Regina di Sicilia* (1988).

Lipinsky, Angelo. "Sicaniae Regni Corona: Il Kamelaukion detta Cuffia di Costanza nel Tesoro del Duomo di Palermo," *Bizantino-Sicula II: Miscellanea di Scritti in Memoria di Giuseppe Rossi Taibbi* (1975), pages 347-370.

Martellotti, Anna (editor). *I Ricettari di Federico II: Dal Meridionale al Liber de Coquina* (2005).

Mastelloni, Maria Amalia. "Il Sarcofago Antico di Costanza d'Aragona," *Federico e la Sicilia, dalla Terra alla Corona: Arti Figurative e Arti Suntuarie* (1995), pages 46-52.

Mazzarese Fardella, Enrico, "La Condizione Giuridica della Donna nel Liber Augustalis" in *Archivio Storico Siciliano,* series 4, volume 21-22 (1997).

Mielke, Christopher. "From Her Head to Her Toes: Gender-Bending Regalia in the Tomb of Constance of Aragon, Queen of Hungary and Sicily," *Royal Studies Journal,* volume 5, number 2 (2018), pages 49-62.

Mumelter, Maria Luise. *Irene von Byzanz,* University of Innsbruck (1936); Universitäts und Landesbibliothek Tirol, C87782809. Unpublished.

Neville, Leonora. *Anna Komnene: The Life and Work of a Medieval Historian* (2016).

Oster, Uwe. *Die Frauen Kaiser Friedrichs II* (2008).

Radici, Benedetto. "Il Casale e l'Abbazia di Santa Maria di Maniace," *Archivio Storico Siciliano* (Palermo 1909), pages 1-104.

Runde, Ingo. "Konstanze von Aragon," *Die Kaiserinnen des Mittelalters* (2011), pages 232-248.

Simeti, Mary Taylor. *Travels With a Medieval Queen: The Journey of a Sicilian Princess to Reclaim Her Father's Crown* (2001).

Skinner, Patricia. "Halt, Be Men! Sikelgaita of Salerno, Gender and the Norman Conquest of Southern Italy," *Gender and History*, volume 12, issue 3 (2000), pages 622-641.

Skinner, Patricia. *Family Power in Southern Italy: The Duchy of Gaeta and Its Neighbors 850-1139* (1995).

Storey, Gabrielle. "Berengaria of Navarre and Joanna of Sicily as Crusading Queens: Manipulation, Reputation and Agency," *Forgotten Queens in Medieval and Early Modern Europe: Political Agency, Myth-Making, and Patronage* (2018), pages 41-59.

Vagnoni, Mirko. "La Sacralità della Regina nella Sicilia Normanna: Il Caso dell'Ordo Coronationis," *Mirabilia,* volume 17 (2013), number 2, pages 174-187.

Van Landingham, Marta. "The Hohenstaufen Heritage of Costanza of Sicily and the Mediterranean Expansion of the Crown of Aragon in the Later Thirteenth Century," *Across the Mediterranean Frontiers,* volume 1 (January 1997), pages 87-104.

HISTORIA HV-
GONIS FALCANDI SICVLI DE
rebus geſtis in Siciliæ regno, iam primùm typis
excuſa, ſtudio & beneficio Reuerendi D. Domini
Matthæi Longogçi Sueſsionũ pontificıs & regni
Galliæ ab interiore ac penitiore conſilio.

Huc accefsit in librum præfatio, & hiſtoricæ lectionis Encomi
um per Geruaſium Tornacæum Sueſsionenſem.

PARISIIS

Apud Mathurinum Dupuys via Iacobea,
ſub inſigni Hominıs ſylueſtris, & Frobenij.
M. D. L.

CVM PRIVILEGIO REGIS.

*The 1550 edition of the chronicle of Hugh Falcandus was
the first publication to consider a Queen of Sicily at length*

Appendix 1
PLACES

We cannot literally see all of the people who lived in times past, and some of our queens are not commemorated by artistic renderings in illuminations, coins, effigies or seals, or even surviving tombs. It is for this reason than much space in this volume is dedicated to social context and topics such as words spoken, poems heard and foods enjoyed by our queens. Beyond these things, we can learn something of a historical woman by seeing the places that she saw, especially where she lived for extended periods.

A few dwellings in the realm familiar to the countesses and queens of Sicily can still be seen, and readers may wish to visit these. Apart from actual residences, a handful of places known to our queens are strikingly similar to the state of their medieval existence. Monreale's cathedral and abbey are such an example (Chapter 8). Another is Palermo's Ballarò street market, effectively a souk that has stood on the same spot for over a thousand years. Photographs of some of these places appear in *Queens of Sicily*.

Considering that most of our queens were born and raised beyond the kingdom's borders, and that as imperial consorts a few lived at times in the Holy Roman Empire, they also set foot in a good number of castles and localities outside Italy.

Unfortunately, many of the residences known to them are in ruin. Adelaide resided at times in the castles of Messina,

Mileto, San Marco d'Alunzio and Patti. Little is left of these edifices, largely destroyed by earthquakes rather than sieges.

Therein lies the problem in listing these structures as places to visit, for while a historian will find the sites themselves interesting, some castles are not much to see. This one may compare to the state of our ancient Greek temples; Segesta, Agrigento and Paestum are impressive, while those at Selinunte are fallen and scattered, attracting rather few visitors.

Therefore, the queenly homes mentioned here, mostly in southern Italy, are those still standing. To this list could be added Winchester and Poitiers (Joanna), the Tower of London (Isabella), Pamplona (Margaret), Trifels (Constance Hauteville), the Jerusalem Citadel (Adelaide), Acre (Yolanda), Sigena (Constance of Aragon) and others, some standing and others not.

We should make a distinction between a woman actually residing in a place or simply visiting. It should be noted that chronicles and charters do not always tell us precisely where a queen was lodged at a specific time unless a particular incident or event is mentioned. We know that Constance Hauteville was present in Salerno's castle during a siege because she was forced to surrender. Isabella's movements in England are known to us. It should be remembered that the Holy Roman Empire did not have a single, centralized capital, so Frederick II, along with his consort of the moment, traveled most of the time.

Our noble list begins, appropriately enough, with the capital.

Palermo

The greatest concentration and number of residences will be found in Palermo, a city that has more churches and royal homes of the twelfth century than any other locality in Europe (only a few of these are shown in the accompanying map). One will find that Palermo is an uncut, unpolished diamond. The city is unkempt, chaotic, usually noisy and sometimes rather dirty. Some landmarks, such as the Norman Palace and Zisa, stand beside gardens, whilst others, such as the Scibene and Cuba, are surrounded by ugly modern buildings. The Ballarò and Capo street markets, both known to the queens of Sicily, occupy streets punctuated by small, open squares formed by the bombings of 1943. Nevertheless, the last decade has witnessed successful efforts to make our city more appealing to visitors, and while it is not quite as attractive as Seville, Cordoba or Granada, Palermo has become one of Europe's more interesting "undiscovered" destinations.

A number of streets and walls survive from the Phoenician era; a sixteenth-century map at the end of this chapter shows many that still exist.

Little remains of the Favara in Brancaccio or the Scibene near Via Nave in what was once the royal hunting ground. Our queens and their children may have spent time in these Fatimid-inspired palaces during the summer. The Norman-Arab Cuba along Corso Calatafimi near a Punic cemetery, and the more impressive Zisa at the end of Via Dante, are in visitable condition, even if the restoration of the latter leaves something to be desired.

Nevertheless, it was probably in the Zisa that Joanna lived as a young bride and later as a widow.

The Norman Palace houses the Palatine Chapel. The royal apartments were in the Pisan Tower.

Unfortunately, the castle overlooking Monreale is little more than a shell, and the royal palace next to the town's magnificent abbey and cathedral (described in Chapter 8) has been incorporated into a modern building. The Martorana and San Cataldo churches are worth visiting. Little is left of the sea castle in the Cala district, which was not a royal residence.

Located near Porta Nuova and the Norman Palace, the church dedicated to Mary Magdalene has been much altered over time compared to San Cataldo. The royal tombs once housed there were translated to Monreale or, in a few cases, have disappeared, with the mortal remains placed in the church's crypt but unmarked. Standing within what is now a military complex, this church is not visible from the street and is not usually open to the public.

Sicily Beyond Palermo

Cefalù's castle is in ruins except for a mediocre reconstruction of a tiny part of it for the benefit of tourists, but its cathedral is splendid. The Osterio Magno in town was a royal residence and a stop for the kings and queens when traveling between Palermo and Messina.

Only the foundations and one wall remain of the Hauteville castle at San Marco d'Alunzio where Adelaide sometimes resided with her young children and where Beatrice of Rethel lived for a few years with young Constance Hauteville.

Impressive as its setting is, the castle of Caltabellotta, to which Sibylla of Acerra may have fled in 1194 (an alternate possibility is that she sent her children there but remained in Palermo to defend the city) is essentially a ruin. A single crumbling tower remains. The site is significant for the "Peace of Caltabellotta," the treaty officially ending the War of the Vespers in 1302.

Erected by Frederick II, Ursino Castle, at Catania, was located along the shore until a lava flow extended the coast further into the sea. This fortress bears some semblance of its original condition.

Venus (Pepoli) Castle at Erice, formerly Monte San Giuliano, was essentially a military fortification rather than a royal demesnial castle and there is little indication that any of our queens ever lived there. The same is true of the castle at Kasr' Janni (Enna). Yet both structures boast impressive locations.

Apulia

The term *Apulia* was meant to embrace what is now Puglia as well as Basilicata (Lucania), Molise and some territories into the March of Ancona.

Erected in 1240, Castel del Monte, outside Andria, is a unique fortification designed in the form of an octagon. This may have been a royal hunting lodge. It is possible that Bianca Lancia lived here for a few years with her children. The sons of Queen Helena Angelina were imprisoned here.

Manfredonia Castle, as its name implies, was built by King Manfred in 1256. This is a military fortress more than a royal residence, but Beatrice of Savoy may have stayed here briefly.

Mount Sant'Angelo was the traditional dower of the queens of Sicily but we do not know that many of these ladies ever visited more than once or twice.

Isabella of England died in the castle of Foggia in 1241. When in Apulia, Frederick held court here, where scholars such as Michael Scot resided. Virtually nothing of the castle still stands.

Oria Castle was the site of the infamous wedding feast where Frederick reputedly snubbed his bride, Yolanda of Jerusalem, for her pretty cousin.

Lecce Castle, where Sibylla of Acerra lived occasionally, has been altered beyond its medieval incarnation.

Campania

Though largely reconstructed, the castle in Ariano Irpino, near Avellino, is still impressive, but it seems doubtful that any queens ever stayed here except perhaps briefly.

The castle overlooking Salerno is a shadow of its former self yet its site on a mountain is spectacular.

The castle at Melfi (this is actually in Basilicata) was erected by the Normans as their first major stronghold in Italy. Though largely rebuilt, it still has a few walls that date from the eleventh century.

On a hill overlooking Nocera Inferiore we find the ruined Castello del Parco, where Helena Angelina was imprisoned and died.

Calabria

Little remains of the castle at Mileto. Saint Mary's, probably the abbey at Bagnara where Joanna of England stayed whilst her brother, Richard, was at Messina, was destroyed by an earthquake in 1783.

Germany

Here the two major castles known to most of the Hohenstaufen consorts (except Manfred's) are Staufen, in Göppingen, an edifice that was mostly destroyed during the Peasants' War in 1525, and Trifels, at Annweiler, which, though largely reconstructed, can at least be visited.

PLACES

This map dated 1570 shows some streets that existed in Palermo in medieval times. The city wall seen here was erected in 1536.

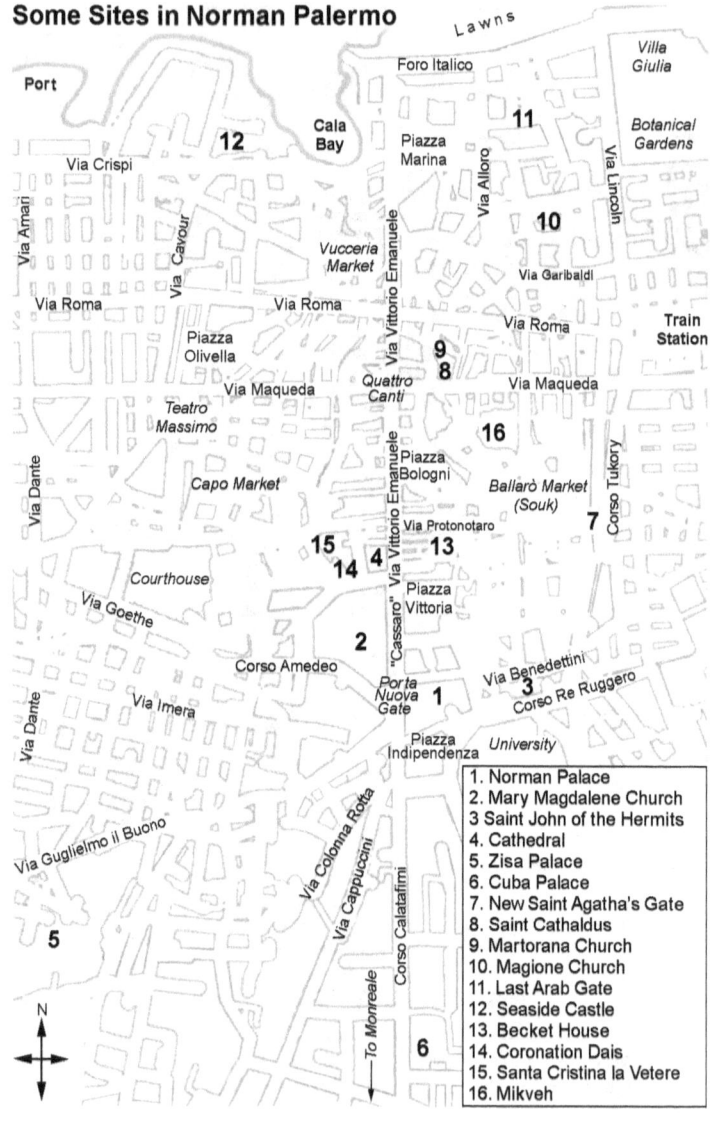

PLACES

Pisan Tower of the Norman Palace seen from the north

The much-altered southern side of the Norman Palace

Remaining loopholes and arches of Monreale's palace

Appendix 2
NINA OF MESSINA

So little is known of the poetess called "Nina of Messina," and so sparsely is her presence attested in the historical record, that her very existence has been questioned. In this she is not alone; another woman of her era who composed poetry is known generically as *la Compiuta Donzella di Firenze,* "the Accomplished Damsel from Florence." Either of these poets may have been the first woman to compose poetry in a medieval Italian vernacular, the former in Sicilian and the latter in Tuscan, although Nina seems to have executed her work earlier.[1] Both were influenced by the Occitan tongues and the troubadour tradition of the time, which already included many female poets in France; the style of Nina's work has been compared to that of Alamanda de Castelnau. Like much surviving poetry of the Sicilian School (see Chapter 7), the extant texts of the poems attributed to Nina have been "tuscanized."

Nina's talent was recognized by Dante of Maiano, an elder contemporary of Dante Alighieri influenced by Occitan movements and the Sicilian School. Maiano, who seems to have been entranced by Nina, albeit from afar (the poem written to her suggests they have not actually met), is a rather enigmatic figure, but that is the case of a number of poets of this era.

The elusive Nina, perhaps *Antonina,* may have been born

as early as 1245, possibly in Messina as her posthumous name suggests. She was clearly an aristocrat, and we may speculate that she was the daughter of a courtier of Frederick II or his immediate successors, Conrad and Manfred. It is thus possible that Nina met one of our queens, perhaps even Helena Angelina, though this is hypothetical. Nina was a contemporary of another well-known woman from northeastern Sicily, Macalda of Scaletta (whom we met in the Introduction).

Nina's exchange, or "dialogue," with Dante of Maiano offers us a rare glimpse into the kind of letters that could be (and occasionally were) exchanged between men and women in Italy during this period, and the poetry that might be composed by a noblewoman or queen influenced by the Sicilian School. As we shall see, there is some lingering doubt about the authenticity of this poem.

Otto delle Colonne, who lived at Messina, seems to have influenced Nina's work. For centuries, Nina's more important poem, found in the same codex as those of other Sicilian poets, was simply considered anonymous, being of unknown authorship.

Bernardo Giunti's early compilation of Italian poetry, first published in 1527, included Nina's better-known sonnet along with the work of Dante of Maiano that preceded and followed it.[2] During the seventeenth century, scholars such as Alessandro Ziliolo and Leone Allacci accepted the historicity of Nina of Messina and this poem.

In her compendium published in 1726, Luisa Bergalli (1703-1779) was unequivocal in attributing at least this one poem to Nina, who seems to have composed it around 1275 as a response to her admirer.[3] During the following century, Francesco Trucchi and other scholars followed in accepting Nina's authorship; Trucchi also attributed to her a second poem, from *Codex Vaticanus Latinus 3793,* namely *Tapina me che amava uno sparviero* (translated below), sometimes *Lamento d'Amore Tradito,* which compares a knight or other suitor to a faithful hawk.[4] The style and form of *Tapina* are similar enough to the poem sent to Dante of Maiano to suggest common authorship and Provençal influences.

Timewise, her work seems to place Nina at the *coda* of the Sicilian School, which had flowered decades earlier during the reign of Frederick II. It was Manfred's defeat at Benevento in 1266 that precipitated the demise of the movement, but not the end of the use of the Sicilian language. It should be remembered that the War of the Vespers of 1282 left Sicily politically separated from the peninsular kingdom ruled from Naples. The intrinsically Guelphic orientation of the Tuscan poets, led by Dante Alighieri and Giovanni Boccaccio, was implicitly anti-Ghibelline and arguably anti-Sicilian; it certainly did not seek to glorify Frederick II or his dynasty. Nevertheless, Dante recognized the importance of the Sicilian tongue in his *De Vulgari Eloquentia* and Boccaccio mentioned Palermo's Cuba palace in his *Decameron*.

The Neapolitan and Sicilian languages survived, and are still spoken today, but by the middle of the fourteenth century Tuscan had emerged as the chief literary language in most of peninsular Italy, even if some time were to pass before it became so in Sicily. Until quite recently, very little was written in English about the Sicilian language, and the Kingdom of Italy (1861-1946) tried to suppress its public use.

Lacking a manuscript tradition but long accepted as genuine, the sonnet attributed to Nina, sometimes "Monna Nina" or "Nina Siciliana," *Qual sete voi, sì cara proferenza,* is a reply to Dante of Maiano, whose solicitation is presented here for context.[5] Though its provenance has sometimes (if rarely) been questioned, it is certainly reasonable to believe that Dante of Maiano received such a letter.

We are on firmer ground with *Tapina,* for which there is a medieval manuscript. Its original orthography follows the translation and a photo of the manuscript appears at the end of this appendix.

In addition to the two sonnets translated here, several additional poems, most notably *Pàrtite amore adeo,* are thought to be the work of "Nina" or another woman of her era.[6]

Two others sometimes mentioned are *Onde si muove e donde nasce amore,* usually attributed to Guido Cavalcanti, and *Ahi lassa innamorata,* generally considered to have been written by Otto della Colonne.[7]

Dante of Maiano to Monna Nina

Le lode e 'l pregio e 'l senno et la valenza,
Ch'haggio sovente audito nominare,
Gentil mia donna di vostra plagienza,
M'han fatto coralmente ennamorare;

> The praise, merit, judgment and worth,
> That have so often been ascribed to you,
> At your pleasure, gentle lady,
> Have made me fall in love with you;

E misso tutto in vostra conoscenza,
Di guisa tal che già considerare,
Non degno mai che far vostra vollienza,
Sì m'ha distretto amor di voi amare;

> And to tell you everything,
> In a manner already contemplated,
> Never worthy to meet you,
> So that love has burdened me with loving you;

Di tanto prego vostra segnoria,
In loco di mercede e di pietanza,
Piacciavi sol ch'eo vestro servo sia;

> So I pray that your ladyship,
> Instead of showing mercy and pity,
> Shall be pleased to make me your slave;

Poi mi terraggio dolze donna mia,
Fermo d'haver compita la speranza,
Di ciò che lo meo core ama e disia.

> I'll prostrate myself my sweet lady,
> Knowing that I'll have the hope,
> Of what my heart loves and desires.

NINA OF MESSINA

Qual sete voi, sì cara proferenza
(Nina's Response to Dante of Maiano)

Qual sete voi, sì cara proferenza,
Che fate a me senza voi mostrare?
Molto m'agenzeria vostra parvenza,
Perché meo cor podesse dichiarare.

> Who are you, who has such a dear preference
> Towards me without identifying yourself?
> I would much rather have you here,
> So that I can declare my love to you.

Vostro mandato aggrada a mia intenza;
In gioja mi conteria d'udir nomare
Lo vostro nome, che fa proferenza
D'essere sottoposto a me innorare.

> Your request pleases my intentions;
> With joy I hope to hear pronounce
> Your name, which chooses
> To be honored by being placed in my trust.

Lo core meo pensare non savrì
Nessuna cosa, che sturbasse amanza,
Così affermo, e voglio ognor, che sia,

> My heart wouldn't know how to think
> Of anything that would get in the way of love,
> This I declare and I want it forever to be so.

D'udendovi parlar è vollia mia:
Se vostra penna ha bona consonanza
Col vostro core, ond' ha tra lor resia?

> I wish to be able to listen to you speak:
> If what you write with your pen is what you say
> With your heart, where is the heresy between the two?

Tapina me che amava uno sparviero

Tapina me che amava uno sparviero,
Amaval tanto ch'io me ne moria;
A lo richiamo ben m'era maniero,
Ed unque troppo pascer nol dovia.

> Sad me who loved a sparrow-hawk,
> So much that I was dying over him;

> When I called him he would heed me,
> And I never had to feed him very much.

Or è montato e salito sì altero,
Assai più altero che far non solia;
Ed è assiso dentro a un verziero,
E un'altra donna l'averà in balìa.

> Now he has flown off and he has soared,
> So high that he cannot rise any further;
> And he is perched in a garden,
> Where another woman has him under her power.

Isparvier mio, ch'io t'avea nodrito;
Sonaglio d'oro ti facea portare,
Perchè nell'uccellar fossi più ardito.

> My sparrow-hawk, whom I had nurtured myself;
> I had you wear a golden bell,
> So that you were more daring in your hunt.

Or sei salito siccome lo mare,
Ed hai rotto li geti e sei fuggito,
Quando eri fermo nel tuo ucciellare.

> Now you have risen just like the sea tide,
> You have torn your jesses and you have fled,
> While you were resting from your hunting.

Original Orthography in the Manuscript

Tapina jnme camaua vno fparuero, amaualu tanto chio menemoria, alorichiamo bene mera manero, edumque troppo pafciere noi douia. ore montato efalito fialtero, afai più alto chefare nomfolia, edè afifo dentro auno uerzero, vnaltra dona lotene jm balia. Jsparuero mio chio tauea nodrito, fonalglio doro tifaciea portare, p'che delluciellare foffe piu ardito. Orfe falito ficome lomare, edarotti ligieti efe fugito, quando eri fermo neltuo vciellare.

NOTES

1. See: Malpezzi Price, Paola, "Uncovering Women's Writings: Two Early Italian Women Poets," *Journal of the Rocky Mountain Medieval and Renaissance Association,* volume 9 (1988), pages 1-15; Cherchi, Paolo, "The Troubled Existence of Three Women Poets," *The Voice of the Trobairitz: Perspectives on the Women Troubadours* (1989), pages 197-210; Arriaga Flórez, Mercedes, *Poetas Italianas de los Siglos 13 y 14 en la Querella de las Mujeres* (Seville 2012), pages 8, 10, 19, 29-43. For an overview of the secondary literature see Cerrato, Daniele, "Monna Nina: Nuove attribuzioni e stato della questione," *En Ligne,* Varia, 2014, number 6.

2. Giunti, Bernardo, *Sonetti e Canzoni di Diversi Antichi Autori Toscani* (1727 edition of work published in 1527), numbers 22-24 in book 11, pages 276-278.

3. Bergalli, Luisa, *Componimenti Poetici delle più Illustri Rimatrici d'Ogni Secolo* (1726), part 1, page 1 (Nina Ciciliana). Although Nina's poem to Dante of Maiano was traditionally dated to around 1290, some scholars have suggested *circa* 1275 as more likely; see Bertacchi, Giovanni, *Le Rime di Dante da Maiano* (1896), pages xx, xxii and liv. The poem is generally accepted as authentic; see note 5.

4. Biblioteca Apostolica Vaticana, *Codex Vaticanus Latinus,* volume 3793, folio 158v. Trucchi, Francesco, *Poesie Italiane Inedite di Duegento Autori* (1846), volume 1, pages 53-54. See also Cancrini, Luigi, *Gemme o Collezione di Poetesse Italiane dal 1290 al 1855* (1855), pages vii, 1, 282. It should be remembered that Frederick II wrote a treatise on falconry.

5. For completeness, Dante's reply to Nina's poem: *Di ciò audivi dir primieramente, Gentil mia donna di vostro laudare, Havea talento di saver lo core, Se fosse ver ciò compitamente. Non come audivi il trovo certamente, Ma per un cento di menzogna fore; Tanto v'assegna saggia lo sentore, Che move e ven da voi sovra saccente. E poi vi piace ch'eo vi parli bella, S'el cor va da la penna svariando, Sacciate no che ben son d'un volere. E se v'agenza e 'l vostro gran savere, Per testa lo meo dir vada cercando, Se di voler lo meo nome v'abbella.* (Giunti, op.cit., page 278.) For more about the poet and his work see Bertacchi, op.cit. supra; Bettarini, Rosanna (editor), *Dante da Maiano: Rime* (1969). For the historicity of Nina based on her poem to Dante of Maiano and the lack of a known manuscript source for it, see Borgognoni, Adolfo, *Dante da Maiano* (1882), also Cherchi, op.cit. It should be noted that the failure to indicate precise manuscript records in such publications as Giunti's was not unusual during the incunable and post-incunable periods, and that many manuscripts were lost before our time, some to be rediscovered, *quod vide* the author's comments in the Preface regarding the rediscovery of certain manuscripts (the Assizes of Ariano, the Ferraris Chronicle).

6. Occcasionally attributed to Nina of Messina: *Pàrtite, amore, adeo, ché tropo ce sé stato; lo maitino è sonato, zorno me par che sia. Pàrtite, amor, adeo, che non fossi trovata, in sì fina cellata como nui semo stati; or me bassa, oclo meo; tosto sia l'andata, tenendo la tornata como di 'namorati; siché per speso usato nostra zoglia renovi, nostro stato non trovi la mala celosia. Pàrtite, amore, adeo, e vane tostamente ch'one toa cossa t'azo pareclata in presente.* Usually dated to around 1286, this is retained by the Archive of State of Bologna in *Memoriali,* volume 64, folio 152v.

7. This was first suggested by Agostino Gallo, though there has never been a scholarly consensus on his theory. See Gallo, Agostino, "Lettera di Agostino Gallo all'ornatissimo signor Cavaliere Antonio Di Giovanni Mira intorno ad alcuni dé primi poeti siciliani in volgare," *Effemeridi Scientifiche e Letterarie per la Sicilia,* January-March 1833, year 2, tomo (part) 5, pages 53-81.

Sad me who loved a sparrow-hawk is the first poem known to be written by a woman in one of the Italian vernacular languages

SOURCES AND BIBLIOGRAPHY

These are source records and scholarly works mentioned in this volume's text and notes, or otherwise considered useful for reference. To avoid redundancy, some additional primary sources will be found in *Queens of Sicily,* pages 669-703. Charters mentioned in Chapter 3 are listed there under "Figures." In the following lists translations are found under either the primary sources or the secondary literature, depending upon the amount of annotation in the work. Relevant secondary works are also listed in Chapter 12. This bibliography is "selective" insofar as no attempt has been made to list *every* secondary work on any particular subject, with preference given to *published* works rather than "unpublished" dissertations or papers uploaded to websites but otherwise unarchived.

Manuscript Sources

Archivio Storico Diocesano di Palermo: Tabulario della Cattedrale di Palermo.

Archivio di Stato di Palermo: Tabulario di Cefalù, Tabulario dei Monasteri di San Filippo di Fragalà e di Santa Maria di Maniace, Tabulario di Santa Maria Maddalena di Messina.

Archivo de la Catedral de Pamplona (Pamplona, Spain): Gran Cartulario.

Biblioteca Centrale della Regione Siciliana (Palermo), Manoscritti.

Biblioteca Comunale di Casa Professa (Palermo), Manoscritti.

Biblioteca Monumento Nazionale Badia di Cava, Manoscritti.

Biblioteca Nazionale Centrale di Firenze: Manoscritti, Banco Rari.

Bourbon Two Sicilies Family Archive (Rome).

Fundación Casa Ducal de Medinaceli: Fondo Messina.

Vatican Apostolic Library: Manuscripts, Vaticanus Latinus and Palatinus Latinus series.

Some Primary Sources in Print

Alio, Jacqueline. *The Ferraris Chronicle: Popes, Emperors, and Deeds in Apulia 1096-1228* (2017).

Batman, Stephen. *De Proprietatibus Rerum* (1585).

Broadhurst, Ronald. *The Travels of Ibn Jubayr* (1952, 2008).

Brühl, Carlrichard. *Rogerii II Regis Diplomata Latina (Codex Diplomaticus Regni Siciliae), Diplomata Regum et Principum e Gente Normannorum,* series 1 (1987).

Cusa, Salvatore. *I Diplomi Greci ed Arabi di Sicilia Pubblicati nel Testo Originale, Tradotti ed Illustrati* (1868).

Del Re, Giuseppe. *Cronisti e Scrittori Sincroni Napoletani,* volume 1 ("Normanni"), pages 5-71 and 559-563 (Romuald of Salerno); pages 88-156 (Alexander of Telese); pages 160-276 (Falco of Benevento); pages 277-391 (Hugh Falcandus); pages 405-439 (Peter of Eboli); pages 461-480 (Cassino Chronicle); pages 571-616 (Catalogus Baronum); (1845).

Del Re, Giuseppe. *Cronisti e Scrittori Sincroni Napoletani,* volume 2 ("Svevi"), pages 5-100 (Richard of San Germano); pages 101-200 ("Nicholas Jamsilla"); pages 201-408 (Saba Malaspina); pages 409-627 (Bartholomew of Nicastro); (1868).

Elze, Reinhard. "Tre Ordines per l'Incoronazione di un Re e di una Regina del Regno Normanno in Sicilia," *Atti del Congresso Internazionale di Studi sulla Sicilia Normanna* (1974), pages 438-459.

Forester, Thomas. *The Ecclesiastical History of England and Normandy,* the *Historia Ecclesiastica* of Orderic Vitalis (1854), 4 volumes.

Garufi, Carlo Alberto. *Catalogo Illustrato del Tabulario di Santa Maria Nuova in Monreale* (1902).

SOURCES AND BIBLIOGRAPHY

Garufi, Carlo Alberto. *I Documenti Inediti dell'Epoca Normanna in Sicilia* (1899).

Garufi, Carlo Alberto. *Necrologio del Liber Confratrum di San Matteo di Salerno* (1922).

Garufi, Carlo Alberto. "Per la Storia dei Secoli XI e XII," in *Archivio Storico per la Sicilia Orientale,* volume 9 (1912), number 2.

Gaztambide, José Goñi. *Colección Diplomática de la Catedral de Pamplona,* volume 1 (1997).

Geoffroy of Beaulieu. *Vita Ludovici Noni,* in *Recueil des Historiens des Gaules et de la France* (1840), volume 20, pages 1-26.

Giles, John. *The Anglo-Saxon Chronicle* (1914).

Giles, John. *Petri Blesensis Opera Omnia,* volumes 1 and 3 (1847).

Hofmeister, Adolf. *Ottonis de Sancto Blasio Chronica,* in the *Scriptores Rerum Germanicarum* series (1912).

Hood, Gwenyth (translator). *Book in Honor of Augustus by Pietro da Eboli* (2012).

Howlett, Richard. *The Chronicle of Robert of Torigni* (1889).

Howlett, Richard. *Chronicles of the Reigns of Stephen, Henry II and Richard I,* volume 2 (1885).

Huillard-Bréholles, Jean. *Historia Diplomatica Friderici Secundi,* volume 5, part 2 (1857).

Kehr, Paul. *Italia Pontificia* (1975).

Kölzer, Theo. *Urkunden und Kanzlei der Kaiserin Konstanze, Königin von Sizilien 1195-1198,* in *Monumenta Germaniae Historica,* volume 6, part 3 (1983).

Loud, Graham. *Roger II and the Creation of the Kingdom of Sicily* (2012).

Luard, Henry. *Matthaei Parisiensis, Chronica Majora* (1877).

Luard, Henry. *The Winchester Chronicle,* in *Annales Monastici,* volume 2 (1865), pages 3-128.

Mendola, Louis. *Federick, Conrad and Manfred of Hohenstaufen, Kings of Sicily: The Chronicle of Nicholas of Jamsilla 1210-1258* (2016).

Mendola, Louis. *Sicily's Rebellion against King Charles: The Story of the Sicilian Vespers* (2015).

Migne, Jacques Paul. "Opuscula Varia," in *Patrologiae Cursus Completus,* series 2, book 145 (1853).

Migne, Jacques Paul. *Patrologiae Cursus Completus,* series 2, book 214 (1855).

Muratori, Lodovico. *Annales Siculi,* in *Rerum Italicarum Scriptores,* volume 5 (1774).

Pasca, Cesare. "Cenno Storico e Statistico del Comune di San Giovanni e Camerata," *Giornale di Scienze Lettere e Arti per la Sicilia,* volume 60, number 178 (October 1837), documents 1-3, pages 41-46.

Pegge, Samuel. *The Forme of Cury* (1780).

Pontieri, Ernesto. *De Rebus Gestis Rogerii Calabriae et Siciliae Comitis et Roberti Guiscardi Ducis Fratris Eius* of Godfrey Malaterra, *Rerum Italicarum Scriptores,* volume 5 (1928).

Powell, James. *The Liber Augustalis or Constitutions of Melfi* (1971).

Riley, Henry. *The Annals of Roger de Hoveden* (1853), 2 volumes.

Robertson, James. *Materials for the History of Thomas Becket, Archbishop of Canterbury* (1885).

Sewter, Edgar Robert Ashton (translator). *Alexiad* of Anna Comnena (1969).

Siragusa, Giovanni Battista. *Liber ad Honorem Augusti di Pietro da Eboli* (1906).

Stevenson, Joseph. *The History of William of Newburgh and the Chronicles of*

SOURCES AND BIBLIOGRAPHY

Robert de Monte in *The Church Historians of England: Pre-Reformation Period,* volume 4, part 2 (1856).

Stubbs, William. *Chronicles and Memorials of the Reign of Richard I,* volume 1 (1864).

Stubbs, William. *The Historical Works of Ralph de Diceto, Dean of London,* volume 2 (1876).

Walz, Dorothea, and Willemsen, Carl (photography). *Das Falkenbuch Friedrichs II* (2000).

Zanetti, Girolamo Francesco. *Chronicon Venetum* (1765).

Secondary Literature

Abulafia, David. *Frederick II: A Medieval Emperor* (1988).
Agius, Dionisius. *Siculo Arabic* (1996).
Alio, Jacqueline. *Margaret, Queen of Sicily* (2017).
Alio, Jacqueline, and Mendola, Louis. *The Peoples of Sicily: A Multicultural Legacy* (2014).
Allen, Nick. "Nancy Pelosi: Donald Trump's Steely Nemesis Shattered Glass Ceilings Along the Way," *The Telegraph* (25 September 2019).
Amt, Emilie (editor). *Women's Lives in Medieval Europe: A Sourcebook* (second edition, 2010).
Anderson, Melitta Weiss. *Food in Medieval Times* (2004), pages 130-121.
Armstrong, John. *Nations Before Nationalism* (1982).
Armstrong-Partida, Michelle. "Concubinage, Illegitimacy and Fatherhood: Urban Masculinity in Late-Medieval Barcelona," *Gender and History,* volume 31, number 1 (March 2019), pages 195-219.
Arriaga Flórez, Mercedes, *Poetas Italianas de los Siglos 13 y 14 en la Querella de las Mujeres* (2012).
Backman, Clifford. *The Decline and Fall of Medieval Sicily: Politics, Religion and Economy in the Reign of Frederick III, 1296-1337* (1995).
Balakrishnan, Anjana, and Cleveland, Mark. "Appreciating versus Venerating Cultural Outgroups: The Psychology of Cosmopolitanism and Xenocentrism," *International Marketing Review,* volume 36, number 3 (May 2019), pages 416-444.
Balcells, Albert. *El Nacionalismo Catalán* (1991).
Balzaretti, Ross. "Sexuality in Late Lombard Italy c.700-c.800 AD," *Medieval Sexuality: A Casebook* (2007), pages 7-31.

Banner, Lois. "Biography as History," *The American Historical Review*, volume 114, number 3 (June 2009), pages 579-586.

Barber, Richard. *The Knight and Chivalry* (revised edition, 2000).

Barber, Richard. *The Reign of Chivalry* (1980).

Barber, Richard. *The Prince in Splendour: Court Festivals in Medieval Europe* (2017).

Bartlett, Robert. *England under the Norman and Angevin Kings 1075-1225* (2000).

Bastiani, Federica, et al. "Mental Distress and Sexual Harassment in Italian University Students," *Archives of Women's Mental Health*, volume 22, number 2 (April 2019), pages 229-236.

Beccalli, Bianca. "The Modern Women's Movement in Italy," *Mapping the Women's Movement* (1996), pages 152-183.

Bellestri, Joseph. *English-Sicilian Dictionary* (1988).

Bennett, Jessica. "Alyssa Milano: Celebrity Activist for the Celebrity Presidential Age," *The New York Times* (25 October 2019).

Bennett, Judith. *History Matters: Patriarchy and the Challenge of Feminism* (2006).

Bennett, Judith. "Medievalism and Feminism," *Studying Medieval Women* (1993), pages 7-29.

Bennett, Judith, and Karras, Ruth Mazo (editors). *The Oxford Handbook of Women and Gender in Medieval Europe* (2013).

Benz, Lisa, and Rohr, Zita (editors). *Queenship, Gender and Reputation in the Medieval and Early Modern West 1060-1600* (2016).

Bergalli, Luisa. *Componimenti Poetici delle più Illustri Rimatrici d'Ogni Secolo* (1726).

Bertacchi, Giovanni. *Le Rime di Dante da Maiano* (1896).

Bettarini, Rosanna (editor). *Dante da Maiano: Rime* (1969).

Birk, Joshua. *Norman Kings of Sicily and the Rise of the Anti-Islamic Critique: Baptized Sultans* (2017).

Blud, Victoria. *The Unspeakable, Gender and Sexuality in Medieval Literature 1000-1400* (2017).

Bonner, Kirk, and Cipolla, Gaetano. *Introduction to Sicilian Grammar* (2001).

Bordone, Renata (editor). *Bianca Lancia d'Agliano: Fra il Piemonte e il Regno di Sicilia* (1992).

Borgognoni, Adolfo. *Dante da Maiano* (1882).

Boström, Ingemar. *Due Libri di Cucina: Anonimo Meridionale* (1985).

Boulton, D'Arcy Jonathan. "Classic Knighthood as Nobiliary Dignity: The Knighting of Counts and Kings' Sons in England 1066-1272," *Medieval Knighthood V: Papers from the Sixth Strawberry Hill Conference 1994* (1995), pages 41-100.

Bourassé, Jean Jacques. *Dictionnaire d'Épigraphie Chrétienne* (1852), volume 1, columns 908-939.
Bowie, Colette. *The Daughters of Henry II and Eleanor of Aquitaine: A Comparative Study of Twelfth-century Women* (2014).
Bowie, Colette. "To Have and Have Not: The Dower of Joanna Plantagenet, Queen of Sicily," *Queenship in the Mediterranean: Negotiating the Role of the Queen in the Medieval and Early Modern Eras* (2013), pages 27-50.
Brett, Roberts, Johnson, Wasserug, "Eunuchs in Contemporary Society," *Journal of Sexual Medicine*, volume 4 (2007), pages 930-955.
Brooke, Christopher. *The Medieval Idea of Marriage* (1989).
Brooke-Little, John. *Boutell's Heraldry* (1978).
Brown, Virginia. *Giovanni Boccaccio: Famous Women* (2003).
Brundage, James. *Law, Sex and Christian Society in Medieval Europe* (1987).
Brundage, James, and Bullough, Vern (editors). *Handbook of Medieval Sexuality* (1996).
Bubola, Emma. "Locker-room talks: Italian politics and normalized sexism," *Al Jazeera*, 11 March 2018.
Bynum, Caroline. "Fast, Feast and Flesh: The Religious Significance of Food to Medieval Women," *Representations*, number 11 (summer 1985), pages 1-25.
Cancrini, Luigi. *Gemme o Collezione di Poetesse Italiane dal 1290 al 1855* (1855).
Cannadine, David. *What is History Now?* (2002).
Carr, Edward. *What is History* (1961).
Castor, Helen. *She-Wolves: The Women Who Ruled England before Elizabeth* (2012).
Catlos, Brian. "Who Was Philip of Mahdia and Why Did He Have to Die?" *Mediterranean Chronicle*, volume 1 (2011), pages 73-103.
Charlier, Philippe, et al. "Schistosomiasis in the Mummified Viscera of Saint Louis (1270 AD)," *Forensic Science, Medicine and Pathology*, volume 12, number 1 (March 2016), pages 113-114.
Chassen-Lopez, Francie. "Biografiando mujeres: ¿qué es la diferencia?" *Secuencia*, number 100 (Jan-Apr 2018), pages 133-162.
Cherchi, Paolo. "The Troubled Existence of Three Women Poets," *The Voice of the Trobairitz: Perspectives on the Women Troubadours* (1989), pages 197-210.
Chevigny, Bell Gale. "Daughters Writing: Toward a Theory of Women's Biography," *Feminist Studies*, volume 9, number 1 (Spring 1983), pages 79-102.
Chiarelli, Leonard. "The Ibadi Communities in Muslim Sicily," *Ibadi Jurisprudence: Origins, Development and Cases*, in the series *Studies on Ibadism and Oman*, volume 6 (2015), pages 159-166.

Chiarelli, Leonard. *A History of Muslim Sicily,* second edition (2018).

Chibnall, Marjorie. *The Empress Matilda: Queen Consort, Queen Mother, and Lady of the English* (1991).

Chibnall, Marjorie. "The Empress Matilda as a Subject for Biography," *Writing Medieval Biography 750-1250: Essays in Honour of Frank Barlow* (2006), pages 185-194.

Cipolla, Gaetano. *Learn Sicilian* (2013).

Clinton, Hillary Rodham. "Nancy Pelosi," *Time Magazine: The 100 Most Influential People* (29 April 2019).

Conti, Emanuele. "L'Abbazia della Matina," *Archivio Storico per la Calabria,* volume 35 (Rome 1967), pages 11-30.

Correnti, Santi. *Storia di Sicilia come Storia del Popolo Siciliano* (seventh edition, Catania, 1995).

Crouch, David. *William Marshal: Knighthood, War and Chivalry 1147-1219* (2002).

Croutier, Alev. *Harem: The World Behind the Veil* (1989).

Cuozzo, Errico. *La Cavalleria nel Regno Normanno di Sicilia (*2008).

Dalli, Charles. "Contriving Coexistence: Muslims and Christians in the Unmaking of Norman Sicily," *Routines of Existence: Time, Life and After Life in Society and Religion* (2009), pages 30-43.

Dalton, Heather. "Frederick II of Hohenstaufen's Australasian Cockatoo: Symbol of Detente between East and West and Evidence of Ayyubids' Global Reach," *Parergon,* number 35, volume 1 (January 2018), pages 35-60.

Damousi, Joy. "Feminist Biography," *Hecate,* volume 15, number 1 (May 1989).

Davanzati, Domenico Forges. *Dissertazione sulla Seconda Moglie del Re Manfredi e sù Loro Figliuoli (*1791).

Davies, Norman. *Vanished Kingdoms* (2012).

Davies, Rees. "Nations and National Identities in the Medieval World: An Apologia," *Belgisch Tijdschrift voor Nieuwste Geschiedenis: Revue belge d'historie contemporaine,* volume 34, number 4 (2004), pages 567-577.

Davis-Secord, Sarah. "Medieval Sicily and Southern Italy in Recent Historiographical Perspective, *History Compass,* volume 8, number 1 (2010), pages 61-87.

Del Giudice, Giuseppe. *La Famiglia di Re Manfredi* (1896).

De Stefano, Antonino. *Federico III d'Aragona Re di Sicilia 1296-1337* (1937).

De Wailly, Natalis. "Examen Critique de la *Vie de Saint Louis* par Geoffroi de Beaulieu," *Bibliothèque de l'École des Chartes* (1844), volume 5, pages 205-231.

Di Blasi, Giovanni. *Storia del Regno di Sicilia* (1844).
Di Girolamo, Costanzo, et al. *Poeti della Corte di Federico II*, in *I Poeti della Scuola Siciliana,* volume 2 (2008).
Di Marzo, Gioacchino. *Opere Storiche Inedite sulla Città di Palermo* (1873), volume 3.
Dinshaw, Minoo. *Outlandish Knight: The Byzantine Life of Steven Runciman* (2016).
Donadio, Rachel. "The Missing Piece in Italian Politics: Women," *The Atlantic* (Washington, 10 March 2018).
Downs, Laura. *Writing Gender History,* second edition (2004).
Drell, Joanna. *Kinship and Conquest: Family Strategies in the Principality of Salerno during the Norman Period 1077-1194* (2002).
Dresvina, Juliana, and Sparks, Nicholas (editors). *Authority and Gender in Medieval and Renaissance Chronicles* (2012).
Duggan, Anne (editor). *Queens and Queenship in Medieval Europe: Proceedings of a Conference Held at King's College, London, April 1995* (1997).
Dunbabin, Jean. *France in the Making 843-1180* (1985, 2009).
Eads, Valerie. "Sichelgaita of Salerno: Amazon or Trophy Wife?" *Journal of Medieval Military History,* volume 3 (2005), pages 72-87.
Earenfight, Theresa. "Absent Kings: Queens as Political Partners in the Medieval Crown of Aragon," *Queenship and Political Power in Medieval and Early Modern Spain* (2005), pages 33-54.
Earenfight, Theresa. "Highly Visible, Often Obscured: The Difficulty of Seeing Queens and Noble Women," *Medieval Feminist Forum,* volume 44, issue 1 (2008), pages 86-90.
Earenfight, Theresa. "Where Do We Go From Here? Some Thoughts on Power and Gender in the Middle Ages," *Medieval Feminist Forum,* volume 51, number 2 (2015), pages 116-121.
Earenfight, Theresa. "Without the Persona of the Prince: Kings, Queens and the Idea of Monarchy in Late Medieval Europe," *Gender and History,* volume 19, number 1 (April 2007), pages 1-21.
Earenfight, Theresa. *Queenship in Medieval Europe* (2013).
El-Azhari, Taef. *Queens, Eunuchs and Concubines in Islamic History 661-1257* (2019).
Elliott, John. "A Europe of Composite Monarchies," *Past and Present,* volume 137, number 1 (November 1992), pages 48-71.
Elton, Geoffrey. *The Practice of History* (1967).
Elze, Reinhard. "Tre Ordines per l'Incoronazione di un Re e di una Regina del Regno Normanno in Sicilia," *Atti del Congresso Internazionale di Studi sulla Sicilia Normanna* (1974), pages 438-459.

Epstein, Stephan. *An Island for Itself: Economic Development and Social Change in Late Medieval Sicily* (2003).

Erler, Mary C, and Kowaleski, Maryanne (editors). *Gendering the Master Narrative: Women and Gender in the Middle Ages* (2003).

Evans, Richard. *In Defence of History* (1997).

von Falkenhausen, Vera, and Johns, Jeremy. "An Arabic-Greek Charter for Archbishop Nicholas of Messina, November 1166," *Rivista di Ricerche Bizantinistiche,* number 8, for 2011 (2012) pages 153-170.

von Falkenhausen, Vera. "Zur Regentschaft der Gräfin Adelasia del Vasto in Kalabrien und Sizilien 1101-1112," *AETOS: Studies in Honor of Cyril Mango Presented to Him on April 14, 1998* (Stuttgart 1998), pages 87-115.

Farmer, Sharon, and Pasternack, Carol (editors). *Gender and Difference in the Middle Ages* (2003).

Fazello, Thomas. *De Rebus Siculus* (1558-1560).

Ferrara, Francesco. *Storia Generale di Sicilia* (1831).

Flood, Alison. "Popular history writing remains a male preserve, publishing study finds," *The Guardian* (11 January 2016).

Fodale, Salvatore. "Blanca de Navarra y el gobierno de Sicilia," *Principe de Viana,* volume 60 (1999), pages 311-322.

Folda, Jaroslav. "Melisende of Jerusalem: Queen and Patron of Art and Architecture in the Crusader Kingdom," *Reassessing the Roles of Women as Makers of Medieval Art and Architecture* (2012), pages 427-477.

Foot, Sarah. "Finding the Meaning of Form: Narrative in Annals and Chronicles," *Writing Medieval History* (2005), pages 88-108.

Fornaciari, Mallegni, De Leo. "The Leprosy of Henry VII: Incarceration or Isolation?" *The Lancet,* volume 353 (27 February 1999), page 758.

Fösser, Amalie. "The Political Traditions of Female Rulership in Medieval Europe," *The Oxford Handbook of Women and Gender in Medieval Europe,* pages 68-84.

Fox-Davies, Arthur. *A Complete Guide to Heraldry* (1909).

Frascadore, Angela. "Le Badesse del Monastero di San Giovanni Evangelista di Lecce," *Tancredi Conte di Lecce Re di Sicilia* (2004), pages 233-286.

Fraser, Antonia. "Step Back in Time," *The Guardian* (24 September 2008).

Freeman, Edward. *The History of the Norman Conquest of England,* third edition (1877).

Friedan, Betty. *The Feminine Mystique* (1963).

Friedman, Bonita. "Envy: The Writer's Disease," *The New York Times* (26 November 1989).

Fröhlich, Walter. "The Marriage of Henry VI and Constance of Sicily: Prelude and Consequences," *Anglo Norman Studies 15* (1993), pages 99-125.

Funken, Liliane and Fred. *Arms and Uniforms: The Age of Chivalry*, part 1 (1977).
Gajewski, Alexandra. "The Patronage Question Under Review: Queen Blanche of Castile and the Architecture of the Cistercian Abbeys at Royaumont, Maubuisson and Le Lys," *Reassessing the Roles of Women as Makers of Medieval Art and Architecture* (2012), pages 197-244.
Galli, Natalie. *The Girl Who Said No: A Search in Sicily* (2019).
Garufi, Carlo Alberto. "Gli Aleramici e i Normanni in Sicilia e nelle Puglie," *Centenario della Nascita di Michele Amari: Documenti e Ricerche*, volume 1 (1910), pages 47-83.
Gazzetta, Liviana. *Orizzonti Nuovi: Storia del Primo Femminismo in Italia 1865-1925* (2018).
Gillingham, John. *Richard I* (1999).
Gilmour, David. *The Pursuit of Italy: A History of a Land, Its Regions, and Their Peoples* (2011).
Giuffrida, Angela. "Italy's highest court accused of victim blaming over rape case," *The Guardian* (London, 17 July 2018).
Giunti, Bernardo. *Sonetti e Canzoni di Diversi Antichi Autori Toscani* (1727 edition of work published in 1527).
Goldstone, Nancy. "I'm a Historian, and I Think Women's History Month is a Mistake," *Time* (in History-Books), 23 March 2018.
Goldstone, Nancy. *The Maid and the Queen: The Secret History of Joan of Arc* (2011).
Gosden, Chris, and Marshall, Yvonne. "The Cultural Biography of Objects," *World Archaeology*, volume 31, number 2 (October 1999), pages 169-178.
Green, Mary Anne Everett. *Lives of the Princesses of England from the Norman Conquest* (1850).
Green, Monica. *The Trotula: A Medieval Compendium of Women's Medicine* (2001).
Greer, Germaine. *Sex and Destiny: The Politics of Human Fertility* (1984).
Greer, Germaine. *The Whole Woman* (1999).
Gregorio, Rosario. *Considerazioni sopra la Storia di Sicilia dai Tempi Normanni sino ai Presenti* (6 volumes, 1805-1816).
Grimson, Alejandro. "Culture and Identity: Two Different Notions," *Social Identities*, volume 16, number 1 (2010), pages 61-77.
Gruber, Lilli. *Streghe: La Riscossa delle Donne d'Italia* (2008).
Guerri, Giordano Bruno. *Il Sangue del Sud: Antistoria del Risorgimento e del Brigantaggio* (2010).
Hamilton, George. "Trotula," *Modern Philology*, volume 4, number 2 (October 1906), pages 377-380.

Harvey, John. *The Plantagenets* (1948).

Hayes, Dawn Marie. "Significance of the Fleurs-de-Lis in the Mosaic of King Roger II of Sicily in the Church of Santa Maria dell'Ammiraglio, Palermo," *Viator,* volume 44, number 1 (January 2013), pages 201-252.

Hechinger, Fred. "Peer Review in Social Fields is Faulted," *The New York Times* (30 September 1986).

Heilbrun, Carolyn. *Writing a Woman's Life* (1988).

Hieatt, Constance. "How Arabic Traditions Travelled to England," *Food on the Move: Proceedings of the Oxford Symposium on Food and Cookery 1996* (1997), pages 120-126.

Hieatt, Constance, and Jones, Robin. "Two Anglo-Norman Culinary Collections Edited from British Library Manuscripts Additional 32085 and Royal 12,C.xii," *Speculum,* volume 61, number 4 (October 1996), pages 859-882.

Horowitz, Jason. "In Italy, #MeToo is More Like 'Meh'" in *The New York Times* (16 December 2017).

Houben, Hubert. "Adelaide 'del Vasto' nella Storia del Regno di Sicilia," *Itinerari di Ricerca Storica,* number 4 (1990), pages 9-40.

Houben, Hubert. *Roger II: A Ruler between East and West* (2002).

Hoving, Thomas. "A Newly Discovered Reliquary of St Thomas Becket," *Gesta,* volume 4, spring 1965 (1965), pages 28-30.

Howell, Margaret. "Royal Women of England and France in the Mid-Thirteenth Century: A Gendered Perspective," *England and Europe in the Reign of Henry III, 1216–1272* (2002), pages 163–181.

Huneycutt, Lois. "Female Succession and the Language of Power in the Writings of Twelfth-Century Churchmen," *Medieval Queenship* (1993), pages 189-201.

Huneycutt, Lois. "Queenship Studies Comes of Age," *Medieval Feminist Forum,* volume 51, number 2 (2015), pages 9-16.

Ingham, Richard, et al. *The Anglo-Norman Language and its Contexts* (2010).

Jamison, Evelyn. "Judex Tarentinus: The Career of Judex Tarentinus *Magne Curie Justiciarius* and the Emergence of the Sicilian *Regalis Magna Curia* under William I and the Regency of Margaret of Navarre, 1156-72," *Proceedings of the British Academy,* volume I, iii (1968), pages 289-344.

Jamison, Evelyn. "The Norman Administration of Apulia and Capua," *Papers of the British School at Rome,* volume 6, number 6 (January 1913), pages 211-481.

Jenkins, Keith. *Rethinking History* (1991).

Jensen, Frede. *The Poetry of the Sicilian School* (1986).

Jensen, Lotte (editor). *The Roots of Nationalism: Identity Formation in Early Modern Europe 1600-1815* (2016).

Johns, Jeremy. "Paper versus Parchment: Countess Adelaide's Bilingual Mandate of 1109," *Documenting Multiculturalism* (November 2018).
Johns, Susan. *Noblewomen, Aristocracy and Power in the Twelfth-Century Anglo-Norman Realm* (2003).
Jones, Mari. *Variation and Change in Mainland and Insular Norman* (2014).
Jordan, Erin. "Corporate Monarchy in the Twelfth-Century Kingdom of Jerusalem," *Royal Studies Journal,* volume 6, number 1 (2019), pages 1-15.
Kantorowicz, Ernst. *Friedrich der Zweite* (1927).
Karras, Ruth Mazo. *Sexuality in Medieval Europe: Doing Unto Others* (2005).
Katz, Robert. *The Fall of the House of Savoy* (1972).
Kavanagh, Dennis, and Rose, Richard. "The Monarchy in Contemporary Political Culture," *Comparative Politics,* volume 8, number 4 (July 1976), pages 548-576.
Kay, Sarah, and Rubin, Miri (editors). *Framing Medieval Bodies* (1996).
Keen, Maurice. *Chivalry* (1984).
Keene, Catherine. *Saint Margaret, Queen of the Scots: A Life in Perspective* (2013).
King, Michelle. "Alyssa Milano On What Is Next For #Me Too," *Forbes* (New York, 27 February 2018).
Kjaer, Lars. "Food, Drink and Ritualized Communication in the Household of Eleanor of Montfort, February to August 1265," *Journal of Medieval History,* volume 37, number 1 (2011), pages 75-89.
Krueger, Christine. "Why She Lived at the Public Records Office: Mary Anne Everett Green and the Profession of History," *Journal of British Studies,* volume 42 (January 2003), pages 65-90.
La Grua, Gregorio. *La Corona di Costanza di Aragona Regina di Sicilia* (1988).
Langley, Ernest. *The Poetry of Giacomo da Lentini* (1915).
Lansing, Richard. *The Complete Poetry of Giacomo da Lentini* (2018).
Leahy, Robert. *Emotional Schema Therapy* (2015), pages 246-248.
Lee, Carole, et al. "Bias in Peer Review," *Journal of the American Society for Information Science and Technology,* volume 64, number 1 (January 2013), pages 2-17.
Lehmann, Claire. "Camille Paglia: It's Time for a New Map of the Gender World," *Quillette,* 10 November 2018, quillette.com/2018/11/10/camille-paglia-its-time-for-a-new-map-of-the-gender-world/.
Levin, Carole, and Bucholz, Robert (editors). *Queens and Power in Medieval and Early Modern England* (2009).
Leyser, Henrietta. *Medieval Women: A Social History of Women in England 450-1500* (1995).
Leyser, Karl. "Concepts of Europe in the Early and High Middle Ages," *Past and Present,* volume 137, number 1 (November 1992), pages 25-47.

Lipinsky, Angelo. "Sicaniae Regni Corona: Il Kamelaukion detta Cuffia di Costanza nel Tesoro del Duomo di Palermo," *Bizantino-Sicula II: Miscellanea di Scritti in Memoria di Giuseppe Rossi Taibbi* (1975), pages 347-370.

Lledó-Guillem, Vicente. *The Making of Catalan Linguistic Identity in Medieval and Early Modern Times* (2018).

Llobera, Josep. *Foundations of National Identity: From Catalonia to Europe* (2004).

Lochrie, Karma. "Situating Same-Sex Female Love in the Middle Ages," *The Cambridge Companion to Lesbian Literature* (2015), pages 79-92.

Lombardo, Francesca, and Alio, Jacqueline. *Sicilian Food and Wine: The Cognoscente's Guide* (2015).

Lucas, Angela. *Women in the Middle Ages: Religion, Marriage and Letters* (1983).

Kjaer, Lars. "Food, Drink and Ritualized Communication in the Household of Eleanor of Montfort, February to August 1265," *Journal of Medieval History*, volume 37, number 1 (2011), pages 75-89.

La Lumia, Isidoro. *Storia della Sicilia sotto Guglielmo il Buono* (1867).

Lerner, Gerda. *The Creation of Feminist Consciousness: From the Middle Ages to 1870* (1994).

Letronne, Antoine. *Examen Critique de la Découverte du Prétendu Coeur de Saint Louis* (1844).

Lochrie, McCracken, Shultz (editors). *Constructing Medieval Sexuality* (1997).

Loud, Graham. *The Latin Church in Norman Italy* (2007).

Louda, Jiri, and Maclagan, Michael. *Heraldry of the Royal Families of Europe* (1988).

Lussana, Fiamma. *Il Movimento Femminista in Italia: Esperienze, Storie, Memorie* (2012).

Maggiorella, Antonia. *Il Principe Poeta: Manfredi di Svevia* (2005).

Mairey, Aude. "Gender and Written Culture in England in the Late Middle Ages," *Clio: Women, Gender, History* ("Working Women, Working Men"), volume 38 (2013), 264-288.

Mallette, Karla. *The Kingdom of Sicily 1100-1250: A Literary History* (2005).

Malpezzi Price, Paola. "Uncovering Women's Writings: Two Early Italian Women Poets," *Journal of the Rocky Mountain Medieval and Renaissance Association,* volume 9 (1988), pages 1-15.

Mandalà, Giuseppe. "The Sicilian Questions," *Journal of Transcultural Medieval Studies,* volume 3, issues 1-2 (2016), pages 3-31.

Mangieri, Cono Antonio. *Il Contrasto di Cielo d'Alcamo: Introduzione, testo manoscritto e diplomatico, testo critico-congetturale, traduzione e note* (2005).

Marinoni, Augusto. *Dal Declarus di Angelo Senisio: I Vocaboli Siciliani* (1955).

Martellotti, Anna. *I Ricettari di Federico II: Dal Meridionale al Liber de Coquina* (2005).

Martellotti, Anna. *La Cassata Siciliana: Un Dolce Arabo e la Sua Fortuna in Occidente* (2012).
Martin, Therese. *Queen as King: Politics and Architectural Propaganda in Twelfth-Century Spain* (2006).
Marwick, Arthur. *The Nature of History* (1970).
Mason-Hohl, Elizabeth. *The Diseases of Women* (1940).
Mastelloni, Maria Amalia. "Il Sarcofago Antico di Costanza d'Aragona," *Federico e la Sicilia, dalla Terra alla Corona: Arti Figurative e Arti Suntuarie* (1995), pages 46-52.
Matthew, Donald. "Modern Study of the Norman Kingdom of Sicily," *Reading Medieval Studies,* volume 18 (1992), pages 34-56.
Matthews, Helen. *The Legitimacy of Bastards: The Place of Illegitimate Children in Later Medieval England* (2019).
Maurolico, Francesco. *Sicanicarum Rerum Compendium* (1662).
Maxwell-Lyte, Henry. *Historical Notes on the Use of the Great Seal of England* (1926).
Mazzarese Fardella, Enrico, "La Condizione Giuridica della Donna nel Liber Augustalis," *Archivio Storico Siciliano,* Series 4, Volume 21-22 (Palermo 1997).
McCracken, Peggy. *The Romance of Adultery: Queenship and Sexual Transgression in Old French Literature* (1998).
McCullagh, C. Behan. *The Truth of History* (1997).
McDougall, Sarah. *Royal Bastards: The Birth of Illegitimacy 800-1230* (2016).
Mead, William. *The English Medieval Feast* (1931).
Mendola, Louis. *Sicilian Genealogy and Heraldry* (2013).
Mendola, Louis. "English and Italian Legacy of the Norman Knight Figures of Monreale," *The Coat of Arms,* journal of The Heraldry Society, London, NS volume 10, number 166 (1994), pages 245-254.
Mendola, Louis. "Pre-Armorial Use of the Lion Passant Guardant and the Fleur-de-Lis as Heraldic Badges in Norman Sicily," *The Coat of Arms,* journal of The Heraldry Society, London, NS volume 10, number 165 (1994), pages 210-212.
Menon, Tanya, and Thompson, Leigh. "Envy at Work," *Harvard Business Review,* April 2010, pages 3-7.
Miceli Jeffries, Giovanna (editor). *Feminine Feminists: Cultural Practices in Italy* (1994).
Mielke, Christopher. "From Her Head to Her Toes: Gender-Bending Regalia in the Tomb of Constance of Aragon, Queen of Hungary and Sicily," *Royal Studies Journal,* volume 5, number 2 (2018), pages 49-62.
Missana, Eleonora (editor). *Donne si Diventa: Antologia del Pensiero Femminista* (2014).

Mitchell, Linda. *Joan de Valence: The Life and Influence of a Thirteenth-Century Noblewoman* (2016), pages 1-7.
Möhren, Frankwalt. *Il Libro de la Cocina: Un Ricettario fra Oriente e Occidente* (2016).
Montanari, Massimo. *Medieval Tastes: Food, Cooking and the Table* (2012).
Morrison, Susan Signe. *A Medieval Woman's Companion: Women's Lives in the European Middle Ages* (2016).
Mortimer, Ian. *The Time Traveller's Guide to Medieval England* (2008).
Mortimer, Ian. *What Isn't History?* (2017).
Mortimer, Ian, and Vincent, Nicholas. "Was Edward II Really Murdered," *BBC History Magazine,* January 2016, pages 44-47.
Mount, Harry. "How the Queen fused the medieval traditions of the Coronation with the modern world," *The Telegraph* (London), 31 May 2019.
Mumelter, Maria Luise. *Irene von Byzanz* (Innsbruck 1936).
Munslow, Alun. *Deconstructing History* (1997).
Murray, Jacqueline. "Historicizing Sex, Sexualizing History," *Writing Medieval History* (2005), pages 133-152.
Murray, Jacqueline. "Twice Marginal and Twice Invisible: Lesbians in the Middle Ages," *Handbook of Medieval Sexuality* (1996), chapter 8, pages 191-214.
Musso, Pasquale. "Il 'Ricettario di Cucina' di San Martino delle Scale," *Bollettino del Centro di Studi Filologici e Linguistici Siciliani,* volume 21 (2007), pages 243-321.
Nasrallah, Nawal. *Annals of the Caliph's Kitchens: Ibn Sayyar al-Warraq's Tenth-Century Baghdadi Cookbook* (2007).
Nelson, Janet. "Medieval Queenship," *Women in Medieval Western European Culture* (1999), pages 179–207.
Neubecker, Ottfried. *Heraldry: Sources, Symbols and Meaning* (1976).
Neville, Leonora. *Anna Komnene: The Life and Work of a Medieval Historian* (2016).
Norton, Elizabeth. *She-Wolves: The Notorious Queens of Medieval England* (2008).
Norwich, John Julius. *Sicily: A Short History, from the Greeks to Cosa Nostra* (2015).
Norwich, John Julius. *The Kingdom in the Sun 1130-1194* (1970).
Oliva, Gianni. *Un Regno Che è Stato Grande: La Storia Negata dei Borboni di Napoli e Sicilia* (2011).
Oster, Uwe. *Die Frauen Kaiser Friedrichs II* (2008).
Paglia, Camille. *Free Women, Free Men: Sex, Gender, Feminism* (2017).
Paglia, Camille. *Provocations: Collected Essays* (2018).

Paglia, Camille. *Sexual Personae* (1990).
Painter, Nell. "Writing Biographies of Women," *Journal of Women's History,* volume 9, number 2 (1997), pages 154-163.
Panvini, Bruno. *Le Rime della Scuola Siciliana,* volume 1 (1962).
Parsons, John C. (editor). *Medieval Queenship* (1993).
Parsons, John C. "Family, Sex, and Power: The Rhythms of Medieval Queenship," *Medieval Queenship* (1993), pages 1-11.
Partner, Nancy. "Preface," *Writing Medieval History* (2005), pages xi-xvi.
Partner, Nancy. "No Sex, No Gender," *Studying Medieval Women* (1993), pages 117-141.
Partner, Nancy. "The Post-Traditional Middle Ages: The Distant Past Through Contemporary Eyes," *Writing Medieval History* (2005), pages xi-xvi.
Parzen, Jeremy. *The Art of Cooking* (2005).
Pasca, Cesare. "Cenno Storico e Statistico del Comune di San Giovanni e Camerata," *Giornale di Scienze Lettere e Arti per la Sicilia,* volume 60, number 178 (October 1837), pages 3-46.
Pianigiani, Gaia. "Women Could Decide Italy's Election, but They Feel Invisible," *The New York Times* (3 March 2018).
Pierson, Ruth, and Prentice, Alison. "Feminism and the Writing and Teaching of History," *Atlantis,* volume 7, number 2 (1982), pages 37-46.
Pitrè, Giuseppe. *Grammatica Siciliana* (1875).
Povoledo, Elisabetta. "Jews Find a New Home in Sicily 500 Years After They Were Forced Out," *The New York Times* (25 April 2017), Section A (city edition), page 4.
Prestwich, Michael. "Medieval Biography," *Journal of Interdisciplinary History,* volume 40, number 3 (Winter 2010), pages 325-346.
Puff, Helmut. "Same-Sex Possibilities," *The Oxford Handbook of Women and Gender in Medieval Europe* (2013), chapter 24, pages 379-395.
Putnam, Robert. *Making Democracy Work: Civic Traditions in Modern Italy* (1993).
Radici, Benedetto. "Il Casale e l'Abbazia di Santa Maria di Maniace," *Archivio Storico Siciliano* (Palermo 1909), pages 1-104.
Rapisarda, Stefano. "Federico II," *I Poeti della Scuola Siciliana* (2008), volume 2, chapter 14, pages 437-494.
Reilly, Bernard. *The Kingdom of León-Castilla Under Queen Urraca* (1982).
Riall, Lucy. "The Shallow End of History? The Substance and Future of Political Biography," *Journal of Interdisciplinary History,* volume 40, number 3 (Winter 2010), pages 375-397.
Richard, Alfred. *Histoire des Comtes de Poitou* (1903).

Richardson, Henry. "The Letters and Charters of Eleanor of Aquitaine," *The English Historical Review,* volume 74, number 291 (April 1959), pages 193-213.

Riley-Smith, Jonathan. *The Crusades: A History* (third edition, 2013).

Riley-Smith, Jonathan. *The First Crusade and the Idea of Crusading* (1986).

Robertson, Elizabeth. "Medieval Feminism in Middle English Studies: A Retrospective," *Tulsa Studies in Women's Literature,* volume 26, number 1 (2007), pages 67-79.

des Roches de Chassay, Arnaud. *Yolande d'Aragon ou l'Unité de la France* (2006).

Rogers, Katie. "Inside the Derailed White House Meeting," *The New York Times* (16 October 2019).

Romito, Patrizia, et al. "Sexual Harassment and Menstrual Disorders Among Italian University Women: A Cross-sectional Observational Study," *Scandinavian Journal of Public Health,* volume 45, number 5 (May 2017), pages 528-535.

Rosin, Dowd, Moran, Paglia. *Are Men Obsolete? The Munk Debate on Gender* (2014).

Rubenstein, Jay. "Biography and Autobiography in the Middle Ages," *Writing Medieval History* (2005), pages 22-41.

Ruddick, Andrea. *English Identity and Political Culture in the Fourteenth Century* (2013).

Runde, Ingo. "Konstanze von Aragon," *Die Kaiserinnen des Mittelalters* (2011), pages 232-248.

Salloum, Habeeb. "Medieval and Renaissance Italy: Sicily," in *Regional Cuisines of Medieval Europe: A Book of Essays* (2002), pages 113-123.

Salloum, Habeeb. *Scheherazade's Feasts: Foods of the Medieval Arab World* (2013).

Sauer, Michelle. *Gender in Medieval Culture* (2015).

Schaus, Margaret (editor). *Women and Gender in Medieval Europe: An Encyclopedia* (2006).

Schofield, Phillipp (editor). *Seals and their Context in the Middle Ages* (2014).

Scholz, Piotr. *Eunuchs and Castrati: A Cultural History* (1999).

Schulman, Sarah. "White Writer," *The New Yorker* (21 October 2016).

Schuman, Rebecca. "Revise and Resubmit," *Slate,* 15 July 2014, slate.com/human-interest/2014/07/the-easy-way-to-fix-peer-review-require-submitters-to-review-first.html.

Schutte, Valerie, and Paranque, Estelle (editors). *Forgotten Queens in Medieval and Early Modern Europe: Political Agency, Myth-making and Patronage* (2018).

Sciascia, Laura. "Bianca di Navarra, l'ultima regina: Storia al femminile della monarchia siciliana," *Principe de Viana,* volume 60 (1999), pages 293-309.

Scully, Terence. *The Art of Cookery in the Middle Ages* (1995).
Scully, Terence. *The Neapolitan Recipe Collection* (2000).
Segal, Lynne. *Why Feminism? Gender, Psychology, Politics* (1999).
de Senneville, Gérard. *Yolande d'Aragon: La reine qui a gagné la guerre de Cent Ans* (2008).
Seward, Desmond. *The Monks of War: The Military Religious Orders* (1972).
Shahar, Shulamith. *Fourth Estate: A History of Women in the Middle Ages* (1983).
Simeti, Mary Taylor. *Pomp and Sustenance: Twenty-Five Centuries of Sicilian Food* (1989).
Simeti, Mary Taylor. *Travels With a Medieval Queen: The Journey of a Sicilian Princess to Reclaim Her Father's Crown* (2001).
Siri, Simona. "Having a misogynist leader has consequences. And no, I don't mean Trump." *The Washington Post* (Washington DC, 14 December 2017).
Skinner, Patricia. *Family Power in Southern Italy: The Duchy of Gaeta and Its Neighbors 850-1139* (1995).
Skinner, Patricia. "Halt, Be Men! Sikelgaita of Salerno, Gender and the Norman Conquest of Southern Italy," *Gender and History*, volume 12, issue 3 (2000), pages 622-641.
Skinner, Patricia. "The Light of My Eyes: Medieval Motherhood in the Mediterranean," *Women's History Review*, volume 6, number 3 (1997), pages 391-410.
Skinner, Patricia. *Women in Medieval Italian Society 500-1200* (2001).
Skinner, Patricia. *Studying Gender in Medieval Europe: Historical Approaches* (2018).
Smith, Anthony. "Chosen Peoples: Why ethnic groups survive," *Ethnic and Racial Studies,* volume 15, number 3 (1992), pages 436-456.
Smith, Denis Mack. *Italy and Its Monarchy* (1989).
Smith, Lesley. "Medieval Marriage and Superstitions," *Journal of Family Planning and Reproductive Health Care,* volume 38 (2012), pages 60-62.
Smith, Richard, et al. *Envy at Work and in Organizations* (2016).
Sommers, Christina Hoff. *Who Stole Feminism? How Women Have Betrayed Women* (1994).
Soncini, Guia. "The Failure of Italian Feminism," *The New York Times* (26 October 2017).
Sottile, Roberto. *L'Atlante Linguistico della Sicilia* (2019).
Stafford, Pauline (editor). *Gendering the Middle Ages* (2001).
Stafford, Pauline. *Queens, Concubines and Dowagers: The King's Wife in the Early Middle Ages* (1983).

Stafford, Pauline. "Writing the Biography of Eleventh-Century Queens," *Writing Medieval Biography 750-1250: Essays in Honour of Frank Barlow* (2006), pages 99-110.

Stein, Robert. "Literary Criticism and the Evidence for Hstory," *Writing Medieval History* (2005), pages 67-87.

Stenton, Doris. *The English Woman in History* (1957).

Stolberg, Sheryl Gay. "Nancy Pelosi, Icon of Female Power, Will Reclaim Role as Speaker and Seal a Place in History," *The New York Times* (2 January 2019).

Storey, Gabrielle. "Berengaria of Navarre and Joanna of Sicily as Crusading Queens: Manipulation, Reputation and Agency," *Forgotten Queens in Medieval and Early Modern Europe: Political Agency, Myth-Making and Patronage* (2019), pages 41-59.

Strayer, Joseph. *On the Medieval Origins of the Modern State* (1970).

Stuard, Susan Mosher (editor). *Women in Medieval History and Historiography* (1987).

Stuard, Susan Mosher. *Women in Medieval Society* (1976).

Sucato, Ignazio. *La Lingua Siciliana: Origine e Storia* (1975).

Summerfield, Giovanna. *Le Siciliane: Così sono se vi pare* (2011).

Taleb, Nassim. *The Black Swan* (2007).

Tanner, Heather (editor). *Medieval Elite Women and the Exercise of Power 1100-1400: Moving Beyond the Exceptionalist Debate* (2019).

Tanner, Heather. "Women's Legal Capacity: Was the Thirteenth Century a Turning Point?" *Paradigm Shifts During the Global Middle Ages and Renaissance* (2019), pages 81-98.

Tosh, John. *The Pursuit of History* (1984).

Thomas, Sandra. "Current Controversies Regarding Peer Review in Scholarly Journals," *Issues in Mental Health Nursing,* volume 39, number 2 (2018), pages 99-101.

Thornton, Hermann. "The Poems Ascribed to Frederick II 'Rex Fredericis' and King Enzio," *Speculum,* volume 2, number 4 (October 1927), pages 463-469; "The Poems Ascribed to Frederick II and Rex Fredericis," *Speculum,* volume 1, number 1 (January 1926), pages 87-100.

Toor, Rachel. "Scholars Talk Writing: Camille Paglia," *Chronicle of Higher Education,* 9 November 2015, chronicle.com/article/Scholars-Talk-Writing-Camille/234124.

Trucchi, Francesco. *Poesie Italiane Inedite di Duegento Autori* (1846).

Tuchman, Barbara. *Practicing History: Selected Essays* (1981).

Urban, Misty. "Margaret, Queen of Sicily," *Medieval Feminist Forum: A Journal of Gender and Sexuality,* volume 55, issue number 1 (summer 2019), pages 319-321.

Van Cleave, Rachel. "Rape and Querela Law in Italy: False Protection of Victim Agency," *Michigan Journal of Gender and Law,* volume 13, January 2007 (Ann Arbor 2007), pages 273-310.
Van Cleve, Thomas Curtis. *The Emperor Frederick II of Hohenstaufen, Immutator Mundi* (1972).
Van Landingham, Marta. "The Hohenstaufen Heritage of Costanza of Sicily and the Mediterranean Expansion of the Crown of Aragon in the Later Thirteenth Century," *Across the Mediterranean Frontiers,* volume 1 (January 1997), pages 87-104.
Varvaro, Alberto. *Vocabolario Storico-Etimologico del Siciliano* (2014).
Vigo, Julian. "Tight Jeans, Rape and Technology," *Forbes* (New York, 22 July 2018).
de Waal, Kit. "Don't dip your pen in someone else's blood: Writers and 'the other,'" *The Irish Times* (30 June 2018).
Wagner-Martin, Linda. *Telling Women's Lives: The New Biography* (1994).
Walker, Gina Luria. *The Invention of Female Biography* (2017).
Walker, Rose. "Leonor of England, Plantagenet Queen of Alfonso VIII of Castile, and Her Foundation of the Cistercian Abbey of Las Huelgas. In Imitation of Fontevraud?" *Journal of Medieval History,* volume 31, number 4 (2005), pages 346-368.
Ware, Susan. "Writing Women's Lives: One Historian's Perspective," *Journal of Interdisciplinary History,* volume 40, number 3 (Winter 2010), pages 413-435.
Weikert, Katherine, and Woodacre, Elena. "Gender and Status in the Medieval World," *Historical Reflections,* volume 2, issue 1, (2016), pages 1-7.
Weiler, Björn. "Knighting, Homage and the Meaning of Ritual: The Kings of England and their Neighbors in the Thirteenth Century," *Viator,* volume 37 (2006), pages 276-299.
Weiss, Bari. "Camille Paglia: A Feminist Defense of Masculine Values," *The Wall Street Journal* (New York, 28 December 2013).
Whatley, Laura (editor). *A Companion to Seals in the Middle Ages* (2019).
White, Lynn Townsend. *Latin Monasticism in Norman Sicily* (1938).
Williams, Lynn. "National Identity and the Nation State: Construction, Reconstruction and Contradiction," *National Identity* (1999), pages 7-18.
Wilson, Bee. *Consider the Fork: A History of How We Cook and Eat* (2012).
Winfield, Nicole. "Italian Court Ruling That a Woman Was Too Ugly to Be Raped Sparks Outrage," *Time* (USA), 14 March 2019.
Winstead, Karen. *The Oxford History of Life-Writing, Volume 1, The Middle Ages* (2018).
Wolf, Armin. "Reigning Queens in Medieval Europe: When, Where, and Why," *Medieval Queenship* (1993), pages 169-188.

Woodacre, Elena. "Blanca, Queen of Sicily and Queen of Navarre: Connecting the Pyrenees and the Mediterranean via an Aragonese Alliance," *Queenship in the Mediterranean: Negotiating the Role of the Queen in the Medieval and Early Modern Eras* (2013), pages 207-227.

Woodacre, Elena (editor). *Queenship in the Mediterranean: Negotiating the Role of the Queen in the Medieval and Early Modern Eras* (2013).

Zaouali, Lilia. *Medieval Cuisine of the Islamic World: A concise history with 174 Recipes* (2007).

INDEX

aaneth, 167
Abruzzi, 5, 176, 291
Abulafia, David, vii, 28n2, 149n40, 341
Abu'l Kasim (Bulcassis), 138
Accardi, Carla, 16
Acre, 372
Acton, Harold, 20
Adam of Cammarata, 81-82, 98, 144
Adelaide del Vasto, 1, 21, 38, 57, 70, 76-78, 84, 89-91, 133, 140, 146n4, 154, 237n3, 267-283, 307
Adelisa of Adernò, 82
adultery, 120, 142-143, 144
Aghlabids, 81, 153, 156, 157
Agrigento, 32, 34, 81, 156, 372
Ahmed es-Sikeli. *See* Caïd Peter
Al Adil (Saphadin), 45, 123
Alaimo of Lentini, 12, 63
Alamanda de Castelnau, 381
Albright, Madeleine, 354
Alcherio, archbishop, 76, 88, 279

Aleramids, 133
Alexander III, Pope, 226
Alexander of Telese, 117, 119, 146n5, 277, 279, 282, 283
Alferio of Salerno, 219
Alfonso I of Aragon, 120
Alfonso VII of León and Castile, 272
almonds, 155, 157, 158, 166, 171-178 passim
Amari, Michele, 295, 299, 341
Amato of Montecassino, 154
amir. *See* emir
Anacletus II, 118, 120, 147n7
Ancona, 375
Andria, 32, 33, 69, 131, 305, 346, 375
Anna Comnena, 301, 336, 342
Apulia (Puglia), 5, 32, 33, 43, 58, 74, 163, 270. *See also* Andria, Bari, Brindisi, Lucera, Taranto, *etc*.
Arabic, 58, 73, 74, 77, 90, 153
Arabs, 10, 13, 19, 56, 58, 77, 154, 159, 162, 180, 226, 252-253, 277, 281. *See also* Agh-

labids, Kalbids, Fatimids, Muslims, *et al.*
Aragon, 13, 26, 35-36, 58, 63, 80, 334, 347
arancina, 159-161
architectural movements, 181, 223-266, 373
Ariano: Assizes of, vi, 104, 107n3, 114, 121, 141-142, 144, 269, 270; town of, 32, 33, 181, 375
aristocracy. *See* barons
Arthurian legend, 274-276
artichokes, 153, 167
Aspremont, Chanson of, 191, 274
aubergines. *See* eggplant
Avellino, 33, 118, 375
Badiazza. *See* Santa Maria della Scala
Bagnara, 376
Balarah souk. *See* Ballarò
Baldwin I of Jerusalem, 78, 282
Baldwin III of Jerusalem, 272
Ballarò, 6, 138, 155, 304, 371, 378
Barber, Richard, 190n22, 284n5
Barcelona, 155, 334
Bari, 32-33, 283, 286, 338
Barisani of Trani, 232
barons (and baronage), 21, 38, 39, 41, 57, 63, 71, 118, 134, 136, 154, 183, 268, 269, 275, 355n10
Bartholomew of Nicastro (Neocastro), 13
Basilicata (Lucania), 5, 32-33, 291, 375
bastardy, 48, 133-135 passim, 275, 276
Beatrice of Rethel, vi, 17, 47, 57, 125, 127, 220, 221, 234, 374
Beatrice of Savoy, 336, 375
beef, 152, 156, 160, 173
Benedictines, 219, 220, 226, 233
Benevento, Battle of, 56, 199, 273, 348, 383
Bennett, Judith, 146n2, 355n7, 359n37
Bertram of Gurdun, 45-47
Bianca Lancia, 132-136, 197, 375
Bible, 140, 229, 230, 232
Bixio, Nino, 300
boar, 125, 153, 159, 164, 230, 255
Boccaccio, Giovanni, 307, 383
Bohemond II, 50
Bonanno of Pisa, 232
Borsellino, Paolo, 313n11
bottarga, 157
Brindisi, 32-33, 49
broccoli, 156, 165, 170, 173
Bronte, 220, 227, 300

INDEX

Byzantine Greeks (and Byzantine Empire), 6, 19, 81, 139, 179, 183, 196, 223, 228, 309
Caiazzo, 117
Cala. *See* Kala
Calabria, 5, 7, 18, 32-33, 44, 51n2, 58, 71, 76, 156, 181, 193, 276, 280. *See also* Catanzaro, Fiore, Mileto, Stilo, *etc*.
Caltabellotta, 34, 374
Cammarata, 12, 81
Campania, 5, 32-33, 182, 291. *See also* Capua, Naples, Salerno, *etc*.
canals. *See* kanats
Cannadine, David, 352
cannoli, 157, 161
caponata, 159, 161, 169
Capua, 32-33, 75, 80, 88, 117, 120
Carr, Edward, 352
cassata, 157-158
Les Cassés, 45
Cassino (Montecassino), 32-33, 48, 154, 219, 224, 226
Castel del Monte, 180, 375
Castellaccio, 222, 249
Catalan language, 58, 193, 200
Catalogus Baronum, 268
Catalonia, 20, 155, 239n22, 298, 311. *See also* Barcelona.
Catania, 8, 12, 32, 34, 82, 177, 305, 374

Catania, University of, 8, 300, 360n40
Catanzaro, 32, 33, 269
cauliflower, 165, 170
Cava, 32, 33, 219, 226, 338
ceci. *See* chickpeas
Cecilia of France, 273
Cefalù, 32, 34, 81, 144, 223, 230, 263
Cereta, Laura, 16
Chalus, 45
Chanson d'Aspremont, 191, 274
Charles of Anjou, King of Naples, 63, 83, 232, 306
Charles II of Naples, 289
Charles III de Bourbon, 298, 300
charters (decrees and letters), 56, 69-98, 221, 345
chess, 13
Chiarelli, Leonard, 86n3
Chibnall, Marjorie, 23, 328
chicken, 152-153, 156, 161-174 passim, 183
chickpeas, 159, 166, 173
chivalry. *See* knighthood
Christine de Pizan, 332
Cielo of Alcamo, 195, 331, 332
Cistercians, 219, 232, 234
Clementia of Catanzaro, 269-270
coats of arms. *See* heraldry
coinage, 71, 75, 104, 194, 287

Conrad I of Sicily, 132, 136, 382
Conradin, 136, 219
Constance of Antioch, 50
Constance of Aragon, 58, 69, 80-81, 97, 105, 198, 218, 235, 306, 335
Constance (Hauteville) of Sicily, Holy Roman Empress, 2, 21, 45, 57, 61-62, 79-80, 96, 99, 136, 270, 306, 372
Constance (Hohenstaufen) of Sicily, Queen of Aragon, 12-13, 63, 136
Contrasto (poem), 195, 196, 332
copyright, 327, 345
Corleone, 226
Correnti, Santi, 8, 299-300
corruption. *See* nepotism
Cosenza, 32, 33
couscous, 157, 169
crespelle, 169, 177
Croce, Benedetto, 8
Crusades. *See* First, Third
Cuba palace, 186, 373, 378, 383
cuccagna, 163
cuisine, 151-190
cultural appropriation. *See* xenocentrism
Cyprus, 45
Dante Alighieri, 19, 191, 383

Dante of Maiano, 383-384
Declarus (dictionary), 169, 200
deconstructionism, 343
decrees. *See* charters
deer, 152, 164, 297
De la Mia Disïanza, 205
Di Blasi, Giovanni, 11
dining. *See* cuisine
diwan (treasury), 141
DNA. *See* genetics
Drengot family, 82, 117, 121
dubbing. *See* knighthood
Earenfight, Theresa, 335
Edrisi (geographer). *See* Idrisi
eggplant, 159, 169
Eleanor of Aquitaine, 48, 55, 192
emir *defined*, 90
Emma Hauteville, 82
Elisabeth of Bavaria, 219, 291
Elizabeth II, Queen, 291, 315n29
Elton, Geoffrey, 352
Elvira of Castile, 2, 120, 155, 158, 182
Enna. *See* Kasr'Janni
Enzo (Enzio) of Sardinia, 134-135, 195
Erice, 316, 374
ethnology. *See* Sicilianità
eucabam, 167
eunuchs, 41, 137, 139-141, 189n19
St Euphemia (abbey in Cal-

abria), 218
Evans, Richard, 352
Excalibur, 274
Falco of Benevento, 119-121 passim, 147n7
Fallaci, Oriana, 16, 22
familiares (royal counsellors), 42-44 passim, 127, 225
Fascism, xi, 23, 195, 300, 306, 311
Fatimids, 13, 105, 137, 141, 153, 154, 160, 219, 228, 230
Favara palace, 180, 186, 281, 373
Fazello, Thomas, 11, 30, 298-299, 337
female inheritance. *See* Sicilian Succession
feminism, vi, xii, xiii, 3, 4, 13, 16, 22, 26, 332, 350-351
fennel, 166, 170, 172
Ferrara, Francesco, 11
Ferraris Chronicle, vi, 73, 119, 337
fertility. *See* infertility
feudalism. *See* manorialism
figs, 153, 177
Fiore (abbey in Calabria), 218
First Crusade, 268, 280
fleur-de-lis, 79-80, 103, 105, 109
Foggia, 375
food. *See* cuisine
forgeries, 72-73, 77

Forges Davanzati, Domenico, 333
fork, 179, 185
Forme of Cury, 165
Francesco II of the Two Sicilies, 20, 168, 291
Fraser, Antonia, 360n45
Frederick I, 127
Frederick II, vi, vii, 15, 34, 37, 69, 77, 129, 132, 137, 141, 178, 196-211 passim, 322, 374
Freeman, Edward, 341
Friedan, Betty, 15
fritedda, 167
furusiyya, 281
Garufi, Carlo Alberto, 9
gender bias. *See* sexism
gender studies, 3, 24, 351
genetics (DNA), 116, 292, 346
Genoard, 42, 123, 224
Geoffrey of Anjou, 104, 112
Geoffrey Malaterra. *See* Godfrey Malaterra
Geoffrey of Monmouth, 274
Geoffrey of Perche, 47
Geoffroy of Beaulieu, 239n22
Gervase of Tilbury, 55
Ghibellines, 199, 383
Giacomo of Lentini, 195
Gilbert of Perche, 18
Girgentan goat, 156
Girgenti. *See* Agrigento
goat meat, 153, 156, 164, 174,

175
Godfrey (Geoffrey) Malaterra, 154, 158, 192, 347
Goldstone, Nancy Bazelon, 325, 327
Greek church. *See* Orthodox Church
Greeks, 19, 20, 24. *See also* Byzantine Greeks
Green, Mary Anne Everett, vii, 130
Greer, Germaine, 15
Gregorio, Rosario, 298-299
Gruber, Lilli, 22, 351
Guelfs. *See* Guelphs
Guelphs, 18, 23, 126, 307, 383
gynecology, 124
Halkah district, 281
ibn Hamdis, Abd al-Jabbar, 191
hare (and rabbit), 125, 153, 164, 184
harems, 41, 123, 137-139, 143
Haskins, Charles Homer, 9
Hauteville dynasty. *See* Roger II, William II, *et al.*
ibn Hawqal, Mohammed, 153
hazelnuts, 156
Helena Angelina of Epirus, 375, 382
Henry VI, Emperor, 39, 48, 58, 61, 79, 140
Henry Aristippo, 41, 138
Henry (Rodrigo) of Montescaglioso, 18, 43, 47, 57
Henry del Vasto, 278
heraldry (coats of arms), 71, 102-112, 274
herring, 174, 330
Hildegard of Bingen, 336
historicism, 13, 295
historiography, xiii, 1, 7, 9, 13, 17, 20, 23, 114-117, 124, 293, 299, 300-304, 321-354 passim
Hohenstaufen dynasty. *See* Henry VI, Frederick II, *et al.*
Holy Spirit (church in Palermo), 232, 264
homosexuality, 128
honor killings, 144
Hospitallers, 268, 271, 280
Hugh Falcandus, 11, 39, 41, 43, 47, 55, 57, 114, 137, 138, 300, 307, 337
Huneycutt, Lois, 356n11
icons, 229
identity (as social concept), xii, 201, 289-315
al Idrisi, Abdullah, 81, 153, 157
infertility, human, 113, 123-125, 152
Innocent II, 118, 121
Innocent IV, 306
Isabella of Angoulême, 128
Isabella of England, vii, 15, 69, 128-132

Isabella of Jerusalem. *See* Yolanda
San Isidore (basilica in León), 220
Islam. *See* Muslims
Italy (after 1860), v, 2, 3, 4, 8, 9, 15, 20, 22, 23, 135, 144, 306
itria, *See* spaghetti
Jamison, Evelyn, x, 9, 23, 340
Jamsilla Chronicle, 336
Jato, 226
Jean de Meun, 332
Jenkins, Keith, 352
Jensen, Frede, 196, 331
Jerusalem Citadel, 372
Jerusalem, Kingdom of, 57, 69, 78, 83, 132, 181, 272, 282
Jews, 6, 21, 138, 200, 311
Jiménez dynasty, xi, 2, 50, 155, 158, 220. *See also* Elvira, Margaret, *et al*.
Joan of Arc, 325
Joanna of England, vii, 37-39 passim, 44-47, 79, 106, 123-125, 181, 183, 192, 220, 270, 349
Joanna I of Naples, viii, 326, 329
Jocelmo of Cefalù, 81
John of Brienne, 194
John of England, 15, 128
St John of the Hermits, 219, 226
John of Procida, 12, 63, 199, 200
Johns, Susan, 29n12
ibn Jubayr, 137, 138, 153, 156
Judaism. *See* Jews,
Judith of Evreux, 82, 192, 270
Justinian, Code of, 350
Kala (Cala) district, 377, 378
Kalbid dynasty, 76, 137
kanats, 153, 186
Kantorowicz, Ernst, vii, 341
Kasr (Cassaro) district, 42, 281
Kasr'Janni (Enna), 32, 34, 76
Keen, Maurice, 284n5
Kitab al-Tabikh (Baghdad Cookery Book), 156
knighthood, 57, 71, 103-104, 118, 231, 267-288
Koran, 140, 295
La Lumia, Isidoro, 339
La Mantia, Giuseppe, 349
lamb. *See* mutton
lardo *defined,* 170
lasagna, 168, 177
Lecce, 32-33, 49, 61, 134, 234
lemons, 153, 172, 175, 176, 186
Leonor (Eleanor) of England, 220
leprosy, 346
Lerner, Gerda, 15
letters. *See* charters
Levi-Montalcini, Rita, 15
Liber de Coquina, 165, 171

lion (in art), 103, 104, 106
livestock. *See* beef, mutton, etc.
Lombards, 19, 57, 58, 119
Lonzi, Carla, 16
Louis IX of France, 232, 306
Lucania. *See* Basilicata
Lucera, 137-138, 140
Lucy of Cammarata, 12, 81-82, 98, 144
Macalda of Scaletta, 12-13
maccu, 166, 167
Madonian Mountains, 34, 51n2
Mafia, 10, 313n11
Magione church, 49, 234, 310
Magna Graecia, 20
Maio of Bari, 42, 347, 362
majolica, 162, 179, 309
Malcolm, John, 301-302
malik, malikah *defined*, 74-75, 277
Maliki Law, 141
mamonia, 174
Mancuso, Elvira, 333
Manfred of Sicily, 12, 63, 132, 133-140 passim, 198, 333, 375
Manfredonia Castle, 375
Maniace, 220-224 passim, 233
manorialisn (feudalism), 12, 43, 81, 118, 268-269, 271, 304
Marchadés, 45-46
Margam bin Sebir, 13

Margaret of l'Aigle, 220
Margaret of Navarre, 2, 11, 18, 40-44, 59-61, 78-79, 217-241, 328-331
Margaret of Scotland, 306
Margaritus of Brindisi, 49
Maria Argyropoulina, 179
Maria of Montferrat, 133
Maria Sophia of Bavaria, 20, 291, 318
marionettes, 309
Caïd Martin, 41, 139
Martorana church, 105, 229, 373
Marwick, Arthur, 352
Mary Magdalene church, 231-235 passim, 373
Matilda of England. *See* Maude
Matilda Hauteville, 17, 38, 82, 117-123, 143, 277
matronage. *See* patronage
mattanza, 157
Matthew of Aiello, 42, 48, 49, 225, 234
Matthew Bonello, 42, 137, 138, 221, 269, 347, 362
Matthew, Donald, 303
Matthew Paris, 130, 131
Maude, Empress, 21, 23, 50, 83, 270
Maurolico, Francesco, 11, 299
Maximilla Hauteville, 276
McCullagh, C. Behan, 352

medicine, 76, 124, 158, 349
Melfi: Constitutions of, 19, 56, 70, 114, 141; town of, 181, 375
Melisende of Jerusalem, 50, 83, 220, 237n5, 272
mental health, 128-132
Meridionale (codex), 165-172 passim
Messina, 12, 13, 18, 32, 34, 45, 47, 56, 154, 371
Messina, Maria, 333
#MeToo movement, 15, 28-29n5
Michael Scot, 375
Mikalis (sword), 274
Milano, Alyssa, 16
Mileto, 32, 33, 181, 237n4, 276, 372
Misura, Providenzia e Meritanza, 201
misogyny. *See* sexism
Molise, 5, 32, 33, 43, 375
monasticism. *See* Benedictines, *et al*.
Monreale, 6, 70, 105, 106, 180, 186, 217-262, 274, 347
Montessori, Maria, 15
Moreso, Salvadore, 299, 313n15
Mortimer, Ian, 6, 352
mosaicry, 105-106, 109, 223, 227, 228-230, 241, 257-260, 262

Mount Sant'Angelo, 375
Mozzoni, Anna Maria, 16
mulberries, 153
multiculturalism, x, 6, 14, 19, 335, 351
Munslow, Alun, 352
murri, 157
Muslims, 19, 21, 39, 58, 59, 74, 81, 137-139, 141, 153, 187, 223, 280-281, 346
Mussomeli, 82, 361
mutton, 158, 167, 174
Naples, viii, 20, 32, 33, 56, 133, 219, 290, 326, 334, 383
Neapolitan language, 63, 165, 170, 193, 297, 326, 383
Nebrodian fir, 88, 231
Nebrodian Mountains, 34, 48, 88, 77, 159, 346
nepotism and corruption, xiii, 3, 15, 360n40, 351
Sts Nicholas and Catald (abbey in Lecce), 218-219
Nicodemus, bishop, 76
Nina of Messina, vi, 17, 195, 381-389
nobility. *See* barons
Nocera Inferiore, 376
Norman French language, 57, 59, 61, 159, 160, 191, 194, 292, 345
Norman Palace (Palermo), 123, 154, 229, 307-308, 330, 373, 377-379

Normans, 9, 19, 23, 105, 119, 154, 183, 281. *See also* Roger II, *et al*.
Norwich (Cooper), John Julius, 302, 311, 328, 340
nougat. *See* torrone
numismatics. *See* coinage
Odo of Bayeux, 281
oeniculture. *See* wine
olives (and olive oil), 152-153, 156, 166, 170, 182
open access, 327
oranges, 153, 159-160, 186, 194
Orderic Vitalis, 277, 281
Oria, 375
Orthodox Church, 21, 41, 76, 140, 223, 238n10, 306
Osterio Magno (Cefalù), 374
Paglia, Camille, xiii, 16, 21-22, 358n22
paleopathology, 346
Palermo, xi, 6, 7, 10, 17, 27, 49, 56, 71, 76, 119, 154, 162, 180, 185, 221, 231, 265, 362, 377, 378. *See also* Kasr, Norman Palace, Zisa, *etc*.
Palmeri Abate, 63
Pamplona, 18, 120, 147n6, 220, 372
Pantocrator, 229-230, 253, 257-259
Panvini, Bruno, 212n1
paper, 56-57, 72, 73, 76, 77

Papyrus River, 155
Partner, Nancy, 146n2
partridge, 153, 164, 173
Parzival, 276
patriarchy, 14, 16, 355n7
patronage (by queens), 26, 76, 81, 217-224, 235, 328
Patti, 70, 181, 218
peer review, 342
Pelosi, Nancy, 16, 21
Pepoli Castle (Erice), 316, 374
Peter III of Aragon, 13, 63
St Peter la Bagnara church, 76, 218
Peter of Blois, 55, 114, 225, 233, 294
Caïd Peter (Ahmed es-Sikeli), 42, 43, 139
Peter of Eboli, 39, 48, 52, 53, 55, 61-63 passim, 69, 79
Peter of Rievaulx, 130
Peter della Vigna, 195
pheasant, 153, 173, 184
St Philip of Fragalà, 233
Philip II of France, 45, 108n6
Philip of Mahdia, 139
philology, 193
Pisan Tower, 154, 379
pistachios, 156, 161, 188n9
Pitrè, Giuseppe, 295
poetry. *See* Sicilian School
Poi ch'a Voi Piace, Amore, 202-205
Poitiers, 372

polyculturalism. *See* multiculturalism
pork, 159, 164, 169, 172. *See also* boar
postmodernism, 335, 343
prandium (pranzo) *defined,* 152
Provençal culture, 192, 194, 196, 219, 230
publishing industry, 322-330
Puglia. *See* Apulia
Purpura, James, 331-332
queenhood *defined,* 31
queenship *defined,* vi, 4, 31
Quran. *See* Koran
rabbit. *See* hare
Rainald of Avenella, 82
Rainulf of Alife, 117-123 passim
rais (title), 157
rape laws, 15, 139, 142-144
ravioli, 164, 167-168, 174
Raymond VI of Toulouse, 79, 123, 220
Raymond VII of Toulouse, 47, 79, 123
Rebellamentu di Sichilia contra Re Carlu, 63, 199
regalità, 15
regicide, 46
reginalità, 15
reginezza, 15
Renaissance, 20
revisionism, historical, 300, 340, 351-353
Ribera, 160
rice, 159-161, 174
rice ball. *See* arancina
Richard I Lionheart, 13, 45-47, 72
Caïd Richard, 139
Richard of Acerra, 49
Richard of Cornwall, 131
Richard of Molise (Mandra), 43-44
Richard Palmer, 42, 59, 294
Richard of San Germano, 48
ricotta, 157-158, 168
Risorgimento (Italian unification), 20, 160, 195, 293, 299
Robert of Capua, 118, 120
Robert Guiscard Hauteville, 38, 57, 74, 75, 101, 218, 278, 280, 352
des Roches de Chassay, Arnaud, 325
Rodrigo of Navarre. *See* Henry of Montescaglioso
Roger I, viii, 71, 74, 81, 82, 91, 133, 144, 218, 274, 276, 280, 287
Roger II, 1, 7, 12, 17, 38, 47, 82, 85, 105, 109, 134, 144, 154, 182, 218, 235, 268, 293-294
Roger III, 49, 235
Roger of Andria, 48
Roger of Apulia, 134

Roger of Howden, 46, 274
Roland, Song of, 276
Rome, 59, 118, 228, 301
Romuald of Salerno, 124, 234, 329, 339
St Rosalie, 290, 296-297
Rudolf of Montescaglioso, 82
Runciman, Steven, 341
Salerno, 118, 119
San Marco d'Alunzio, 17, 47, 77, 125, 126, 180, 221, 374
Sancho VI of Navarre, 220
Santa Maria della Scala, 72
Saphadin. *See* Al Adil
Sari al Kadi district, 155
sausage, 169, 175
ibn Sayyar al Warraq, 156
scapece, 169, 183
Scarlata, Marina, 23
Schuman, Rebecca, 359n29
Scibene palace, 186, 373
seals, 69-100 passim
Senisio, Angelo, 169, 200
de Senneville, Gérard, 325
serfdom, 13, 76, 80, 144, 281
Seward, Desmond, 284n1
sexism, 2, 7, 14-16
sexual harassment, 15
sexuality, 113-150
sfince, 158
Sforza, Caterina, 2
sheep. *See* mutton
she-wolf *defined,* 37
Sibylla of Acerra, 49, 57, 62, 218-219, 235, 290, 374, 375
Sibylla of Burgundy, 55
Sichelgaita of Salerno, 17, 75-76, 88, 101, 218, 270, 336
Sicilian language. *See* Sicilian School
Sicilian School, 191-216, 381-389
Sicilian Succession, 70, 143
Sicilianism *defined,* 290
Sicilianità, 8, 289-315
Caïd Siddiq (Sedictus), 138
Sigena (abbey in Aragon), 220, 372
sigillography. *See* seals
Sila Mountains, 218
silk making, 137, 153
Simeti, Mary Taylor, 325
Simon Hauteville, 76, 218, 276
Simon of Taranto, 134
Siracusa, 32, 34, 161, 349
Skinner, Patricia, 342, 351
Smith, Denis Mack, 8, 300
spaghetti, 157, 169, 179
Spinelli Codex, 199
spousal abuse, 117-123
Stafford, Pauline, 356n11
Stams (abbey in Tyrol), 219
Staufen (locality), 376
Staufen dynasty. *See* Hohenstaufen
Steinem, Gloria, 15
stemperata, 157, 169
Stephen of Perche, 39, 43, 47,

59, 220, 221, 348
Strickland, Agnes, 303, 333
sugar cane, 153, 157
swordfish, 153
swords, 273-274
Sylvester of Marsico, 41-42
Syracuse. *See* Siracusa
Tagliacozzo, Battle of, 23, 348
Tancred of Antioch, 273, 293
Tancred of Lecce, 48, 57, 61, 134, 222, 234, 274
Taranto, 32, 33, 58, 134, 135, 193
tardin, 156
Templars, 268, 280
Testa di Turco, 161-163
Teutonic Order, 268
Theotokos, 5, 230
Thibald of Saint-Arnouldt de Crepy, 56
Third Crusade, 45, 123, 192, 274
Thomas Becket, 56, 59-61, 182, 223, 229, 234, 259
Thomas le Brun, 55
ibn Thummah, Muhammed, 161
titles and styles, 69-100
Titone, Virgilio, 300
torrone, 158
Tosh, John, 352
Trabia, 157
Tramontana, Salvatore, 8
treasury. *See* diwan

Trifels, 372, 376
Troina, 34, 158, 192, 346
Trota of Salerno, 12, 124-125, 336
Trotula. *See* Trota
Tuchman, Barbara, 336, 343, 352, 353
tuna, 153, 157
Tuscan language, 63, 191, 195, 197, 199
Tuscany, 18, 208, 306
Tuttoapposto (film), 360n40
Two Sicilies, Kingdom of, 7, 20, 26, 168, 291, 317-320
Ubaldino della Pila, 178
unification, Italian. *See* Risorgimento
Urban, Misty, 332
Urraca "the Reckless" of Castile and León, 50, 120, 220, 272
Ursino Castle (Catania), 374
Van Cleve, Thomas Curtis, vii, 341
Van Dyck, Antoon, 296
vermicelli. *See* spaghetti
Vespers War, 12, 63, 236, 289, 296, 341, 383
Victoria, Queen, 7, 291
Viola, Franca, 150n52
walnuts, 156
Walter, Archbishop, 84, 114, 221, 225, 227, 234
Walter of Caltagirone, 63

Walter of Capparone, 273
watermelon, 158
Weir, Alison Matthews, 324, 325
wheat, 153, 157, 170
White, Lynn Townsend, 9
William I, 41, 125, 134, 137, 221, 234-235, 269, 273
William II, 11, 17, 23, 37, 44, 78, 92, 93, 94, 182, 222, 260, 273
William III, 49
William of Apulia (chronicler), 154
Wiliam, Duke of Apulia (son of Roger Borsa), 278
William of Blois, 233
William Marshal, 104, 283
Winchester, 347, 372
wine, 125, 157-159 passim
Wise, Timothy, 14
women's studies, 3, 13, 24, 333, 351
wren pie, 178
xenocentrism, 301, 328
Yolande of Aragon, 325
Yolanda (Isabella) of Jerusalem, 69, 131, 132, 133, 372
zibibbo, 159
Zisa palace, 45, 123, 181, 186, 373

This book was first printed simultaneously in Italy and in the United States of America in January 2020. The text is set in Garamond, a typeface developed in Paris by the engraver Claude Garamont during the sixteenth century.

www.ingramcontent.com/pod-product-compliance
Lightning Source LLC
Chambersburg PA
CBHW030048100526
44591CB00008B/67